DATE DUE

FE 2 02			
MY 0 02			
DE 6 06			

DEMCO 38-296

Plutarch and Arrian have contributed more than any other ancient authors to our picture of Alexander the Great, but since they wrote four or more centuries after his death the value of what they said depends upon the sources of information on which they themselves drew. In this book the attempt is made (surprisingly for the first time) to define and to evaluate those sources in a detailed study, analysing the historians' works section by section and comparing them with other accounts of the same episodes. Plutarch and Arrian rank among the finest writers of antiquity, and their charm is not ignored in this appreciative study.

Professor Hammond maintains that a close analysis of the sources is essential for a balanced view of the history of Alexander the Great. After writing his *Alexander the Great: King, Commander and Statesman* (1980; 2nd edn 1989) he published *Three Historians of Alexander the Great* on Diodorus, Justin and Curtius (Cambridge University Press, 1983). The present book completes his study of the five Alexander-historians and lays a new basis for work in this area.

This book will be of particular value to ancient historians but also has much to offer to anyone seriously interested in the life of Alexander the Great.

CAMBRIDGE CLASSICAL STUDIES

General Editors

M. F. BURNYEAT, M. K. HOPKINS, M. D. REEVE,
A. M. SNODGRASS

SOURCES FOR ALEXANDER THE GREAT
AN ANALYSIS OF PLUTARCH'S *LIFE* AND ARRIAN'S *ANABASIS ALEXANDROU*

SOURCES FOR ALEXANDER THE GREAT

An analysis of Plutarch's *Life* and Arrian's
Anabasis Alexandrou

N. G. L. HAMMOND, C.B.E., D.S.O., F.B.A.
Honorary Fellow of Clare College, Cambridge

CAMBRIDGE
UNIVERSITY PRESS

the University of Cambridge
Street, Cambridge CB2 1RP
k, NY 10011-4211, USA
Victoria 3166, Australia

© Faculty of Classics, University of Cambridge 1993

First published 1993

Printed in Great Britain at the University Press, Cambridge

A catalogue record for this book is available from the British Library

Library of Congress cataloguing in publication data

Hammond, N. G. L. (Nicholas Geoffrey Lemprière)
Sources for Alexander the Great: an anlysis of Plutarch's Life
and Arrian's Anabasis Alexandrou / N.G.L. Hammond.
p. cm. – (Cambridge classical studies)
Includes bibliographical references and index.
ISBN 0 521 43264 2
1. Arrian. Anabasis. 2. Plutarch. Alexander. 3. Alexander, the
Great, 359-323 B.C. 4. Greece – History – Macedonian Expansion,
359-323 B.C. 5. Generals – Greece – Biography. 6. Greece – Kings and
rulers – Biography. I. Title. II. Series.
DF234.2.H34 1993
938′.07′092–dc20
[B] 92-12772 CIP

ISBN 0 521 43264 2 hardback

IN MEMORIAM
J. L. AND L. B. HAMMOND

CONTENTS

PREFACE

This book is the second part of a comprehensive study of the sources which lie behind the five main extant accounts of Alexander the Great. Thus it is a companion volume to my publication of 1983, *Three Historians of Alexander the Great: the so-called Vulgate authors, Diodorus, Justin and Curtius.* The preliminary part of the comprehensive study was conducted as the basis of my book, published in 1980, *Alexander the Great: King, Commander and Statesman,* in which the reader was informed of the divergencies in the sources of information at each critical event and encouraged to make his own evaluation of those sources.

The need for an analysis of the sources of Plutarch's *Alexander* is obvious and undisputed, and in the Prolegomena I have written about previous work in that field, culminating in the commentary by J. R. Hamilton, published in 1969. The need for a similar analysis of the sources which lie behind Arrian's *Anabasis Alexandrou* is equally great despite the fact that important commentaries have been published during the last fifteen years. P. A. Brunt revised the text and the translation of the Loeb edition, and he added a new Introduction and twenty-eight Appendixes, which constituted an extensive, if uncoordinated, commentary; the first volume appeared in 1976 and the second in 1983. Meanwhile, A. B. Bosworth published in 1980 a full-scale commentary on the first three books of the *Anabasis*. Both commentaries are of great value in collecting and collating a mass of relevant material. However, they have defects. The Greek text and the English translation of the Loeb edition are both faulty in my opinion, and the unindexed Appendixes are difficult to use. Bosworth's commentary is marked by a continuous and, in my view, unjustified distrust of Arrian, and by a tendency to seek errors

xi

in Arrian's work of which some at least are due to modern misunderstanding. But the serious defect in both is a dependence on the concept of 'The Vulgate Tradition' and in consequence a failure to analyse the sources and thus the merits and demerits of the versions of the three authors who are grouped together under that label – Diodorus, Justin and Curtius. Moreover, there has been a tendency to prefer the versions of one or more of those authors to the version supplied by Arrian, e.g. for the attack on Thebes, Diodorus 17.9–13 being preferred to Arrian 1.7–8; and the preference seems at times to be based on personal taste rather than any comparison of the sources used respectively by Diodorus, writing three centuries after the event, and Arrian, writing nearly five centuries after the event. Indeed it has become customary with some recent writers that they turn more to the 'Vulgate' authors and cut Alexander down to an ordinary size.

In this book, as in my earlier book on three authors, I am breaking new ground, because a detailed analysis has not previously been attempted. It has therefore been possible to keep the footnotes within a reasonable length and to concentrate on fairly recent literature. The help which I have received has been from colleagues and especially pupils in recent years when I have lectured on Philip and Alexander, for instance at Trinity College, Hartford, Carleton College, and the University of Newcastle, New South Wales. It has been a great pleasure, as always, to work with the staff of the Cambridge University Press in the production of this book.

Clare College, Cambridge   N. G. L. Hammond
October 1991

ABBREVIATIONS AND SELECT
BIBLIOGRAPHY

A	Alexander the Great
AG[2]	N. G. L. Hammond, *Alexander the Great: King, Commander and Statesman* (2nd edn, Bristol Classical Press, 1989)
Anc. Mac.	*Ancient Macedonia*, papers read at the International Symposia held in Thessaloniki, 4 vols. (Institute of Balkan Studies, Thessaloniki, 1970, 1977, 1983, 1986)
Arr.	Arrian, *Anabasis Alexandrou*
Atkinson	J. E. Atkinson, *A Commentary of Q. Curtius Rufus' Historiae Alexandri Magni Books 3 and 4* (Amsterdam, 1980).
Beloch	K. J. Beloch, *Griechische Geschichte* III and IV (Berlin–Leipzig, 1922–7)
Berve	H. Berve, *Das Alexanderreich auf prosopographischer Grundlage*, 2 vols. (Munich, 1926)
Bosworth *AA*	A. B. Bosworth, *From Arrian to Alexander* (Oxford, 1980)
Bosworth *C*	A. B. Bosworth, *A Historical Commentary on Arrian's History of Alexander* I–III (Oxford, 1980)
Bosworth *CE*	A. B. Bosworth, *Conquest and Empire: the reign of Alexander the Great* (Cambridge, 1988)
Brown *Ones.*	T. S. Brown, *Onesicritus* (Berkeley, 1949)
Brunt *L*	P. A. Brunt, *Arrian* I (Cambridge, Mass. – London, 1976), II (1983), Loeb edition
Ellis	J. R. Ellis, *Philip II and Macedonian Imperialism* (London, 1976)
Epit. Metz.	*Epitome rerum gestarum Alexandri et liber de morte eius* ed. P. H. Thomas (Leipzig, 1966)
FGrH	F. Jacoby, *Die Fragmente der griechischen Historiker* (Berlin, 1923–30; Leiden, 1940–58)

FHG	Müller, *Fragmenta Historicorum Graecorum* (Paris, 1841–70)
Goukowsky	P. Goukowsky, in the Budé edn of Diodorus Siculus 17 (Paris, 1976)
Habicht	C. Habicht, *Gottmenschentum und die griechischen Städte* (Munich, 1970)
Hamilton *C*	J. R. Hamilton, *Plutarch, Alexander: a Commentary* (Oxford, 1969)
Hamilton *L*	J. R. Hamilton, 'The letters in Plutarch's *Alexander*', *PACA* 4 (1961) 9–20
H*A*	N. G. L. Hammond, ed., *Atlas of the Greek and Roman World in Antiquity* (New Jersey, 1981; Bristol Classical Press, 1991)
H*AAJ*	idem, 'Aspects of Alexander's journal and ring in his last days', *AJPh* 110 (1989) 155–60
Hammond *Ep*	idem, *Epirus* (Oxford, 1967)
Hammond *MS*	idem, *The Macedonian State* (Oxford, 1989)
H*AT*	idem, 'Army transport in the fifth and fourth centuries', *GRBS* 24 (1983) 27–31
H*CR*	idem, 'Casualties and reinforcements of citizen soldiers in Greece and Macedonia', *JHS* 109 (1989) 56–68
H*CU*	idem, 'A cavalry unit in the army of Antigonus Monophthalmus: ASTHIPPOI', *CQ* 28 (1978) 128–35
H*GR*	idem, 'The battle of the Granicus River', *JHS* 100 (1980) 73–88
H*KA*	idem, 'The kingdom of Asia and the Persian throne', *Antichthon* 20 (1986) 73–85
HM	*A History of Macedonia* I by N. G. L. Hammond (Oxford, 1972); II by N. G. L. Hammond and G. T. Griffith (1979); III by N. G. L. Hammond and F. W. Walbank (1988)
H*MAT*	idem, 'The march of Alexander the Great on Thebes in 335 B.C.', in Μέγας Ἀλέξανδρος 2600 χρόνια ἀπὸ τὸν θάνατόν του, ed. K. Babouskos (Thessaloniki, 1980) 171–81
H*PF*	idem, 'Papyrus British Library 3085 verso', *GRBS* 28 (1987) 331–47
H*RJ*	idem, 'The Royal Journal of Alexander', *Historia* 37 (1988) 129–50

H*RP*	idem, 'Royal pages, personal pages, and boys trained in the Macedonian manner during the period of the Temenid Monarchy', *Historia* 39 (1990) 261–90
H*SPA*	idem, 'Some passages in Arrian concerning Alexander', *CQ* 30 (1980) 455–76
H*VG*	idem, 'The various guards of Philip II and Alexander III', *Historia* 40 (1991)
LCM	*Liverpool Classical Monthly*
Mederer	E. Mederer, *Die Alexanderlegenden bei den ältesten Alexander-historikern* (Stuttgart, 1936)
M–G	*Macedonia and Greece in Late Classical and Early Hellenistic Times*, ed. B. Barr-Sharrar and E. N. Borza (Washington, 1982)
Mossman	J. M. Mossman, 'Tragedy and epic in Plutarch's *Alexander*', *JHS* 108 (1988) 83–93
OCD	*The Oxford Classical Dictionary*², ed. N. G. L. Hammond and H. H. Scullard (Oxford, 1970)
P*A*	Plutarch, *Life of Alexander*, in the Loeb edition (1971)
Papazoglou *CBT*	F. Papazoglou, *The Central Balkan Tribes in Pre-Roman Times* (Amsterdam, 1977)
PCPS	*Proceedings of the Cambridge Philological Society*
Pearson *LHA*	L. Pearson, *The Lost Historians of Alexander the Great* (New York, 1960)
Perrin	B. Perrin, *Plutarch's Lives* VII (1971), Loeb edition
Powell	J. E. Powell, 'The sources of Plutarch's *Alexander*', *JHS* 59 (1939) 229–40
Rabe	I. Rabe, *Quellenkritische Untersuchungen zu Plutarchs Alexanderbiographie* (Hamburg, 1964)
RE	Pauly–Wissowa, *Realencyclopädie der classischen Altertumswissenschaft*
Robson *L*	E. I. Robson, *Arrian* I (New York and London, 1929), II (1933), in the Loeb edition
Schachermeyr	F. Schachermeyr, *Alexander der Grosse: das Problem seiner Persönlichkeit und seines Wirkens* (Vienna, 1973)
Stadter	P. A. Stadter, *Arrian of Nicomedia* (Chapel Hill, N. C., 1980)

Stadter *P*	idem, *Plutarch's Historical Methods* (Cambridge, Mass., 1965)
Studies	N. G. L. Hammond, *Studies in Greek History* (Oxford, 1973)
Studies Edson	*Ancient Macedonian Studies in honor of Charles F. Edson* (Thessaloniki, 1981)
Tarn	W. W. Tarn, *Alexander the Great* II (Cambridge, 1948 and 1979)
THA	N. G. L. Hammond, *Three Historians of Alexander the Great: the so-called Vulgate authors, Diodorus, Justin and Curtius* (Cambridge, 1983)
Tod	M. N. Tod, *Greek Historical Inscriptions* II (Oxford, 1948)
Walbank *C*	F. W. Walbank, *A Historical Commentary on Polybius* I–III (Oxford, 1957–79)
Wardman	A. E. Wardman, 'Plutarch and Alexander', *CQ* 5 (1955) 96–107
Wilcken	U. Wilcken, *Alexander the Great* (London, 1932)

Full bibliographies are provided in *HM* III xviii-xxx and Bosworth *CE* 300–14.

References to Plutarch's *Lives* are to the sections in the Loeb edition.

PROLEGOMENA

In 1983 when I published in this series *Three Historians of Alexander the Great: the so-called Vulgate authors, Diodorus, Justin and Curtius*, I wrote on p. 169 that I hoped to conduct a separate inquiry on the same principles into the sources of Plutarch's *Life of Alexander* and of Arrian's *Anabasis of Alexander*. Those principles are a detailed, specific analysis of each section of one work and a detailed comparison of its specifications with the treatment of the same topic in the other four main accounts of Alexander's career. One may wonder why such an inquiry into the sources, for instance, of so widely read a work as Plutarch's *Alexander* has never been undertaken. An answer was offered by J. E. Powell in his article, 'The sources of Plutarch's Alexander', *JHS* 59 (1939) 229–40: 'The sources of Plutarch's *Alexander* have hitherto been a subject passed by without examination in detail, not because examination was superfluous but because the task was considered hopeless on account of its complexity' (238).

Powell implied that he had conducted such an examination. However, even if his conclusions had been accepted, he would only have deferred the real issues. He argued that Plutarch used only two sources. The first was a collection of Letters of Alexander, which Powell held to be entirely spurious. The second was 'a *variorum* source' or 'Sammelwerk', 'an encyclopaedic work', to quote Powell's words (234), 'in which the divergent versions of each successive event in a large number of historians of Alexander were collated and registered'.[1] Even if we accept the existence in antiquity of such a work 'of stupendous size and detail', as Powell remarks, and the contin-

---

[1] As Tarn remarked (307 n. 3), Powell acknowledged that A. Schoene had advanced the theory of a common source for Plutarch and Arrian in 1870. However, that theory did not win acceptance; see Hamilton *C* xlix n. 4.

uous use of it by Plutarch, we are no further towards knowing the ultimate source of what Plutarch wrote; for Plutarch did not give the names of the authors, one by one, of the variant versions in the source-book which he supposedly was copying.

In fact no one has accepted Powell's view. Tarn demolished it in 1948 (306–9). Rabe published a dissertation in 1964, in which she re-examined the six topics which Powell had examined (Medius, A's illness, Bucephalus' death, Callisthenes' death, A's illness at Tarsus, the Gordian knot) and found his theory unproven in all cases. Hamilton endorsed the views of Tarn and Rabe in his *Commentary* in 1969. Moreover, Hamilton had written in 1961 an important article in which he showed that some of the Letters cited by Plutarch were genuine.

There are, of course, general works on Plutarch's methods as a biographer and general surveys of possible sources for his *Alexander*. An example of the latter is Tarn's study (296–309), in which he argued that Plutarch's picture of a deteriorating Alexander owed much to the influence of the Peripatetic school of philosophy, that some Letters were genuine and each had to be judged on its own merits, and that Powell's theory of 'a *variorum* source-book' (306) was untenable. Hamilton argued in his *Commentary* (xlix-liii) that Plutarch consulted directly Onesicritus, Aristobulus and Aristoxenus, and probably Callisthenes and Chares (li, it 'may reasonably be assumed'), and that in addition Plutarch probably 'consulted Cleitarchus directly'. On the basis of these general probabilities Hamilton listed the passages in the *Life* which, he wrote, 'we may tentatively assign' to five of these writers (he excluded Aristoxenus).[2] In the course of the *Commentary* he made proposals of source at some points, which I shall usually mention in my own analysis.

Thus we return to my opening quotation from Powell's article, and we can reinforce it with a companion-piece from Tarn (296): 'No one has yet made any real attempt to analyse its [Plutarch's *Life*'s] sources, and it is not likely that anyone

---

[2] He added Theophrastus and Ctesias with one passage each in the *Life*.

ever will, for its ultimate sources must have embraced the whole Alexander-literature, whether known or unknown to ourselves.'

In grasping this particular nettle I acknowledge my debt to my predecessors and especially to Hamilton for his fine *Commentary*. I can make the attempt to analyse Plutarch's sources only because I have already studied the works of Diodorus, Justin and Curtius in depth and I have made much use of Plutarch and Arrian in writing about Alexander.

Plutarch's *Life* partakes of biography and of history. There are a number of passages in which he reflects upon the personality, the character and the changing nature of Alexander. Powell called them 'digressions illustrative of character' (op. cit. 229). I shall call them 'the reflective passages'.[3] It is reasonable to put them in one category because they are in one style and of one kind of content. History entered into the bulk of the *Life* in that Plutarch proceeded through the life of Alexander from his birth to his death, and he had to have a chronological, narrative thread to which he attached his chosen incidents. That thread could be tenuous (e.g. 67.1 Carmania, 67.7 Gedrosia, 69.1 Persis, 70.3 Susa and so on), but it had to be more or less continuous. I shall call the record of the incidents 'the narrative passages'. Because the incidents are very diverse, and because, as we shall see, he used many sources, the narrative passages are remarkably uneven, both in style and in content (e.g. in narrative compare 6 with 9.4–11; in attitude compare 13 with 35, in coherence compare 50 and 63 with 50 and 68).

---

[3] Such passages occur in other Lives. H. D. Westlake, for instance, called them 'enlargements' in his article, 'The sources of Plutarch, *Pelopidas*', *CQ* 33 (1939) 12.

PART ONE

PLUTARCH'S SOURCES FOR THE NARRATIVE PASSAGES

1

ALEXANDER'S ORIGIN, BOYHOOD AND RELATIONS WITH PHILIP

1. The introduction

In the introduction, covering the two *Lives* which he knew would attract both interest and criticism more than any other *Life*, Plutarch warned his readers that he was writing 'not Histories but Lives' of Alexander and of Caesar. In the immediate context he pointed out that he was not committed to recording all the famous acts of the two men, and that he should be allowed to find indications of personality often in their sayings and even their jests.[1] What he did not say but may have expected his readers to infer from this introduction was that he would be treating his evidence not with the historian's insistence on accuracy but with the biographer's love of traditional anecdotes.

The first sentence of the actual *Life of Alexander* lives up to Plutarch's warning words. 'Alexander's descent, as a Heraclid on his father's side from Caranus, and as an Aeacid on his mother's side from Neoptolemus, is one of the matters which have been completely trusted.' While the Heraclid and Aeacid descent went unquestioned by ancient writers,[2] the citation of

---

[1] Sayings of Alexander appear first in 4.11 and 5.4; the sayings and the jests of Caesar during his stay with the pirates are recorded in *Caes.* 2.

[2] That Alexander, son of Amyntas, was a 'Hellen' from Argos was confirmed by the Hellanodicae at Olympia *c.* 500, no doubt by checking that his ancestors were members of the Temenid house there (Hdt. 5.22 with *HM* 2.3f.); and the descent of the Molossian royal house from Aeacus was asserted in a poem by Pindar *c.* 485

5

Caranus as the founding father in Macedonia – and so analogous to Neoptolemus in Molossia – was not only controversial
but must have been known to be controversial by Plutarch.
For he was conversant with the histories of Herodotus and
Thucydides, which had looked to Perdiccas as the founding
father in Macedonia.[3] Caranus was inserted as a forerunner of
Perdiccas in Macedonia only at the turn of the fifth century;
he appeared as such in the works of fourth-century writers,
such as Marsyas the Macedonian historian (*FGrH* 135/6 F 14)
who on my analysis[4] was used by Pompeius Trogus (*Prologue*
7 'origines Macedonicae regesque a conditore gentis Carano').
Thus the dogmatic statement of Plutarch, that Caranus was
the forerunner, should have been qualified, if he had been
writing scientific history. But because the statement conveyed
a belief which Alexander certainly held in his lifetime it was
justified in the eyes of a biographer and in the eyes of those
who were more concerned with biographical background than
with historical facts. If Plutarch had been challenged, he would
no doubt have claimed that his belief was based on his own
wide reading of authors who had studied the origins of
Macedonia and provided 'completely trusted' data.[5]

2. Chapters 2.2, 9.5–10 and 10.6–7

When Plutarch wished to express doubt about the historicity
of an event or an anecdote, he made use of the conventional
expressions 'it is said', 'they say', 'it seems' (we shall encounter them again in Arrian's *Anabasis*). The next sentence (2.2)
provides an example. It opens with the word λέγεται: Philip

(Hammond *Ep.* 490f.). Alexander I advertised his Heraclid descent by showing the
forepart of a lion on his coinage. Genealogies were carefully preserved and were
regarded as genuine for royal houses (as at Sparta) and other houses in the sixth
century.

[3] Hdt. 137.1 and 139; Thuc. 2.100.1, giving the same number of generations; see *HM*
II 4.

[4] In *CQ* 41 (1991) 501. The head of a young man wearing a diadem without string-
ends, which appeared first on the coins of Archelaus and was repeated on coins of
Aëropus and Pausanias, was probably the head of Caranus.

[5] He no doubt read Pompeius Trogus, *Historiae Philippicae*, who described the
coming of Caranus to Macedonia, as we see from Just. 7.1.7–10 (cf. 33.2.6).

'is said' to have fallen in love etc. The reader is thereby warned that in Plutarch's opinion this episode is less worthy of trust than what preceded (Alexander's descent) and than what is to follow (the dreams of Philip and of Olympias). The doubt which Plutarch raised has been stated more emphatically by modern writers, e.g. by G. T. Griffith in a footnote: 'the love match ... seems ruled out by chronological improbability'.[6] The chronological factors which bear on Philip 'still a lad' (μειράκιον ὢν ἔτι) and Olympias 'an orphaned child' (παιδὸς ὀρφανῆς γονέων) falling in love and 'so' marrying are as follows. Born in 383 or 382, Philip ceased to be a lad by 363/2;[7] Olympias was orphaned probably in 360;[8] and the marriage, which Plutarch implies followed quickly[9] on their meeting in Samothrace, did not take place until 358/7, when Philip was some twenty-five years old. Individual details may have been true (e.g. meeting in Samothrace, falling in love); but the combination of them is certainly false,[10] Arybbas was wrongly described as the brother of Olympias, whereas he was her uncle. Whoever first publicised this false account lacked the knowledge of the Macedonian and Molossian royal houses which was characteristic, for instance, of Hieronymus of Cardia (he died *c*. 260), and assumed that his readers also were ill-informed. When we try to identify the originator of the false account, we shall look for someone writing after 260, careless of detail and substance, and distrusted by Plutarch (see. p. 9 below).

There are some links between this passage (2.2) and two later passages (9.5–10 and 10.6–7). At 9.5–6 Philip, though

---

[6] *HM* II 215 n. 2. He did not give his own reasons but referred the reader to the excellent arguments of H. Strasburger in *RE* 18.1 (1939) 178.

[7] Hamilton *C* 2f. cites authorities for putting the upper limit at 21 years of age (cf. P*A* 11.6 and Demosth. 23.2); Plutarch called Caesar 'a lad' at what he thought to be a similar age (*Caes.* 1.7–2.7).

[8] So G. N. Cross, *Epirus* (Cambridge, 1932) 37.

[9] As implied by οὕτως; thus Strasburger loc. cit. 'unmittelbar darauf geschlossen'. The translation by Perrin, 'Philip betrothed himself to her at once' is inaccurate; the literal meaning is 'and so Philip fixed the marriage'.

[10] It has been suggested that Curtius referred to the meeting in reporting Alexander's retorts to Cleitus and others (8.1.26); but Alexander was referring to events after the battle of Chaeronea, and he censured Philip and others for being at the mysteries when they ought to have been invading Asia.

'beyond the age' for such an affair (in 337 he was forty-five!), fell in love with 'the girl' Cleopatra and married her. This marriage caused quarrels within the women's quarters to spread like an infection into the kingdom, and it led to 'many grievances and great differences which were still further aggravated by the viciousness of Olympias, a jealous and passionate woman, who exacerbated Alexander'. It has to be borne in mind that marrying for love at any level and especially at that of royalty was an aberration: for as Sophocles showed, a man who yields to love 'is mad' (*Antigone* 790). The evil consequences of Philip's mad passion, which had led him to marry Olympias and now Cleopatra, followed rapidly. For in Plutarch's account a dreadful quarrel ensued between Philip and Alexander. In consequence of it Olympias and Alexander left Philip's court (9.11).

But worse was to follow. Cleopatra and her uncle Attalus were responsible for the outrageous treatment of a young man, called Pausanias, who failed to obtain redress (10.6) and assassinated Philip.

Though most of the blame rested with Olympias, who had exhorted and exacerbated the young man, yet a degree of accusation attached also to Alexander. For it is said (λέγεται) that, when Pausanias met Alexander after that outrage and complained to him, Alexander quoted the verse of Medea: 'the giver of the bride, the bridegroom and the bride'.[11]

The expression 'it is said' had been used of the love-match at 2.2. It shows now, as it did then, that Plutarch doubted the veracity of his source.

Athenaeus, writing towards A.D. 200, has left us a summary of what Plutarch appropriately called Philip's 'marriages and passionate loves' (9.5). Whereas Philip generally married 'with war in view' (we might say with policy in mind, for the Macedonian state was continuously at war),[12] 'he fell in love with Cleopatra, the sister of Hippostratus and the niece of

---

[11] The implication was that Pausanias should kill Attalus, Philip and Cleopatra; and there was the further idea that Alexander's words were prophetic.
[12] I gave this meaning in *HM* II 153. Griffith agreed with me in *HM* II 214 but he translated 'in the course of war' which seems to me mistaken. See L–S–J s.v. κατά B III 1.

Attalus, married her and by bringing her in alongside Olympias ruined his whole life' (557d). The climax was mentioned by Athenaeus at 560c: 'entire households were overturned through women – that of Philip, father of Alexander, through the marriage with Cleopatra'. In other words the marriage with Cleopatra led to the quarrels with Alexander and to the assassination of Philip at the instigation of his wife Olympias, events which Athenaeus did not trouble to report but which are retailed by Plutarch at 9.7–11 and 10.6–7. In both cases Philip's surrender to passionate love was a fatal folly. Olympias brought him the loss of his right eye (3.2); and thereafter Cleopatra (10.6) and Olympias worked on Pausanias until he murdered Philip.

That Plutarch at 2.2, 9.5–10 and 10.6–7 and Athenaeus at 557b–e and 560c were abbreviating drastically a common source which gave a much longer account is certain.[13] Thus at 10.6 Plutarch's mentions of Pausanias and of his failure to obtain redress are so abbreviated that they are almost unintelligible; and similarly Athenaeus failed to explain how the marriage with Cleopatra proved fatal to the life of Philip. The missing information was no doubt in the common source. We owe to Athenaeus the name of the source: Satyrus, *Life of Philip*, which was written around the middle of the third century B.C. and no longer survives.

We may pause to consider the extent to which Satyrus' account was used by later authors. Plutarch and Athenaeus both liked Satyrus' story of the unseemly quarrel between Attalus and Alexander at the wedding-feast of Philip and Cleopatra (9.7–10, and 557d–e). Justin referred briefly to Philip drawing his sword and chasing Alexander, as an incident arising from Alexander's fears of a rival being considered for the throne (9.7.3–4). Plutarch retailed the throwing of a tankard by Alexander, Philip drawing his sword against his son but tripping and falling in a drunken stupor (9.7–10); Athenaeus had Alexander and Attalus throw tankards at each other but did not mention the fall of Philip (557d–e). The account of

---

[13] As I argued in *THA* 87–90.

Satyrus had already been used by Pompeius Trogus, whose version is indicated in the abbreviated reports of Justin.

Philip marries Olympias, daughter of Neoptolemus, king of the Molossians, the marriage being procured by her cousin on the male side ('fratre patrueli'),[14] the guardian of the virgin,[15] namely Arybbas, king of the Molossians, who was already married to Olympias' sister, Troas. This was the cause of death and of all evils for him; for instead of gaining additional territory through kinship with Philip Arybbas lost his own kingdom and died in exile. (Just 7.6.10–11).

Plutarch simply had Philip 'persuade her brother Arybbas' to agree to the marriage (2.2). Athenaeus had Philip acquire the kingdom of Molossia by marrying Olympias, and he transferred (or repeated) the cliché about marriages leading to disasters to the clash between the two wives, Olympias and Cleopatra (557d and 560c).

The reader of Athenaeus will wonder how the marriage with Cleopatra resulted in the death of Philip. The answer is provided most fully by Justin, the ultimate source being Satyrus, *Life of Philip*. According to him the assassin of Philip, Pausanias, a young Macedonian noble ('nobilis ex Macedonibus adulescens'),[16] had been violently raped in his first years of puberty by Attalus, and at a later date he had been the victim of a dirty trick by Attalus; for he was made drunk at a dinner and was submitted like a male prostitute to the lust of Attalus and Attalus' guests. Thereafter Attalus made him the butt of his contemporaries. Pausanias complained often to Philip, and when he saw his enemy promoted and himself put off 'not without mockery', Pausanias transferred his anger to Philip himself and exacted from the unfair judge the revenge which he was unable to take upon his enemy (9.6.4– 8). 'It has been believed', continued Justin, 'that he had been also incited by Olympias, and that Alexander himself had manifestly been not unaware of the plan to kill his father ... the two of them

[14] Arybbas was not a cousin but an uncle of Olympias. Plutarch may have misread the common source, when he called Arybbas the brother of Olympias at 2.2.
[15] This virgin condition was stated for Cleopatra at 9.6, παρθένον, where his source was probably Satyrus.
[16] Plutarch at 10.6 called Pausanias a νεανίσκος.

are believed to have impelled Pausanias to commit so great a crime' (9.7.8). The expressions 'creditum est' and 'creduntur' warn us that Justin doubted the veracity of the source. Plutarch was briefer. He mentioned an outrage committed on Pausanias (but without describing what it was), Pausanias' inability to obtain 'justice', Olympias inciting Pausanias, and Pausanias' murder of Philip. Like Justin, Plutarch entered a cautionary phrase, 'it is said', when he went on to incriminate Alexander as being privy to Olympias' plan (10.6–7).

Justin seems, then, to have been totally uncritical in accepting the sensational account of Satyrus, except that he warned us by adding 'creditum est' and 'creduntur' when he wrote of Olympias and Alexander planning the death of Philip. Plutarch showed a doubt about the love story of the young prince and princess when they were being initiated at Samothrace; and he carelessly changed Attalus' relationship from cousin to brother (2.2). He swallowed the full account of the quarrel at the wedding-feast, the drunkenness of Philip, and the exacerbation of Alexander by the evilly jealous Olympias (9.5–10). But he chose to omit the racy account of the sexual assaults on Pausanias and the inattention 'not without mockery' which Philip gave to Pausanias' complaints. Like Justin, Plutarch entered a *caveat* when he came to the suggested complicity of Alexander in the plot to kill Philip; but he seems to have accepted without any reservation the involvement of Olympias as the instigator of Pausanias.

The doubts which Justin and Plutarch expressed about the veracity of their source, Satyrus, on certain points (the love-match at Samothrace, the instigation by Olympias of the assassin Pausanias, and the complicity of Alexander in the plot) were fully justified. Satyrus simply did not know certain facts: the ages of Philip 'the lad' and Olympias 'the orphan' at their supposed love-match in Samothrace, the date of their marriage, the relationship of Arybbas and Olympias, and the age of Pausanias who, as we shall see, was no 'youth'. Satyrus' version of some of the events was more sensational and less likely to be true than that of Diodorus, who was following a

11

different source, probably Diyllus.[17] Thus, whereas Satyrus
had Attalus rape Pausanias when he was a boy and then
after making him drunk organise a gang-rape of Pausanias, in
which Attalus himself took the lead, Diodorus gave a different
and more detailed story, which ended with the sexual abuse of
Pausanias by Attalus' muleteers, Philip's anger at the outrage,
Philip's promotion of Pausanias, and Philip's need of the services of Attalus as a general in Asia. The assassination was
staged differently by Satyrus and by Diodorus. According to
Satyrus there were no Bodyguards ('sine custodibus corporis'
in Just. 9.6.3) and Philip was killed in a narrow place (i.e. in
the *parodos*) when he was between the two Alexanders. According to Diodorus Philip sent his Friends ahead and entered
the *orchestra* alone, his various guards being at some distance
from him, and it was one of the Bodyguards, Pausanias, thus
a high-ranking officer,[18] who ran forward and killed the king.
Of these two accounts that of Diodorus is certainly to be
preferred; for it is very detailed and is derived without doubt
from an eyewitness.

Satyrus made Pausanias a young lad, a victim of sexual
abuse on a grand scale. Diodorus had a young Pausanias
(probably a Page) and an older Pausanias, who was promoted
to be a Bodyguard (one could not go higher).[19] He provided
an account of their relations with Attalus and with the king,
mentioned only one instance of sexual abuse (that by Attalus'
muleteers), and explained the reasons for the actions which

---

[17] See my article in *CQ* 31 (1937) 84, 86 and 90 and *THA* 32ff. with n. 20.

[18] In *HM* II 403 Griffith argued that the word 'Bodyguard' was wrongly used of
Pausanias and others in Diodorus 16.93.3 and 94.4, and that the error was due
to a confused use of the term. But Diodorus is perfectly clear: he applied the
term σωματοφύλαξ to Pausanias, Leonnatus, Perdiccas and Attalus and the term
δορυφόροι to the guards who were to stand far off (16.93.1 and 94.3); and
the promotion of Pausanias was κατὰ τὴν σωματοφυλακίαν and not κατὰ τὴν
δορυφορίαν. Berve II 233 n. 1 thought that the Somatophylakes were Hypaspists;
but why did Diodorus not call them that? Berve is followed by J. R. Fears,
'Pausanias, the assassin of Philip II', *Athenaeum* 53 (1975) 115 n. 14. See also *LCM*
4.10 (1979) 215f. and W. Heckel in *Phoenix* 40 (1986) 279f.

[19] According to Diodorus the older Pausanias had once been the favourite of the
king, φίλος γεγονώς (16.93.3); it was later that he saw another Pausanias in that
position. Griffith in *HM* II 684 missed the meaning of the perfect tense of γεγονώς,
when he wrote of the two Pausaniases as rivals for the king's favours.

Philip took (16.93.3–9). Again the account of Diodorus is far superior to that of Satyrus.

Satyrus, unlike the surviving Alexander-historians, made Olympias and Alexander privy to the plan of Pausanias. Justin doubted the truth of Satyrus' interpretation; Plutarch limited his own doubt to one element in that interpretation, Alexander's complicity. The rest of Satyrus' account of Olympias' participation in the affair, as it is reflected in Justin 9.7.9–11, is utterly fantastic. Olympias provided horses for the assassin's flight, ran to join in the funeral of Philip, put a gold wreath on the head of the crucified Pausanias that very night, cremated Pausanias' corpse, covered the remains with a tumulus and inaugurated annual sacrifices in honour of Pausanias. The placing of the gold wreath was 'something which no one other than she could have done while the son of Philip was alive', the implication being that Alexander, being privy to the plot, let his mother go scot-free. It is evident that Satyrus was writing not history but propaganda, which was as false as it was malicious.

The circumstances under which such propaganda was started are not in doubt. When Olympias engineered the deaths of Philip Arrhidaeus and Eurydice, whose claims had been supported by Cassander, the son of Antipater, Olympias accused Antipater and his sons of having caused the death of Alexander by a deadly poison.[20] Plutarch reported that accusation, but he made it clear that he did not believe it to be true (77.1–5; see p. 147 below). When Cassander engineered the death of Olympias in 316 B.C., he circulated the rumour that Olympias had instigated the murder of Philip and had honoured the assassin Pausanias.

Now that we have analysed the sources of these chapters of the *Life* and made comparisons with accounts in other writings we can see that Satyrus was a most untrustworthy author, and that accounts which derived from other sources for the same events are generally to be preferred by the modern historian. Where source-analysis has not been attempted, most

[20] See *HM* III 140f.

scholars have simply felt free to pick and choose such incidents as appealed to them personally and suited their subjective idea of the personalities of Philip and Alexander.[21] Such an approach is uncritical and unsound.

3. Chapters 9.11 to 10.5

We have seen that Plutarch was drawing on Satyrus for 9.5–10 and for 10.6–7. The question, then, is whether he was using Satyrus for the intervening passage, with which we are now dealing. That he did so for the withdrawal of Olympias to Epirus, and of Alexander to Epirus and thence to Illyria (9.11), is clear from the similar statement in Justin 9.7.6 ('in Epirum cum matre, inde ad reges Illyriorum').[22] In 9.12–14 Plutarch reported the persuasion of Philip by Demaratus and the persuasion of Alexander by Demaratus which resulted in the return of Alexander (nothing being said of Olympias). Justin also referred very briefly to the difficulty which attended the reconciliation: 'vixque revocanti mitigatus est patri precibusque cognatorum aegre redire conpulsus' (9.7.6). Justin went on to say that Olympias would have engaged her brother Alexander in war against Philip, if Philip had not diverted Alexander by staging the wedding of Alexander and his

---

[21] The contemporary and unassailable evidence is that of Aristotle. While listing examples of outrageous treatment (ὕβρις) such as killing a ruler, he included 'the attack on Philip by Pausanias for letting Pausanias be outraged by Attalus and company', ὑπὸ τῶν περὶ Ἄτταλον (*Pol.* 1311a33f.). Aristotle was concerned simply to give an example; his aim was not to 'give the lie to the official version that he [Pausanias] was merely a tool of others'. (Brunt *L* I lx). Ellis, accepting Diyllus as the probable source of Diodorus (306 n. 56), nevertheless called it 'the official version' and divided Justin's account into two versions. Macedonia had no Ministry of Information; what was made public was the verdict of the State Court, that two sons of Aëropus had been privy to the plot. Most writers repeat the longer version, that of Diodorus (e.g. Ellis 223), but yield to the temptation of adding a colourful point or two from Justin (e.g. Griffith in *HM* II 684ff. adding Olympias making the journey of return from Epirus 'as fast as the horses could travel', an elaboration of Just. 9.7.10 'ad exequias cucurrisset'). To entertain the idea that Olympias or/and Alexander were privy to the plot, as E. Badian did, for instance, in *Phoenix* 17 (1963) 244ff., is to put faith in passages which we have been warned by Justin and Plutarch not to trust.

[22] The plural indicated that there were 'kings' in Illyria and not a single 'king of Illyrians' as F. Papazoglou has maintained; see my article in *BSA* 61 (1966) 239ff.

daughter Cleopatra.[23] It seems likely that Plutarch and Justin (Trogus) were using a common source which devoted attention to the immediate aftermath of the quarrel between father and son and between husband and wife. In the case of Justin that source was certainly Satyrus; and it follows that Plutarch too was probably using Satyrus.

The Demaratus of Plutarch 9.12–14 is a well-attested citizen of Corinth. He was listed among the traitors helping Philip when Philip was weak (Demosth. *De Corona* 295), served as ambassador at Syracuse in 345 (Plu. *Tim.* 21, 24, 27), fought beside Alexander at the River Granicus in 334 (Arr. 1.15.6), visited Susa in 331 as a friend of Alexander's father (Plu. *Alex.* 37.7 πατρῷον φίλον), and died at Alexander's court as 'a more elderly man' in 328/7 (Plu. *Alex.* 56.2).[24] Demaratus, according to Plutarch, brought Philip to his senses by contrasting Philip's concern for Greece [i.e. after Chaeronea when the Hellenic League was being established] with the 'dissension and disaster with which he had filled the royal household'. Such an anecdote, whether true or not, would have appealed to a Greek writer such as Satyrus.

The next section, 10.1–3, describes another rift between Alexander, now back at court, and his father – a rift during which Olympias exacerbated Alexander. The story is as follows. Pixodarus, the satrap of Caria, sent an agent to arrange with Philip a marriage between Pixodarus' eldest daughter and Arrhidaeus, Philip's son. Olympias and others told Alexander that Philip was planning thereby to make Arrhidaeus his successor rather than Alexander.[25] Alexander was confounded; he sent off an agent (Thessalus the actor) to Pixodarus to say that Arrhidaeus was an illegitimate child[26]

---

[23] This is an absurd suggestion to anyone who was aware of the military position in 337, when Macedonia and the Greek states were in alliance.

[24] Bosworth *C* i 122f. postulated a different Demaratus who fought at the River Granicus; this is unnecessary since Parmenio fought there when he was already elderly.

[25] Such an inference was far from compelling in a court where all members of the royal house were married off to obtain political alliance or military support.

[26] This is a Greek idea deriving from the practice of monogamy. Macedonian kings were polygamous and the children of their wives were all legitimate. See *HM* II 153.

and not *compos mentis*, and that the marriage should be arranged instead with Alexander. Pixodarus was delighted. But Philip, taking Philotas, son of Parmenio, with him, entered Alexander's room and ticked him off severely. Philip upbraided Alexander as 'ignoble and unworthy of his high station in desiring to become the son-in-law of a Carian fellow who was the slave of a barbarian king [i.e. of the Persian monarch]'.

The absurdity of the story is obvious. While Pixodarus was a subject of Persia (as he was at the time), there was no attraction in forming a marriage alliance with him. If he should rebel at some future date and maintain his independence, he would still be relatively unimportant. The supposed negotiations had to be strictly secret while Caria was in Persian hands; it is nonsensical to suppose that they were common knowledge for Olympias and Alexander's friends. Again the supposed message of Olympias to Alexander and his supposed proposals to Pixodarus had to be kept secret, especially from Philip. Finally, the supposed remarks of Philip to Alexander were known only to them and to Philotas, who was surely under an oath of secrecy until his death in 330. The taunt about becoming the son-in-law of a barbarian fellow was absurd on the lips of Philip, who was himself the son-in-law of the Illyrian Bardylis and the son-in-law of the Getic king, Cothelas. The story has features common to passages which, we have argued, were inspired by Satyrus: Olympias exacerbating Alexander against his father (9.5), conversations reported verbatim from dinner-parties (9.7–10) and from a tête-à-tête between Philip and Demaratus (9.13), and a treasonable remark by Alexander to Pausanias, which neither would have divulged (10.7). It follows that the author from whom Plutarch took the Pixodarus affair was Satyrus. His account of the affair has rightly been regarded as unhistorical by critical historians.[27]

---

[27] Most recently by M. B. Hatzopoulos in *M–G* 5ff.; and by myself in 1981 in *AG²* 36f. On the other hand, A. R. Burn in *Alexander the Great and the Hellenistic Empire* (London, 1947) 49f. accepted the affair *in toto*, as 'a pretty kettle of fish'; so too most recently but more cautiously Bosworth *CE* 21f. Arguments for accepting the affair are advanced best by V. French and P. Dixon in *The Ancient World* 13 (1986) 72–86.

4. Chapters 2.3–6, 7–9 and 3

The dreams in 2.3–5 are related by Plutarch as facts. Yet they were surely *somnia post eventum*, like the *vaticinia post eventum* in chapter 3. If Olympias had had such a terrifying dream, she would not have revealed it; nor would Philip have revealed his supposed dream, as it was generally supposed to suggest that Olympias had been, was being or would be unfaithful. It was only after Alexander's triumphs in Asia that he was to be identified as the lion of such dreams. The story of the snake lying with Olympias is common to 2.6, 3.1–2 (when the snake is identified by Apollo with Zeus Ammon) and 3.3 (when Olympias told Alexander of his begetting 'and him alone'). The story of Philip seeing the snake in his wife's bed (2.6) is common to the prophecy that Philip would lose his eye (as he did three years later at Methone); thus this part of the story probably arose after 354.

Plutarch included two warnings. He added 'they say' (λέγουσιν) to his report that the sight of the snake at work blunted Philip's desire and led to a cooling of relations between him and Olympias, for which two alternative reasons on Philip's part were provided. The plural 'they say' and the two alternatives indicate that Plutarch had consulted more than one source on this topic, and in 2.7–9 he gives in addition 'another story' (ἕτερος λόγος), which explained the presence of the snake as due to the Macedonian–Thracian Orphic rites. He added that Olympias was particularly well versed in these rites and was expert in handling giant tame snakes. Then at 3.3 Plutarch cited Eratosthenes as saying that Olympias told Alexander and him alone the secret of his begetting, when she sent him off to Asia and bade him have corresponding ambitions. Plutarch went on to report a witty saying by unnamed persons other than Eratosthenes.

That Plutarch here used several sources, one being Eratosthenes, the Librarian at Alexandria from *c.* 246, is to be believed; for contemporary scholars would have commented if his claim had been untrue. The reports of the alleged dreams circulated probably before Alexander died and certainly soon after his death. For they figured in versions of *The Alexander*

Romance.[28] Plutarch had an 'implicit faith in the veracity of dreams along with stress on their prophetic quality' and he often reserved them 'for predictions of the future greatness of the hero'[29], as he does in the case of Alexander. They are of interest to us in that they reveal the mentality of the generation after the birth of Alexander and the reporting of them gives us an insight into the mentality of Plutarch.

In 3.5 A's birth was dated by Plutarch to 'the 6th day of early Hecatombaeon'. This was the first month of the Attic year, and it ran approximately from 21 June (midsummer) to 20 July. Plutarch noted that the Macedonians called it Loüs (a variant form of Λώιος, meaning 'better').[30] This month was the tenth of the Macedonian year, which began with Dius (running approximately from late September into October), and it corresponded approximately with late July into August. The birth lying in the overlap of the two calendar months was thus in late July.[31] Plutarch continued in the same sentence: 'it was on this day that the temple of Artemis at Ephesus was burnt'. That date would have been recorded in the priestly records at Ephesus; it evidently coincided with the 6th of Hecatombaeon. Plutarch went on to mention some synchronisms. One of them was Philip's victory in the Olympic Games, which were held every fourth year. Thus the year was 356 B.C. The news of the victory of his race-horse reached Philip together with the news of A's birth (we do not know where Philip was at the time).[32] Since the sacred month of the Olympic festival fell in July and August,[33] it is acceptable that the two items of news reached Philip at the same time, say in early August.

---

[28] Dreams of the snake, the snake's actual behaviour and the dream of the womb of Olympias being sealed figured in the Greek version (ed. W. Kroll, 1.5; 1.6.3; 1.8.3.) together with the explanation that one does not seal an empty vessel.

[29] F. E. Brenk, *In Mist Apparelled* (Leiden, 1977) 233f.

[30] See J. N. Kalléris, *Les anciens Macédoniens* I (Athens, 1954) 235 and II (Athens, 1976) 557f., connected the name of the month with a prayer to Demeter (cf. s.v. Ὁμολώιος) for a good harvest, which falls in late June into July in Lower Macedonia.

[31] So G. T. Griffith in *HM* II 54 and 772 but without analysing the sources of information; see also Hamilton *C* 7 'about 20 July'.

[32] He may well have been in Thessaly; see Diod. 16.14.2 under the year 357/6, and my chronology in *JHS* 57 (1957) 44ff., *pace* G. T. Griffith in *HM* II 225.

[33] J. E. Sandys, ed., *A Dictionary of Classical Antiquities* (London, c. 1894) 429.

Who was the author of this information, on whom Plutarch relied? He was a Greek writer because he used the Attic chronology for the month and day and the burning of the temple at Ephesus for confirmation of the day. It was presumably he who provided the other synchronisms: two from Greek affairs – the victory at the Olympic Games and the recent fall of Potidaea, an Athenian possession (ἄρτι ᾑρηκότι) – and one Macedonian affair, Parmenio's defeat of the Illyrians.[34] This author was evidently able to correlate different chronological systems: Attic, Macedonian, Ephesian and Olympic.

In 3.6–7 Plutarch enlarged on the fire at Ephesus as follows:

Hegesias the Magnesian [*FGrH* 142 F 3] uttered a witticism frigid enough to have put that fire out. He said 'naturally the temple was burnt down because Artemis was occupied with the delivery of Alexander'. All the Magi who happened to be staying in Ephesus, regarding the disaster of the temple as the portent of another disaster, ran about beating their heads and shouting that a great disaster and calamity for Asia had been born that day.

It is to be noted that Plutarch cited Hegesias only for the feeble joke, and neither for the synchronisation in 3.5, nor for the behaviour of the Magi; for they were both in a narrative tense and not in the accusative and infinitive.[35] It so happens that Cicero had mentioned both parts of Plutarch's statement: for he said that Artemis attended the birth of A and her temple at Ephesus was burnt (*N.D.* 2.69), and that the night when Olympias gave birth to A was agreed to be the night of the burning of the temple, and as dawn broke next day the Magi had shouted that a plague and calamity for Asia had been born that night (*Div.* 1.47). It is evident that Cicero and Plutarch had a common source, directly or ultimately. Fortunately Cicero named his source for the first passage as Timaeus (*FGrH* 566 F 150a). Plutarch, then, drew on Hegesias for the feeble joke, but on Timaeus for the rest, namely 3.5 and 3.7–8.

---

[34] Tod II 157 shows that three kings, including the Illyrian Grabus, were in league against Philip before 26 July 356 B.C., but had not recently been defeated. Diodorus reported that they were defeated while 'they were collecting their forces' (16.22.3), perhaps in early August.

[35] Jacoby, *FGrH* II B 807 failed to notice the distinction. Hamilton *C* 8 saw 'no good reason to credit' Hegesias with more than the remark about Artemis, i.e. 3.6.

Why should Timaeus have concerned himself with these matters, when he did not write about A? Two reasons may be advanced. Timaeus was born in the same year, 356 B.C. (he lived until 260 B.C), and he may well have been interested in the birthday of his greatest contemporary. He was particularly famous for his control of precise chronology; and Polybius cited as an example Timaeus' correlation of Attic data, priestly records, lists of Olympic victors, and records of ephors and kings at Sparta (12.10.4 and 12.11.1).[36] Similarly in the dating of A's birth Timaeus correlated, as we have seen, Attic data, Macedonian months and events, priestly records at Ephesus, and Olympic victor lists. He probably recorded it as an example of his expertise.

Since Timaeus retailed the prophecy of the Magi, he was probably responsible for the prophecy made by the diviners at Philip's court, that A would be invincible (3.9 ἀνίκητον ἔσεσθαι). Both prophecies were clearly *vaticinia post eventum*.

5. Chapters 4.8 to 6.8

The anecdotes which Plutarch provided were appropriate to A as a boy in his early teens. At that age he could have contemplated competing in the boys' events at the Olympic Games, entertained Persian envoys in the absence of Philip, been educated by Leonidas and Lysimachus, and mastered the horse Bucephalus. In other words A was already a member of the School of Pages, which he entered about the age of fourteen, i.e. in 342. By that date Philip had recorded his Olympic victories on his coins (4.9), had won a leading position in central Greece and in the Balkans (4.4–6), and was powerful enough in Thrace to be approached by Persian envoys (5.1–3).[37] A was then of an age to master the undisciplined stallion,

---

[36] See G. L. Barber in *OCD*[2] 1074, and Walbank *C* II 347f. Polybius was evidently relying on Timaeus in giving the reign of A as lasting 13 years, i.e. *c.* July 336 to 10 June 323 (Livy 45.9.5, based on Polybius).

[37] This passage is a shorter version of what Plutarch had written in *Moralia* 342b–c. Neither passage was used by G. T. Griffith in *PCPS* 14 (1968) 46f. and *HM* II 485ff. and Bosworth *C* I 229; for they were sceptical of the mention by Arrian of a treaty of 'friendship and alliance between Philip and Artaxerxes' (2.14.2). In fact this

Bucephalus; indeed he was said to have been fourteen years of age on that occasion in the Armenian version of *The Alexander Romance* (trs. A. M. Wolohojian) 47.

That the account came from someone who was an exact contemporary and a fellow-Page of A seems highly probable. Such a man could have recalled A's remark 'to his fellows' (πρὸς τοὺς ἡλικιώτας): 'Boys, everything will be achieved first by my father, and no great and brilliant deed will be left for me to accomplish together with you.' He could have understood A's frugality in regard to bodily pleasures, his high-minded, serious ambition 'beyond his years' (4.8 παρ' ἡλικίαν), and his longing for 'excellence and glory' (5.5). And he could have realised how difficult it was for A to grow up in the shadow of Philip.

We know of two works which described the upbringing of A: Marsyas Macedon, αὐτοῦ Ἀλεξάνδρου ἀγωγή (*FGrH* 135/6 τ 1), and Onesicritus, πῶς Ἀλέξανδρος ἤχθη (*FGrH* 134 τ 1). Plutarch evidently used the former of these; for Marsyas Macedon was 'brought up with A' (Souda s.v.),[38] was a brother of Antigonus Monophthalmus, and was surely a fellow-Page. On the other hand, Onesicritus was not a Macedonian and was not brought up in Macedonia. Being a Greek islander, he probably joined A's expedition in 334 as a member of the Greek fleet. There is a vividness and a perceptiveness about A's emotions as a boy that are best attributed to the memories of a contemporary in the School of Pages. Thus the descriptions of Leonidas as 'a man of stern disposition' and of Lysimachus as 'lacking in refinement' came probably from Marsyas.[39]

The account of A mastering Bucephalus (6.1–8) is so vivid

passage enables us to offer as a date for the treaty '*c.* 342', which is in line with Beloch III².1 538 and F. R. Wüst, *Philip II von Makedonien und Griechenland* (Munich, 1938) 89. A date in the early forties, as suggested by Hamilton *C* 13, is less appropriate, because Philip was then a minor power, engaged in the Chalcidian and the Sacred Wars. G. L. Cawkwell in *CQ* 13 (1963) 128 favoured 351, but A would then have been only five years old.

[38] σύντροφος Ἀλεξάνδρου τοῦ βασιλέως. His history of Macedonia was used probably by Trogus 7.1 to 7.4.2; see my article in *CQ* 41 (1991) 501f.

[39] Rather than Onesicritus for Leonidas and Chares for Lysimachus. See Hamilton *C* 14 for references.

that it must have come ultimately from an eyewitness. We see Philonicus with the horse and Philip with his entourage descending (from the palace at Aegeae or at Pella) 'into the plain', so that the horse could show its paces. Its wild behaviour caused Philip to reject it, whereupon A intervened. The conversation and the wager between father and son led to general laughter. The mastering of Bucephalus was told by someone who understood horses as well as A himself did. The details are convincing. A threw off the cloak (*chlamys*) which was part of the Page's dress (it is shown in the Royal Hunt Fresco in Philip's Tomb).[40] Riding bareback, he guided the horse with the pressure of his leg rather than with the bit (6.7).[41] And the emotions of the spectators ranged from apprehension to relief and in Philip's case to tears of joy, 'it is said' (6.8). The doubt thereby implied referred rather to Philip's remark. 'My boy, look for a kingdom to match yourself; Macedonia is not large enough for you.'

Some points in the account invite comment. It was not a question of 'breaking' a stallion, which is normally done at the age of two or soon after. He was already bridled and had no doubt been ridden. He was offered for sale probably at the age of four or soon after, because it is then that training begins, whether for dressage or for war.[42] Thus he was born around 346. The statement of Onesicritus that Bucephalus was aged thirty in 326 (61.1), and thus that he was born in 356, is

---

[40] A was then 14 or so, rather than 9 or 10 as suggested by Th. Sarikakes in K. Babouskos, ed., *Megas Alexandros* (Thessaloniki, 1980) 240. The traditional dress of the Royal Page was described by Plu. *Mor.* 760b as cloak, high boots and *kausia*. This dress is worn by the Royal Page in the Royal Hunt Fresco of Philip's Tomb on the viewer's extreme right. The idea that the *kausia* was not worn until after A's conquest of Asia is thus rendered untenable. The arguments of E. A. Fredricksmeyer in *TAPA* 116 (1986) 215ff. are thereby strengthened and in my opinion unanswerable.

[41] See Tom Roberts, *Horse Control – the Rider* (Adelaide, 1982) 43. Perrin 239 mistranslates as 'the foot' in this context.

[42] Plutarch described the horse as ἀκόλαστος 'undisciplined' and not as ἀδάμαστος, 'unbroken', *pace* Perrin 237, Hamilton *C* 169 and A. R. Anderson in *AJPh* 51 (1930) 11 'Alexander broke him'. In fact a horse was broken early, as the word πωλοδάμνης 'colt-breaker' indicates. I am most grateful for advice I received in the University of Newcastle, New South Wales, from Justin Holland, who has worked in racing stables, and Dr E. Baynham; both of them had ridden bareback at a young age.

untenable; for no one would pay a very high price for a stallion some fourteen years old in 342, unless it was for stud purposes, whereas Bucephalus was to become a war-horse. Onesicritus probably started the romanticising about Bucephalus. For A too was thirty in 326, and later, in *The Alexander Romance*, Bucephalus was said to have been conceived from the seed of Nectanebo, as A was conceived, and to have died of a broken heart at the death of A.[43] The author of the account of the mastering of Bucephalus was a practised horseman himself; for the use of the leg, i.e. the inner side of the calf, is best in riding bareback (6.7). The price which Philonicus was asking for Bucephalus – 13 talents – has been doubted, because it was exceptionally high.[44] The figure occurred not only at 6.1 but also in Gellius 5.2.1, where it was attributed to Chares of Mytilene (*FGrH* 125 F 18); but in Gellius the horse was bought for 13 talents and given to Philip, whereas in Plutarch's account the horse was offered for sale at that price to Philip. Consequently Plutarch was not drawing on the account of Chares.[45] As regards the high price, Bucephalus was exceptionally large, handsome and spirited (6.6, and Arr. 5.19.5) and Philip was the wealthiest owner in the European world. As an asking price 13 talents was not impossible. I conclude that Plutarch was drawing on Marsyas Macedon, *Upbringing of Alexander* in chapters 4.8 to 6.8. For the end of Bucephalus see pp. 110ff. below.

---

[43] See A. R. Anderson, op. cit. 15f. Onesicritus might have been the source used by Arrian at 5.19.4, where the age was given as 'about thirty years'; but by the second century A.D., when Arrian wrote, the myth about Bucephalus as a magical horse was common to many authors. It is surprising that Arrian attributed such an age to Bucephalus without adding that it was a *legomenon*.

[44] Pliny, *N.H.* 8.154 gave the price for which he was bought as XVI talents. It should be emended to XIII.

[45] I disagree here with Jacoby, *FGrH* 2 D 437, who thought it 'very probable' that Cleitarchus used Chares for the price of the purchase of Bucephalus; and J. R. Hamilton, 'Alexander's early life', *Greece and Rome* 12 (1965) 118 thought that the Bucephalus episode was 'probably' from Chares.

2

BALKAN CAMPAIGN, SACK OF THEBES
AND LANDING IN ASIA

1. The Balkan campaign and the sack of Thebes (11–13)

In 11.1–4 the situation facing the young king, just twenty
years old (see above, p. 18), was described by Plutarch in
a sensational manner and in an unusually florid style. For
example, 'after mastering Greece by force of arms Philip
did not have time to yoke and tame her but merely caused
upset and turmoil, so that he left Greek affairs in a state of
great surge and commotion, all due to the novelty of the situation'. A contrast was drawn between the fearfulness of the
Macedonians,[1] ready to withdraw entirely from Greece and
appease the barbarians with mild measures, and the daring
and the great-mindedness of the young king. Here hostility to
the Macedonians is coupled with the initial portrayal of the
headstrong king.

In 5–6 there is no mention of A's first descent into Greece
and his election as leader of the joint forces of the Greeks and
the Macedonians against Persia. The omission must have been
deliberate; for Plutarch had to be selective in order to keep the
Life to a reasonable length. The narrative which he does give
is brief: A's rapid campaign to the Danube, victory there in a
great battle (μάχῃ μεγάλῃ) over Syrmus, king of the Triballi,
and an immediate response to news of a rising by Thebes
and of Athens' collusion by marching through the Gates (of
Thermopylae).[2] He did not derive this from Ptolemy and/or
Aristobulus; for the account based on them, which Arrian
gave (1.2. and 1.4.6), had no 'great battle' at the Danube

---

[1] Perrin mistranslates 11.3 by interpolating 'counsellors of Alexander', which is not
in the Greek text.

[2] These are 'the Gates' (meaning a pass) *par excellence*; cf. Arr. 1.7.5, which refers
also to Thermopylae and not, as Brunt *L* I 33 n. 4 says, to a pass on 'an unusual
easterly route.' See H*MAT* for A's route.

between A and Syrmus.³ However, reference to such a battle was made by Justin at 11.2.8, where A and his army were reported in the Assembly at Athens to have been wiped out by the Triballi 'in that battle' ('in eo proelio'). It is likely, then, that Plutarch and Justin had a common source for the false information about a great battle; and this likelihood is increased by both of them stressing the speed with which A responded to the news of a rising (εὐθύς and 'tanta celeritate'). The source which I suggested for Justin 11.2 was Cleitarchus (*THA* 94f.).

Plutarch had A declare that Demosthenes had called him a boy when campaigning against the Illyrians and the Triballians and a lad when he was in Thessaly (περὶ Θετταλίαν γενόμενον), and that A intended to present himself at the walls of Athens as a man. A stay in Thessaly *en route* from the Balkans towards Athens is assumed in this passage. Whereas in Arrian's account A marched post-haste through Thessaly (1.7.5), Justin reported a stay in Thessaly 'in transitu' (11.3.1), during which A reminded the Thessalians of 'Philip's benefactions and of the descent from the Aeacidae [Achilles' family] which his mother and they shared'. Here, too, a common source is indicated, namely Cleitarchus.⁴

When A approached Thebes, there were according to Plutarch preliminary negotiations. A asked for the surrender of two men, Phoenix and Prothytes (perhaps the Boeotarchs of Arr. 1.7.11), and the Thebans demanded the surrender of Philotas and Antipater. Arrian said that A delayed in the hope that Thebes would negotiate, but that no negotiations followed (1.7.7–11); and he did not mention the four named men. However, Diodorus mentioned Philotas as commander of the Macedonian garrison inside Thebes (17.8.7). Arrian said that Antipater was named as the commander of the Macedonian army by the leaders of the Theban rising (1.7.6);

---

³ There was only a minor engagement with the Triballi at the Lyginus River, at which time Syrmus was taking refuge on an island in the Danube. For this campaign see my article in *JHS* 94 (1974) 66ff. and briefly in *AG²* 45–8.
⁴ He laid particular emphasis on the Aeacid connection; see *THA* 91f., referring especially to Just. 11.3.1.

and Polyaenus had an Antipater command a successful ambush, which is incompatible with Arrian's account of the capture of the city (4.3.12). It is likely that Plutarch, Diodorus
and Polyaenus had a common source which provided these
names.[5] Next, according to Plutarch, the Thebans asked all
who wished to join in liberating Greece to join their ranks.
Diodorus reported this as the Theban riposte to a proclamation by A, asking the Thebans to join in the Common Peace
of the Greeks (17.9.5). When action started, the Thebans
fought with a gallantry and a zest beyond their actual strength
'against many times their number' (πολλαπλασίοις). The same
claim was made by Diodorus, who had the Macedonians 'many
times as numerous' (17.11.2 πολλαπλασίοις) and described
the Theban spirit as 'exalted' (17.11.4). The final collapse was
brought about by the sortie of the Macedonian garrison from
the Cadmea according to Plutarch and Diodorus (11.10 and
17.12.5). These coincidences between Plutarch and Diodorus
indicate that they were using a common source, namely Cleitarchus, as I argued in the case of Diodorus in *THA* 13–15 and
27. To clinch the matter, we may refer to the figures which
Plutarch and Diodorus gave later for Theban losses, more
than 6,000 dead and more than 30,000 sold as slaves (11.12
and 17.14.1).[6]

At 11.11 Plutarch mentioned that the Phocians and the
Plataeans 'accused the Thebans'. Where? The answer appears
in Justin, where they are the first two of the peoples denouncing the Thebans 'in the council', i.e. of the Greeks of the
Common Peace (11.3.8). When it was decided to destroy
Thebes, the expectation of A was that 'the Greeks would be
terrified, cower down and keep still' (*PA* 11.11); and Diodorus
made the same point in writing that 'A instilled great fear into
those of the Greeks who might rebel' (17.14.4).

In 12 the action of Timoclea and the release of her and her
children by A were recorded. They were set out also in *Moralia*
259d–260d and with slight variations in Polyaenus 8.40.

---

[5] For a discussion of these passages see *THA* 168.
[6] In 17.4.1 Diodorus gave for the sale of the captives 440 talents; that is the figure
given by Cleitarchus (*FGrH* 137 F 1); see *THA* 26.

Plutarch gave his source as Aristobulus not here but in *Moralia* 1093c.

In chapter 13 there is the same exaggeration and florid writing as in chapter 11: Athens' exceeding grief for Thebes, A like a lion in his savagery but now sated and merciful to Athens, A regarding Athens as the future ruler of Greece if anything should happen to A, and A finally overcome with remorse and superstitious dread. For later on A used to attribute to the wrath of Dionysus and to retribution (νέμεσις) 'the episode of Cleitus which happened *in vino*' (ἐν οἴνῳ γενόμενον) and 'the cowardice in India of the Macedonians who abandoned his expedition and his glory to incompleteness' (13.4).[7] Here Plutarch envisaged Dionysus as the god of wine and made drunkenness responsible for A killing Cleitus. That, however, is not the explanation in Plutarch's version of the episode; for it was the portent, the vision and the incomplete sacrifice (50.4–7) which made the death preordained (52.2).[8] But in the accounts of Justin and Curtius drunkenness was the main feature (12.6.2 'inter ebrios' and 6 'pocula'; and 8.1.22 'multo mero', 8.1.43 'mero sensibus victis', 8.2.1 'ebrietate', 8.2.6 'inter vinum et epulas', and mention of Liber, the god of wine). In *THA* 104 and 146 I proposed Cleitarchus as the source for these two versions, and I therefore propose him as Plutarch's source here. The cowardice of the Macedonians was one of Cleitarchus' themes, as in 11.9 and in Diodorus 17.23.1–3 and 27.2, passages based on Cleitarchus (*THA* 38f.).

To sum up, I conclude that Plutarch used as his source Cleitarchus for chapters 11 and 13, and Aristobulus for chapter 12.

2. Antecedents to and then the landing in Asia (14–15)

The meeting of Alexander and Diogenes (14.1–5)

This episode pleased Plutarch, for he mentioned it also in *Moralia* 331e–f, 605d and 782a. The meeting was related to

---

[7] The reference is to the Macedonians being afraid to cross the Hyphasis and face Indian forces beyond the Ganges.

[8] See below, p. 94 for Plutarch's source at 50–2.

the appointment of A as *Hegemon* of the Greeks, because that appointment was made at the Isthmus and Diogenes lived in a suburb of Corinth called Craneion. We may accept Plutarch's statement that at the time many politicians and philosophers came to visit A, but that A had to go to Diogenes, who was lying in the sun (14.1–3). 'At the approach of so many fellows Diogenes sat up a little.' Who were these fellows? The answer is provided for us by Arrian, who said that A found Diogenes lying in the sun on the Isthmus and that A halted, accompanied by his Hypaspists and his Pezhetairoi (7.2.1). We may thus infer that Plutarch and Arrian were drawing on a common source which had given a fuller account of the meeting.

The source was well informed of the circumstances at the time; for already in A's early years as king A had these two Royal Infantry Guards.[9] The source was also an admirer of Diogenes. The most likely writer is Onesicritus. For he was a pupil of Diogenes (*FGrH* 134 T 1, 2 and 5a) and, as such, he might well have been present at the meeting. It should be noted that Arrian reported the meeting as historical; for his qualification, λέγεται, applied only to A's reaction (see p. 282 below). I conclude that Plutarch probably drew on the work of Onesicritus, and that Arrian's account came – perhaps through Aristobulus – ultimately from Onesicritus.[10] The meeting, then, was historical despite modern doubts,[11] and Alexander may well have said. 'Indeed, were I not Alexander, I would be Diogenes.'

---

[9] The Guards are mentioned in Arr. 1.8.3 where the MSS τὰ δὲ ἀγήματα should not be emended, and at 1.8.4 where τὸ ἄγημα τὸ τῶν Μακεδόνων is the Guard of Pezhetairoi. See H*VG*.

[10] Onesicritus wrote earlier than most of the Alexander-historians; see Jacoby in *FGrH* 2 D 469.

[11] Hamilton *C* 34, for instance, called it 'doubtless a fiction'. He misinterpreted Arr. 7.2.1 when he said that Arrian 'gives it only as a λεγόμενον'. Arrian in fact applied λέγεται only to A's wonder (θαυμάσαι λέγεται) which was similar to his reaction to the Indian philosophers described in 7.1.5–7. Similarly Brown *Ones.* 28 'the safest view is probably that it [the meeting with Diogenes] did not take place at all'; cf. Brunt *L* II 205 n. 1. These commentators did not realise the significance of the two sets of Guards.

Prophecies and portents (14.6–9)

Plutarch's report that the Pythia at Delphi called A 'invincible' (ἀνίκητος) finds an echo in Diodorus 17.93.4. There were, according to Diodorus, two oracles which encouraged A to advance beyond the Hyphasis: one from the Pythia that A was 'invincible', and the other from Ammon granting to A 'rule over all the earth'. The context within which Diodorus mentioned the two oracles was a highly coloured and probably untrustworthy narrative about the country beyond the Hyphasis. He had already reported the oracle of Ammon at Siwa: there A asked for 'rule over all the earth' and the oracular spokesman told A that he would be 'invincible for ever' (17.51.2–3). There too the account was sensational and untrustworthy. As I maintained in *THA* 43f. and 63f., the source in both passages (51.2–3 and 93.4) was Cleitarchus.[12] I conclude that Plutarch derived from Cleitarchus his statement that A visited Delphi and was told he was invincible.[13] The story is unhistorical.[14]

Plutarch reported 'other signs from heaven and especially the sweating of the cypress-wood statue of Orpheus at Leibethra' (in Pieria), adding the qualification 'it seems'. He went on to say that Aristander interpreted this as a happy omen. Arrian too had a report of the sweating statue of Orpheus in Pieria and of Aristander bidding A to be of good cheer. In both accounts Aristander went on to say that A and his achievements would cost poets and musicians much labour and sweat (P*A* 14.9 and Arr. 1.11.2). It is clear that Plutarch and Arrian followed the same source. Since Arrian added no qualification, he was drawing on one or both of his pair, Ptolemy and Aristobulus; and of the two it was Aristobulus

[12] So too Goukowsky xxix and 74 'sans doute Clitarque'.
[13] Hamilton *C* 34 'it is probable that his source was Cleitarchus'.
[14] Cleitarchus expected his readers to see A as a second Philomelus, a desecrator of the shrine. See Diod. 16.27.1 for Philomelus forcing the priestess to make a response. H. W. Parke, *The Delphic Oracle* (Blackwell, 1939) 252 dismissed the story of A forcing the priestess to serve as 'obviously a fictitious doublet of the earlier incident'.

whom Plutarch was apt to follow rather than Ptolemy.[15] On the whole it is likely that the common source was Aristobulus.[16]

A's forces and finances (15.1–3)

The figures for A's forces which the ancient sources provide do not include those already in Asia. In his earlier work, *Moralia* 327d–e, Plutarch cited the figures of Anaximenes, Aristobulus and Ptolemy, to which we can add those of Callisthenes (Plb. 12.19.1). Here Plutarch cited only the lowest figures for infantry (30,000 from Ptolemy) and cavalry (4,000 from Aristobulus), and the highest figures for infantry (43,000 from Anaximenes) and cavalry (5,000 from Ptolemy, although he had given 5,500 from Anaximenes in *Moralia*). Plutarch omitted Callisthenes, presumably because he distrusted Callisthenes' 'official figures' (40,000 infantry and 4,500 cavalry). He was not prepared to be dogmatic about the precise number of A's forces.[17]

Plutarch described the financial position of A when setting out for Asia (15.3 ὁρμώμενος), in spring 334: namely not more than 70 talents to provision his forces according to Aristobulus, debts of 200 talents according to Onesicritus, and rations for thirty days only according to Duris. A different figure for A's debts, contracted on setting out for Asia, namely 800 talents, was given in A's speech at Opis according to Arrian (7.9.6 δανεισάμενος ... ὁρμηθείς).

Thus Plutarch had consulted a number of writers on A's forces and finances but not apparently the source to which Arrian owed his figure of 800 talents (see p. 288 below).

Gifts to Alexander's Friends (15.3–7)

In *Moralia* 342d, when describing A's generosity, Plutarch had said that Perdiccas alone refused to accept a gift. Here

---

[15] For Aristobulus' interest in natural phenomena and their mystical significance see *FGrH* 139 F 6, F 13 (6), F 54, F 55 (22) and F 58 (3).

[16] Hamilton *C* 35 remarked that Arrian 'was perhaps following Aristobulus' and cites in support H. Strasburger, *Ptolemaios und Alexander* (Leipzig, 1934) 23.

[17] See a discussion in *THA* 36f.

Plutarch added 'and some of the other Friends'. What A distributed were lands, villages, and revenues from hamlets or harbours. That Macedonian kings did make such gifts is attested,[18] except in the case of a 'hamlet', which was probably a part of a scattered village (Plutarch's συνοικία being comparable to a *mahalas* in modern Epirus).[19] But Plutarch's account of what happened in spring 334 is exaggerated beyond belief. For he said that A gave away 'almost all the royal property' and 'the bulk of his possessions in Macedonia', so that when Perdiccas asked 'What are you left with?' A replied 'My hopes.'

A similarly exaggerated account was given by Justin in a concise manner. 'He divided among his Friends all the inheritance which he had in Macedonia and in Europe, declaring that for himself Asia was enough' (11.5.5). Thus Plutarch and Justin were drawing on a common source, who on my interpretation in *THA* 96 was Cleitarchus. Contemporary Greek writers tended to regard the Macedonian kings as immensely wealthy and yet so prodigal that they impoverished themselves.[20] This view of A appealed to Plutarch.

[18] See Hammond *MS* 178f. and 187.
[19] See Hammond *Ep.* 28.
[20] See, for instance, Theopompus F 217 and 224 (*FGrH* 115). He was probably the source of Just. 9.1.5 and 9, and 9.8.6; see my article in *CQ* 41 (1991) 499, 502f.

3

THE SET BATTLES IN ASIA

1. Aristobulus and Callisthenes

Plutarch gave very much shorter accounts of A's set battles than Arrian did. It was purely a matter of choice. Plutarch could have reproduced from Aristobulus a Persian battle-order as easily as Arrian did; but it would not have shed any light on A's personality, which was Plutarch's primary concern. On the other hand, Plutarch did provide some details of A's motivation and some of A's sayings, which are not to be found in Arrian's accounts. For these he must have turned to the work of any author who was himself interested in A's personality and who either as a participant or as one close to participants in all the set battles became aware of A's motives and sayings. In fact we know of only two writers who fit these requirements, Ptolemy and Aristobulus. When we consider the fragments of their works, there is no doubt that Aristobulus was more concerned with A's personality than Ptolemy was. We shall therefore approach these battles with Aristobulus in mind as a probable source.

In his account of the Battle of Gaugamela Plutarch twice quotes statements by Callisthenes. The question therefore arises: how far was Callisthenes used by our main sources of information, namely Ptolemy and Aristobulus, as condensed and reported by Arrian? The position of Arrian is abundantly clear: 'I record what Ptolemy and Aristobulus both have written.' He does not mention Callisthenes, and we have no grounds for supposing that Arrian was lying. One reason for neglecting Callisthenes was the contempt which Arrian personally had for Callisthenes as a flatterer of A and as a boorish, tactless and excessively conceited man (4.12.6f.). Another reason was the distrust of Callisthenes' history which was avowedly and officially published for purposes of propaganda. We can be grateful that Arrian made no use of Callisthenes.

Ptolemy and Aristobulus did not accept the 'official' figures for the number of troops which crossed with A to Asia. Each preferred to give his own figure, and Arrian chose to give not Callisthenes' figures (40,000 infantry and 4,500 cavalry) but Ptolemy's figures in his version (1.10.3 'not much more than 30,000 infantry and over 5,000 cavalry'). The points which Plutarch included for the Battle of Gaugamela – the prayer of A and the incompetence of Parmenio (see p. 40) – were not given by Arrian, and presumably not by his sources, Ptolemy and Aristobulus. For in Arrian's account Parmenio's cavalry engaged keenly in the pursuit and captured the Persian camp (3.15.1, 3 and 4).

It has been suggested that Callisthenes' 'official version' was 'passed on through Ptolemy and Aristobulus and enshrined in the *Anabasis* of Arrian', with particular reference to the Battle of Issus.[1] Something of Callisthenes' version is known from Polybius 12.17–22, who found it illogical, paradoxical and untrustworthy. Callisthenes' version overlaps most with Arrian's version in matters arising from the terrain: namely, A's infantry deploying gradually from column into line as the level ground extended and the cavalry attack delivered by the Persians of the right wing where the river was not an obstacle. Callisthenes and Arrian agreed on the number of the Greek mercenaries, but that number was probably given by many Alexander-historians.

The differences are striking. Callisthenes placed all the Persian cavalry on the Persian right wing, whereas Arrian had some Persian cavalry on the left wing (2.8.10). Callisthenes gave 30,000 as the number of the Persian cavalry, whereas Arrian included 30,000 cavalry in a force which was sent ahead to cover the deployment of the main body (2.8.5 and 10). Callisthenes had Darius make a change in his battle-order by moving his Greek mercenaries from his right wing to his centre 'when the enemy were drawing near' (Plb. 12.18.9). This

---

[1] A. M. Devine in *The Ancient World* 12 (1985) 25.

change is not in Arrian; indeed, as Polybius rightly said, such a change is incredible. Then Callisthenes stated that A arranged his battle-order so that he should confront Darius, and that Darius did likewise but later changed his mind. In Arrian's account Darius stayed in the centre and A's attack was delivered from a point on his right wing, far from Darius. The reinforcements reported by Callisthenes – 'from Macedonia' 5,000 infantry and 800 cavalry – were different from the numbers given by Arrian: 3,000 Macedonian infantry, 300 Macedonian cavalry and 350 Greek cavalry (1.29.4). These differences show, beyond doubt in my opinion, that Callisthenes' version was not adopted by Ptolemy and Aristobulus and was not transmitted through them to Arrian.

Finally, there is in Arrian no echo of Callisthenes' reporting of oracular utterances about A's divine birth (*FGrH* 124 F 14), of the sea off the coast of Pamphylia doing obeisance to A (F 31), and of the crows squawking at night to bring the laggards to the oasis at Siwa (F 14b). Indeed Ptolemy and Aristobulus took so little notice of Callisthenes that they did not even agree on the manner of his death (4.14.3).

2. The River Granicus (16)

There are very strong similarities between the account by Plutarch and the account by Arrian.[2] For example, they both record Parmenio's advice and A's retort (P*A* 16.3; Arr. 1.13.3 and 6), the depth of the river and its steep banks causing alarm (P*A* 16.2; Arr. 1.13.4), A and his cavalry entering the river-bed (P*A* 16.3; Arr. 1.15.4), the desperate fighting round A (P*A* 16.7–11; Arr. 1.15.6–8), the last stand by the Greek mercenaries (P*A* 16.13; Arr. 1.16.2) and the wording of the inscription on the spoils (P*A* 16.18; Arr. 1.16.7). These similarities are so marked that Plutarch and Arrian must have been drawing on a common stock of information. In Arrian's case we know that he followed the accounts of Ptolemy and Aristobulus. Plutarch, then, was drawing on one or other or on both.

[2] For the course of the battle see H*GR*, and for the sources especially 86f.

The differences between the account by Plutarch and the account by Arrian are considerable. Plutarch provided points about A which are not in Arrian's account at all. Thus A was 'perhaps under compulsion' to fight the battle. He named the month a second Artemisius, in order to evade the Macedonian practice of not campaigning in the month Daesius.[3] He seemed to be exercising his command in a mad and desperate manner rather than sensibly. A's shield and helmet had conspicuous features. A was asked for terms under oath by the Greek mercenaries. In leading the charge and losing his horse A was actuated by passion rather than by calculation.[4] A sent most of the spoils, other than armour, to Olympias. Because all these additional points are concerned with A personally, they may be attributed to Plutarch's use of Aristobulus.

Plutarch differed from Arrian in some matters which both of them covered. During the fighting A wounded Rhoesaces with his lance and then fought with his sword (PA 16.8), whereas in Arrian's account A killed Mithridates and then Rhoesaces with his lance (1.15.8). Then Cleitus killed Spithridates with his lance (PA 16.11), whereas in Arrian's account Cleitus severed the arm of Spithridates at the shoulder with his scimitar (1.15.8). According to Plutarch the Persian losses 'are said to be' 20,000 infantry and 2,500 cavalry (PA 16.5), whereas Arrian mentioned only cavalry losses as 'up to 1,000' (1.16.2). On the Macedonian side Plutarch reported 34 killed, of whom 9 were infantrymen[5] (PA 16.15), whereas Arrian reported 25 Companion Cavalrymen killed at the first assault, more than 60 other cavalrymen, and 'up to 30' infantrymen (1.16.4). Plutarch reported the sending of two sets of spoils to Greece and the words of the inscription on the second set (not on that sent to Athens), whereas Arrian mentioned

---

[3] Daesius was the month leading up to the harvest (*Et. Magn.* s.v.). A prosaic explanation of A inserting a second Artemisius is that he was adding an intercalary month in this way in the Macedonian year 335/4.

[4] Plutarch refers to A's personal attack and not to A's response to the mercenaries' request for terms, as Hamilton *C* 41 implies and as Bosworth *C* 124 states.

[5] Bosworth *C* 125 finds 'no problem with the [9] infantry' but only by including them among those who were commemorated by statues; yet that is not what Plutarch was saying in his phrase νεκροὺς γενέσθαι.

only one set which was sent to Athens and had the inscription (1.16.7).

How do we account for these differences? Since Plutarch wrote first and Arrian must have read Plutarch's *Life of Alexander*, Arrian is deliberately correcting Plutarch and thereby Plutarch's source. The simplest explanation is that Plutarch was following Aristobulus, who wrote from memory, and that Arrian was following Ptolemy, who had access to A's *Royal Journal*, in which details of A's actions and of Macedonian losses were recorded.[6] This explanation is strongly supported by Plutarch citing Aristobulus for the Macedonian losses (16.15). A corollary of this conclusion is that Aristobulus wrote before Ptolemy did so.[7]

At two places Plutarch seems to have used a source other than Aristobulus. The Persian losses 'are said' to be 20,000 infantry and 2,500 cavalry, the qualification indicating a departure from the main source; and 'most of the Macedonian killed and wounded' fell in the action against the Greek mercenaries, a statement incompatible with Aristobulus' report of only 9 infantrymen killed. We do not know who that other source was.[8] Both Plutarch and Arrian made careless mistakes. For Plutarch had A order 34 bronze statues of the Macedonian dead, whereas Arrian rightly limited the statues to the 25 Companion Cavalrymen. On the other hand, Arrian failed to mention the sending of spoils to the Greeks 'generally', i.e. to the Council of the Greeks of the Common Peace.

3. Issus (20.1–9)

Plutarch had more interest in Darius' folly and A's good fortune than in the details of the campaign and Battle of Issus. Darius, says Plutarch, failed to heed the wise advice

[6] See H*RJ*.

[7] As I have argued in *AG*² 3f., *THA* 182 n. 71 and 193 n. 20; *HM* III 23f. and 27f.; and H*AAJ*, correcting a misrepresentation of my views by E. Badian, 'The Ring and the Book', *Zu Alexander d. Gr.* (Amsterdam, 1987) 605ff.

[8] The figures in Diodorus are again different, namely 10,000 infantry and not less than 2,000 cavalry (17.21.6). They were derived probably from Cleitarchus (*THA* 25f.).

of Amyntas, a Macedonian refugee, who had a knowledge of
A's temperament. The same failure was recounted by Arrian,
but not by any other Alexander-historian. In the accounts of
Plutarch and Arrian the same points appear. Darius should
have stayed in his position in an extensive plain, which was
suitable for his superior numbers (PA 20.2; Arr. 2.6.3); Darius
was afraid that A would hold back or run away (PA 20.3; Arr.
2.5.4–5); and Amyntas was certain that A would seek Darius
(PA 20.3; Arr. 2.5.6). Arrian presented Amyntas' advice in his
narrative and not as a *legomenon*. Accordingly, he drew on
Ptolemy or Aristobulus or on both. Plutarch must have done
so too.

Each author added his own reflections. Plutarch stressed the
good fortune of A (20.5 τῇ συντυχίᾳ and 20.7 ἡ τύχη ... τῆς
τύχης), who found the ground favourable to his small numbers, whereas Darius wanted to go back to his previous position but was caught on ground unsuitable for his cavalry
(20.5f.). Arrian saw the hand not of fortune but of some divine
power (2.6.6 καί τι καὶ δαιμόνιον τυχόν, 2.6.7 ἐχρῆν and
2.7.3 ὁ θεός), which led Darius into a position unsuitable for
his cavalry and his vast array of missile-throwers, whereas for
A victory was easy and the ground just right for deploying
the Macedonian phalanx (2.6.6 and 7.3).[9]

Thereafter Plutarch devoted one sentence to the course of
the battle. He then reported that A was wounded in the thigh,
according to Chares by Darius in personal combat, but according to A in a letter 'not seriously', without naming his
attacker (20.9). Arrian gave a very full account of the battle in
some five chapters. He mentioned A's wound in the thigh,
which did not prevent him from visiting his wounded men
(2.12.1).

There is enough common ground in the reflections of
Plutarch and Arrian to show that they were continuing to
draw on their common source. As we shall see below (p. 224),
that source was probably Aristobulus. The one sentence sum-

[9] The reflections were not fully substantiated in the narrative of the battle which
Arrian and others gave. See my account in *AG*² 95–110.

marising the course of the battle is Plutarch's own piece. He
then cites both Chares and a letter of A.

4. Gaugamela (31.6–33.11)

Plutarch provided a full programme of the events which preceded the engagement of the forces in battle. There are analogies for this in other writers. The events may be summarised
as follows:

(1) A and Aristander sacrificed (P*A* 31.9; Curt. 4.13.15).
(2) The senior Companions and Parmenio advised a night attack, and A
rejected the advice with the reply 'I will not steal my victory' (P*A* 31.10–
14; Curt. 4.13.4–10; reported as a *legomenon* by Arrian at 3.10.1–2).
(3) A fell into a deep sleep, was roused by Parmenio and explained why he
was happy (P*A* 32.1–3; Diod. 17.56.1–4; Just. 11.13.1–3; Curt. 4.13.17–
24).

Although there are variations from one author to another,
there is no doubt that this programme of events came from a
common source. In *THA* 20, 25ff., 100, 123 and 128 I argued
that the source of the passages which I have cited from
Diodorus, Justin and Curtius was Cleitarchus. This conclusion is compatible with Arrian's mention of item (2) as a
legomenon, i.e. as deriving not from Ptolemy and Aristobulus
but from a less trustworthy writer. Plutarch also had doubts
with regard to item (3); for he introduced his account with the
word λέγεται 'A. is said to have slept'. The author whom
Plutarch was following in 31.6–32.3 was thus Cleitarchus.

The account of the battle which Plutarch gave was very
disjointed.[10] The various parts are as follows:

(1) 32.4–7. The battle opened with a Persian cavalry onslaught which drove
back Parmenio and his cavalry on the Macedonian left wing, and with
Mazaeus sending cavalry round that left wing to capture the Macedonian
(overnight) camp.[11] This led Parmenio to send messengers to A, who
made a tart reply.
(2) 32.8–12. After sending his message to Parmenio A put on his helmet. His

---

[10] For a general account see *AG*² 138ff.
[11] For A's two camps see *AG*² 136 and 143. Arrian described the base camp at
3.9.1, and he implied the existence of an advanced camp at 3.11.1.

dress and equipment, and his sparing of Bucephalus until the moment of attack were then described.

(3) 33.1–3. A addressed the Greeks, Aristander pointed to an eagle, 'the cavalry charged and the phalanx flowed on behind them.'

(4) 33.4–8. The enemy fled without even engaging. Darius in turn fled, abandoning his chariot and armour and mounting a mare.

(5) 33.9–11. Darius would not have escaped if a second set of messengers had not reached A from Parmenio, who was being 'sluggish and incompetent'. Thereupon A sounded the recall. While on his way towards Parmenio, A learnt that the enemy had fled there also.

The disjointed nature of the account is due to Plutarch's changes of source. In particular the disjunction of (1) and (5) is striking; for they seem to have been consecutive in the original source, because the mention of a second set of messengers in (5) at 33.9 (πάλιν ... ἕτεροι) picked up the mention of the first messengers in (1) at 32.6. Moreover, in both (1) and (5) Parmenio was harshly criticised (32.7 and 33.10f.). I infer, then, that Plutarch derived (1) and (5) from the same source or sources, and (2), (3) and (4) from other sources.

There are unusual features in passages (1) and (5). The actions on the Macedonian left, the capture of the camp and Parmenio's message to A preceded A's own attack (at 33.7). Then after the flight of Darius the poor performance of Parmenio on the left wing is described (33.9–11). The same unusual sequence of events in two separate sections of narrative was similarly provided by Curtius.[12] In the first section, 4.15.2–9, Darius had ordered the cavalry under Bessus to outflank and charge A's left wing (4.15.2 'in laevum Alexandri cornu latere invehi') and Mazaeus' 1,000 cavalry, 'wheeling round' ('circumvehi', i.e. outside Parmenio's left wing), headed for the Macedonian camp (4.15.5).[13] Thereupon Parmenio sent Polydamas to A, whose reply was in the nature of a reprimand (4.15.6–8). In the second section, 4.16.1–7, after the flight of Darius, Parmenio, hard pressed by the cavalry of

---

[12] Atkinson 446f. and 454f. discussed the sources of Curtius, but he did not stress the sequence of events in Curtius' account being like the sequence in Plutarch's account.

[13] These two victorious movements, both allegedly happening before A went into action, are a feature of Diodorus' account at 17.60.1 δευτέρου δὲ προτερήματος, which came from Cleitarchus in my opinion (*THA* 21ff.).

Mazaeus, sent cavalrymen to A to ask for help. When they reached A, who was already in close pursuit of the fleeing enemy, A gnashed his teeth and halted the pursuit. Meanwhile Mazaeus had slackened his attack and his men too were soon in flight. However, Parmenio held his own men back. It is thus certain that Plutarch and Curtius were using the same source or sources for these sections of their narratives.

One source which Plutarch named in passage (5) was Callisthenes, who said that Parmenio's slackness was due 'to envy and abhorrence of the authority and of the overbearing nature of A's power' (33.10). But the main source was different; for it gave the alternative explanation that Parmenio's slackness was due to 'his old age undermining his courage somewhat'.[14] There are some pointers to Cleitarchus as the main source. He usually paid attention to the Thessalian cavalry and to Parmenio as their commander. On this occasion they were in action first (PA 32.5) and last (PA 33.11 and Curt. 4.16.6). He represented A as prone to rage (see THA 16 at Thebes, 24 and 26). In this case A was 'vexed' (PA 33.11 ἀνιαθείς) and 'gnashed his teeth' (Curt. 4.16.3) at the message sent by Parmenio. There is also in the accounts of Plutarch and Curtius a complete failure to understand the tactical development of the battle. That is typical of Cleitarchus (THA 23).

In passage (3) the Thessalians and the other Greeks were addressed by A. The words of A's prayer were cited from Callisthenes, that Zeus 'should defend and strengthen the Greeks, if indeed A was descended from Zeus' (33.1). Here too we suspect that the sources were Cleitarchus and Callisthenes. Plutarch and Curtius both reported an eagle flying above the head of A, and the seer Aristander, wearing a white mantle, pointed to it as a good omen (PA 33.2; Curt. 4.15.26). They were drawing on the same source, who was probably still Cleitarchus. In passage (4) the part of the Macedonians in the battle was despatched in a single sentence, 'the cavalry charging and the phalanx flowing on behind it' (33.3). The enemy

---

[14] The alternatives are clearly stated; only the second is taken from Callisthenes.

fled without a blow and A pressed on towards Darius. A picturesque description follows of Darius 'towering conspicuous, a fine-looking man and tall, standing on a lofty chariot, fenced about by a numerous and brilliant array of horsemen'; 'the noblest of them slaughtered and falling in heaps, weaving and twining themselves in their last agonies about riders and horses'; and Darius in flight 'on a mare they say which had just foaled' (33.5–8). Such sensational and impressionistic writing was typical of Cleitarchus, and we may infer that he was one of the sources used here by Plutarch; but there were certainly other writers such as the one who introduced the mare into the picture. The descriptions which Diodorus and Curtius gave, drawing partly at least on Cleitarchus (*THA* 21ff. and 128), are very similar in tone but differ in many details.

The arming of A in passage (2) was composed as part of the epic nature of the battle, even though Plutarch was going backwards somewhat in time, for the arming had taken place in the 'tent', i.e. in what corresponded to a palace (32.8 ἀπὸ σκηνῆς εἶχε). The description provides detail and provenance: an undergarment from Sicily, a helmet and gorget from Theophilus' workshop, a sword from Citium in Cyprus, and a cloak woven by Helicon from Rhodes.[15] That it was a true description of the items is rendered almost certain by the similar dress of A in the Alexander Mosaic (whether it represented him at Issus or at Gaugamela) and by the features of the weapons and armour found in Philip's Tomb – especially the iron pieces, helmet, gorget and sword. Such a description must have come from a contemporary, who was a close attendant on the king. The most likely person was Chares, the Palace Chamberlain, who described such palace ceremonies as the mass wedding at Susa (*FGrH* 125 F 4 = Athen. 538b–539a). That likelihood is increased by the sentence about Bucephalus, whom A was wont to ride only into action

---

[15] An interesting detail is the attachment of the gorget to the helmet (συνήρμοστο δὲ αὐτῷ), not to the cuirass as was generally supposed. The iron helmet shone 'like pure silver', which implies a recent development in the treatment of iron. That may have been due to Paeonian metallurgists; for Clement, *Strom.* 1.16.76 said that the Nōropes, a Paeonian tribe, were the first to work copper and to 'refine iron'.

(32.12); for Chares was cited by Gellius as his authority about Bucephalus (Gellius 5.2; see below, p. 111). I conclude, then, that Plutarch drew on Chares for 32.8–12.

It is evident that Plutarch indulged his own taste for graphic writing in this case, because he regarded the Battle of Gaugamela as the decisive battle of Alexander's career. Throughout his account in 32.4 to 33.11 he made free use of Cleitarchus' writing and added colourful touches from Callisthenes, Chares and other writers.

5. The Battle of the River Hydaspes (60.1–11)

Plutarch derived his description of this battle from a letter (or letters) of A with the exception of a remark quoted from Onesicritus' account and mentioned by another or others (60.6). That some forms of royal correspondence were kept in the King's Archive and also by the recipient or the writer, is known from a report in Plutarch, *Eumenes* 2.3, that, when a fire occurred, A ordered his satraps and generals to send to him copies of the destroyed papers. There were also fictional letters, sometimes posing as genuine letters and sometimes being a conventional form of romantic writing. The question in this instance is whether Plutarch had before him a genuine or a fictive letter. The answer may emerge from a comparison of Plutarch's account with that of Arrian, which was based on the accounts of Ptolemy and Aristobulus, and in particular with the résumé of Ptolemy's account for one phase of the action in Arr. 5.14.4–15.2.[16]

The following divergences may be noted.

(1) In Plutarch there was only one island 'not large' (60.3 and 4). In Arrian there were two islands (5.11.1, 12.2, 4, and 13.1; and the second one 'large' at 5.13.2). In Plutarch A's force crossed over to the 'not large' island (60.3). In Arrian the boats and rafts went past that island (5.13.1) and landed on

---

[16] My account of the battle is in *AG*² 210ff., and the sources are discussed in 215f. Later accounts, such as that of A. M. Devine in *The Ancient World* 16 (1987) 92, have not led me to change my views.

what they thought to be the far bank but was in fact the second, 'the large island' (5.13.2). In Plutarch the troops were already on the 'not large' island when torrential rain and many tornadoes and thunderbolts fell upon them, so that some men were killed and burnt up by the thunderbolts (60.4). In Arrian there was violent rain during the night; 'but towards dawn the wind and rain had quietened down, and the cavalry embarked' for the crossing (5.12.4).[17]

(2) In Plutarch when A landed on the far bank there were no enemy around until he had covered four kilometres with his cavalry (60.7). When he did make contact, A routed 1,000 cavalry and 60 'of the chariots' and (later)[18] captured all the chariots and killed 400 cavalry. In Arrian three versions were presented. (1) 'Some say' there was a battle at the landing in which A was wounded and Bucephalus was killed by an Indian advance force under the command of Porus' son (5.14.4).[19] (2) Aristobulus said that Porus' son arrived first and could have prevented A from landing; but instead he drove past with his 60 chariots. Then, when A's force had landed safely, his mounted archers attacked and routed them, inflicting casualties (5.14.3). (3) Ptolemy said that A had already made the crossing when Porus' son was coming up with 2,000 cavalry and 120 chariots; and that A attacking them with his mounted archers and his own group of cavalry killed some 400 Indians and captured all the chariots (5.14.5–15.2). Thus the account given by Plutarch is incompatible with versions (1) and (2). But it is compatible with (3), if we assume that the

---

[17] The leading troops crossed by daylight, taking a route 'by the island', in order not to be seen by the Indian scouts on the far bank (5.12.4 ὡς μὴ πρόσθεν ὀφθεῖεν). I see no justification for the remark of Devine, loc. cit., that 'the crossing itself seems to have taken the whole night'. To cross during the night was impractical; for the violent rain meant that it was pitch-black during the night, and one could not then have been embarking some 5,000 horses and searching for a landing-place.

[18] The genitive case in the phrase τῶν ἁρμάτων ἑξήκοντα indicates that there were more than sixty chariots. The aorist tense τρεψάμενος separates the routing of the 1,000 cavalry and 60 chariots from the subsequent capture of all the chariots. Thus Devine, loc. cit. 100, is mistaken in putting the detachment at 1,000 cavalry and 60 chariots 'apud Plut. Alex. 60.8'.

[19] For the end of Bucephalus see below, p. 110.

forces of Porus' son came up in two separate groups, each consisting of 1,000 cavalry and 60 chariots.[20]

To the main battle Plutarch devoted a couple of sentences (60.10f.), which contained the statement not found elsewhere that the enemy gave up 'during the eighth hour', i.e. after sunrise when the crossing was made.[21] Here Plutarch must have abbreviated the letter drastically.

Was the letter genuine? The divergences in the accounts of the crossing are such that either the letter is false or else the account based on Ptolemy and Aristobulus is false.[22] We must remember that Arrian will have read the passage in Plutarch and will have been aware of the so-called letters of A. He chose to follow Aristobulus and Ptolemy, and in particular Ptolemy (5.14.4 fin.). His judgement was based on his knowledge of those writers' works, of which we have only sparse fragments, and upon the fact that they – and in this case Ptolemy as a Bodyguard attendant on A (5.13.1) – were participants in the campaigns. On such grounds Arrian's account is to be accepted as accurate. On the other hand, the letter exaggerated the dangers of the crossing and the horrors of the weather to epic proportions – a fault which was in no way characteristic of A. It should be regarded as fictitious.[23]

---

[20] On this hypothesis we can see why Aristobulus came to attribute 60 chariots to Porus' son (Arr. 5.14.3) through confusing the first clash with the main action between A and the Indian advance force.

[21] The eighth hour is reasonable if we allow one hour to complete the crossing, five hours for the infantry to march fifteen miles during which Porus advanced some four miles towards them (5.15.4), and two hours for the battle.

[22] For instance, in the letters according to Plutarch A ordered Coenus to attack the enemy right wing (60.10). In Arrian's account Coenus was to move 'as towards the right' (a feint) and then to attack from the rear those of the enemy cavalry who would be facing A's main body of cavalry (5.16.3); see AG^2 211f. and fig. 20. One has to choose one account or the other. Devine, loc. cit. 92, holds that both have A order Coenus 'to move against the Indian right', but the Greek texts are more precise. In the letter A ordered Coenus, to attack the right, τῷ δεξιῷ προσβαλεῖν κελεῦσαι, and in Arrian A 'sends Coenus as towards the right', πέμπει ὡς ἐπὶ τὸ δεξιόν and later to attack the enemy from behind.

[23] As I suggested in AG^2 216 the author of this letter drew in part on the account by Aristobulus.

4

ALEXANDER AND DARIUS

1. Courses open to Alexander and to Darius (17.1–20.4)

In Plutarch's account A was 'in two minds about his next move' after the capture of the coast as far as Halicarnassus (17.2 ἀμφίβολος ἦν πρὸς τὰ λοιπὰ τῇ γνωμῇ). 'Many times he was eager to meet Darius and put the whole issue to the hazard, and many times he intended to defer his march inland to meet Darius until he had gained additional practice and strength in the coastal region with its resources.' A was represented as still dithering almost a year later. For when he heard of the death of Memnon, 'he was encouraged rather to undertake the march inland' (18.5 ἐπερρώσθη πρὸς τὴν ἄνω στρατείαν μᾶλλον).

This picture of an irresolute A is very different from that provided by Diodorus 17.22.5, who was drawing probably on Diyllus (see *THA* 38), and by Arrian 1.20.1, who was following Ptolemy and Aristobulus as usual. For Diodorus had A disband his fleet because it was useless and expensive; and Arrian, giving the same reasons, added the far-sighted policy 'of capturing the coastal cities and breaking up the Persian fleet by denying to it the possibility of replacing crews and of putting in anywhere in Asia'.[1] According to Diodorus and Arrian that decision was taken after the fall of Miletus, some weeks before the siege of Halicarnassus. A different theory about A's reason for disbanding his fleet was introduced by Diodorus with the words 'some say' (17.23.1): namely that 'Darius was being expected [to reach the coastal area] and the Macedonians would fight more ardently if the hope of escape

---

[1] 'Asia' included Egypt. A had in mind the bases of the Persian fleet, which were in Cyprus, Phoenicia and Egypt, and he saw that once the army captured Phoenicia and Egypt the Persian fleet would collapse. Bosworth *C* 143 underestimated A's ability when he wrote 'it is difficult to suppose that A saw so far ahead'.

45

[by sea] was removed from them'. The source of this passage, which suggests that A was waiting in summer 334 for Darius to reach the coast, was Cleitarchus, as I argued in *THA* 38f.[2] It is probable that Plutarch was following Cleitarchus in presenting A as a ditherer then in 17.2–3 and later into summer 333.

A series of events in 17.4–18.5 appears to come from the same source; for they are presented as influencing A during this period of irresolution. The events are as follows.

(1) A bronze tablet was regurgitated by a spring near Xanthus in Lycia. It bore an inscription which revealed that Persian rule would be terminated by Greeks.[3] 'Encouraged by this, A pressed on with clearing up the coastal region as far as Phoenicia and Cilicia.'

(2) A's (main) army passed along the Pamphylian coast (instead of taking an inland route). This event gave 'many historians' the opportunity to engage in startling and bombastic writing, to the effect that 'the sea made way for A through some heaven-sent chance' (17.6 θείᾳ τινὶ τύχῃ παραχωρήσασαν Ἀλεξάνδρῳ). One such producer of bombast was Callisthenes who suggested that the sea seemed to bow down to A (*FGrH* 124 F 31 ἐν τῷ ὑποκυρτοῦσθαί πως δοκῇ προσκυνεῖν).[4] At a time when natural phenomena were thought to be controlled by gods, Arrian at 1.26.2 was no doubt correct in saying that 'A and those around him considered that the change of wind was not without divine direction' (οὐκ ἄνευ τοῦ θείου). Plutarch added from his own reading a jest by Menander at the expense of the bombastic writers, and he said that A did not suggest anything as portentous when he described in a letter his making of a road and his 'passing through' (the sea).[5]

---

[2] The same idea was advanced in 17.23.2 for the tactics attributed to A at the River Granicus, of which the description came from Cleitarchus (*THA* 16 and 25f.).

[3] One might expect 'Macedonians'. The source was then a Greek writer, such as Cleitarchus.

[4] The implication of worship was present in the text of Callisthenes; for the whole passage is in the accusative and infinitive, *pace* Pearson *LHA* 36f.

[5] Perrin is incorrect in translating ὁδοποιῆσαι as 'he marched' and διελθεῖν as 'passed through it', i.e. the road. A had a road made inland by the Thracians, and

(3) On taking over Gordium A saw the waggon of Midas and learnt of the barbarians' belief that 'the loosener of the knot was fated to become king of the inhabited world' (18.2 εἵμαρται βασιλεῖ γενέσθαι τῆς οἰκουμένης). Plutarch gave the following two versions 'of the loosening. 'Most writers' say that A was at a loss how to loosen it, and that he cut through the knot with his sword; but Aristobulus says that he loosened it quite easily by removing the so-called 'pin'. Arrian mentioned these two versions, saying 'some writers' instead of 'most writers'. The first version has survived also in Justin 11.7.3–16 and Curtius 3.1.14–18; the second also in a fragment of Marsyas of Philippi (*FGrH* 135-6 F 4). The source which has been suggested by most scholars for the first version is Cleitarchus.[6] Plutarch alone says that the loosener of the knot was destined to become king 'of the inhabited earth', τῆς οἰκουμένης sc γῆς, the sense of the expression being 'the inhabited world' in the time of Aristotle.[7] The idea that A wanted to be a world-ruler is a sure mark of Cleitarchus,[8] as for instance in Diodorus 17.51.2 (A.'s questions at Siwa).

Thus the interconnection of 17.2f. and 18.5 and the relevance of the events in 17.4–18.4 to the subject of the whole passage, namely the indecision of A and the events which swayed him, have been derived by Plutarch from one main source. The sum of probabilities for the theme and for the events leave no room for doubt that the main source was Cleitarchus. We can see also that Cleitarchus wrote with Herodotus in mind; for the miraculous events in the form of oracles and dreams which swayed Xerxes were paralleled in

---

he himself took the main body through the sea (Arr. 1.26.1). Plutarch repeated διελθεῖν from his citation of Menander διελθεῖν δηλαδὴ διὰ θαλάσσης. This point is missed by Hamilton *L* 12, who accepted the translation by Perrin.

[6] So Jacoby, *FGrH* 2 D 511, Mederer 10, Schachermeyr 161f. (from Callisthenes via Cleitarchus), Rabe 44f., and E. A. Fredricksmeyer in *CP* 56 (1961) 160f. The description of the knot in Justin 11.7.15 and in Plutarch 18.5 came from a common source, since the following terms correspond: 'capita' and ἀρχαί, 'loramenta' and δεσμοί, 'nodi' and ἑλιγμοί, and 'gladius' and μάχαιρα. What Plutarch omitted was Justin's comment that A treated the oracle with more violence ('violentius oraculo usus'). In *THA* 97 I argued that the source of Justin might have been Cleitarchus.

[7] See L–S–J[9] s.v. *pace* Tarn 79 n. 5, who thought it meant 'the Greek world'. All other writers said that A would be 'king of Asia'; see Hamilton *C* 46.

[8] See *THA* 96, as in Just. 11.6.3 'universum terrarum orbem'.

the account of A's period of indecision. Cleitarchus continued with the same recipe for the indecision of Darius, with the addition of good advice disregarded, as in the account by Herodotus.

Darius too was undecided for some time. He was influenced by a series of events.

(1) He was encouraged by a dream which the Magi interpreted as foretelling the destruction of the Macedonian phalanx and the rapid disappearance of A. But the true meaning of the dream, 'as it seems',[9] was that A would become master of Asia and speedily end his life with glory (18.7f.). Curtius 3.3.2–7, giving a longer version of the dream and the two interpretations, drew on the same source. Curtius added an omen which suggested that the Greeks would overthrow Persia.[10] The probable source was Cleitarchus, who exaggerated the importance of the Greeks.[11]

(2) A delayed for a long time at Tarsus in Cilicia. Darius thought that the reason for the delay was cowardice in A. But the cause in fact was an illness which afflicted A. Plutarch described the circumstances at some length, fitting it in here rather than in a historical sequence. The illness was due to exhaustion as 'some say' (one of them was Aristobulus, as cited in Arr. 2.4.7), or to bathing in the icy waters of the river Cydnus, as 'others say' (Just. 11.8.3f. and Curt. 3.5.1–4). The dramatic account which Plutarch gives has points in common with the much longer account of Curtius: the close friendship of A and the doctor (19.4 and 3.6.1), money and a royal marriage offered by Darius according to Parmenio (19.5 and 3.6.4), hiding of the letter under A's pillow (19.5 and 3.6.5), A swooning after the dose (19.9 and 3.6.13 'interclusus spiritus'), and speedy recovery (19.10 and 3.6.16). In *THA* 121 I maintained that the source of Curtius (and also of Justin, whose

---

[9] Plutarch is expressing support for this interpretation, which was evidently in his source.

[10] This omen in Curtius is analogous to the inscription on the tablet at Xanthus in Plutarch's account. Curtius introduced Roman features – the form of the camp instead of the phalanx, Babylon for the temple of Belus and a horse for A.

[11] Cleitarchus emphasised also the analogies between A and Achilles, such as the early death with glory.

account is very short) was Cleitarchus. Plutarch, then, drew on Cleitarchus as his main source for the illness and the speedy recovery.[12]

(3) The advice given by Amyntas, son of Antiochus, to Darius was good, that Darius should stay in broad and extensive plains to exploit his greatly superior numbers. But Darius did the opposite and realised his folly too late (20.1f., 4 and 6). Also Amyntas as a Macedonian in exile knew the nature of A and warned Darius of it. Similarly Herodotus had presented Demaratus, the Spartan king in exile, as giving good advice to Xerxes, who then disregarded it to his cost (Hdt. 7.235 and 237.1). As I shall argue below (p. 223), comparison of this account with the longer one in Arrian 2.6.3–7 leads to the conclusion that Plutarch and Arrian drew on a common source or sources, namely Ptolemy and/or Aristobulus.

The whole passage, 17.1–20.4, affords an insight into Plutarch's method. He adopted the account and the interpretations of Cleitarchus, that A was undecided for more than a year whether to march inland or to await the coming of Darius to the coast, that Darius was misguided into leaving the open spaces and seeking to encounter A on narrow ground, and that fortune gave a happy chance to A. Plutarch followed Cleitarchus in listing the events which swayed the two kings. But in describing those events he mentioned or followed other sources, namely for events in Pamphylia 'many historians', a Menander play and a letter of A; at Gordium 'most writers' and Aristobulus; at Tarsus 'some writers' including Aristobulus; and for the advice of Amyntas Ptolemy and/or Aristobulus.

2. Alexander and the family of Darius (20.10–21.11, and 24.1–3)

Arrian gives clear guidance on this subject. In his narrative of the pursuit of Darius and of the capture of the camp, in which Arrian was following Ptolemy and/or Aristobulus, he reported

---

[12] A was incapacitated by illness for a month or more; see AG^2 92f.

the capture by A of the chariot, shield, mantle (*kandys*) and bow which Darius abandoned in his flight (2.11.5f.), and the capture in Darius' camp of Darius' mother, wife (she was his sister), infant son, two daughters and other top-ranking Persian ladies (2.11.9). 'The bulk of his money and everything else which accompanies a Great King on campaign for his extravagant way of life had been sent by Darius to Damascus' (2.11.10).

For what happened on the day of the capture Arrian gave only the one account but he qualified it as follows. 'Some of those who wrote of A's achievements say that during the night on which he came back from his pursuit of Darius he heard, on passing into the tent of Darius, a lamentation of women' (2.12.3). Whereupon A was told: 'It is the mother, wife and children of Darius, because it has been reported to them that you have the bow and the royal mantle, and that Darius' shield has been brought back.' A then sent Leonnatus to tell them that Darius was alive but had left his arms and the mantle in the chariot, and that they were all Alexander had. Leonnatus added a further message that A granted them all the rights of royalty, including the title of queen, since his war with Darius was not a matter of enmity but was for the rule over Asia. 'This indeed', wrote Arrian, 'is what Ptolemy and Aristobulus say' (2.12.6).[13]

Arrian then added a *logos*, i.e. not from Ptolemy and Aristobulus, which was concerned with 'the next day'. Then A and Hephaestion, dressed alike, paid a visit, and the mother of Darius did obeisance to Hephaestion as the taller man. Hephaestion backed away. One of the ladies-in-waiting pointed out which was A. The mother of Darius drew back in confusion, whereupon A said that she had not made a mistake, since Hephaestion too was 'Alexander' ('a protector of men').

---

[13] In this passage Arrian is not saying that the account so far was peculiar to Ptolemy and Aristobulus; rather, that they were among 'some of those writers' who gave that account (2.12.3). Bosworth *C* I 220, 'Arrian claims [this account] to be the consensus of Ptolemy and Aristobulus', does not give the full picture.

Plutarch's account ran as follows. A captured the chariot and the bow of Darius (20.10). On returning from the pursuit A found the Macedonians carrying off a superabundance of rich loot but reserving for him the tent[14] of Darius, which was crammed full with his brilliant retinue and with equipment and great wealth. Stripping off his armour A had a bath in a tub, complete with pitchers, bowls, basins and caskets, all made of gold. Plutarch reported verbatim a conversation between A and one of his Companions, and a comment by A: 'This, it seems, was what it was to be a king.'

This account differed from the accounts of Ptolemy and Aristobulus and others as reported in Arrian 2.11.5–10. For Plutarch had A capture only the chariot and the bow, and not the mantle and the shield. Whereas Arrian reported that Darius and the other Persians had sent all their equipment to Damascus (2.11.10), Plutarch emphasised the immense amount of loot and the enormous wealth of Darius' own tent. Plutarch, then, was drawing on a source other than Ptolemy and Aristobulus.

On the other hand, Plutarch's account has much in common with that of Diodorus 17.35f. The immense quantity of loot which was seized in the Persian camp had belonged to the king's Friends, Kinsmen and Commanders as well as to the royal wardrobe and treasury (17.35.1–4). The victors maltreated the Persian ladies, some of whom appealed to the royal family for help (35.4–36.4). Meanwhile the Royal Pages of A were preparing a bath and a banquet in the tent of Darius (36.5). On his return from the pursuit A enjoyed the bath and was about to relax and dine. The similarities in the accounts of Diodorus and Plutarch are such that we may conclude that they came from a common source.

The next part of the story is told by Plutarch as follows. A was informed that the mother, wife and two daughters of

---

[14] The 'tent' was the mobile headquarters of Darius, and it was famous for its wealth and luxury; see the descriptions in PA 20.13 and Diod. 17.35.1–4. The tent of Ptolemy Philadelphus was in this Persian tradition (Athen. 196a–197c).

Darius were lamenting at the sight of Darius' chariot and bow. 'After a long time' A sent Leonnatus to tell them that Darius was not dead, that A was at war with him for hegemony, and that the ladies would enjoy royal treatment as before.[15] Moreover, A permitted them to bury any Persian as they wished, and to use the spoils for adornment of the funeral, and he doubled the allowances hitherto paid to the ladies (21.4). The permission for such burial was reported by Curtius (3.12.13), and the doubling of the Queen Mother's retinue and other benefactions figured in Diodorus (17.38.1).

In conclusion, then, Plutarch may have taken such points as the message delivered by Leonnatus from the accounts of Ptolemy, Aristobulus and others, as indicated by Arrian (2.12.3 and 6). But in general he preferred a more colourful account which included such details as the looting of enormous wealth, the bath and its gold fittings, and the doubling of the ladies' allowances. These details were also given by Diodorus and Curtius. Thus Diodorus, Curtius and in these items Plutarch were using as common source a very full and colourful account. That source was Cleitarchus.[16] It is interesting that Plutarch did not repeat from Cleitarchus, as Diodorus and Curtius did, the story of A and Hephaestion visiting the ladies next day. He may have had the doubts which Arrian was to express later (2.12.6–8).

The account of Cleitarchus, as revealed by Diodorus, Curtius and Plutarch, was a splendid example of journalistic, fictional writing. The facts were known to Ptolemy, who was in attendance on A during the pursuit (Arr. 2.11.8), and to Aristobulus who was on the campaign. They were aware, for instance, that the bulk of the Persian treasure and most of the aristocratic ladies had been sent to Damascus. Cleitarchus, however, provided a brilliant account of looting and raping by

---

[15] This is common to Arr. 2.12.5, i.e. to the versions of Ptolemy, Aristobulus and some others.

[16] Jacoby, *FGrH* 2 D 503 wrote that Cleitarchus was the source behind the accounts of Diod. 17.37–8, Curt. 3.11.20–2, and Just. 11.9.11f. See also Goukowsky 192f., 'tableau pathétique qui doit provenir de Clitarque ... peut-être une invention de Clitarque'. My arguments for Cleitarchus are in *THA* 19f., 27 and 118.

the soldiers, and of oriental extravagance. The bath-tub scene was superb. In fact there were no Royal Pages in Asia at the time, for the first batch came out from Macedonia in winter 331/0,[17] and it may be doubted whether the mobile bath-tub unit of Darius was quite so lavishly equipped with gold accoutrements.

In 21.5–11 Plutarch praised A for not raping any of the captured women but treating them honourably. He gave his own opinion, when he wrote 'as it seems' in this sentence:[18] 'A, as it seems, considered mastery of oneself more kingly than conquest of enemies' (21.7). His continence was a commonplace for the Alexander-historians. Plutarch made two points not mentioned elsewhere. 'A said in jest that the Persian women were a pain to the eyes.' This may be authentic; for A would have had in mind the passage in which Herodotus had reported the saying of the Persian envoys that the Macedonian women were a pain to the eyes (5.18.4). The second point is that 'Parmenio urged A, as Aristobulus says,' to cohabit with Barsine, the daughter of Artabazus, who was a widow of exceptional beauty.[19] Once again Plutarch was reading the work of Aristobulus.

Plutarch resumed his narrative with the phrase 'after the Battle of Issus' at 24.1. The treasures and the women sent on to Damascus by Darius were captured by the Thessalian cavalry, whom A sent to enrich themselves, because they had proved exceptionally brave in the battle. The rest of the army got plenty too. In other accounts it was Parmenio who was sent to capture Damascus (Curt. 3.8.12, 3.12.27 and 4.1.4; Arr. 2.11.9f. and 15.1; Polyaen. 4.4.5). 'Then for the first time the Macedonians tasted the joys of gold, silver, women and barbarians' way of life, and like dogs they were eager to follow the trail in pursuit and track down the wealth of the Persians'

---

[17] Diod. 17.65.2 and Curt. 5.1.42; and H*RP* 265f.

[18] So too Hamilton *C* 55f. Plutarch had expressed his opinion earlier in *Mor*. 338d–e.

[19] She had been the wife of Mentor (Arr. 7.4.6) and of Memnon (Curt. 3.13.14), and she bore a son to A called Heracles (Just. 11.10.2–3 and Plu. *Eum*. 1.7) in 327/6 (see *HM* III 100 and 165). Her beauty was mentioned by Just. loc. cit. For the text of Plutarch see Hamilton *C* 55 fin.

(24.3). The emphasis on the Thessalian cavalry as the finest cavalry in A's army and on the Macedonian (not the Thessalian or Greek) thirst for loot is typical of Cleitarchus,[20] who was probably still being used for the narrative.

[20] See *THA* 17, 21f. and 23f. with 25f. for the Thessalian cavalry, and *THA* 96 on Just. 11.5.8–9.

PHOENICIA, EGYPT, MESOPOTAMIA AND PARTHIA

1. Tyre and Gaza (24.4–26.2)

'Instead [of pursuing the acquisition of wealth by marching inland] A decided to gain control of the sea-coasts. As for Cyprus the kings came at once and delivered it into A's hands, but Tyre he besieged for seven months with causeways, siege-engines and at sea 200 triremes' (24.4f.). Plutarch was not interested here in strategic or military details. Indeed he was inaccurate in saying that Cyprus came over 'at once'; for that happened half-way through the siege.[1] His figure of 200 triremes was made up presumably of the 80 Phoenician ships and the 120 Cyprian ships, which deserted from the Persian fleet;[2] it omitted other ships which A already had.

Plutarch's interest was in the following dreams and oracles. (1) A dreamed of Heracles welcoming him into Tyre (24.5). (2) Many Tyrians dreamed that Apollo announced his intention of leaving Tyre and joining A, whereupon they chained his colossal statue and nailed it down to its base, calling him an 'Alexandriser' (24.6f.). (3) A dreamed he was pursuing a mocking satyr who finally surrendered. The seers interpreted this as 'Tyre is thine' (*sa-tyros*). 'The spring by which A dreamed of seeing the satyr is pointed out by them' (? the Tyrians). (4) Aristander the seer interpreted omens to mean that Tyre would fall in the current month. As this happened on the last day of the month, his interpretation was greeted with mocking laughter. But A ordered the day to be back-dated to become the twenty-eighth. In fact the city was taken on that very day (25.1–3).

Dream (1) and an interpretation of it by Aristander were

---

[1] Curt. 4.3.11; Arr. 2.17.1 and 2.20.3.
[2] Arr. 2.20.1–3.

reported by Arrian, who was as usual following Ptolemy and/
or Aristobulus (2.18.1). The introductory words 'something
indeed divine' (καί τι καὶ θεῖον) could be due to Arrian or to
his source. On the other hand Curtius had A 'as one experienced in working on the minds of his men' announce the
dream to his troops (4.2.17), this trick occurring in a passage
which came probably from Cleitarchus as source (*THA* 124
and 128).[3] Dream (2) occurred also in Diodorus, who said the
statue's chains were of gold (17.41.7f.), and in Curtius, who
had a chain of gold attached to an altar of Heracles (4.3.21).
The common source of Diodorus and Curtius has been
identified as Cleitarchus.[4] Where Plutarch called Apollo
an 'Alexandriser', Diodorus called him a 'Philalexander'
(17.46.6). Dream (3) occurred also in Eustathius, *ad Dion.
Perieg.* 911. The source proposed by Jacoby, *FGrH* 125 F 7,
was Chares. Omen (4) is reminiscent of A changing the name
of the month before the Battle of the River Granicus in 16.2,
a passage which we have ascribed to Aristobulus as source (p.
35 above). Probably this omen (4) came also from him; for in
each case A was supporting a religious belief.

It seems, then, that Plutarch may have derived his versions
from the following sources: dream (1) from Ptolemy and/or
Aristobulus; dream (2) from Cleitarchus; dream (3) perhaps
from Chares; and omen (4) from Aristobulus.

In 24.10–14 Plutarch interposed between the dreams and
the omen an escapade by A in the Antilebanon mountains,
during which his old tutor Lysimachus collapsed from exhaustion and was carried along by A. An expedition to the
Antilebanon was reported by Curtius 4.3.1, Arrian 2.20.4 and
Polyaenus 4.3.4 init., but not the escapade involving Lysimachus and A. As I argued in *AG*[2] 119, the escapade is to be
regarded as fiction, since the king was always accompanied by
Bodyguards and Companions on such expeditions. Plutarch
himself tells us his source: Chares (24.14).

During the siege of Gaza the following omen occurred,

---

[3] Like the other omens of Curt. 4.2.13–14, one being also in Diod. 17.41.7.
[4] Hamilton *C* 63 'from Cleitarchus'; Atkinson 319 opted for Cleitarchus as the
possible source. *THA* 42 and 128.

according to Plutarch. A clod of earth, dropped by a bird, hit A on the shoulder, and the bird alighting on a siege-engine got caught in the torsion-sinews (of a catapult). Aristander's inter- pretation was proved right; for A was wounded in the shoul- der and the city was taken (25.4–5). This omen was described elsewhere but with variations. (1) Curtius had A sacrificing at sunrise, when he was struck by a clod on his head. The raven which had dropped it alighted on a tower smeared with tar, in which it stuck and was captured. Aristander interpreted this as meaning that the city would fall but that A was in danger of being wounded that day (4.6.1–12). (2) Arrian had A sacrific- ing when a carnivorous bird dropped a stone on his head, and Aristander said 'You will take the city, O king, but you must take care for yourself this day' (2.26.4). Both Curtius and Arrian went on to say that A disregarded the warning and was wounded by an 'arrow' according to Curtius and by a 'cata- pult' (firing an arrow) according to Arrian. Because Arrian reported this as part of his narrative and added that the wound was treated 'with difficulty', he was drawing on his declared sources, Ptolemy and/or Aristobulus. Curtius has his own variations. The omen occurred not at the start, as in Arr. 2.26.4, but after a reverse, and 'A's mind was not unaffected by superstition' in the matter. He escaped being wounded by an Arab posing as a suppliant, and he thought he was now safe. However, 'fate is inescapable'. A was wounded, and after being treated by Philip the doctor he fainted. This more elab- orate account may have come from Hegesias (*FGrH* 142 F 5) and from Cleitarchus.[5] Plutarch owed his account not to them but to Ptolemy and/or Aristobulus.

After the capture of Gaza A sent many of the spoils to Olympias, Cleopatra and his Friends, and a large amount of frankincense and myrrh to 'Leonidas the tutor' (25.6). He had been mentioned at 5.7 as 'a man of stern disposition' (p. 21 above). Plutarch then explained that the gift was connected with an incident in the boyhood of A. Leonidas, 'as it seems', had stopped A from throwing a lot of incense onto an altar-fire

[5] See *THA* 127f.

and remarked: 'You can be as lavish as you like, Alexander, once you are master of the land of incense.' So now A wrote to Leonidas. 'We have sent you myrrh and frankincense in abundance, so that you may stop being niggardly with the gods.'

For A's boyhood Plutarch was not quoting from A's letter to Leonidas. The qualification 'as it seems' was added, because Plutarch had some reservation about the reliability of his source, who was probably Onesicritus,[6] as we shall see for the next item.

The finest object among the spoils was a casket. A asked his Friends what they thought he should place in it, and he received many suggestions. He said he would place the *Iliad* in it for safe keeping. 'This is attested by no few of the trustworthy [writers]' (26.2). Plutarch had already mentioned at 8.2 'the *Iliad* of the casket as they call it', which A kept under his pillow, 'as Onesicritus has recorded'. It is evident that Onesicritus was one of 'the trustworthy writers' in this matter.

2. Alexandria, Siwa and Egypt (26.3–27.9)

Plutarch begins by citing 'men of Alexandria who trust in Heracleides' and by adding the qualification 'if what they say is true'. It is not clear whether Plutarch had met them at Alexandria or was writing from hearsay. The Heracleides was probably Heracleides Lembus,[7] a resident in Alexandria in 170 B.C., whose writings included an epitome of Satyrus, *Lives*. Their story was that A dreamed of a grey-haired, venerable man who appeared to him and recited the two lines of the *Odyssey* which described the island of Pharos; that the dream occurred when A wished to found a city; and that he visited Pharos and declared Homer to be a very wise architect. The ultimate source of this puerile story may have been Satyrus, *Life of Alexander*.[8]

---

[6] From his work entitled *How A Was Brought Up*.

[7] See *OCD*[2] 500. He is more likely than Heracleides Ponticus. See Hamilton *C* 66 on the matter.

[8] This is a more likely source than a work of Heracleides Lembus, which was perhaps about Homer.

As there was no chalk available, barley-meal was used to mark out the plan of the city, which was shaped like a Macedonian cloak (*chlamys*). A was pleased with the plan; but then a swarm of birds devoured every bit of the barley-meal and A was distressed (26.8–9). However, the seers cheered him, saying that the city would be most bountiful and would become the nurse of men of all kinds. This account differs from that of Strabo 792 and from that given by Arrian as a *logos* at 3.2.1; but it is close to that of Curtius 4.8.6,[9] which reported the swarm of birds, the initial despondency and then the interpretation of the seers. I argued in *THA* 123f. that Curtius was following the account of Cleitarchus, who lived for some years at Alexandria. If he and Plutarch had a common source, then Plutarch was also drawing on Cleitarchus.

There are two parts to Plutarch's account of Siwa: the journey (26.11–27.4) and the consultation (27.5–9). There are points about the journey which are common to other accounts, such as the heat, sand, rain and crows acting as guides; but the exaggerated nature of Plutarch's account is closer to the accounts of Diodorus (17.49.3–6) and Curtius (4.7.10–15). The second part differs radically from the account of Callisthenes in Strabo 814, who said that the priest's responses were nods and signs except for 'the spoken words to the king that he was son of Zeus', and from the account of Arrian, who reported only A's own words that 'he had heard all his heart desired'. On the other hand, this part has the following points in common with Diodorus 17.51.1–4, Justin 11.11.6–11 and Curtius 4.7.25–8. I cite from Plutarch first in each case.

(1) The priest gave greetings to A 'from the god as from [his] father' (Plutarch ἀπὸ τοῦ θεοῦ χαίρειν ὡς ἀπὸ πατρός). Diodorus had these words: χαῖρε, εἶπεν, ὦ παῖ· καὶ ταύτην παρὰ τοῦ θεοῦ ἔχε τὴν πρόσρησιν. Justin wrote 'Hammonis filium salutant', and Curtius 'filium appellat, hoc nomen illi parentem Jovem reddere affirmans'.

(2) A asked whether any of his father's murderers had escaped, and the priest told him 'to mind his words (εὐφημεῖν)

---

[9] Curt. 4.8.6. Atkinson 368 commented on the closeness of the two accounts.

since his father was not mortal'. Diodorus had A ask the same question and the priest reply εὐφήμει 'for no one of men can plot against A's father'. Justin reported the same question and the answer 'his father can neither be killed nor die', and Curtius gave as the reply to the same question 'his father cannot be damaged by anyone's criminal deed'.

(3) A then reshaped his question, asked if all the murderers had been punished and received the answer that this was so. The same question and answer occur in Diodorus, Justin and Curtius.

(4) A asked whether the god grants him rule over 'all men', and he was told this was so. Diodorus had him granted τὴν ἁπάσης γῆς ἀρχήν, Justin 'possessionem terrarum' and Curtius to be 'terrarum omnium rectorem'.

(5) A gave offerings to the god and gifts to the priests. Diodorus mentioned offerings to the god, and Curtius gifts to the priests and the god.

It is thus certain that Plutarch, Diodorus, Justin and Curtius were following a common source.[10] It is generally agreed that that source was Cleitarchus.[11]

However, Plutarch had some more to say. At 27.4 he reported as most amazing the report of Callisthenes that the crows recalled stragglers at night and guided them to the track by their cawing.[12] At 27.8 he stated that the second part – the consultation – was so reported by 'most writers', but that A himself said in a letter to his mother that he had had some secret responses which he would tell to her alone on his return. As Hamilton observed of this letter, 'there is no good reason to doubt its authenticity'.[13] Further, 'some say'[14] that the

---

[10] They varied the order and the diction, in order not to be repeating one another's phrases.

[11] See *THA* 43f. (for Diodorus), 99 (for Justin) and 122 (for Curtius). Goukowsky xix and 203–7 passim for Cleitarchus as the source used by Diodorus. For a discussion see Hamilton *C* 69–72 and Brunt *L* I 467–74.

[12] The citation of Callisthenes here shows that Plutarch was following another author in describing the actions of the crows in helping laggards by daylight. Similarly he had not followed Callisthenes when he had the priest answer in clear language and not by nods and signs.

[13] One cannot see any reason for writing a fictitious letter of such an unexciting and uninformative kind.

[14] Plutarch is warning us that what follows may not be true.

priest, wishing to speak in Greek as a form of friendliness pronounced ὦ παιδίον [literally 'O little child'] mistakenly as ὦ παῖ Διός, meaning 'O son of Zeus'.

Plutarch's method in 26.11–27.9 is now clear. He made an abbreviated version of the account of Cleitarchus (it had already been published in short forms by Diodorus, Trogus and Curtius). To it he added a reference to Cambyses' army, drawn from Herodotus 3.26, and a mention of Callisthenes' amazing crows cawing at night. On completing his version he said that this version of the consultation was given by most writers (we can name Cleitarchus, Diodorus, Trogus and Curtius among them). He added the letter of A to Olympias, and the improbable story of the muddled Greek expression.

3. Phoenicia and Mesopotamia (29.1–31.5)

'On returning to Phoenicia from Egypt A proceeded to organise in honour of the gods sacrifices, processions and contests of circular dances and tragic dramas' (29.1). Plutarch did not say where the festival was held. Of the Alexander-historians Curtius mentioned a sacrifice to Heracles of Tyre before A set out for the Euphrates (4.8.16). Arrian placed at Tyre a sacrifice to Heracles and a festival of athletics and the arts (3.6.1).

In 29.2–6 Plutarch gave a report of the dramatic competition in which A's favourite actor, Thessalus, was defeated by Athenodorus. He recounted a saying by A and reported A's generosity in paying a fine imposed on Athenodorus by Athens, and in granting ten talents to a comic actor, Lycon, who begged for that sum by inserting a line into a comedy. Diodorus, Justin, Curtius and Arrian had nothing similar. Plutarch, however, was already familiar with the material; for he had included it in his earlier work (*Mor.* 334e). The most likely source is Chares, who wrote of such occasions. For instance, Chares described the ceremonies associated with the marriages of A and some ninety Friends, which lasted for five days and included performances in which Thessalus, Athenodorus and Lycon were mentioned (Athen. 538b–539a = *FGrH* 125 F 4).

In 29.7–9 'when Darius sent a letter and friends to A, begging him to accept 10,000 talents in exchange for the captives, and to be his friend and ally with possession of all territory west of the Euphrates and with the hand of one of his daughters in marriage, A shared the matter with his Companions'. These are the terms of the offer reported by Arrian 2.25.1. Plutarch then tells the anecdote of Parmenio saying 'If I were A, I would accept this offer', and of A replying 'I too by Heaven, if I were Parmenio'. Arrian told this same anecdote in his next sentence (2.25.2). Finally, Plutarch reported that A wrote, that if Darius should come to A, he would receive every kindness (τῶν φιλανθρώπων), but that otherwise A in person was on the march towards him (29.5). Arrian gave a fuller summary of A's letter, which ended with the command that Darius was to come to him, if he wished to receive any kindness (εἴ τι εὑρέσθαι ἐθέλοι φιλανθρώπων). The passages in Plutarch and those in Arrian are so close that they must have either used a common source or drawn upon a common stock of material.

The choice between a common source and a common stock is easily made when we consider the chronological setting. Plutarch placed the peace-offer in summer 331; Arrian at least a year earlier during the siege of Tyre. It follows that Plutarch drew on a common stock and did not accept the date which Arrian later accepted from his acknowledged sources, Ptolemy and/or Aristobulus.[15]

The next event in Plutarch's narrative is the death of Darius' wife, Stateira, in captivity, 'soon' after A's reply to Darius, i.e. in late summer to autumn 331, when A 'was marching against Darius' (31.1). To this event Plutarch attached a long account of a eunuch of Stateira's entourage escaping to Darius with the news of the magnificent funeral accorded by A to the dead queen. Darius suspected at every turn that Stateira had been

---

[15] Ptolemy had access to the *Royal Journal* of A, and it was in the *Journal* that copies of letters (Plu. *Eum.* 2.3) and records of diplomatic negotiations (Polyaen. 4.6.2) were kept. See H*RJ* 130f. Ptolemy would not have been in error about the date. Bosworth *CE* 76 thinks that Arrian dated the peace-offer 'erroneously' to the siege of Tyre and that Plutarch's date is the historical one. His attempt in *C* 256 to explain how Arrian might have misunderstood his sources is far-fetched.

repeatedly raped by A (30.3–10). Assured at last that A had behaved 'with self-control and with magnanimity', Darius in the presence of his 'Companions' prayed that if Persia should be overthrown 'no other than A should sit upon the throne of Cyrus'. The tête-à-tête speeches between Darius and the eunuch are clearly apocryphal, and the prayer is unhistorical, since Darius would never have made such an avowal in public on the eve of the great battle.

At the end of his account Plutarch added: 'The majority of the historians say that these things happened and were said.' Which historians were they? Diodorus reported in the same sequence Darius' peace-offer, A's interchange with Parmenio, A's reply that Darius should yield or fight, and then, as A was advancing towards the enemy camp, the death and sumptuous funeral of Stateira. There Diodorus stopped (17.54.2–7). Justin gave similar events but in a different order. He began with the death of Stateira, the tears of A, and the funeral attended by A 'not for love but for decency'. Darius saw himself outdone in kindness and reckoned he would prefer, if necessary, to be conquered by such a man above any other. Darius then sent his peace-offer to A and A made his reply (11.12.6–16). Curtius had a much fuller account (4.10.18–4.11.22). He began with the death of Stateira (as Justin had done), the tears of A, his mourning and his part in the funeral with Persian rites. He then went on to a eunuch of Stateira's entourage escaping and informing Darius, who believed at every stage that Stateira had been raped repeatedly by A. There were even more tête-à-tête speeches than in Plutarch's account. In the end Darius was convinced. He prayed that, if his own rule should end, his successor as king of Asia might be none other than so just and merciful a man (4.10.34). Darius then made his peace-offer (again as in Justin). The oldest envoy made a lengthy speech, Parmenio deployed arguments for accepting, A made a similar but clumsier quip than that in the account of Diodorus. A's reply to the peace-offer provided another piece of direct speech. The manoeuvres which preceded the Battle of Gaugamela commenced at once.

It is evident that there was in existence before the time of

Diodorus a very long and sensational account of A's continence and gallantry, Darius' opposite opinion of A's treatment of his wife, and Darius' prayer that A should, if need be, succeed him. The account is indeed an extension of the story of the gallantry shown by A and Hephaestion when they visited the captive women.[16] The author of that story was Cleitarchus (see p. 52 above). I conclude, then, that Cleitarchus was the author of the prototype which was the model for Diodorus, Trogus as reflected in Justin, Curtius and Plutarch.[17] Each of these four writers felt free to modify and arrange the events and the details as he thought fit.

Finally, we note that Arrian, writing after Plutarch, expressed his own opinion of the story that A and Hephaestion visited the captive women. He said that Ptolemy and Aristobulus did not record it (2.12.6). So he added 'I have written down this [*logos*] neither as being true nor as being utterly incredible' (2.12.8). Similarly Arrian mentioned as a *logos* the story that a eunuch in charge of Stateira escaped to Darius and overcame Darius' suspicions that Stateira was being raped by A, whereupon Darius prayed that, if need be, none other than A should be king of Asia. This happened 'after the battle' of Issus (4.20.1). Here too Arrian is warning us that the story was not in the accounts of Ptolemy and Aristobulus. As we have seen, it occurred, probably for the first time, in the history of Cleitarchus, and it was dated, as Arrian indicated, to the winter of 333/2.

To return to Plutarch, he chose to describe only one peace-offer, whereas the other Alexander-historians described two or three according to taste.[18] He chose to follow the sequence of events which had been given by Diodorus for the early part of the story, and to proceed thereafter with his own version of much that Curtius had reported. He chose to place these

---

[16] There is an interesting connection between A's visit to the captive women and the statement after Stateira's death that A had seen her only once (Just. 11.12.7 'semel tantum'; Curt. 4.10.24 'semel omnino eam viderat, quo die capta est').

[17] As I argued in *THA* 45, 100 and 122; see Goukowsky 208f. 'cette source est vraisemblablement Clitarque'.

[18] For a list of these see Bosworth *C* 227f. and Atkinson 277f.

events in 331. Thus he had Stateira die 'in childbirth'[19] a year and a half after she had been taken captive, and yet did not speculate who the father might have been. His version says little for his sense of historical probability. It was a story to which he had committed himself in his earlier work (*Mor.* 338e–f), but then without providing a date for Stateira's death and Darius' prayer.

Chapter 31 opens with the familiar idea that Darius was 'coming down' (καταβαίνοντα) i.e. towards the Mediterranean coast. As we have seen (above p. 49), Plutarch adopted this idea from Cleitarchus. Darius is said by Plutarch to have been bringing 1,000,000 men. This number was provided in the form of 800,000 infantry and 200,000 cavalry by Diodorus at 17.39.4 and 53.3, both being passages which I attributed to Cleitarchus as source (*THA* 42 and 44). There follows a strange story of something which happened just before the Battle of Gaugamela. The camp-followers divided themselves into two teams, named their captains 'Alexander' and 'Darius', pelted one another with clods of earth, then engaged in fisticuffs, and finally attacked one another with stones and sticks. A intervening ordered the captains to fight it out in single combat (μονομαχῆσαι), weapons being provided by A for 'Alexander' and by Philotas for 'Darius'. The army watched the fight, regarding the outcome as an omen for the future (of victory or defeat in the forthcoming battle). After a hard fight 'Alexander' won. He was rewarded with twelve villages and the right to wear Persian dress. 'This at any rate is what Eratosthenes has recorded.'

The story of camp-followers, single combat and an omen which was of course a true forecast is so puerile that it should be attributed to Cleitarchus. The only other single combat of this kind which occurred in the accounts of the Alexander-historians was that between a Macedonian Corragus and an Athenian Dioxippus. A named the day and 'many myriads of men' watched the fight. The duel and its sequel were narrated

---

[19] So too Justin 'ex conlisione abiecti partus' (11.12.6), whereas Curtius attributed her death to the exhaustion of continual marching and to grief of mind (4.10.19).

65

with some childish comments by Diodorus at 17.100f. and Curtius 9.7.16–26. In *THA* 66 and 154f. I argued that both writers were drawing on Cleitarchus as their common source. It follows, then, that Eratosthenes was responsible only for the reward.[20] This is reasonable, because we should not expect Eratosthenes, writing in the second half of the third century B.C., to have made up this story, let alone have thought it worth recording, and because Eratosthenes was a writer whom Plutarch consulted on the matter of Persian dress and A's form of it (*Mor.* 329f–330c; see below, p. 79, on this subject).

4. From the victory of Gaugamela to the death of Darius (34–43)

'The battle having had this result, the empire of the Persians seemed to be utterly terminated (ἡ μὲν ἀρχὴ παντάπασιν ἡ Περσῶν ἐδόκει καταλελύσθαι), and A having been proclaimed King of Asia sacrificed to the gods in a magnificent manner and gave his Friends money, houses and commands'[21] (34.1). A similar view was taken by Justin. 'By this battle A seized for himself rule over Asia ('hoc proelio Asiae imperium rapuit'), five years after his accession; and his fortune was so happy that thereafter no one dared to rebel and the Persians accepted the yoke of slavery after so many years of imperial power' (11.14.6f.). It is evident that Plutarch and Justin were following a common source for their opening sentences. Yet, to suppose that Persian rule was ended by defeat at Gaugamela was premature; for Persis and Media were intact and Darius was in command of armed forces. The words of Justin overlook the further fighting by Persian forces (e.g. at the Persian Gates), the rebellion of Bessus and later that of Spitamenes. Plutarch described next the dealings of A with the Greeks both of Asia and of the homeland just after the battle (34.2–4);[22] and he then moved without any

---

[20] Jacoby, *FGrH* 241 F 29, published too much of the text as a fragment of Eratosthenes.

[21] Similar gifts to A's Friends were mentioned by Plutarch at 15.3–6, a passage ascribed to Cleitarchus as source (above, p. 31). He is probably the source here.

[22] The passage is poorly translated by Perrin, and one phrase is misunderstood by

description of military events to Babylonia (35.1) and to Susa (36.1). On the other hand, Justin had the troops rewarded with gifts and refreshed for 34 days while A reviewed the loot; and then A found 40,000 talents 'in the city Susa' (11.14.8f.).

The other Alexander-historians did not mark the Battle of Gaugamela as such a climacteric event. If we may judge from Arrian 3.15.5 and 3.16.3–9, Ptolemy and Aristobulus reported that A captured the Persian camp at Arbela, proceeded at once (εὐθύς) to Babylon, sacrificed to Ba'al and pressed on to Susa, which he reached in twenty days at a marching rate of some 20 miles a day.[23] At Susa he sacrificed 'in the traditional manner' and held a torch-race and athletic contests, and from Susa he sent to Athens the statues of Harmodius and Aristogeiton.[24] For Ptolemy and Aristobulus the capture of Susa 'the most important imperial centre'[25] of the Persian empire and its hoarded treasure was the climax of the campaign. It was here that A celebrated the victory of the Macedonians and the Greeks over Persian despotism. Diodorus and Curtius, who were following Cleitarchus,[26] had A capture the

---

Hamilton C 91. It should be taken as follows: 'Seeking honour for himself A wrote to the Greeks [cf. 29.9 πρὸς τὸν Δαρεῖον ἔγραψεν], that all the tyrannies were put down and they [the Greeks] were living in free states with their own laws; and individually he wrote to the Plataeans that he was rebuilding their city etc.' A was proclaiming the liberation of all Greek states from the pro-Persian tyrannies, which had been in power on the Asiatic mainland and in some of the islands.

[23] Hamilton's 400 miles (C 95), i.e. 20 miles a day, is nearer the mark than Bosworth's 'c. 25 km a day' (C 316). We may compare A's marching rate of some 20 miles a day in 335 and in 334 in Europe (AG² 58 and 67). See C. Neumann, 'A note on A's march rates', Historia 20 (1971) 196f.

[24] Arrian stressed this by using a vivid tense (πέμπει), as he had done at 1.16.4 (ἑστᾶσιν). The latter tense was misunderstood by Bosworth C 11 'a startling oversight' and 126 (see HSPA 460). Arrian referred later at 7.19.2 to a logos that A gave to visiting Greek ambassadors statues removed by Xerxes for them to take to their cities, whether the statues were located at Babylon, Pasargadae, or Susa or elsewhere in Asia; and 'it is said that the bronze statues of Harmodius and Aristogeiton were so taken back to Athens' (οὕτω λέγεται ἀπενεχθῆναι ὀπίσω). A's aim, of course, was to give credit to the Greeks for their part in the campaign; they brought back what they had lost. Bosworth C 317 misunderstands the passage in saying 'Arrian later implies that A sent it [the statue-group] back during his second visit to Susa in 325/4.' Arrian was referring to the way in which the statues were taken back to Greece, not to the time of their despatch. Bosworth concluded that the statues were not sent back until the reign of Seleucus I and Antiochus I (see below, p. 301 n. 62).

[25] CAH² IV (1988) 79.

[26] See THA 54.

Persian camp at Arbela, press ahead because of the stench of the Persian dead,[27] and let the army relax in Babylon for 'more than 30 days' and for '34 days' respectively (Diod. 17.64.3f.; Curt. 5.1.10 and 36–9, complete with strip-tease shows). Thereafter progress was slow to Susa. Diodorus and Curtius are at odds with Ptolemy and Aristobulus.[28]

That A was proclaimed King of Asia[29] is confirmed by A's wording on the spoils which he dedicated after the battle: 'King Alexander, having mastered Darius in battle and having become Lord of Asia, made sacrifice to Athena of Lindus in accordance with an oracle' (*FGrH* 532 F 1, 38). This proclamation was more important to A than it was to Ptolemy and Aristobulus, who saw fighting ahead. What, however, was the source of Plutarch? A clue is provided by Justin's statement of relaxation for 34 days (11.14.8); for the same number of days was provided by Curtius (5.1.39). Thus they had a common source, namely Cleitarchus, who was followed by Curtius. A similar clue appears in Plutarch's figure of 40,000 talents at Susa (36.1); for Justin also has this figure (11.14.9). They were then both following Cleitarchus. On the other hand, Diodorus has 40,000 talents plus 9,000 darics (17.66.1f.) and Curtius has 50,000 talents (5.2.11). In my analysis of sources I attributed these passages of Diodorus and Curtius to a use of Diyllus (*THA* 55 and 129f.). If Plutarch was following Cleitarchus, as we have now deduced, we can understand that he took the account of A's dealings with the Greeks from Cleitarchus, who was interested in emphasising their part in the Panhellenic crusade.

In chapters 35 and 36 Plutarch wrote about naphtha and properties of the soil in Babylonia, and at the end he said that it was a digression (παρέκβασις), which implies that he had

[27] Cleitarchus thought the battlefield was at Arbela and therefore the stench there was intolerable (see *THA* 54). Arrian reported that the battlefield was 500 to 600 stades (102 to 111 kilometres) from Arbela (3.8.7; cf. 6.11.5).

[28] Some troops may have stayed behind in Babylon, but A pressed on with the main army. A had sent Philoxenus 'at once after the battle' (εὐθὺς ἐκ τῆς μάχης) to Susa, and A was already 'on the way' to Susa (κατὰ τὴν ὁδόν), when he met Philoxenus' despatch-carrier. There was no time for A to have sat at Babylon for 34 days.

[29] For this see H*KA* 73f. and especially 77.

moved away to an author or authors not directly concerned with A. He certainly began with A's wonder at 'the chasm from which, as from a spring, naphtha wells up continually ... like asphalt except that naphtha ignites from a distance' (35.1f.). Naphtha in Persian, asphaltos in Greek and bitumen in Latin are the same thing. Curtius 5.1.16 mentioned A's visit to Mennis (in Babylonia), where 'there is a cave from which a spring pours out a huge quantity of bitumen'. It is evident that Plutarch and Curtius were drawing on the same source, who was very probably Cleitarchus, as in chapter 34.

Plutarch then tells in 35.5–9 how one of A's bath-attendants, an Athenian called Athenophanes,[30] proposed to anoint with naphtha a young boy, called Stephanus, who was singing gracefully to A in the bathroom. The youth agreed and anointed himself, whereupon the naphtha ignited and he was severely burnt. The fire was quenched only by the large number of bath-attendants holding jars of water, with which they swamped the boy. Strabo 743, having described how liquid naphtha ignites from a distance, cited the instance of the boy being 'ignited by A' and the fire being extinguished only by the bystanders with a great deal of water. That Plutarch and Strabo drew on a common source is most likely; and there is the added evidence that in both texts it was said to have been done 'for an experiment' (πρὸς τὴν πεῖραν and πείρας δὲ χάριν). It is probable that Plutarch and Strabo were continuing with the author followed in 35.1–4. In any case it was not Poseidonius, whom Plutarch cited in the next sentence for the different colours of two kinds of naphtha.

Plutarch turned next to the question whether Medea used naphtha to kill her rival, and then to what it was in the Babylonian soil that brought naphtha into being and made barley-grains jump of their own accord. There is no clue to his source for these points. He returned to A at 36.15. For Harpalus, being left behind (by A) 'as supervisor of the terri-

---

[30] As an Athenian citizen he was one of those who accompanied A to his bath, anointed him etc. and 'relaxed his mind suitably', presumably by conversation. In Plutarch's citation from the *Royal Journal* Nearchus talked to A 'as he lay in the bathroom' (76.3).

tory, naturalised some Greek plants in the palace grounds of Babylon but failed with ivy, because the soil was 'fiery' (πυρώδης). Now Plutarch had already told this anecdote in *Moralia* 648c, and he had then named Theophrastus as his source, correctly because the anecdote has survived in Theophrastus, *Hist. Plant.* 4.4.

We have seen that Plutarch began chapter 36 with Cleitarchus as his source. As what follows – the purple dye and the reason for its long life – is qualified twice by the expression 'they say', it is probable that Plutarch has departed from Cleitarchus and is using some one else. Then at 36.4 Plutarch quotes Dinon on the water of the Nile and the Danube which was brought regularly to the Persian monarchs at Susa. As Hamilton wrote, Plutarch 'used him extensively, evidently at first hand'. Plutarch may have turned to Dinon here, or he may have found the citation in the work of his son, Cleitarchus.

In chapter 37 Plutarch described the advance through Persis to Persepolis, during which A was able to turn an enemy position by taking a circuitous route. His guide was bilingual, being the son of a Lycian father and a Persian mother. The Pythian priestess, 'they say', foretold his part in guiding A – still a boy at the time of the prophecy – towards the Persians 'as a wolf' (punning on Λύκιος and λύκος, 'a wolf').[31] The Lycian and the prophecy were mentioned also by Curtius 5.4.4–13, especially 11, and by Polyaenus 4.3.27, who described the turning operation through very difficult country;[32] and the Lycian guide figured in the account of Diodorus 17.68.5. In *THA* 56 and 131 I argued that an account by Cleitarchus was followed by Diodorus and by Curtius, the latter at least for the later stage, 5.4.21–34.[33] Thus Plutarch could have based his chapter 37.1f. on Cleitarchus.

---

[31] The oracle was *post eventum*. See H. W. Parke, *The Delphic Oracle* (Oxford, 1939) 251f.

[32] Curtius described the dense branches forming a hedge across their path (5.4.24), Polyaenus had 'the path concealed by the roofing-over of the forest' (ἄτραπος εἴη τῷ συνηρεφεῖ τῆς ὕλης ἀποκεκρυμμένη) and Diodorus had the unusual phrase 'by the treed-over path' (διὰ τῆς καταδένδρου).

[33] Arr. 3.18.1–10 did not include the oracle or the Lycian, and he had A take guides from among 'his prisoners'. Polyaenus followed a different source. Since Ptolemy was present in the action (3.18.9), his account as abbreviated by Arrian is to be preferred.

'There [i.e. in the two-sided attack according to Arrian and three-sided according to Curtius (5.4.27–30)] it happened that much slaughter occurred of those who were being caught (τῶν ἁλισκομένων); for A himself writes that, considering it to be to his advantage, his order was that the men be killed' (37.3). If we accept Arrian's account as historical, we see that A with some 6,000 infantry and 700 cavalry and Craterus with some 3,500 infantry and 500 cavalry were attacking 40,000 Persian infantry and 700 Persian cavalry.[34] Moreover, for the surprise attacks the Macedonian forces were split into three detachments which were not in contact with one another during the action. A could not afford to have each detachment take thousands of prisoners in this situation. Thus his order, made in advance of setting off from the camp of Craterus, is understandable, and of those who were caught in the trap Ariobarzanes and a few cavalrymen only escaped. Plutarch was evidently quoting from a written document, whether a letter of A or an entry in the *Royal Journal*,[35] and there is no reason to doubt the authenticity of the order.

An alternative interpretation has often been advanced.[36] This begins with the postulates that there is a lacuna in Plutarch's text after 'the march against the Persians' (at 37.2), and that in the lacuna there was a description of the capture of Persepolis, although Plutarch gave no description of the capture of Babylon or of Susa. Given those postulates, then ἐνταῦθα refers to the postulated place, Persepolis, and the order was to kill the inhabitants of Persepolis. Quite apart from the postulates, there are difficulties in the Greek words. For when Plutarch writes of captured persons, he uses either οἱ αἰχμάλωτοι (as at 21.1) or οἱ ἑαλωκότες (as at 29.7), and

---

[34] Diod. 17.68.1 had 25,000 infantry and 300 cavalry, and Curt. 5.3.17 had 25,000 infantry, both from Cleitarchus on my interpretation in *THA* 56 and 131.

[35] Plutarch gave an account of particulars concerning A's illness which were in the *Royal Journal* (76.1; cf. 77.1). In the present instance Plutarch may have consulted the *Journal* himself, or he may have taken the written order from a source which had used the *Journal*.

[36] See Hamilton *C* 97 and add Bosworth *CE* 92f. 'the men cut down and the women enslaved in Persepolis', citing *PA* 37.3–5. That the city was looted is likely. Horrific descriptions were given by Diod. 17.70.1–6 and by Curt. 5.6.1–9, despite the statement of Curtius that the population left the city at 5.6.2 'barbari deserto oppido ... diffugerant'. Their common source was probably Cleitarchus; see *THA* 56 and 131.

never the present participle οἱ ἁλισκόμενοι. Next, the order was to kill τοὺς ἀνθρώπους, an expression used by Plutarch, for instance, of the Greek mercenaries at the Battle of the Granicus and of the priests at Siwa (16.14 and 27.7), but not of men, women and children. Thus the alternative interpretation does not fit the Greek words. And as regards the postulates, it is simpler to postulate that Plutarch, writing carelessly, omitted the words ἐν Περσεπόλει in his next sentence: νομίσματος δὲ εὑρεῖν πλῆθος ὅσον ἐν Σούσοις. For there is no evidence of a lacuna in the manuscripts.

At 37.3f. Plutarch qualified with 'they say' the statements that as much coined money was found as at Susa (i.e. 40,000 talents), and that 10,000 mule-pairs and 5,000 camels carried away the rest of the gear and the wealth. These figures came from a source other than that followed by Diodorus at 17.71.2, who had A collect 120,000 talents and summon a multitude of mules and 3,000 camels, i.e. from a source on my interpretation other than Cleitarchus. However, the next two items are worthy of Cleitarchus. (1) A accosted an overthrown statue of Xerxes, pondered in silence and passed on. This is a good example of the puerility which was a mark of Cleitarchus according to Cicero. (2) Demaratus of Corinth, a loyal friend of Philip and A, wept, 'it is said', as an old man will, to see A sitting for the first time on the throne of Darius under its gold canopy and to think that Greeks of the past had not lived to see this. Plutarch had told this anecdote earlier in *Mor.* 329d, but he had then had him sitting on the throne in Susa, which made more sense.[37]

In the next chapter Thaïs is reported to have instigated the burning of the palace of Xerxes at Persepolis during a drunken party, at which A and his Companions were accompanied by women who joined in the drinking with their lovers.[38] Thaïs was the most famous of these prostitutes, her lover being

---

[37] Diod. 17.66.3 and Curt. 5.2.13 had A mount his throne first in Susa, but they told a different story, inherited probably from Diyllus (see *THA* 55 and 130).

[38] This description fits a Greek dinner, at which prostitutes were present, but it does not fit a Macedonian dinner, at which men only were present both traditionally (Hdt. 5.18.3) and in A's time, as at the dinner when Cleitus was killed. Thus the author whom Plutarch was following here was a Greek writer.

Ptolemy, and she was applauded for a speech, in which she proposed the burning as a demonstration that the women followers of A exacted a greater revenge from Persia on behalf of Greece than the Greek commanders had ever done. Then a tipsy A, wearing a wreath and grasping a torch, led the way into the palace, and all the Macedonians joined in the arson, thinking that this was a sign that they would go home to Macedonia. 'Some writers say that it was done thus; others say it was an act of policy [literally 'from intention'].[39] In any case it is agreed that A quickly repented and ordered the fire to be put out.'

Of other writers who gave the initiative to Thaïs we have accounts by Diodorus at 17.72 and Curtius at 5.7.2–7. These will have been known to Plutarch. However, there is no doubt that Diodorus, Curtius and Plutarch were all drawing ultimately on a common source, and that that source was Cleitarchus.[40] For we learn from Athenaeus that 'Cleitarchus wrote of Thaïs as having been responsible for the burning of the palace at Persepolis' (576d–e).[41] As a Greek writing for Greeks, Cleitarchus was eager to mark the punishment of Persia on behalf of Greece and to show the words of an Athenian beauty as mightier than the swords of the great commanders, whereas the Macedonian leaders were portrayed as crazy with drink and the Macedonian soldiers as simply wanting to go home.

Among the authors who said that it was 'an act of policy' we can count Ptolemy and Aristobulus. For they were the sources of Arrian's version at 3.18.11:

A burned the Persian palace, though Parmenio advised him to preserve it, advancing various arguments and especially that it was not good to destroy what was already A's own property and that the peoples throughout Asia would not turn to A so readily, for they would think that even he had

---

[39] 38.8 ἀπὸ γνώμης. The contrast is with the burning by Thaïs, which was intentional, of course, but not an act of policy.

[40] See *THA* 57, 85, 93 and 132. Hamilton *C* 99 'this is evidently the version of Cleitarchus' and Bosworth *C* 331 'the main lines of the story certainly go back to Cleitarchus'.

[41] *FGrH* 137 F 11.

decided not to exercise the rule over Asia but simply to conquer and pass on. A used to say that he wished to punish Persia for having sacked Athens and burnt the temples during their invasion of Greece and to exact revenge for all the other injuries they had done to the Greeks.

Another author, one known to Plutarch, was Strabo. 'A burnt the palace at Persepolis, taking revenge for the Greeks, because the Persians sacked with fire and sword the temples and the cities of the Greeks' (Strabo 729/30).

In both sets of accounts the palace was burnt as an act of revenge for the Greeks. We can see the importance of this when we recall that Agis and his allies, with the help of Persian subsidies, held the bulk of the Peloponnese from October 331 to April 330. Throughout that period there was a fear that other states and especially Athens might join the insurgents. A therefore did everything possible to emphasise the victory of Greek arms in Asia, the liberties of the Greek states and the overthrow of Persian might in the months after the victory at Gaugamela in October 331. Nothing was more striking than the burning of Xerxes' palace at the capital of the Persian empire, Persepolis (Diod. 17.70.1 and Just. 11.14.10 'caput Persici regni'). The news of the burning in January 330 reached the Greek mainland some two months later, at a critical time just before Antipater was able to assume the offensive.[42]

Plutarch's next narrative step is at 42.5, when A set off from Persepolis in April/May 330, 'expecting to fight another battle' against Darius. But on hearing that Darius had been arrested by Bessus, A sent the Thessalians home with a bounty totalling 2,000 talents. (So too Arrian 3.19.5 but adding 'the other allies', i.e. the other Greek troops of the League.) Then came 'the long, arduous pursuit of Darius, during which A covered 3,300 stades in eleven days'.[43] Lack of water was a special difficulty. Plutarch reported an anecdote about A handing

[42] The importance of the situation in Greece is overlooked in the commentaries of Hamilton and Bosworth.

[43] In Arr. 3.20.2 A was said to have reached Rhagae from Ecbatana on the eleventh day. Plutarch says only that A began on hearing that Darius had been arrested by Bessus. On the other hand, Arr. 3.20.3 had A learn of the arrest only at Rhagae. It is not clear in Plutarch's vague account which the eleven days were. On the pursuit in general see my article in *CQ* 28 (1978) 136f.

back an offered drink of water, which we shall consider later
(see below p. 275). In 43.1 Plutarch gave a highly coloured
account of the finale.

A with only 60 men, they say, breaking into the camp of the enemy, riding
over much discarded gold and silver, passing many waggons full of women
and children, which were coursing this way and that without their drivers,
and bent on pursuit of the leaders, among whom they expected to find
Darius. With difficulty they found him, his body full of many javelins, lying
in a waggon, a little short of death.

Being given a drink of cold water, he uttered his last words in
direct speech to a soldier Polystratus, took his hand and expired (43.4).

At this point we may pause to note that in two accounts
Darius was dead when he was found. So Diodorus wrote at
17.73.3 'it was just after his death that A rode up in pursuit
with his horsemen'. Arrian ended his account with the words
'Darius died of his wounds a little later, before he could be
seen by A' (3.21.10). However, Plutarch was not alone in his
version. For Justin 11.15.1–13 and Curtius 5.13.13–25 had
Darius, chained with golden fetters, discovered in a waggon by
a soldier, whom Curtius named as Polystratus. Darius was
pierced with multiple wounds but he was 'still breathing' (so
Justin, while Curtius' text broke off with the word 'semivivi',
'half-alive'). Justin reported a long speech for a dying man,
in which there were points similar to those in Plutarch's version, and he ended with the same climax: 'post haec porrexit
manum expiravit⟨que⟩' (11.15.13). It is evident that Justin,
Curtius and Plutarch were following a common source, namely on my interpretation Cleitarchus (see *THA* 101, 133 and
137). Diodorus was aware of yet another version. For he
added at 17.73.4: 'as some have written, A found Darius still
breathing, commiserated with his misfortunes, and was
requested by him to avenge his murder'. It was so in *The
Alexander Romance* of Ps.-Callisthenes.[44]

To return to Plutarch at 43.3, 'when A came, he was clearly
distressed by the disaster, and unfastening his own cloak he

---

[44] R. Merkelbach, *Die Quellen des griechischen Alexanderromans* (Munich, 1954) 20.

threw it over the body and covered it'. He had mentioned this in his earlier work (*Mor.* 332f). He was continuing, no doubt, with Cleitarchus. 'Later, when he found Bessus, he rent him asunder (διεσφενδόνησεν)[45] by having him tied to two trees bent together and then letting the trees go to split him apart' (43.6). This was the final form of torture to which Bessus was submitted by the Persian aristocrats in Diodorus 17.83.9. 'They inflicted every outrage and torture, cut his body a little bit at a time and then rent his limbs asunder (διεσφενδόνησαν).' A lacuna follows in the text of Diodorus, wherein the method of rending apart may have been added. I have argued in *THA* 52, 61 and 141 that the source of Diodorus was Cleitarchus. It follows that Plutarch was drawing on Cleitarchus in the *Moralia* and in 43.5f. He continued to do so in 43.7, where the burial of Darius and the elevation of Exathres to the rank of Companion are common to Diodorus 17.73.3, Justin 11.15.15 and Curtius 6.2.11.

5. Hyrcania and Parthia (44–7)

In ancient times there were two theories about the 'Hyrcanian' or 'Caspian' stretch of water. 'The early naturalists' (44.2) held that it was an inlet or gulf of the 'Outer Sea' or 'Sea' (τῆς ἔξω θαλάσσης or πελάγους) which was believed to encircle the inhabited earth.[46] The other theory was that the water was landlocked, a lake, which was connected with the 'Maeotic Lake' (our Sea of Azov) probably by the river Tanaïs (Don). Because A claimed to be King of Asia and because the river Tanaïs was said to form the boundary between Europe and Asia, it was important for A and his contemporaries to determine which theory was correct.

One of the scientists accompanying A was Polycleitus of Larissa. His views were described by Strabo as pleasing to A (Strabo 509). According to him the Caspian and the Maeotic

---

[45] Plutarch transferred the execution to A himself, thus making him comparable to Theseus, who dealt with the robber Sinis in this manner. Diodorus, having a favourable view of A, left the job to the Persian nobles.
[46] Such as Hecataeus and Herodotus.

Lake were linked together through the course of the Tanaïs, which flowed under the name Jaxartes into the Caspian and later flowed into the Maeotic Lake.[47] Polycleitus lent support to this theory by pointing out that the Caspian bred snakes and its water was sweetish (ὑπόγλυκυ), and that the Scythians beyond the Jaxartes made their arrows of fir, which grew only in Europe. Thus, when A reached the Jaxartes, he was at the boundary of Asia.[48]

When Curtius brought A to the Caspian, he described it as 'sweeter than others, breeding huge snakes ... and some think the Maeotic Marsh flows into it, and argue that its sweetness in comparison with other seas is due to the water of the Marsh reducing the salinity' (6.4.18). As these points are like those attributed to Polycleitus by Strabo, it seems that Curtius was also following Polycleitus. Plutarch wrote that, since A was unable to gain clear information, the conjecture he rated highest was that the Caspian was a 'recoil' or 'backflow' of the Maeotic Lake (44.1 μάλιστα δὲ εἴκασε τῆς Μαιώτιδος λίμνης ἀνακοπὴν εἶναι). Plutarch could have obtained this much from Polycleitus or from any writer familiar with A's views, such as Aristobulus,[49] or at second hand from Cleitarchus. Indeed there is a link between Plutarch and Cleitarchus in Plutarch's remark, that the Caspian proved no smaller than the Pontus (Black Sea), and a fragment of Cleitarchus (*FGrH* 137 F 12) giving his belief that it was 'not less than Pontus Euxinus'. Plutarch himself believed in the other theory, that the Caspian was a gulf of the Outer Sea (πελάγους ἰδὼν κόλπον).[50]

Plutarch placed the capture of A's war-horse Bucephalus 'here', that is vaguely in Hyrcania (44.3). The capture was represented as almost accidental: 'some of the barbarians

---

[47] The Macedonians knew an analogy in the Strymon, which flowed then through two lakes before reaching Amphipolis and the sea.

[48] He therefore named his city on the Asian side of the Jaxartes 'the farthest Alexandria', Alexandria Eschate. He was influenced by Aristotle, who expressed similar views, as revealed in *Meteor.* 350a–351a.

[49] Arr. 3.30.7 cited Aristobulus for the Jaxartes being the Tanaïs and flowing into the 'Hyrcanian Sea'. See below, p. 299. Further comments are given by Hamilton *C* 116–19 and in *CQ* 21 (1971) 108f., and by Bosworth *C* 377f.

[50] See *AG*² 177 for a map of the world as A conceived it to be.

happened unexpectedly on those who were leading his horse Bucephalus and captured him'. He differed in these matters from Diodorus and Curtius, who both had A at war with the Mardi and in the midst of operations when the horse was captured (17.76.5 and 6.5.11 and 17–18). He differed also from Arrian who said that the horse 'disappeared in the land of the Uxians' (5.19.6), who lived far away to the south; moreover, Arrian seems to represent the kidnapping as happening in a time of peace (perhaps after the reduction of the Uxii). Plutarch continued as follows. A was very angry and issued dire threats, which were enough to result not only in the return of Bucephalus but also in the surrender of their cities. 'A treated them all kindly and gave ransom-money to those who took the horse' (44.4–5). Here too Plutarch differed from Diodorus and Curtius, who had A carry out his threats and terrorise the Mardians into returning the horse, and even then A kept some Mardians as hostages (17.76.7–8 and 6.5.19–21).

We see, then, that Plutarch did not draw on the account of Cleitarchus, which was most probably the common source of Diodorus and Curtius (see *THA* 135),[51] nor on the accounts of Ptolemy and Aristobulus, on which Arrian drew presumably at 5.19.6. He chose instead a source which portrayed A as treating the barbarians 'kindly' (φιλανθρώπως) and even being generous to the kidnappers. We have argued that Marsyas Macedon was the author on whom Plutarch drew for the early history of Bucephalus (above, p. 23); and we shall suggest that he preferred Onesicritus in discussing the end of Bucephalus (below, p. 113). Of these two Marsyas Macedon may be preferred on the ground that he was writing favourably of A.[52]

'Moving on from there [Hyrcania] into Parthia and being at rest A for the first time put on the barbarian dress.' Plutarch

---

[51] See also Hamilton *C* 120 'a common source, perhaps Cleitarchus'.

[52] There is an analogy in Just. 7.6.16, where Philip is said to be 'generous to the vanquished' ('mitis adversus victos'), namely to the people of Methone who were banished with one garment each. In an article in *CQ* 41 (1991) 505 I argue that this passage was derived from Marsyas Macedon. If the work of Marsyas stopped with events of 331, the statement about Bucephalus might well have been in a digression concerning the horse.

had written of A's dress in *Moralia* 329f–330c. There he had cited Eratosthenes, who wrote in the second half of the third century B.C., as his source for the statement that A adopted a dress which was a combination of Persian and of Macedonian elements, and that he abjured the tiara, *kandys* and trousers (*anaxyrides*). Here Plutarch described the dress as intermediate between the Persian and the Median styles, and noted the same three features which A avoided (45.2f.). His source was presumably Eratosthenes here also.[53] In *Moralia* Plutarch was arguing that this mixed dress was in line with A's policy of uniting 'the two greatest and most mighty peoples' (329e), and so he wrote of a mixture of Persian and Macedonian features; but in the *Life*, while he repeated this idea, his emphasis was more on the effect the adoption of Persian and Median features might have and indeed did have on the Macedonians. At first – and he is writing of the first time A did this – he was beginning a gradual process of accustoming the Macedonians to a change in his way of life which might lead to an attempt (ἀπόπειρά τις) at introducing obeisance (*proskynesis*). So he tried out the new dress at first on the barbarians and his Companions, and then later he was seen so dressed by the many when he was riding out and giving audience. 'The Macedonians found it distressing, but they felt they should make some allowance in matters which led to his pleasure or his glory because they admired his excellence in the other respects' (45.4).

Plutarch resumed this topic at 47.1. The distress which the Macedonians felt was the background, it seems, to 'A's fear that they might refuse to undertake the rest of the campaign [to conquer all Asia]'. He therefore divided his forces. He left the main body in place, and he took his best troops, numbering 20,000 infantry and 3,000 cavalry, on a special operation in Hyrcania. During it he attacked them in a speech to the effect that, if the army should merely throw Asia into confusion and then depart, the barbarians would at once attack them as women (47.1).

[53] So too Hamilton *C* 121 'probably Eratosthenes'.

Nevertheless, he let any depart who wished to do so, but he called any such to witness that at a time when he was winning the inhabited world for the Macedonians he had been deserted, so that he would be campaigning with his Friends and with his volunteers.[54] This is almost literally what was written in the letter to Antipater.

And the letter said that after his speech they all shouted out: 'Lead us wherever in the world you like.' Thereafter, adds Plutarch, the main body was easily persuaded to follow.

The restlessness of the Macedonians, their desire to return home and the persuasion of them by A to continue featured also in Diodorus 17.74.3 (very briefly), Curtius 6.2.15–6.4.1 (with a lengthy speech) and Justin 12.3.2–4. In all three passages A summoned 'the Macedonians' or 'the army [meaning the Macedonians]' to an assembly (Diod. εἰς ἐκκλησίαν; Just. 'ad contionem'; Curt. 6.2.21 'ad contionem'), and received an enthusiastic response (Diod. παρορμήσας εὐπειθεῖς; Just. 'incitatis militum animis'; Curt. 'summa militum alacritate'). Indeed 'the soldiers ordered him to lead them wherever he might wish' (Curt. 6.4.1). It seems then that Diodorus, Justin and Curtius followed a common source. In addition, Diodorus and Curtius had the same general location for the event: Diodorus placed the meeting and A's speech two days' march before reaching Hecatompylus (17.75.1), and Curtius placed it at Hecatompylus (6.2.15). In *THA* 58 and 134f. I argued that the common source was Diyllus.

Plutarch, however, placed the meeting and the speech much later, namely after the conquest of Hyrcania and not, as Diodorus, Justin and Curtius had it, before the entry into Hyrcania (Diod. 17.75.3; Just. 12.3.4; Curt. 6.4.2). It is thus evident that Plutarch did not share their common source, being Diyllus, but followed an author who was less accurate. There is also a difficulty in the number of troops which Plutarch says were taken as 'the best', namely 20,000 infantry and 3,000 cavalry, as opposed to the main body (47.1 and 4). For A's concern was only with the citizen troops in his army, that is the Macedonians proper, who in 330 numbered probably some 13,500 Infantry Companions and 2,000 Cav-

---

[54] Reading τῶν ἐθελοντῶν rather than in the Loeb edition τῶν ἐθελόντων.

alry Companions.[55] For this inaccuracy we need a Greek author, and the most likely candidate is Cleitarchus.[56]

Cleitarchus was certainly in Plutarch's mind in the preceding chapter, 46, where the visit of the Amazon queen was under consideration. Plutarch gave the names of the authors who reported a visit: Cleitarchus, Polycleitus, Onesicritus, Antigenes and Ister; and of those who denied such a visit: Aristobulus, Chares, Ptolemy, Anticleides, Philo, Philip of Theangela, Hecataeus, Philip the Chalcidian and Duris. 'And A seems to support the latter group.' For A made no mention of the Amazons in a letter to Antipater which described everything accurately and said that 'the Scythian' offered A his daughter in marriage.[57] This letter must have been written after the Scythian king made that offer in summer 329 (Arr. 4.15.2). Plutarch said 'seems to support', because Plutarch was making the inference that the Scythian king would have mentioned the Amazons if they had existed. He strengthened his inference by citing the story (λέγεται) that many years later, when Lysimachus was king and Onesicritus was recounting the visit of the Amazon queen, Lysimachus smiled and said 'And where was I at the time?'

In 45.5f. Plutarch digressed to enlarge on A's excellence in the eyes of the Macedonians. Thus he endured severe wounds – a splintering of his tibia, and a blow on the neck which impaired his sight for a considerable time – but he did not stop exposing himself to danger recklessly. Indeed 'on crossing the Orexartes, which he thought was the Tanaïs, and routing the Scythians he pursued for 100 stades [$18\frac{1}{2}$ kilometers] although suffering from diarrhoea'. There are some indications that Plutarch was drawing here on Aristobulus. For a similar description of the leg-wound in Arrian 3.30.11 came from Ptolemy and/or Aristobulus; the injury to the neck affecting A's sight figures in Curtius 7.6.22, a passage attributed tentatively to Aristobulus in *THA* 142; and the name 'Orexartes',

---

[55] See my argument in H*CR* 64.

[56] It is also to be observed that Plutarch wrote of 'the inhabited world' (47.2 τὴν οἰκουμένην), which was characteristic of Cleitarchus (see *THA* 44 and 63).

[57] Hamilton *L* 14 'it seems excessively sceptical to see in this letter the work of a forger'.

instead of the usual 'Iaxartes', was peculiar to Aristobulus (Arr. 3.30.7 = *FGrH* 139 F 25).[58] Plutarch had already mentioned the leg-wound with the same details in *Moralia* 327a and 341b. The length of the pursuit – 100 stades – was probably taken from Aristobulus; for it is different from the 80 stades of Curtius 7.9.13, a passage attributed to Cleitarchus as source in *THA* 143f.

At 47.5 Plutarch moved on to the second stage of his main theme in these rather disjointed chapters, 45–7, namely the interchange of Macedonian and Persian customs (45.1).

So then [on persuading the Macedonians to continue the campaign] A went still further in likening himself to the native peoples as regards his way of life, and in bringing them[59] closer to Macedonian customs; for he thought that by [this] mingling and sharing he would base his control of the situation on loyalty rather than on force, while he himself was setting off on a distant campaign.

The timing of this second stage is set after the persuasion of the Macedonians, i.e. after the conquest of Hyrcania which was completed by mid-August 330;[60] and the distant campaign which he had in mind was the conquest of the eastern part of 'Asia', including 'India'. 'That was why, also, he selected 30,000 boys, ordered them to learn Greek letters and be brought up in the use of Macedonian weapons, and appointed many men as supervisors (ἐπιστάτας).' Plutarch next looked ahead to a further example of bringing together Macedonian and Persian ways of life, namely the marriage of A and Roxane in 327, which he saw as inspired both by love and by policy (47.7 'it seemed to be not out of harmony with the situation he was establishing'). 'For the barbarians took confidence from the association which this marriage indicated', because even in this case of passionate love A showed a continence and a respect for law, which won their great affection.

The author to whom Plutarch owed this favourable inter-

---

[58] The MSS of Arr. 3.30.7 read 'Ορξάντην, for which Brunt *L* 1 331 substituted 'Ιαξάρτην, despite the reading in Plutarch. See Hamilton *C* 123, citing Tarn 9 with n. 2.

[59] See Hamilton *C* 128 for reading ἐκείνους (rather than ἐκεῖνα which is in all MSS), which resumes 'the native peoples'. It is important to note that Plutarch was writing not of Persians only but of the Asians generally.

[60] See *AG*² 179 for the celebrations then at Zadracarta.

pretation of A adopting some eastern ways and of A's passionate love of Roxane 'in her youthful beauty' (καλὴν καὶ ὡραίαν
... ὀφθεῖσαν) was most probably Aristobulus. We have seen
signs that Plutarch was following his account at 45.4–6 in
assessing the Macedonians' reactions to the first stage of the
new policy. And now at the second stage there is the same
understanding of A's policy as a two-way process, not just A
adopting Persian ways but also the introduction of Asians to
Macedonian ways, both in the case of the 30,000 boys and in
the wedding with Roxane. It is a much more understanding
interpretation than that which was offered by the Alexander-
historians. Thus Diodorus 17.108.3 saw the 30,000 young men
as 'a counterweight' or force opposing 'the Macedonian phalanx';[61] and Curtius 8.5.1 saw them as 'at the same time both
hostages and soldiers'. Next, Diodorus 17.77.4 had A 'begin
to imitate both the Persian luxury and the extravagance of
the Kings of Asia'; Justin 12.3.8 'A assumed the dress of
the Persian kings and the diadem previously unusual for
Macedonian kings, just as if he would accede to the terms of
those he had conquered'; and Curtius 6.6.1f. 'A changed his
continence and self-restraint ... to arrogance and lechery,
... and strove to rival the dizzy heights of the Persian court
which was equated with the power of the gods.' The common
source of these three passages was Cleitarchus (see *THA* 59,
102 and 136). Arrian expressed his own personal opinion that
A was drawn into emulation of Median and Persian opulence,
and that this was a sign that A was losing control of himself
(4.7.4f.).[62]

In 47.9–12 Plutarch mentioned that Hephaestion approved
A's policy and changed his own way of life in sympathy with
him. There followed a digression on the relations between A
and Hephaestion, A and Craterus, and Hephaestion and Craterus with personal anecdotes and sayings. The author who
was most likely to have written about these relations with
insight and sympathy was Aristobulus.

[61] In *THA* 72 I argued that his source was Diyllus.
[62] See also Arrian's own final comment at 7.29.4.

6

CONSPIRACIES AND CALLISTHENES

1. Philotas and Parmenio

There were two phases in the history of Philotas: the first when he was under suspicion and observation, and the second which ended with trial and execution in October 330. Plutarch alone described the first phase at any length. Arrian mentioned it in a single sentence, in which he named his sources specifically. 'Ptolemy and Aristobulus say that a plot by Philotas, son of Parmenio, had already been reported to A even earlier in Egypt, but that it appeared to be incredible because of the long friendship they had had, the honour he had conferred on Philotas' father Parmenio, and the trust he had in Philotas himself' (3.26.1). Curtius described the second phase at great length, but he was apparently either unaware or unaccepting of the first phase. For he said in the course of his description that the excessive boasting of Philotas in the presence of A had laid him 'under suspicion not of crime but of arrogance' (6.8.3). Diodorus too had nothing to say of a first phase. It is thus reasonable to infer that the first phase was described by Ptolemy and Aristobulus, but not by other Alexander-historians.

In the *Moralia* Plutarch described the first phase as an illustration of A's 'most honourable and most kingly use of his authority' (340a). Philotas, son of Parmenio, (he wrote) was one of those who were invincible in battle but subservient to pleasure, women and the lure of gold and silver (339b). He became obsessed with a girl of Pella, called Antigona,[1] who was taken prisoner at Samothrace by a Persian admiral (in 333) and liberated a few months later at Damascus. Talking

---

[1] The word γύναιον suggests that she was less than respectable. It is interesting that he used the Doric form of her name.

freely and boasting of the achievements of his father and himself, Philotas implied that Philip and A would have been nowhere but for them. Antigona told a girl-friend, and she told Craterus. So Craterus took Antigona to A, who did not have sexual relations but made a secret arrangement, that she should pass information to him. 'Working secretly through her A discovered all about Philotas' (339f τὸν δὲ Φιλώταν ὑποικουρῶν δι' αὐτῆς ὅλον ἐφώρασε). Yet A never told anyone, while 'more than seven years passed'. Why seven years? The answer is provided by Arrian's mention of Egypt, where A was in the first part of 330, and the 'more than seven years' takes one down to 323, the year of A's death. It was thus 'most honourable' of A throughout the remaining years of his life not to offset any criticism of himself over the deaths of Philotas and Parmenio by revealing that first phase.[2]

Who then did reveal that first phase? Nothing more is heard of Antigona, who presumably obeyed A's order of secrecy. Craterus alone knew, and he would not have revealed what A was keeping secret. It must have been after the death of A and before the death of Craterus in 321, that Craterus let the secret out; and so news of it would later have reached Aristobulus and Ptolemy. Since Aristobulus wrote his history of A earlier than Ptolemy did, it is likely that Aristobulus first described that first phase.[3] If so, Plutarch was drawing on Aristobulus in *Moralia* 339e–340a.

In the *Life* Plutarch repeated much of what he had written in the *Moralia*. He made Antigona into Antigone, and he called her a girl of Pydna (not Pella). He added examples of Philotas' open-handed generosity, his abundant wealth, and his pretentious way of life, which made others jealous and suspicious, and he cited Philotas calling A 'a stripling'

[2] Hamilton *C* 134 wrote of 'the seven years' that Plutarch 'presumably dated this to the beginning of A's reign ... if it is not a rhetorical exaggeration'. But it was not in the first year of A's reign that Antigona was telling A about the boasts of Philotas (*Mor.* 339f). On the other hand, if the seven years is emended to a couple of years, i.e. 329 and 328, there was nothing so very honourable about A remaining silent.

[3] Since Aristobulus and Ptolemy published in my opinion in the 280s, the earlier writers such as Cleitarchus and Onesicritus would not have known of this first phase.

(μειράκιον). But he explained A's silence differently: 'either because A was confident of Parmenio's loyalty to himself, or because he feared their reputation and their power [i.e. of father and son]'. Why has Plutarch changed his explanation? The reason was surely that Plutarch was leading us up to the executions and suggesting indirectly that A ceased to be confident of Parmenio's loyalty and was influenced by fear of the combined authority of father and son.

Plutarch's account of the second phase is remarkable for the total omission of a trial by the Macedonians. He simply wrote that after the death of Philotas A killed Parmenio also (καὶ Παρμενίωνα ... ἀνεῖλεν). There is, however, no doubt that a trial was held in accordance with Macedonian practice. The clearest statement is that of Arrian. 'Ptolemy, son of Lagus, says that Philotas was brought before the Macedonians, was accused strongly by A, and made his defence in person' (3.26.2). Diodorus and Curtius reported a trial (17.79.6 and 80.1; and 6.8.1f.). So did Justin (12.5.3). The trial was held because a plot had been reported and because one of the suspects had resisted arrest or committed suicide.

Plutarch reported the preliminaries which led to the attempt to inform A in much the same way as the other authors did (there are variations in the name of Plutarch's Limnus). Then differences appear. Plutarch wrote that the informers tried twice to reach A but they were refused entry by Philotas. Ptolemy also used the plural of the informers (Arr. 3.26.2). However, Diodorus and Curtius had only one informer, Cebalinus (17.79.3–5; and 6.7.16f.). On being informed, Plutarch continued, A sent someone to arrest Limnus, but Limnus resisted arrest and was killed; and A, already greatly incensed, was still more disturbed in mind (διεταράχθη). According to Diodorus A was shattered (καταπλαγείς), arrested Dimnus at once and learnt everything from him; but later, while the matter was being investigated, Dimnus killed himself. According to Curtius Dymnus wounded himself fatally, faced a question by the king, and then collapsed and died.

These differences show that different sources were being followed. Plutarch agrees with Ptolemy in using the plural of the informers. In *THA* 59f. I argued that Diodorus was following the account of Diyllus, which was favourable to A; and in *THA* 136 I left the question of Curtius' source open, but it seems likely that he made use of Cleitarchus, who was unfavourable to A. It looks probable, then, that Plutarch was continuing with the account of Ptolemy and/or Aristobulus.[4]

According to Plutarch the informers gradually intimated the involvement of Philotas, seeing that he had disregarded them twice; and A, feeling bitter towards Philotas, consulted those who had long hated Philotas and heard from them 'innumerable charges against Philotas' (49.10). Philotas was arrested and interrogated under torture, the Companions standing by and A listening from behind a curtain.[5] 'They say' that when Philotas was uttering pitiable and abject cries and prayers to Hephaestion and others A said: 'Are you so feeble and so unmanly, Philotas, and yet attempted so great an undertaking?' (49.12). Plutarch then passed abruptly from Philotas being killed to the killing of Parmenio. Of the other writers Ptolemy had the informers come forward in the trial and convict Philotas and his associates (Arr. 3.26.2). Diodorus reported the verdicts of the Macedonians: Philotas and the others accused, among whom was Parmenio, were condemned to death. Philotas was then tortured, confessed the plot and was killed with the others who had been condemned with him (17.80.1f.). Curtius provided interviews with speeches between A and Philotas, a meeting of the council of Friends at which the informer but not Philotas was present, a speech by Craterus, the thoughts of the Friends, and their decision to torture Philotas next day. That evening A had Philotas to dinner – his last. During the night the arrests were made and next morning the trial was held and adjourned, so that Philotas could be tortured in the presence of the leading Companions during the

---

[4] It is probable that Arrian was reporting Ptolemy's account in 3.26.2 only, and that he then resumed the joint account of 'Ptolemy and Aristobulus'; for at 27.1 Arrian used the plural verb λέγουσι, of which the two writers were the implied subject.

[5] This device may have been inspired by Agrippina hiding behind a curtain for the same purpose (Tac. *Ann.* 13.5.2). It was employed by Curtius for a later occasion, when A overheard Callisthenes from behind a curtain ('aulaea', the Latin form of Plutarch's αὐλαία).

night, and having confessed he and others were stoned to death next day (6.7.31–6.11.38).

The differences are again revealing. Plutarch ceased to coincide with Ptolemy. He was like Diodorus and Curtius in having Philotas tortured; but Diodorus put the torture after the verdict by the Macedonians, and Curtius put it after the first part of the trial by the Macedonians. Plutarch was alone in having A hide behind a curtain and taunt poor Philotas, whereas A was absent during the torture in Curtius' account (Curt. 6.11.12). It is evident that Plutarch was not following the source used by Diodorus or that used by Curtius. There were probably many accounts, freely composed, out of which Plutarch took what he wanted.

The killing of Parmenio in Plutarch's account was followed by a brief note of his achievements, his advice to A to cross into Asia, and the fate of his three sons. 'What was done made A feared by many of his Friends, and particularly by Antipater' (49.14). Plutarch then instanced secret negotiations by Antipater with the Aetolians in the context of the restoration of exiles in 323. Of the other writers Ptolemy reported the killing with javelins 'of all Philotas' other accomplices' and the despatch of Polydamas to Parmenio (3.26.3, the word 'other' implying that Parmenio was an accomplice).[6] Diodorus included Parmenio among those accused and condemned to death (17.80.1). Justin said that a trial was held of both Philotas and Parmenio (12.5.3 'de utroque prius quaestionibus habitis'). Curtius had Philotas under torture incriminate his father (6.11.28f.), and Curtius indicated that both were found guilty (6.11.39).

The differences again show Plutarch operating on his own. His chief interest throughout the Philotas episode was in A: his scheming with Antigona, his keeping quiet for the one reason or the other (49.2), his anger at the neglect or suppression of information by Philotas, his perplexity, his bitterness, his

---

[6] καὶ Φίλωταν μέν ... καὶ ὅσοι ἄλλοι μέτεσχον αὐτῷ τῆς ἐπιβουλῆς ἐπὶ Παρμενίωνα δὲ σταλῆναι Πολυδάμαντα. Within the antithetical construction of μέν and δέ Arrian added ἄλλοι to look forward to Parmenio; for the meaning of ἄλλοι is not other than Philotas, to whom αὐτῷ refers, but other than Parmenio.

readiness to hear ill of Philotas, his taunting of Philotas under torture, and his becoming feared by many of his Friends. He was depicting a deterioration both in A himself and in A's relations with his Friends. The holding of a trial and the question of the guilt or innocence of Philotas and Parmenio were not matters which concerned Plutarch in this passage.

2. Cleitus

In 50–1 Plutarch presented the case of Cleitus. He introduced it with a sentence which was intended to influence our judgement of A and of Cleitus in what was to follow.

To those who simply hear the facts this case is more savage (ἀγριώτερα) than that of Philotas, but to those who take the cause and the occasion into consideration what happened is found to have been not intentional but due to some bad luck through the king providing in his anger and his drunkenness a pretext for the demon of Cleitus.

Plutarch's language here combines a malevolent operation of chance (δυστυχία) and the action of some supernatural force, a *daimon* (ὁ Κλείτου δαίμων), which is for us the antithesis of an individual's guardian angel.[7] I shall draw attention to these two factors in giving a summary of Plutarch's narrative.

A was given some fine fruit from Greece and wanted to share it with Cleitus. So he summoned him. Cleitus happened to be sacrificing, but he stopped in mid-sacrifice to proceed to A, and as he went three sheep, already consecrated, followed after him. A consulted his diviners, who said the omen (τὸ σημεῖον) was bad. A then ordered them to make a propitiatory sacrifice for the sake of Cleitus with all speed. For this was the third day after a strange dream in which A said that he seemed to see Cleitus and the sons of Parmenio sitting together in black clothing, all being dead. However, Cleitus did not complete his own sacrifice; instead he went at once to the dinner, for which the king had made sacrifice to the Dioscuri. The relevance of all this was brought out by Plutarch,

---

[7] The *daimon* could be good or bad according to the predestined course of one's life. Hamilton *C* 140 adopted Perrin's translation 'Cleitus' evil genius', and he mentioned the *daimones* in his Introduction p. xx.

when he described the remorse of A at the death of Cleitus. He was inconsolable until the diviner Aristander reminded him both of his dream about Cleitus and of the omen (τὸ σημεῖον, i.e. of the sheep following Cleitus), as indicating that these things had been predestined long ago (52.2 ὡς δὴ πάλαι καθειμαρμένων τούτων).

Of the other writers Trogus, as we infer from Justin's narrative (12.6.1–17), and Curtius (8.1.22–2.11) presented the affair as a matter of anger and drunkenness in A and in Cleitus. The only idea of the gods being involved developed within the mind of A during the first night of his remorse. Then, according to Curtius (8.2.6), as A wondered whether 'the wrath of the gods' might have driven him to such a criminal act, it occurred to him that he had not made his annual sacrifice to Father Liber (corresponding to the Greek god Dionysus) at the appointed time, and that in consequence the god had shown his anger in having the killing done at the drinking of wine and feasting. There is no suggestion by Curtius that this idea was anything more than a mental aberration in A. Arrian, however, began his account with the statement that A sacrificed to Dionysus every year on the day sacred to Dionysus among the Macedonians, but that on this occasion he neglected to do so and sacrificed to the Dioscuri, the sacrifice to the Dioscuri coming into his mind for some reason or other (4.8.2). Then in the sequel Arrian reported that some of the diviners 'sang of the wrath of Dionysus' (Arrian is reminding us of the opening of the *Iliad*: 'Sing, goddess, of the wrath of Achilles'), because A had failed to sacrifice to Dionysus. A began to eat again, and he made the sacrifice due to Dionysus.

Thus Plutarch and Arrian were alone in supplying a religious dimension. There is a link between them in the sacrifice to the Dioscuri. Plutarch merely said that A had sacrificed to them on the day of the dinner. As this was the day on which, according to Arrian, sacrifice was due to Dionysus – a point picked up and reused by Curtius – it is apparent, though not stated by Plutarch, that Cleitus' uncompleted sacrifice was being made to Dionysus; for to a Macedonian that day was Dionysus' name-day. The implication is that the wrath of

Dionysus played a part in the fate which overtook Cleitus. This in itself constitutes a further link with Arrian's report of the diviners singing of the wrath of Dionysus. It seems, then, that for this religious dimension Plutarch and Arrian went back to a common source.

The question of Arrian's source is complicated (see below, pp. 240ff.). At 4.8.1 he began by saying that although the affair occurred a little later, it was not untimely for him to report it at this moment (the point being that the affair afforded another example of A's lack of self-control). The narrative was then introduced with the word λέγουσι, 'they say'. Who are 'they'? If Arrian was drawing only on Ptolemy and Aristobulus, he would either not say λέγουσι at all (in accordance with his usual practice), or he would name them for emphasis, as he did at 3.26.1. I conclude then that he is giving a report based on several accounts, no doubt including those of Ptolemy and Aristobulus. This conclusion is supported by the division of his sources later in the account: 'some say ... others say ... Aristobulus says' (4.8.8f.), and 'there are some who say ... but most writers say' (4.9.2f.). The narrative is given accordingly in the accusative and infinitive (apart from additions by Arrian at 4.8.3 fin., and 5 fin.) until 4.8.7. Then come two sentences in narrative tenses in order to be vivid (they report the cries of A). An accusative and infinitive sentence follows: 'the Companions were no longer able to hold him back' (4.8.8).

Next come the statements by different writers: some say A killed Cleitus (i.e. at once) with a spear, others say with a pike, but Aristobulus says ... and his account continues to the end of 4.8.9. Later, 'some say' A decided to commit suicide, but 'most writers' say otherwise (4.9.2f.). Thus it is apparent that Arrian found more discrepancies in his sources for the latter part of the affair than for the drinking session. He cited the report of Aristobulus at some length, because he thought him 'more trustworthy', as we see in the *Preface*.

To return to Plutarch, as regards the religious element which he and Arrian alone of our writers record, we can say only that they drew on common sources which included Ptolemy and

Aristobulus. From these sources Plutarch took his contribution: the incomplete sacrifice to Dionysus, the dream of A, the omen of the three sheep and the interpretation thereof by Aristander and another diviner, the failure of A to sacrifice to Dionysus (he sacrificing instead to the Dioscuri), and the later explanation by Aristander of the dream and the omen as foreshadowing the fated sequel (the death of Cleitus). Arrian took his part: the day being sacred to Dionysus among the Macedonians, the failure of A to sacrifice to Dionysus (he sacrificing instead to the Dioscuri), some of the diviners 'singing of the wrath of Dionysus' because of that failure by A (no doubt Aristander, A's most trusted diviner, being among them), and A thereupon coming out of his despair and sacrificing to Dionysus.

There are a number of features which seem to come from a contemporary participant or participants in the affair, because there would have been no point in inventing them later: the Greek fruit up from the coast, the name of an otherwise unknown diviner, variant names for otherwise unknown composers of verses, the names of two otherwise unknown Greeks of Cardia and Colophon, and an otherwise unknown Bodyguard. Further, the account comes ultimately from someone well versed in the military-matters of the day: for it involved the presence of Bodyguards (σωματοφύλακες), Guards (δορυφόροι) and a trumpeter in the drinking-room, the nearby camp of the Hypaspists, and the significance of an order issued in the Macedonian dialect (41.6).[8] Ptolemy and Aristobulus would both have had this knowledge.

To make further progress we turn to Arrian 4.8.9, where the account which he gives from Aristobulus contains two points. First, 'Aristobulus did not say from what the drunken behaviour started' (ὅθεν μὲν ἡ παροινία ὡρμήθη). Arrian is referring back to his narrative at 4.8.5f. There the drunken behaviour (ἐν τοιᾷδε παροινίᾳ) started with Cleitus saying that A had done nothing so great and wonderful, since the achievements were those mainly of the Macedonians; and it

---

[8] See H*VG* 397f.

continued with Cleitus awarding top place to Philip's achievements and shooting down those of A, 'Cleitus already behaving drunkenly' (παροινοῦντα ἤδη τὸν Κλεῖτον). These particular sayings do not appear in Plutarch's account. The omission is the more striking because this topic is prominent in the other accounts (Just. 12.6.2f.; Curt. 8.1.23–31; and Arr. 4.8.6).[9] I conclude therefore that Plutarch was following Aristobulus faithfully as his source.

The same conclusion emerges when we compare Plutarch's account of the movements of Cleitus and his death with that of Aristobulus as cited by Arrian at 4.8.9. Whereas two sets of other writers had A kill Cleitus immediately in the presence of the full company, Aristobulus said that Cleitus was taken outside the citadel, 'where this happened', but returned alone, met A and was struck by him with a pike. Plutarch had Cleitus pushed out of the drinking-room by the Friends,[10] but then he came back through a different door and as he was drawing the curtain aside to enter he was killed with a spear[11] by A (51.8f.).

Plutarch, we assume, continued with the account of Aristobulus when he wrote that A would have killed himself with the same spear, that he was prevented and carried forcibly to his room by the Bodyguards, and that he was brought out of his despair by Aristander's assurance that the death of Cleitus was predestined in the dream and the omen (52.2). Callisthenes and Anaxarchus were fetched as philosophers to support Aristander. Callisthenes tried tactful arguments, and Anaxarchus took the line that A, like Zeus, was always right.

According to Arrian, 'some say' that A tried to kill himself (4.9.2), but 'most writers' say that A lay on his bed calling out particularly the name of Cleitus' sister, 'Lanice'.[12] The

---

[9] In Justin Cleitus 'memoriam Philippi tueretur', and in Curtius Cleitus 'Philippi acta bellaque in Graecia gesta commemorat, omnia praesentibus praeferens'.

[10] Aristobulus said that Cleitus was led away by Ptolemy, son of Lagus, the Bodyguard; but that probably means that Ptolemy was the senior officer and had helpers, as Cleitus was no doubt unwilling to go. So Plutarch's 'by the Friends' may be derived from Aristobulus' account.

[11] The word αἰχμή in Plutarch 51.9 means 'the point' of a weapon and could have been used of a pike (sarissa, the word used for the weapon in Arr. 4.8.9 fin.).

[12] A childish shortening of 'Hellanice', the name being given in full by Curt. 8.1.21.

decision to kill himself is in Plutarch's account, that is in Aristobulus' account on my interpretation; it is also in Justin 12.6.8 and Curtius 8.2.4. The lamentation for Lanice is not in Plutarch's account, but it is in Justin 12.6.10f. and Curtius 8.2.8f. Thus Aristobulus did not record the lamentation for Lanice. Next, the arguments of Anaxarchus and their effect in consoling A were reported by Arrian as 'said by some'. Among those 'some' we should include Aristobulus (see also below, p. 242).

My conclusion is that Plutarch followed Aristobulus' account for the affair of Cleitus up to 52.7. When we turn back to the introduction at 50.1f., we can see that Plutarch had his own belief in a combination of bad luck and of the *daimon* or fate of Cleitus. He clearly chose the account of an author which gave a similar explanation, namely that of Aristobulus, because in particular the dream and the omen foreshadowed the march of destiny which was bound to end in the death of Cleitus. According to Arrian Aristobulus said that 'the error' (τὴν ἁμαρτίαν) was 'of Cleitus alone', in that he returned to the drinking-room. Whether Aristobulus was familiar with the theory of Aristotle in the *Poetics* or not,[13] Cleitus fell into disaster through an error (ἁμαρτίαν) on the human level; but supernatural powers, whether they were called destiny, *daimon* or the wrath of Dionysus, were shown in Aristobulus' account to have had a hand in the tragedy.[14]

3. Callisthenes

From the visit to A Plutarch moved on to the personality and the actions of Callisthenes. Whereas Anaxarchus won the favour of the king during the visit, Callisthenes lost it. Indeed A had always found intercourse with Callisthenes lacking in charm, because Callisthenes was so forbidding (αὐστηρός).

[13] A and some at least of his contemporaries and Companions were steeped in Aristotle's theories, and A as an avid reader of tragedies will have heard Aristotle's views on 'the tragic hero'.

[14] The play in which the wrath of Dionysus was at work so ruthlessly was the *Bacchae*, produced originally in the theatre at Aegeae (Vergina). We need to remember that such plays were regarded as revelations of the ways of the gods.

Plutarch then tells a story (λέγεται) to illustrate how abrasive Callisthenes was in conversation with Anaxarchus. (There is no clue to the source of this story, which is not told elsewhere.) Other philosophers at the court also disliked Callisthenes, because the young paid homage to him for his discourse and the older men admired his orderly, dignified and self-sufficient way of life and his patriotic motive for joining A, namely the hope that he might bring about the refounding of his own city, Olynthus. Apart from the envy he excited, he was criticised for his frequent refusal of invitations and, when he did go out, for his glum and apparently disapproving silence, so much so that A once quoted a verse of Euripides to describe him:

> I hate a wise man who is unwise even to himself.[15]

Plutarch then told two stories to support his characterisation of Callisthenes. The first story (53.3 λέγεται) was taken from Hermippus, a writer of biographies in the latter part of the third century B.C. Stroebus, who used to read aloud to Callisthenes, reported the following incident to Aristotle. At a dinner-party Callisthenes was asked to make a speech in praise of the Macedonians, which he did so well that he was applauded and decorated with garlands. A then quoted a line of Euripides:

> It is no great thing to speak well on a noble theme.[16]

A then challenged him to make a speech denouncing the Macedonians, 'so that they could learn their faults and improve themselves'. Callisthenes did this so well, implying that Philip had been 'utterly evil' (πάγκακος), that he incurred the hatred of the Macedonians and a reproof from A. Realising that he had alienated the king, Callisthenes on his departure quoted[17] two or three times a line from the *Iliad*, which implied that Cleitus was a better man than A:

---

[15] *TGF* ed. A. Nauck, F 905.
[16] *Bacchae* 266f.
[17] Plutarch's text has πρὸς αὐτόν 'quoted to him' (i.e. to A). K. Latte suggested reading πρὸς αὑτόν 'quoted to himself'. In either case his quotation was heard, and no doubt it was intended to be heard, by A.

Killed too was Patroclus, a man far better than you are.[18]

When Aristotle heard of this quotation, he remarked that Callisthenes (his nephew) was forceful and great in discourse but he had no sense. Plutarch expressed his own approval of Aristotle's remark (οὐ φαύλως οὖν εἰπεῖν ἔοικεν).

Plutarch showed his doubt about the veracity of this story by beginning it with the word λέγεται, although he mentioned Hermippus as his source later, at 54.1. He was right to have doubts, for Stroebus was no writer and Aristotle would hardly have incorporated that story in his own writings. Hermippus may have obtained the story from the oral tradition. Its authenticity is doubtful.[19]

The second story begins 'Chares of Mitylene says' (54.4). However, Plutarch wrote an introductory sentence, which may be summarised thus. The refusal of Callisthenes in vehement and philosophical terms to make obeisance (προσκύνησις) and his uniqueness in stating his reason publicly (μόνος ἐν φανερῷ) freed the Greeks from a great disgrace and A from a greater disgrace by deflecting the (demand for) obeisance but destroyed Callisthenes himself, because he was thought to have forced rather than persuaded the king. We shall see that there is more in the introduction than in the story which Plutarch tells. For Plutarch described in Chares' story the passing on of a loving-cup at a drinking-party. Each Friend on receiving it drank, made obeisance, kissed A and resumed his place. When it came to Callisthenes, he drank and went to kiss A, who had not been watching but was talking to Hephaestion. However, one of the Friends told A that Callisthenes had not made obeisance. A refused to accept the kiss. So Callisthenes said in a loud voice 'Well, well, away I go the poorer by a kiss' (54.6).

What figures in the introduction is the rejection of obeisance

---

[18] *Iliad* 21.107, spoken by Achilles to Lycaon. The line was particularly apt if the occasion was soon after the death of Cleitus in autumn 328 rather than in spring 327, when the Pages conspired.

[19] The incident was mentioned later by Philostratus, *Vit. Apoll.* 7.2. Some of those who have taken the story to be completely authentic have seen a plot by A to trap Callisthenes. But A could not have been confident that the popularity engendered by the first speech would not stay intact; for Callisthenes could well have played safe in his second speech. See Hamilton *C* 148 for references.

in a public speech of vehemence and philosophical content and the deflection of the demand. However, these are both found in a long account by Arrian (4.10.5–12.7) which ends with the same words 'Away I go the poorer by a kiss.' For in that account the drinking-party was held to introduce obeisance, Anaxarchus and Callisthenes spoke publicly for and against making obeisance to A, and after Callisthenes' speech A withdrew his demand for obeisance in the case of the Macedonians. Arrian introduced this part of his account with the words 'the following story prevails' (τοιόσδε κατέχει λόγος); and what followed was all in the accusative and infinitive down to Leonnatus mocking a clumsy Persian making obeisance, at 4.12.2. He then wrote: 'also the following story (τοιόσδε λόγος) is recorded'. This story is evidently a summary of the story from Chares of Mitylene which Plutarch reported. But there are some differences. Arrian says that the cup went first to those with whom agreement had been made that they would do obeisance. Although Arrian does not say so, the cup evidently came to Callisthenes, because he had made such an agreement.

What Arrian did not say in his account was appended to the story by Plutarch not in the accusative and infinitive but as a narrative fact. 'While such alienation was developing,[20] Hephaestion was being believed, when he said that Callisthenes had promised him that he would make obeisance and then belied the agreement' (55.1). Thus we may conclude that Plutarch and Arrian had a common source, from whose long account of one drinking-party organised to introduce obeisance Plutarch and Arrian each took what was of interest to him.[21] That source was Chares of Mitylene.

At 55.2 Plutarch moved on towards the conspiracy of the

---

[20] The MSS read ὑπογινομένης, a present for an imperfect participle, which is contemporary with the main verb ἐπιστεύετο in the imperfect tense. See Hamilton C 153, although I do not find in the Greek text any grounds for 'Plutarch's obvious disbelief of Hephaestion's statement'. Plutarch was simply reporting this from the account of Chares.

[21] Similarly Curtius drew on the first part for his own version and he added colour from the history of his own time in 8.5.9–8.6.1. Callisthenes was famous for his 'gravitas viri et prompta libertas'. See below, p 243f. I differ here from Hamilton C 150 and from others who set one version against the other as rivals and discard that of Arrian.

Pages. Courtiers like Lysimachus and Hagnon persisted in saying that the sophist was going around with his high-minded thoughts as if he intended the overthrow of a despotism, and that the striplings were running all together to him and treating him as the only free man among so many myriads of people. Accordingly, when the Conspiracy of the Pages was disclosed, the accusations made against Callisthenes by his detractors 'were thought to have verisimilitude'. These were that, when one of them put the question 'How shall I become most famous?', Callisthenes said 'If you kill the most famous', and that while he was inciting Hermolaus to do the deed he kept ordering him not to fear the golden couch but to remember that he would be approaching a man liable to sickness and wounds.[22] Similar allegations were reported by Curtius at 8.6.24f.: for instance, 'it was agreed ('constabat') that Callisthenes used to lend a ready ear to the Pages' censures and accusations of the king'. Arrian also made the point that the detractors of Callisthenes were readily believed when they asserted that he had a part in the plot – indeed some of them said 'he himself incited them towards the plotting' (4.12.7 ἐπῆρεν αὐτὸς ἐς τὸ ἐπιβουλεῦσαι). No doubt Curtius, Plutarch and Arrian drew ultimately on common material, but it is not possible to identify its source.

'And yet', continued Plutarch, 'no one of those with Hermolaus, not even in the extreme agonies [of torture], denounced Callisthenes' (55.5).[23] Plutarch then adduced the evidence of two letters. 'A himself' said in a letter which he wrote 'at once' (εὐθύς) to three officers (who were on a separate mission at the time), that when they were being tortured the boys were unanimous in saying 'they did it of themselves and no one else was in the know'. But later (ὕστερον), in writing to Antipater, after accusing Callisthenes also he said: 'the boys were stoned by the Macedonians, but I shall punish the sophist and those who sent him out and those who receive

---

[22] A typical tête-à-tête conversation, which neither Callisthenes nor Hermolaus would have reported to others.

[23] The distinction has to be kept in mind between reports of Callisthenes' conversations with Pages before the event and the declarations of the arrested Pages.

in their cities the men who plot against me' (55.7). Both letters should be accepted as genuine;[24] and the later letter will have been caused by new evidence, such as arose in the cases of Attalus after the assassination of Philip and of Demetrius after the condemnation of Philotas. Plutarch, and probably his source, did not pass any judgement either way on Callisthenes. His only comment was that A revealed outright his attitude towards Aristotle in the second letter; for Aristotle was said to have sent Callisthenes to accompany A as his official historian.

Of other writers Curtius reported that the names of the conspirators were given by the informer, and that the name of Callisthenes was not among them (8.6.24). Arrian, following Ptolemy and Aristobulus as usual, reported that those named by the informer were arrested and under torture admitted their own plot and named also certain others (4.13.7 fin.). Among the last it is clear that Callisthenes was not named, for if he had been Arrian would have said so. Thus Plutarch was in accord with Ptolemy and Aristobulus and with Curtius on this point, that in the trial the boys declared that Callisthenes was not privy to the plot (Plutarch συνειδείη; Curtius 'conscius'). The other question was this: did the boys say in the trial that Callisthenes had encouraged them? Or was that merely alleged by critics of Callisthenes? Aristobulus, and likewise Ptolemy, according to Arrian, gave the first alternative, the boys saying that Callisthenes incited them towards the deed of daring (4.14.1 ἐπᾶραι, the word used at 4.12.7). Plutarch gave the second alternative, reporting the allegations of the critics. Curtius lay between the two alternatives in saying that 'it was agreed' ('constabat') that Callisthenes encouraged criticism of the king (8.6.24). Plutarch and Curtius were following an author or authors other than Aristobulus and Ptolemy in this matter.

'As regards the death of Callisthenes,' wrote Plutarch,'

---

[24] See Hamilton *C* 155 and for the second letter Hamilton *L* 16. The second letter may refer to new evidence which was held to incriminate Callisthenes. Its vagueness makes it implausible as a forgery.

some say he was hanged by A, others that he was bound in fetters and died of disease, and Chares that for seven months after his arrest he was kept bound under guard, in order that he might be tried in the presence of Aristotle before the Council [of the Greeks], but that he became exceedingly fat and lousy and died during the days when A was wounded in India. (55.9)

Arrian specified Ptolemy as saying Callisthenes was tortured and hanged, and Aristobulus as saying that he was taken along bound in fetters (with the army) and died of disease (4.14.3). Curtius had him die under torture (8.8.21).[25] It seems that Plutarch consulted a number of authors, including Aristobulus, Ptolemy and Chares, of whom Chares is probably to be believed, because he was a Greek at court and his account was circumstantial.

[25] The captivity of Callisthenes was developed by later writers into a tale of horrors, e.g. in Just. 15.3.4f. To be lousy was not debilitating in itself (as I found in 1943). The conditions of detention were not necessarily harsh; for Alexander Lyncestes was held in this way for more than three years.

7

BACTRIA, INDIA AND CARMANIA

1. Bactra to the River Hydaspes (56–9)

In chapter 56 Plutarch recorded the death of Demaratus of Corinth in spring 327. He repeated points he had made earlier about Demaratus: he was elderly (πρεσβύτερος, cf. 37.7 πρεσβυτικῶς), he and A were loyally devoted to one another (εὐνοίας, cf. 37.7 εὔνουν ὄντα ἄνδρα καὶ πατρῷον φίλον), and he said the Greeks who had died before seeing A seated on the throne of Darius were deprived of a great pleasure (cf. 37.7), the last point having been reported already in *Mor.* 329d. Now 'his eager wish was to go inland to A' (56.1 πρὸς Ἀλέξανδρον ἀναβῆναι).[1] This implies that he had returned to the coast and probably to Greece since 330, when he was reported to be at Persepolis (37.7). The author whom Plutarch was following may have described the movements of Demaratus between 330 and late 328 when he set off from the coast. He died at Bactra. 'The army heaped up a mound 40 metres high and great in circumference in his honour, and his remains were carried down to the coast on a four-horse chariot brilliantly equipped.' This is the first grandiose memorial, a cenotaph, to be erected on A's orders. Cleitarchus is a possible source, as at 37.7, but there is not enough evidence to decide.

There are three descriptions of the burning of the Macedonians' excessive baggage. Curtius dated it to 330 before the trial of Philotas. His account is exaggerated. 'The army could hardly move in column, so heavily laden with spoils and the equipment of luxury', and 'no one dared to weep for the loss of what he had gained with his own blood, when the king's wealth was being devoured by the same conflagration'

---

[1] Hamilton *C* 157 thought that this phrase referred to spring 334, but the context does not support his view.

(6.6.14f.). But soon the troops 'were rejoicing, ready for service and prepared for everything'. Plutarch dated it to early 327, when A was setting out for 'the land of the Indi': 'The army was already heavy with the mass of spoils and difficult to move (πλήθει λαφύρων τὴν στρατιὰν ἤδη βαρεῖαν καὶ δυσκίνητον), the great majority, uttering shouts of enthusiasm and engaging in war-cries, ... burnt with their own hands what they did not need ... and they filled A with zest and eagerness' (57.1–2). The similarities are such that the two accounts stem from a common source, which was extolling the spirit of A and the Macedonians. The third account, written by Polyaenus in the second century A.D., had a different date and a different slant. 'A was subduing the land of the Indi' and 'the Macedonians did not think the battle with the Indi necessary, because they had already acquired so much loot'.[2] The time appears to be winter–spring 326, when opposition by Porus was anticipated. Once the excessive baggage was burned, 'the Macedonians ... found themselves in need of acquiring loot again and so set off for the war more eagerly' (4.3.10). This emphasis on the acquisition of loot and on the tricks which A played on his Macedonians, in order to overcome their reluctance to fight, was typical of Cleitarchus (e.g. in *THA* 16f. at the Granicus, 18 at Issus, 38 on the disbanding of the fleet, and 96). On the other hand, the common source of Curtius and Plutarch was expressing admiration for A and his Macedonians. It might well have been Ptolemy and/or Aristobulus.[3]

In 57.3 Plutarch gave two examples of A's being already 'feared and inexorable in punishing offenders', which were not mentioned elsewhere. They are connected not with what preceded or what follows, but with his own theme of a more harsh ruler, as at 42.3f.

[2] Hamilton *C* 157 held that Polyaenus placed this stratagem 'immediately before the invasion of India'; but the reference to 'the battle with the Indi' (τὴν πρὸς Ἰνδοὺς μάχην) is not to a forthcoming campaign. The imperfect tense of κατέστρεφε at the start is commonly used by Polyaenus, because it is graphic (cf. 4.3.4, 8.9.11 and 14).

[3] Either Curtius or Plutarch has misdated the burning of the baggage. Plutarch was probably aware of Curtius' dating and corrected it. So the balance is in favour of 327, the date which I gave in *AG*² 202.

In 57.4–9 Plutarch reported two omens, one depressing and the other cheering for A. The first – the birth of a lamb with a tiara-like swelling and testicles round its head – indicated that through the divine will A might be succeeded by 'a low-born and unwarlike man',[4] the references being clearly to Philip Arrhidaeus, his birth allegedly from a Thessalian harlot (e.g. Just. 13.2.11 'propter maternas ... sordes quod ex Larissaeo scorto nasceretur'), and his physical and mental incompetence. This portent was not only invented after his accession; it must have been put into circulation after his death, probably by the opposing faction which had supported Olympias. According to Plutarch A was so disgusted by the portent that he had himself purified 'by the Babylonians' (they followed him on the campaign, together with the Chaldaeans and the Egyptians of Curtius 10.10.13);[5] this will have been part of the propaganda which represented Philip Arrhidaeus as a foul impostor. The second portent happened when the Master of the King's Bedchamber was digging out a site for the Royal Tent beside the River Oxus in spring 328. He uncovered a spring of oil, which soon flowed with the purity of olive oil; yet the country did not grow olive trees. The diviners interpreted this omen to mean that the expedition would be glorious but toilsome (ἐπίπονος) and difficult (57.9). A was amazingly pleased as he wrote in a letter to Antipater, counting this 'one of the greatest of the things which had come from the god to him'.

There are other versions of this second portent. According to Strabo 518 'they say that while digging near the river Ochus they found a spring of oil'. Strabo went on to show that there was some confusion between the Ochus and the Oxus, the one sometimes being thought to flow into the other. At the beginning of this section, where the text is corrupt, Strabo was citing Aristobulus, and it is thus probable that we may count him among those who 'say' that a spring of oil was found. Curtius

---

[4] Perrin's translation 'an ignoble and impotent man' for ἀγεννῆ καὶ ἄναλκιν ἄνθρωπον misses the point.
[5] Curtius distinguished the priests of the Babylonians from the Chaldaeans and the Magi at 5.1.22.

wrote of a spring of water being found in the very tent of the
king (7.10.14 'in ipso tabernaculo regis'). His story was that
the soldiers were digging wells for drinkable water, because the
Oxus was muddy, but only late in their efforts found this
spring, which they therefore declared had suddenly gushed
out. The king himself wanted it to be believed that it was a gift
of the gods.[6] Arrian provided a spring of oil and a spring of
water in his account, which runs as follows (4.15.7–8): 'While
he was in camp by the river Oxus a spring of water came up
not far from the tent of A himself, and another spring of oil
right by the tent.' When the portent was reported to Ptolemy,
son of Lagus, the Bodyguard, Ptolemy told A, and A sacrificed
at the sign from heaven (ἐπὶ τῷ φάσματι) in as many ways as
the diviners directed. Aristander said the spring of oil was a
sign of toils (πόνων), but that it indicated a victory after the
toils.

The clearest indication of sources is afforded by Arrian,
whose narrative was based on the accounts of Ptolemy and/or
Aristobulus. Moreover, his account contained the discovery of
two springs, one of water, reported also by Curtius – and the
water was vitally important for the army[7] – and the other of oil,
reported also by Strabo and Plutarch, partly because its rarity,
as Strabo said, made its presence paradoxical. The water was
a gift of the gods; that was what A wanted his men to believe,
according to Curtius.[8] The oil was something supernatural; so
A wrote of it to Antipater as something 'from the god', and
the diviners gave their interpretation of the oil according to
Plutarch and Arrian. The original account came from someone who was there at the time; for precise details were supplied
of the positions of the two springs in relation to the Royal
Tent, of the man in charge of the digging (Proxenus by name
according to Plutarch but otherwise unknown), of the un-
drinkable water of the Oxus, and of the absence of olive trees
in Sogdiana. Aristobulus is much more likely to be the source

---

[6] In Curt. 7.10.14 'deum' is provided only in one manuscript, so that the text runs
'deum donum id fuisse'. This reading is adopted in the Loeb text.

[7] See Curt. 7.4.27 and 7.5.2–14 for the lack of water in the area.

[8] See n. 6 above.

than Ptolemy. For Aristobulus was cited by Strabo, he was particularly interested in such natural phenomena as the kinds of trees which grew in newly discovered areas, and he reported often on the reactions of A to events. The mention of Ptolemy, which occurs in Arrian's report, might have come from Aristobulus.[9] For as an analogy, we have Ptolemy's action in removing Cleitus reported in a context which we have ascribed to Aristobulus (above, p. 93). It is not necessary to attribute this mention of Ptolemy to Ptolemy himself; for there was nothing creditable in passing information to A on this occasion. I conclude that Strabo, Curtius, Plutarch and Arrian drew from a longer account by Aristobulus whatever interested each one of them.

Plutarch added two points from elsewhere. 'It is said' that the water of the Oxus, being very soft, leaves the skin of bathers slimy (57.7); this is not mentioned by any known author. The citation from the letter of A to Antipater is typical of his belief in 'the god'; and there is no ground for questioning the authenticity of the letter.[10]

Chapter 58 will be discussed later (below, p. 250). In 59.1 'Taxiles is said (λέγεται) to have a portion of Indike not short of Egypt in size.' A similar statement had been made by Strabo: 'they say (φασίν) that the territory is greater than Egypt' (698). Plutarch could have taken this idea from Strabo, including the qualification 'they say', which means that the source was not entirely trustworthy. The passage in Strabo precedes a description of the realm of Abisares (Cashmir), in which Onesicritus was cited as the authority for snakes there of gigantic length. Thus Onesicritus was probably Strabo's source for the size of Taxiles realm.[11] Plutarch continued as follows: 'Taxiles is said to have been a wise sort of man and to have said on greeting A:

---

[9] Hamilton *C* 158 (citing Jacoby in *FGrH* 2 D 516, 38 and other writers), and Brunt *L* I 391 n. 4 held that Arr. 4.15.7f. was based on Ptolemy.

[10] Hamilton *L* 16 defends its authenticity. Athen. 242f included in a list of springs one of oil in Asia 'of which A wrote that he had found a well of oil'. This may refer to the same letter.

[11] So Hamilton *C* 162 for the size of Taxiles' realm 'the source of Plutarch and Strabo, and ultimately of the accounts in Diodorus and Curtius, is probably Onesicritus; see H. Strasburger in *Bibl. Or.* 9 (1952) 207'.

"What need have we of wars and battle with one another, unless you have come to rob us of water or essential foodstuff etc.?"' Since the philosophical conversation is governed by 'is said', it came from the same source as the opening sentence. The content of the conversation, which is clearly unhistorical, is typical of Diogenes and the Cynics, and it is most probable that it was written by Onesicritus, a pupil of Diogenes (65.2; see above, p. 28).[12] Thus Onesicritus was most probably drawn on by Plutarch in 59.1–4.

Plutarch resumes the narrative tenses at 59.5, in which the exchange of gifts reached a climax in A giving Taxiles '1,000 talents of coined money' and this gift 'grieved A's Friends greatly'. The same information had been given by Curtius at 8.12.16f.: 'M talenta [signati argenti] ... quae liberalitas ... amicos ipsius vehementer offendit.' Plutarch could have taken this from Curtius, or from the source followed by Curtius, namely Cleitarchus in my opinion.[13] In 59.6 the Indian mercenaries were reported by Plutarch to have been the fiercest opponents of A, and for that reason 'after making a treaty with them at a certain city A intercepted them on the way as they were departing and killed them all'. The city was Massaga, and the treaty was that the mercenaries should serve in the forces of A. That was common ground for the authors who described this incident. The breach of faith, however, was attributed to the mercenaries by Ptolemy and/or Aristobulus, whom Arrian followed in his account, saying that the mercenaries 'were intending to make their escape at night' (4.26.3f.). A was held by Diodorus to have broken faith, because 'he followed the barbarians and falling upon them suddenly wrought great slaughter', was accused of bad faith, and then shouted back in a loud voice that he had agreed to their departure from the city but not to friendly relations for ever (17.84.1f.). The source of Diodorus was certainly Cleitarchus (*THA* 52f. and 149). Plutarch added his own judgement of the affair (59.7).

[12] The conversation had been given in a summary form by Plutarch in *Mor.* 181c. Berve II 370 commented on it as 'vielleicht auf Onesikritos zurückgehend'.
[13] *THA* 149f.

A's other bitter opponents were 'the philosophers', who 'reviled any kings joining A and raised the free peoples (τοὺς ἐλευθέρους δήμους) in revolt'. So A killed many of them by hanging. The term 'philosophers' and death by hanging were mentioned by Ptolemy and/or Aristobulus, as we see in Arrian 6.16.5 and 6.17.2. Diodorus referred to 'the race of the so-called Brahmans' (17.102.7).[14] It was Diodorus who wrote of the Sambastae as living in cities 'with a democratic constitution' (17.102.2 δημοκρατουμένας; cf. Curt. 9.8.4). The source of Diodorus in both passages was in my opinion Cleitarchus (*THA* 67 and 154f.).

Thus it seems that Plutarch was drawing on his reading of Cleitarchus for what he wrote in 59.5–8.

2. Postscripts to the Battle of the Hydaspes (60.12–61.3)

According to Diodorus, Porus far exceeded his followers in bodily strength and was five cubits tall, i.e. in standard Greek cubits 7 feet 7½ inches (17.88.5). Curtius said that he 'almost exceeded the limit of human stature' (8.14.13 'humanae magnitudinis propemodum excesserat'). The source behind these passages was in my opinion Cleitarchus (*THA* 23, 25f. and 150). He certainly tended to exaggerate. 'The great majority of writers', said Plutarch, 'agree that Porus exceeded four cubits and a span', i.e. 6 feet 8½ inches (60.12). This seems reasonable.[15] However, Arrian, who was aware of the views of the great majority of writers, took the view that Porus was 'more or less over five cubits' tall (5.19.1).

Praise of the giant elephant of Porus follows. It defended Porus and beat back his assailants, while Porus was still fit (such defence had been mentioned by Strabo 705). Then the

---

[14] See Goukowsky 260 for the large number of Brahmans and their service as soldiers.

[15] Tarn's faith in his supposed short Macedonian cubit (p. 170) seems to be misplaced, because neither Diodorus nor Arrian was a Macedonian and in any case they would not have used a Macedonian measure for their intended readers. In terms of sources, if Cleitarchus lay behind Diodorus, he would have used the standard Greek measures. However, Hamilton *C* 166 found Tarn's arguments convincing.

elephant realised that Porus was failing. Lest Porus should slip off, the elephant lowered itself gently on its knees to the ground; and (when Porus was safely down) it firmly drew the javelins one by one from his body with its trunk (60.13). This episode delighted Plutarch; he had used it in *Moralia* 970d. It was repeated later by Aelian, *N.A.* 7.37. On the other hand Diodorus had none of this: in his account Porus fainted and fell off the elephant (17.88.6). In Arrian's account Porus dismounted from his elephant and went with Meroës to meet A (5.18.7). But Curtius provided a long and colourful account. When Porus began to slide off, his mahout ordered the elephant to kneel. It did so, and all the other elephants followed its example as they had been trained to do, with the result that all the riders were easily captured by the Macedonians. Porus' elephant, however, began to protect him by attacking would-be looters and then lifted Porus and was placing him on its back, when it was overwhelmed with weapons and expired (8.14.39f.).

On my interpretation Diodorus was following Cleitarchus (*THA* 23 and 25f.); Arrian was following Ptolemy and/or Aristobulus; and Curtius based his account of the battle on several sources, which included Cleitarchus, Onesicritus and Chares (*THA* 150f.). Thus the authors whom Plutarch may have been following were Onesicritus and Chares. The elephant's loving care of its master, which is a feature unique to Plutarch, is paralleled by the behaviour of Bucephalus; for weakened by many wounds and failing, Bucephalus collapsed but in such a way that it placed the king on the ground rather than threw him (Curtius 8.14.34). As we shall see in discussing the next chapter, the probable source was Chares.

The conversation between A and Porus in chapter 60.14 had been reported three times already in *Moralia* (181e, 332e, 458b).[16] Curtius had given a different conversation (8.14.41–3). Arrian gave the conversation as in Plutarch's account, but he qualified it as a *logos*, which means that it was not taken

---

[16] Resumed later by Themistius, *Or.* 7.88d.

from Ptolemy and/or Aristobulus[17] (5.19.1–3, on which see below, p. 257). Chares may well have been the source.

There is some confusion about the territories given by A to Porus. Strabo 686 said that A gave as additional territory the land between the Hydaspes and the Hypanis – a variant form of Hyphasis – which had 9 nations and 5,000 cities; but he thought this number to be exaggerated and he entered a cautionary 'it is said' (701 λέγεται). Strabo's numbers were repeated by Pliny, *N.H.* 6.59. Plutarch mentioned the additional territory as containing 'they say' (60.15 φασίν) 15 nations, 5,000 considerable cities and very many villages; and he called the inhabitants 'the independent [i.e. republican] Indians',[18] that is those as far east as the Hyphasis. Arrian reported the proclamation of Porus as king of the land already captured, i.e. up to the Hyphasis, being 7 nations in all and over 2,000 cities among them (6.2.1).[19] As regards the sources of these statements Strabo was probably drawing on Aristobulus, since the form Hypanis has been attributed to him;[20] and if that is so, Arrian drew on Ptolemy at 6.2.1. The discrepancy between Strabo's 5,000 cities and Arrian's 2,000 cities is understandable, when we recall that Arrian described the villages of this area as being 'not less populous than the cities' (5.20.4); and the number of nations may have been defined on differing standards. Plutarch was following a source who was closer to Aristobulus than to Ptolemy but had his own idea of the number of nations. He may have been Onesicritus, who has been suggested by L. Pearson.[21] The last sentence of chapter 60, giving an estimate of the size of Philip's satrapy, will be based then on Onesicritus.

[17] *Pace* Brunt *L* II 59 n. 2.
[18] So called also by Arrian at 5.20.6, 21.5, 22.1 and 24.6.
[19] Arrian had mentioned at 5.21.5 the intention to place some tribes under Porus and at 5.29.2 the addition of territory up to the Hyphasis during A's stay there. Porus was not present at that time. The investiture was made later at 6.2.1. This last passage was not 'perhaps a doublet', as Brunt *L* II 472 suggested.
[20] By Tarn 32. The arguments are not entirely convincing, because they depend on assuming that some texts are corrupt. His discussion is in *The Greeks in Bactria and India* (Cambridge, 1951) 144 n. 3.
[21] In *LHA* 106 and n. 88.

'After the battle with Porus, too, Bucephalus died, not immediately but subsequently; not as a result of wounds, for which he was being treated, as most say, but from old age, being utterly worn out, as Onesicritus says; for Bucephalus, he says, died at the age of thirty' (61.1).

It is obvious from Plutarch's words that many authors had written about the death of Bucephalus and that they had given different accounts. Plutarch mentions two aspects – the timing 'immediately' or 'subsequently', and the cause of death being 'wounds', i.e. in the battle, or 'old age'. In considering the other statements about this event which have survived we shall tackle another aspect, namely where Bucephalus died; for it was believed that Bucephala was founded by A at the place where Bucephalus died. I begin with this last aspect.

One view is summarised by Stephanus Byzantius s.v. βοὸς κεφαλαί: 'Bucephala was founded where he crossed and fought and his horse died, called Bucephalus.' Arrian gave the reports of Ptolemy and Aristobulus about the lack of action at the landing on the east bank, and then continued. 'But some say that there was a battle at the landing ... and that Porus' son wounded A himself and also his horse Bucephalus, and that it died there' (5.19.4 αὐτοῦ); 'but Ptolemy ... with whom I also agree, says otherwise'. Since Ptolemy was a Bodyguard in attendance on A at the landing, it is certain that Ptolemy's account was correct.[22]

Other writers transferred the death of Bucephalus to the clash with Porus himself.[23] In Justin 12.8.3f. Porus and Alexander made a dead set at one another, and 'at the first meeting' A's horse being wounded brought him 'headlong' to the ground, whereupon he was saved by his Bodyguards rushing to him. Curtius 8.14.34 had A in pursuit of Porus who was withdrawing on his elephant, and then A's horse Bucephalus 'severely wounded and failing' falling flat ('procubuit') but in such a way that A was not thrown but put on the ground.

---

[22] See *AG*² 215f. for an evaluation of the sources for the battle.
[23] The Porus medallion, for which see *AG*² 284f., may have contributed to this reshaping of the tradition, if the horse was thought to be Bucephalus.

Gellius 5.2 had Bucephalus, severely wounded, carry A out of the battle and then fall at once ('ilico concidit') to the ground.

In my analysis of the sources I argued that in his description in 8.10 to 8.14 Curtius 'made use of Cleitarchus and of other unidentifiable and equally undependable sources' (*THA* 150). It makes sense that Cleitarchus was the author who established the death of Bucephalus in action against Porus. The variation in Gellius came probably from Chares, whom Gellius cited at the beginning of his note on Bucephalus.[24] Justin's source gave his own variation on the theme (see *THA* 105). Thus we can name two of those who had Bucephalus die 'immediately', as Plutarch put it – Cleitarchus and Chares.

That Bucephalus died of wounds incurred in the battle was stated, as we have seen, by Stephanus Byzantius, Justin, Curtius and Gellius, and in general terms by 'others' than Ptolemy and Aristobulus. It occurred but without elaboration in Diodorus 17.95.5, Strabo 698 and *Epit. Metz* 62. Here too we have seen the hands of Cleitarchus and Chares. The attribution of his death to old age, as reported by Plutarch, was included by Arrian in a short note about the horse at 5.19.4–6, which was appended to the naming of the city Bucephala. Arrian remarked that Bucephalus was 'not wounded by anyone' (a reference to 5.14.4) but died 'exhausted by heat and age'. Plutarch had said that the horse was 'past his prime' at the Battle of Gaugamela in 331 (32.12). His death five years later could well have been due to old age.[25]

Although Plutarch mentioned the founding of Bucephala in memory of Bucephalus, he did not say where the city was. Its position was in dispute. Arrian, who in accordance with his

---

[24] Jacoby in *FGrH* 2 D 437 on Chares (125) F 18 held that Gellius' sections 4–5 came 'gewiss' from Chares.

[25] As I argued above (p. 22), Bucephalus was born *c.* 346 and was 20 or so in 326. As Arrian said at 5.19.3 'he had shared A's hardships and hazards' for some ten gruelling years of hard going and tremendous pursuits, which must have worn him out. Hamilton *C* 169 accepted the age of Bucephalus as 30 in 326, and he cited a Dr Green, who held that a stallion's life-span was most commonly 28 to 32; but the life of a stud-stallion is not comparable to that of a war-horse which was subject to extremes of heat and cold and to the strains of combat. Dr E. Baynham of the University of Newcastle, New South Wales, kindly gave me advice on this matter.

general practice may be assumed to be following Ptolemy and Aristobulus, put Nicaea on the east bank, where the victory was won, and Bucephala on the west bank, 'from which he set out and crossed the Hydaspes' (5.19.4).[26] The same positions were given by Diodorus 17.89.6 (following Diyllus; see *THA* 62), one city being where A defeated Porus, and the other 'beyond the river, where A himself crossed'. But Bucephala was placed on the east bank by Stephanus Byzantius, 'where A crossed and fought', by Gellius 5.2, 'in isdem locis', and by *Epit. Metz* 62, 'in eo loco'. There is no doubt that these three were following Cleitarchus, Chares and others.

The founding and the naming of Bucephala were also controversial. Plutarch was non-committal.[27] There was mention by Arrian of the founding of two cities after the battle (5.19.4) and of Craterus being left behind to build them (5.20.2); and also by Justin 12.8.8; and by Gellius 5.2 fin. These authors mentioned the naming. However, Diodorus and Curtius separated the founding from the naming by an interval of some months (Diod. 17.89.6 and the naming at 17.95.5, and Curt. 9.1.6 and 9.3.23). The explanation is that the death of Bucephalus occurred after A had departed from the Hydaspes, and that it was only when A returned from the Hyphasis to the Hydaspes that he named the city in honour of the horse which had died during his absence. This version is likely to be correct. It fits Plutarch's emphasis on 'subsequently', Arrian's insistence that the horse was not wounded by the son of Porus, and the dependability of Diyllus as the source in Diodorus 17.95.5 and in Curtius 9.3.23, as I argued on other grounds in *THA* 64 and 152.

To summarise our conclusions, Plutarch took the same view as Ptolemy, Aristobulus and Onesicritus in saying that Bucephalus died as a result not of wounds but of old age. When he mentioned 'most writers' who attributed his death to wounds

---

[26] In this passage Arrian stressed that Bucephalus died 'there' (αὐτοῦ), the word being emphasised by the violent hiatus with οὐ βληθείς. The same emphasis with a hiatus occurred also at 5.14.4 αὐτοῦ ἀποθανεῖν. Jacoby took αὐτοῦ as 'there' with ἀποθανεῖν (*FGrH* 2 D 505), as I do, whereas Brunt *L* II 43 translated αὐτοῦ as 'his [horse]'. See Hamilton *C* 168f. with a map.

[27] So too Strabo 698.

in action, he may have had in mind Cleitarchus and Chares, and perhaps their followers, Diodorus, Trogus, Strabo, and Curtius. Then in saying that his death occurred 'later', he was in line with Diyllus, his follower Diodorus, and Curtius. It is evident that Plutarch read several of the above writers and accepted the view of Onesicritus in particular.

Later in the chapter Plutarch reported as a *legomenon* the founding of a city named after a favourite dog, Peritas (mentioned by Theopompus, *FGrH* 115 F 340). The author of the report was Sotion, who said he had had it from Potamon; both these writers wrote in the early decades of the Roman Empire. It is of interest that Plutarch did not check the truth of what Sotion said.

3. From the Hydaspes to the city of the Malli (62–3)

The effect of the battle of the Hydaspes was a blunting of the Macedonians' morale; for they had managed 'with difficulty to defeat 2,000 cavalry and 20,000 infantry' (62.1f.). These numbers for the army of Porus in the main battle are lower than those in other writers. The closest are those in Curtius 8.13.6, where before A crossed the river Porus had 2,000 cavalry, 30,000 infantry, 300 chariots and 85 elephants; and it is thus probable that Plutarch drew on one of several sources which Curtius used (see *THA* 150). It was this blunting of morale which checked A from advancing 'further into Indike' (τοῦ πρόσω τῆς Ἰνδικῆς) and caused the Macedonians 'to resist strongly when A wanted them to cross the Ganges also' (62.1f.). Plutarch differed herein from other writers. For they reported a decline in Macedonian morale only on arrival at the Hyphasis river (Diod. 17.94.1f.; Curt. 9.2.10; Arr. 5.25.2). While modern writers make the crossing of the Hyphasis the critical issue, Plutarch stressed the object of going further, which was to confront an army on the far bank of the Ganges.

According to Plutarch the Macedonians learnt that the forces on the east side of the Ganges, itself a formidable barrier '32 stades wide', 'were said' (ἐλέγοντο) to be 80,000 cavalry, 200,000 infantry, 8,000 chariots and 6,000 elephants. Of other writers Diodorus gave the width of the Ganges as 32 stades and as 30 stades (17.93.2; 2.37.2; 18.6.2), and Megasthenes as 100 stades (in Strabo 702; Arr. *Ind.* 4.7). Of the military figures the 200,000 infantry appear in all sources; but lower figures for the other components were given by Diodorus (2.37.3; 17.93.2) and Curtius (9.2.3f.). It is clear then that Plutarch did not draw on Diodorus and Curtius, nor on their common source, which is agreed to have been Cleitarchus.[28] Plutarch sought to justify his figures by citing the career of 'Androcottus' (Chandragupta), who made a gift of 500 elephants to Seleucus (in 304) and conquered all Indike with an army of 600,000 men.[29] We need as a source for Plutarch a third-century writer who provided information about the Ganges area. Arrian cited two such, Eratosthenes and Megasthenes (5.3.1, 5.5.1, and 5.6.2; *Ind.* 3.1 and 7). Of the two Eratosthenes is to be identified as Plutarch's source; for Megasthenes gave the width of the Ganges at its narrowest point as 100 stades (*Ind.* 4.7).

The Macedonians having checked A's further advance (62.1), A sulked and raged in his tent (62.5). But the exhortations of his Friends and the tears and cries of the soldiers weakened his resolve, so that he began to break camp. But to enhance his glory he resorted to deceitful tricks. For here and there on the banks of the Hyphasis he left outsize armour, high mangers and horse-bits of abnormal size. He also set up altars of the gods, which are revered 'still today' (μέχρι νῦν) by the kings of the Praesii (in the Ganges valley) and are used for sacrifice in the Greek manner. When Androcottus was a boy, he saw A in person. 'It is said' that Androcottus often said subsequently that A came within reach of taking control, because the king then was hated and despised as a pestilential fellow of low birth (62.9).[30]

---

[28] See *THA* 63 and 151, and Hamilton *C* 171f. 'their common source cannot be other than Cleitarchus'.

[29] This figure was given also by Pliny, *N.H.* 6.68, while Strabo 709 made his army 460,000 strong.

[30] This king was said to be the son of a barber and to have won the throne through murder (Diod. 17.93.3).

This account of A yielding so quickly is *sui generis*. In other accounts A consulted a Council of Commanders (Arr. 5.28.1f.), or addressed an Assembly of Macedonians (Diod. 17.94.5; Curt. 9.2.12), or was himself addressed by the soldiers (Just. 12.8.10–15). The examples of A's tricks were different in Diod. 17.95.1f. and Curt. 9.2.16.[31] Here too we need a source who was probably not going back to any Alexander-historian but was making up his own version and included the reminiscences of Chandragupta. Finally, it is probable that 'still today' was lifted from the source; for it is most improbable that Plutarch knew what was happening on the bank of the Hyphasis in his own day, if indeed the kings of the Praesii still reigned in the Ganges valley. Thus the source was probably still Eratosthenes.

In chapter 63 Plutarch described the bravery, the wounding and the survival of A at the city of the Malli. This chapter is by far the finest piece of writing in the *Life*. It is remarkable for its vividness, clarity and colour – all qualities which are attributable to a single account which Plutarch adopted rather than to the pen of Plutarch himself.

The first sentence was Plutarch's own composition, as a link with what preceded. It is inaccurate. 'From there' (ἐντεῦθεν) takes us back to the Hyphasis (the Hydaspes was the start of the voyage). 'Building many ferries under oar and rafts' overlooks the fact that the building had been carried out in advance (Diod. 17.89.4 and 95.3; Arr. 5.3.5, 5.8.4f. and 6.1.1). In the rest of the chapter there are a number of clues which will lead us to the author of the account which Plutarch was following. I list them numerically.

(1) The attack which A made was against the Malli, who 'they say' (φασίν) proved the most warlike of the Indians (63.2). Plutarch had already located the attack 'among the Malli' (*Mor.* 327b and 341c), and Arrian, writing after Plutarch, had A attack the city of the Malli (6.8.4; 6.11.3). This, however, was exceptional. For 'that this incident happened to A among the Oxydracae is maintained by the entire

---

[31] Their common source was Cleitarchus; see *THA* 64 and 152, and Hamilton *C* 174.

logos' (6.11.3 ὁ πᾶς λόγος κατέχει), this word being used like *legomena* in Arrian's preface to mean the report of writers other than Ptolemy and Aristobulus. That this is the meaning at 6.11.3 is made clear in the next section where the same Greek expression was used for the reports that the battle of 331 occurred at Arbela; and then Arrian added that Ptolemy and Aristobulus placed it at Gaugamela (see below, p. 269).[32] If then Arrian is correct and the location among the Malli was peculiar to Ptolemy and Aristobulus,[33] it follows that Plutarch in *Mor.* 327b and here at 63.2 was drawing on either Ptolemy or Aristobulus. The warlike character of the Malli appeared also in Arrian 6.4.3: 'A was informed that the Malli and the Oxydracae were the most numerous and the most warlike of the Indians thereabouts.' This supports the suggestion that Plutarch was drawing on either Ptolemy or Aristobulus.[34]

(2) 'A was almost alone (ὀλιγοστός) when he crouched and threw himself down into the midst of the enemy' (63.3). 'Almost alone' meant that he had very few companions. This was so in Arrian's account, where three other men were on the ladders with him and reached the wall-top (6.9.3 and 6.10.1). On the other hand, A was said to be alone when he jumped down according to Diodorus (17.99.1 ἐρημωθείς ... μόνος),[35] Curtius (9.4.33 'velut in solitudine destitutus') and Justin (12.9.5 'sine ullo satellite desiluit'). Again it appears that Plutarch was using the account either of Ptolemy or of Aristobulus.

(3) 'A was accompanied by two guards' (63.5 ὑπασπιστῶν), by name Peucestas and Limnaeus (63.7). However, Arrian provided three, namely Peucestas, Abreas and Leonnatus (6.10.1); and he added the comment that all authors had

---

[32] Brunt *L* II 132f. translated ὁ πᾶς λόγος κατέχει as 'it is universally told and believed', a phrase which would have included Ptolemy and Aristobulus. Yet Arrian excepted them at 6.11.5.

[33] Curtius placed the incident at 'a town of the Sandracae' (his version of Oxydracae at 9.4.26), and Diodorus probably did likewise (17.98.1f., mentioning the 'Sydracae' first).

[34] Curtius also referred to these two peoples as 'ferocissimae Indiae gentes' (9.4.16; cf. 9.4.24). It was an obvious deduction from the nature of the campaign.

[35] The text here may be corrupt.

Peucestas but they were not in agreement about Abreas and Leonnatus, and that 'some' added Ptolemy, although Ptolemy himself denied that he was there (6.11.7f.). Arrian confirmed later that Peucestas and Leonnatus were there and saved A's life, because he reported that gold crowns were conferred on them for that service (7.5.5). The following were said to be present with A. 'Peucestas ... and after him a good many others' (Diod. 17.99.4 ἕτεροι πλείους); Peucestas, Timaeus, Leonnatus and Aristonus (Curt. 9.5.14–16); Ptolemy and Limnaeus (Plu. *Mor.* 327b); and Limnaeus, Ptolemy and Leonnatus (Plu. *Mor.* 344d). Ptolemy was said to be present by Cleitarchus and Timagenes (Curt. 9.5.21). The conclusion to be drawn from all this is that Plutarch chose for the *Life* an account which was different not only from his own earlier statements in *Moralia* but also from what was found in the accounts of Cleitarchus, Timagenes, Diodorus, Justin and Curtius. It is possible that Arrian followed Ptolemy in his account rather than Aristobulus, and that Plutarch in the *Life* chose to follow Aristobulus.

(4) According to Plutarch A was struck first by an arrow, then suffered many wounds and finally was struck on the neck by a cudgel (63.6–9 τέλος δὲ πληγεὶς ὑπέρῳ). However, according to Arrian Ptolemy said A was wounded only once, by an arrow (6.10.1 and 6.11.7); and this was the version of Diodorus (17.99.3 and 100.1), Curtius (9.5.9) and Justin (12.9.12f.). Plutarch, however, in his *Moralia* had already given A three wounds – an axe-blow through the helmet causing a head-wound, the arrow in the chest and a blow 'from a cudgel on the neck' (*Mor.* 344c–d ὑπέρῳ κατὰ τοῦ αὐχένος; also the last wound at 344d). Who was Plutarch's source for this unique account? For once he gave us the answer, at *Moralia* 341c in listing A's wounds: 'among the Malli from a three-foot arrow through the breastplate into the chest, and ... on the neck (κατὰ τοῦ αὐχένος) as Aristobulus has recounted'. Thus it is certain that Plutarch was following faithfully the account of Aristobulus, at 63.9.

(5) 'They sawed off the arrow-shaft which was of wood'

(63.11). In *Moralia* 345a Plutarch had said that the Macedonians did not dare to saw off the arrow-shaft, because the sawing might split the bone, cause excessive pain and produce a haemorrhage. No other writer mentioned any sawing. On the contrary, Curtius said that they cut off the shaft to prevent the arrow-head from being moved (9.5.22 'abscidunt'), and Arrian mentioned that there were many accounts of the treatment of the wound (6.11.1f.; see below, p. 269). It is remarkable that Plutarch contradicted what he had written in *Moralia*. He must have done so because he was following a single account faithfully.

(6) '[The arrow-head] it is said (λέγεται) was three fingers wide and four fingers long' (63.12).[36] Here again Plutarch contradicted what he had said at *Moralia* 344c, 'four fingers wide and five fingers long'. No doubt he took the reduced measurements from the account which he was following closely. He entered the qualification 'it is said', perhaps as a face-saver for the contradiction.

When we put all these clues together, it is certain that Plutarch was giving in the *Life* a faithful rendering of the account by Aristobulus, probably with some abbreviation. That account included points which are not found in the other surviving accounts. The enemy were cleared off the wall-top by arrow-fire before A went up the ladder (63.3). When A jumped down and brandished his weapons, 'the barbarians thought that a flaming phantom was moving in front of his body' (63.4 σέλας τι καὶ φάσμα). They saw that he was accompanied by two guards (63.5 ὑπασπιστῶν). When help came, 'A was leaning against the wall, looking towards the enemy' (63.9; different in Arr. 6.10.2). The arrow-shaft was sawn off, and the arrow-head was three fingers wide and four fingers long (63.11f.). When A knew from the clamouring of the Macedonians outside that they were eager to see him, he

---

[36] These figures correspond roughly to 2 inches and 3 inches. Hamilton *C* 178 cited with approval the remark of F. C. Babbit in the Loeb edition of Plutarch's *Moralia* v, that 'Plutarch the rhetorician increases by one finger-breadth the dimensions of the arrow-point which are given by Plutarch the biographer in his *Life of Alexander*'. I prefer to attribute the difference to a change of source, because the rhetorical exaggeration is so tiny.

took his coat and went out to them (63.13; different in Arr.
6.13.1–3 and Curt. 9.6.1).

4. Indian philosophers and Alexander's return to Persia (64–9)

'Of the Gymnosophists A captured those who had done most
to persuade Sabbas [elsewhere Sambus] to revolt.' Arrian
reported the capture of a city (unnamed) in the kingdom of
Sambus, where A killed those of the Brahmans – 'who are
sophists for the Indians' – with whom responsibility for the
revolt lay (6.16.5); and the hanging of other Brahmans who
had been responsible for the revolt of Musicanus (6.17.2). This
treatment of rebel-leaders was not censured by Arrian or any
other Alexander-historian; for by Greek and Roman standards such treatment of rebels was not culpable. On this occasion the interrogation was to decide the order of execution
for the ten captured Gymnosophists. The surprising thing
in Plutarch's account was that A let these Gymnosophist
rebel-leaders go free and in addition gave them not nooses to
hang themselves, as Olympias gave to Eurydice, but gifts
(65.1). Thus the source on which Plutarch drew was favourable to A and reported this episode as an example of A's
clemency.[37]

The details of the interrogation of the nine wise men and the
tenth, the oldest, who was acting as judge, are unlikely to be
historical. For they consist of smart answers to smart questions, and they do not show the influence of anything particularly Oriental or of any one Greek philosophical school. It
proved to be a very popular episode with ancient writers. The
earliest text of it, a papyrus of *c.* 100 B.C., reported the ten
questions and answers as Plutarch did later but with some
slight variations, and the same sequel – the freeing of the ten
wise men – with an ironical definition of A.'s gifts, which were
said to consist of clothing for the nudists.[38] Later versions
have survived in *Anecdota Graeca* ed. Boissonade 1.145, Ps.-

[37] For the gifts see Hamilton *C* 179.
[38] Perhaps learnt from the Mallians at the time.

Callisthenes 3.5f., and *Epit. Metz* 71ff., together with derivative excerpts or summaries.[39]

Plutarch set this episode alongside another, recounted in 65.1–3, which included 'Onesicritus says'. If he had obtained the episode of 64 from Onesicritus, he surely would have said so and not have written the antithetical sentences at 65.1: 'these on the one hand he set free with gifts, but to those, on the other hand, who were most in repute and were living in quietness by themselves he sent Onesicritus' etc. The deduction that Plutarch did not draw on Onesicritus for chapter 64 is confirmed by the absence of any Cynic doctrine from the question-and-answer interrogation.[40] Where then did the episode originate? It is possible, as Wilcken suggested,[41] that it was derived from an early Indian folk-tale (in which the moral would have been that A was outwitted and was forced, presumably by some promised condition, to spare the ten wise men) and that it soon was adopted into *The Alexander Romance*. But the Greek love of such philosophical quizzes (ἀπορίαι) and the Greek nature of the questions and answers[42] in the papyrus and in Plutarch's version point in my opinion to a Greek source and to one who was representing A not as a ruthless tyrant but as a king who was merciful. Finally, because Arrian told of the hanging of Brahmans and not of any pardon such as our episode reports, we may exclude Ptolemy and Aristobulus as authors of the episode; and we may also conclude that the episode is unhistorical,[43] in that Aristobulus would surely have reported such a pardon as supporting his

---

[39] I disagree with the opinion of U. Wilcken, 'Alexander der Grosse und die indischen Gymnosophisten', *Sitzber. d. p. Akademie der Wissenschaften* (Berlin) 1923.176, 'Er erscheint als ein grausamer Tyrann'. So too K. von Fritz, *Philologus* Supplbd 1926.1ff. and Hamilton *C* 179 'the setting represents a powerful and unscrupulous ruler face to face with a wise man'. The danger is that we read our own concept of A into Plutarch's account and forget the sequel, namely the conferring of gifts by A on the philosophers (65.1).

[40] Published by Wilcken, loc. cit. This has the variant that A promised freedom to the judge alone, if his judgement should be approved.

[41] See Wilcken, loc. cit. 162f. Brown *Ones.* 46f. and Hamilton *C* 178f.

[42] See Wilcken, loc. cit. 176, 'ich nicht glauben kann dass sie von O stammt'.

[43] Arr. 6.16.5 and 17.2. Hamilton *C* 179.

own view of A, and his report would have been included readily by Arrian.

We are told by Strabo 711–17 of four Greeks who wrote of the Indian philosophers. Two of them, Aristobulus and Onesicritus, we have already excluded as sources for chapter 64. Nearchus, according to Strabo 716–17, drew a distinction between the Brahmans, who engaged in civic life and accompanied the kings as advisers, and the other sophists who considered questions of natural science; and he added that women joined them in philosophising and that they were all ascetic in their way of life. This summary of Nearchus' views does not fit Plutarch's account in chapter 64, because it was Nearchus' first group who were captured as instigators of the revolts but Nearchus' second group who were dealing with questions of natural science. We are left with the fourth, Megasthenes, who divided Brahmans from 'Garmanes'. To the Brahmans he attributed ideas of natural science. Some of these ideas he described as simplistic and based on myth; but in many cases he said they were like those of the Greeks, and he instanced ideas on cosmology, the number of elements, the position of our earth in the universe, the nature of the deity and the indestructibility of the soul (712f.).[44] Megasthenes comes closest to what Plutarch wrote, in naming these philosophers 'Brahmans', regarding them as advisers of the kings and making them like Greek philosophers in some of their ideas on natural science; for that likeness is integral to the Indians' answers to A's questions. Thus the author from whom Plutarch most probably derived his account in chapter 64 is Megasthenes.

In 65 Plutarch dealt with the other philosophers. 'To those in the highest repute living by themselves in quietness (ἐν ἡσυχίᾳ) A sent Onesicritus with the request that they should come to him.' Strabo began a long account of what Onesicritus had written about the philosophers with the mention of this

---

[44] Four of the questions appeared in other Greek contexts, involving for instance Thales and Aristides the Just; see Wilcken, loc. cit. 166, 167, 169 and 171. See also Plu. *Mor.* 153e.

mission, and with the statement that these 'sophists' lived naked, practised endurance and were held in most honour (715). Later in Strabo's account the meaning of 'living in quietness' becomes apparent. Thus Plutarch based his opening sentence on Onesicritus. Plutarch's next narrative step is at 65.5: 'Calanus, however, was persuaded by Taxiles to come to A.' The meaning of 'however' is made clear by a sentence in Strabo's account, where Onesicritus said that the sophists did not go to others on a summons; thus the intervention by Taxiles was needed. Calanus was the first of the sophists whom Onesicritus addressed (Strabo 715 = 15.1.64). Evidently Plutarch was abbreviating drastically the sequence of events in Onesicritus' account.

The conversation which Onesicritus held with Calanus and Dandamis was reported from Onesicritus at some length by Strabo and briefly by Plutarch, both ending with Dandamis (Mandanis in Strabo) saying that Socrates, Pythagoras and Diogenes erred in attaching supreme importance to laws.[45] The explanation of Calanus' name in 65.5 came probably from Onesicritus, although it is not included in the summary by Strabo.

For the other statements in this chapter Plutarch cited other sources. 'Others say that Dandamis asked only one question: Why did A make so long a journey to come here?' (65.4). Sources other than Onesicritus might have included Nearchus.[46] Then at 65.6–8 'it is said' that Calanus set up the illustration (τὸ παράδειγμα) of the empire for A in the form of an outstretched hide, which can be made to lie flat only if you stand on its centre; for when Calanus stood on a part of the outer edge, other parts rose up. As Hamilton pointed out, a 'similar' illustration was related by Aelius Aristides to the empire of Cyrus the Great, and it was suggested by J. H. Oliver that the source used by Aelius Aristides was Ctesias.[47]

---

[45] Strabo 716 = 15.1.65 and PA 65.3.
[46] Pearson LHA 127 'Nearchus never appears as a principal authority on the wise men.'
[47] The story may have taken shape much earlier, but I am concerned only with Plutarch's source of information.

Plutarch, however, did not draw on Ctesias; for Plutarch's conclusion was that A should stay holding down the centre of his empire, but Ctesias' conclusion was that Cyrus must keep marching around to put down the parts which rose up.[48] We cannot provide a name for the origin of this 'saying'.[49]

Plutarch made an error in placing the events of chapters 64 and 65 in that sequence. For the mention of Taxiles persuading Calanus to go to A in 65.5 dated the mission of Onesicritus and the meeting of A with Calanus to before A's entry into Taxila.[50] The capture of the Gymnosophists who had incited the revolt by Sambus in 64.1 happened several months after the arrival of A at Taxila. Plutarch was either unaware of the true sequence or was careless in writing as he did.

In 66.1 'the passage down the rivers to the sea took seven months' time'. Plutarch, resuming his narrative from the recovery of A from his wound at 63.14, brought A down the Hydraotes, Acesines and Indus to the sea, which he reached in July 325. The seven months, then, date the recovery from the wound to December 326. Dating the passage of time by months rather than days is unusual in the Alexander-histories. It was a method used by Aristobulus in describing the voyage from Bucephala on the Hydaspes to the region of Pattala as taking ten months, and it is thus likely that Plutarch was drawing on Aristobulus, as he had done in chapter 63. 'Entering the Ocean, A sailed out to the island which he called Skilloustis and others called Psiltoukis.' Landing there he sacrificed to the gods, observed the nature of the open sea (πέλαγος) and of the coast within reach, prayed that no man after him should pass beyond the limits of his expedition and turned back (66.2). Plutarch differs from the accounts in Diodorus 17.104.1 and Arrian 6.19.3f., in that they have two islands, one being within the river-delta and the other out to sea. Further, Plutarch gave the name Skilloustis to the island

---

[48] Hamilton C 181 suggested that Onesicritus may have adapted Ctesias' illustration to suit this context. But since Plutarch has been reporting what 'Onesicritus says' earlier in the chapter, it is improbable that he would make Onesicritus anonymous here.

[49] See Brown *Ones*. 38 and Pearson *LHA* 96f. for Onesicritus' report.

[50] See Wilcken 180f.

out to sea, whereas Arrian called the island within the delta Killouta. Yet, Plutarch and Arrian have an island name in common; for Skilloustis was close enough to Arrian's Killouta. On my interpretation Diodorus was following an accurate source, Diyllus, and Arrian was following Ptolemy and Aristobulus, so that their accounts should be accepted as correct for the number of islands, and Arrian's location of the named island should be preferred. The best explanation for the similarity of the name and for the divergences in Arrian's account is that Plutarch was still following Aristobulus and that Arrian preferred the account of Ptolemy.[51]

Though Plutarch mentioned the appointment of Nearchus as admiral and Onesicritus as chief pilot and the aim of their voyage, he wrote only of A's movements by land. He seems to have changed to another source, for what follows is much more sensational and inaccurate. The losses in crossing the territory of the Oreitae were, by implication rather than by direct statement, three-quarters of 120,000 infantry and 15,000 cavalry (over 100,000), due mainly to famine, and sixty days later A entered Gedrosia where he had all things in abundance (66.4–7). The losses were incurred in fact in the desert of Gedrosia, not in the territory of the Oreitae, and the huge number of losses is rejected by all scholars.[52] The extraordinary error over the location had already been made by Curtius 9.10.18 'itaque fame dumtaxat vindicatus exercitus tandem in Cedrosiae fines perducitur'. The early arrival of 'all things in abundance' thanks to the nearby satraps occurred also in

---

[51] F 35 = Strabo 692. On inclusive reckoning A left Bucephala in the course of October of our calendar. This corresponds with Aristobulus' time for starting the voyage 'not many days before the setting of the Pleiades', the setting being at the end of October (J. E. Sandys, *A Dictionary of Classical Antiquities* (London, 1894) 495).

[52] A was probably accompanied by Ptolemy as one of the Bodyguards but not by Aristobulus, who in writing from memory much later fell into error but remembered the variant names of the island. Jacoby, *FGrH* 2 D 467 considered Nearchus to be Arrian's source for the name of the island; but Arrian has not indicated any departure from his standard procedure of following Ptolemy and/or Aristobulus, and the work of Nearchus seems to have started with events a month or two later. The source of the long account in Curtius 9.9 is unknown (*THA* 155).

Diodorus 17.105.7f. and Curtius 9.10.17f., and it was certainly unhistorical.[53] In my analysis of sources I thought that the source of Diodorus and Curtius was probably Cleitarchus (*THA* 69f. and 156). If I am correct, Plutarch was taking a few points from a long account by Cleitarchus either directly or through an intermediate author such as Curtius.[54]

In 67.1–6 Plutarch described a drunken revel through Carmania. He drew on the source followed by Curtius 9.10.24–8. For they share the following points: seven days of continuous drunkenness, Friends and Commanders garlanded (φίλους καὶ ἡγεμόνας ἐστεφανωμένους; 'amici et cohors regia, variis redimita floribus coronisque'), canopied waggons with rich hangings (ἅμαξαι ... ἀλουργοῖς καὶ ποικίλοις περιβόλα-ιοις; 'vehicula constrata ... in tabernaculorum modum ornari ... alia veste pretiosa'), mixing bowls and huge containers, flutes and stringed instruments, and drunken licence. The source of Curtius was probably Cleitarchus (see *THA* 156). It seems then that Plutarch was continuing with Cleitarchus. This is consistent with Arrian's dismissal of this story as a fiction, not recorded by any reputable author (6.28.2; see below, p. 278).

At 67.8 'it is said' (λέγεται) that A when drunk (μεθύοντα) was watching a festival of dancing. His beloved Bagoas won the dance, was decorated, walked through the theatre and sat beside A. Seeing this the Macedonians clapped and shouted 'give him a kiss', until A embraced him and kissed him passionately' (κατεφίλησεν). The point of this story is not that A was drunk[55] but that he was unashamedly in love with this boy-dancer. The opening word 'it is said' indicates that the story did not come from the source of what preceded, namely from Cleitarchus, whose account had been accepted without

---

[53] See *AG*² 238 and n. 162.

[54] See *THA* 156.

[55] The 60 days mentioned by Plutarch as having been passed in the territory of the Oreitae occurred in Strabo 723 (= 15.2.7) and Arrian (6.27.1) for the journey from Ora to the capital of Gedrosia. In Plutarch's account the revel through Carmania happened before the army reached the capital of 'Gedrosia' (67.7), which is an error in geography or a verbal confusion by Plutarch (see E. Badian in *CQ* 8 (1958) 151).

qualification. Thus Plutarch implied that the source of the story was less to be trusted than Cleitarchus.

The story is not mentioned in the usual Alexander-histories, but it occurs in a passage in Athenaeus, *Deipnosophists*, where Athenaeus said A was 'madly fond of boys' (φιλόπαις). Athenaeus continued as follows. 'At any rate Dicaearchus, *On the Sacrifice at Ilium*, says that he was overwhelmed (ἡττᾶσθαι) by the eunuch Bagoas, that in the sight of the whole theatre he bent over and was kissing Bagoas passionately (καταφιλεῖν), and that on the spectators shouting and clapping he did not disobey but bent over and kissed him again' (Athen. 603a–b). Here A is not said to be drunk, and we learn that the boy Bagoas was a eunuch, presumably a castrated slave.[56] Thus he was the Bagoas described by Curtius as a eunuch boy in the flower of boyhood (6.5.23 'spado atque in ipso flore pueritiae').

Despite the slight differences of A being drunk in Plutarch and Bagoas being a eunuch in Dicaearchus it is clear to me that both accounts referred to the same incident (for one can hardly suppose that it all happened twice in different places). Dicaearchus, a pupil of Aristotle, was writing within the lifetime of, for instance, Aristobulus and Ptolemy; it is thus probable that he was the originator of the account, and that Athenaeus quoted him as such. Whether Plutarch took his account directly, as I should suppose,[57] or indirectly from Dicaearchus is unimportant. His source of information in either case was Dicaearchus.[58]

In 68.1–5 Plutarch produced a rambling and muddled ac-

---

[56] Hamilton C 186 and E. Badian, op. cit. 151 n. 3 held that 'the emphasis' or 'main *motiv*' in Plutarch's account was A's drunkenness. Yet Plutarch did not enlarge on his one word μεθύοντα. Many incidents of A being drunk were listed by Athenaeus (434a–f), but this was not one of them.

[57] According to Curt. 6.5.23, who was drawing on Cleitarchus (*THA* 135 and 157), he had been the beloved of Darius, whose court was served by a large number of eunuchs. Incidentally, a boy of this age was not the host of A near Babylon in 323; for the Bagoas of Aelian, *V.H.* 2.23 was evidently the outstanding 'Persian' who was made a trierarch (Arr. *Ind.* 18.8), *pace* Badian, loc. cit. 156 n. 3, following Berve 2.99.59.

[58] Tarn 320 'Plutarch . . . repeats Dicaearchus' story.' Badian, loc. cit. 151 n. 3 argues for 'no common source'. See also *THA* 194 n. 24, written at a time when I did not analyse Plutarch's source as thoroughly as I do here.

count which can only be of his own making. The narrative thread was provided by Nearchus, meeting A at 68.1 and leaving him at 68.6, in January 324. Confusion begins with the first word ἐνταῦθα resuming the palace of Gedrosia (67.7), a mistake or a confusion by Plutarch for the palace of Carmania. The meeting of Nearchus and A took place not there but five days inland from Harmozia (Hormuz) (Arr. *Ind.* 33.7, following Nearchus) rather than at Salmus (Diod. 17.106.4). The plan for a large fleet to sail down the Euphrates with ships built at Thapsacus and with crews 'from all parts' is a jumble of A's arrangements in 323 (Arr. 7.19.3–5; 7.21.1). The idea of circumnavigating Arabia and Africa and of entering the Mediterranean Sea through the Straits of Gibraltar was certainly not entertained when Nearchus was reporting on his voyage from India; it was at Persepolis, according to Arrian 7.1.2, that 'some writers' attributed this project to A. Plutarch turned next to the restlessness of the subject peoples and the misrule of generals and satraps; for they had thought that A would not return safe from India. His summary is minimal (cf. Arr. 7.4.1–3). Next, Plutarch moved to friction between Antipater and the royal ladies and the moving of Olympias to Epirus and Cleopatra to Macedonia, which took place probably late in 324.[59] The remark that Macedonia would not submit to rule by a woman was probably a vague echo in Plutarch's mind of Antipater's dying words in 319.[60] This jumble of episodes is an excellent example of what happened when Plutarch failed to follow the guidance of a narrative source.

At 68.6f. Nearchus returned to the fleet and A marched into Persis. There he punished generals who had misgoverned. He killed a son of Abuletes called Oxyartes with a pike[61] (Arr. 7.4.1 called him Oxathres), and he imprisoned Abuletes himself, satrap of Susiane, for failing to provide essential supplies.

---

[59] See H*SPA* 475 for the date.
[60] Diod. 19.11.9 'never permit a woman to be head of the kingdom'.
[61] Tarn's objection (p. 299) that A did not use the *sarissa* as a weapon is absurd. A, like Philip, fought sometimes in the phalanx, and he could take a *sarissa* from one of his guards on a ceremonial occasion.

Plutarch appended the delightful story of Abuletes bringing 3,000 talents of coinage which on A's order were thrown to the horses. When they did not eat the coins, A exclaimed: 'What use to us is your provision?' The occasion for this episode is not stated. If Plutarch thought it was when A emerged from the Gedrosian desert (a back-reference to 66.7 'the nearest satraps'), he was mistaken because Susiane was too far away to be involved.[62] On the other hand, it was perhaps a timeless story. Arrian's account is different. When A was at Susa, he arrested and executed Abulites (Arrian's version of the name) and his son Oxathres, 'because he [Abulites] was administering[63] the Susii badly' (7.4.1). No doubt Arrian, following Ptolemy and/or Aristobulus, was correct, and Plutarch was incorrect as regards the charge against and the fate of Abuletes. The source of Plutarch is not discernible.

[62] Berve II 5 thought that the supplies were for the army leaving Gedrosia. Badian in *CQ* 8 (1958) 148 held that Abuletes was killed as 'a scapegoat' for A's own mistake in Gedrosia. Yet Susa was 1,000 kilometres from the fringe of the Gedrosian desert, and no one could have expected Abuletes to send supplies that far.

[63] The manuscript reading ἐπεμελεῖτο should not be altered, as it is in Brunt *L* II 210; for it refers to Abuletes.

8

PERSIA AND BABYLONIA

1. Alexander in Persis and Susiane (69–71)

In 69.1–5 Plutarch recorded two happenings in Persis (ἐν δὲ Πέρσαις). (1) 'A distributed the money to the women in accordance with the custom of the Persian kings, who whenever they entered Persis gave each woman a gold piece.' Plutarch had already mentioned this custom in *Moralia* (246a–b), where his source was Ctesias; here Plutarch may have written from memory of *Moralia*.[1] 'That, they say (φασίν), is the reason why some kings did not visit Persis often and Ochus not even once, alienating himself from his fatherland through stinginess.' This is childish, not least because Ochus built a palace at Persepolis in Persis, and that is why Plutarch added 'they say'. He obtained it from a less dependable source. (2) A not undistinguished Macedonian, Poulamachus of Pella, was executed for having desecrated the Tomb of Cyrus (69.3). Herein Plutarch was not following Aristobulus, who said that no one was incriminated by the Magi (Arr. 6.29.11), nor the source of Curtius' statement that Orxines was executed as the criminal (10.1.37), namely Cleitarchus on my interpretation (*THA* 157). Whatever Plutarch's source was, it was incorrect.

Plutarch went on to an inscription in Greek letters, which on A's orders was to be engraved under the Persian one on the Tomb of Cyrus. A translation of the latter was then given by Plutarch which does not correspond with that of Aristobulus in Arrian (6.29.8) and in Strabo (730 = 15.3.7), nor with the absurd version of Onesicritus in Strabo (ibid.).[2] Plutarch's

---

[1] The custom may have been a reward for the Persian women's bravery as described by Justin at 1.6.13ff.; see also *FGrH* 90 (Nicolaus Damascenus) F 60 and Polyaen. 7.45.2.

[2] Onesicritus said that the epigram was 'Greek inscribed in Persian letters'. He was equally incorrect in describing the Tomb of Cyrus as ten storeys high (δεκάστεγον).

source, then, was neither Aristobulus nor Onesicritus. The addition of a Greek inscription underneath the Persian one on the Tomb was not mentioned in any surviving work except that of Aristus of Salamis, a third-century B.C. writer (*FGrH* 143 F 1). He might perhaps have been Plutarch's source. Plutarch reported that A was deeply moved by the inscription, for he had in mind the uncertainty and the mutability of life – a sentiment which fitted Plutarch's version of the inscription and should therefore be associated with it.

The spectacular suicide of Calanus, the Indian philosopher, and the celebrations after it were mentioned by many writers. Plutarch devoted 69.6–70.2 to the subject. For our analysis of the sources it will be best to start with 70.1f.

On his return from the pyre A assembled many of his Friends and Commanders for a banquet and proposed a competition with a prize for the victor in the drinking of neat wine (ἀγῶνα ἀκρατοποσίας). Promachus, who drank most, reached four pitchers.[3] He took the prize, which was a crown worth a talent, and survived for three days. Of the others, as Chares says (ὡς Χάρης φησί) forty-one drank and died, bitter cold coming on top of strong drink.

For once the text of a passage to which Plutarch referred is preserved, in Athenaeus (437). It may be translated as follows:

Because of the Indians' fondness for wine, he [Chares] says, A set up also a competition in drinking neat wine (ἀκρατοποσίας ἀγῶνα) with prizes – a talent for the first, 30 minae for the second and 10 minae for the third. Of those who drank the wine 35 died at once because of the cold (παραχρῆμα μὲν ἐτελεύτησαν ὑπὸ τοῦ ψύχους τριάκοντα καὶ πέντε), and six died in their tents a little later. The winner, who drank most, downed four pitchers of neat wine and took the talent. He survived for four days. His name was Promachus.

Plutarch was not quoting verbatim, though he said 'as Chares says'. In fact, in abbreviating, he attributed 41 deaths – not 35 – to the cold, and he repeated the main points in his own order and phrasing.

The opening sentence of 70.1, as translated above, is differ-

---

[3] A pitcher held some six pints. Promachus is named as the winner in Aelian, *V.H.* 2.41.

ent from the preceding sentence in Athenaeus, which may be translated thus:

Chares of Mitylene in *Histories of Alexander*, after saying of the Indian philosopher Calanus that he hurled himself onto a pyre and died, remarks (φησίν) that at his tomb A organised a contest of athletic events and of the arts in praise of Calanus.

Chares writes here of a festival with events – including the drinking – open to all ranks in the army. Plutarch, however, wrote of Friends and Companions at a banquet. Thus he was not drawing on Chares. There is a further indication that Plutarch changed his source within 70.1f.; for he has produced the *reductio ad absurdum* that 41 of A's Friends and Commanders died as a result of the drinking.

We should note here the practice of Plutarch. He does not give the name of the author whom he is following for his main account. On the other hand, when he introduces a point from another author, he names that author, in this case Chares.

To return to Chares. He had Calanus 'hurl himself onto a pyre' (ῥίψας ἑαυτὸν εἰς πυράν). So also did Onesicritus (*FGrH* 134 F 18). This was not customary in India; for, as Onesicritus pointed out (F 17a; in Strabo 716 = 15.1.65), the philosopher should 'anoint himself, sit on the pyre, order it to be lit and not move while being burnt'. On the other hand, Plutarch did have Calanus die in just this customary manner at 69.8, adding that 'he sacrificed himself auspiciously in the traditional manner of the sophists there'. Herein Plutarch was of the same mind as Arrian 7.3.5, where Arrian was following Ptolemy and/or Aristobulus. Since we are ruling out Chares and Onesicritus at this stage, did Plutarch follow Ptolemy or/and Aristobulus in 69.6–8?

'After suffering from a stomach disorder for a short time, Calanus asked', wrote Plutarch,

that a pyre be prepared for him. Conveyed on horseback to it, he prayed, sprinkled himself, cut off some hair as an offering, and while mounting the pyre raised a hand in greeting to those Macedonians who were present. He asked them to treat that day as one of pleasure and of drinking deep with the king, and he said he would be seeing him in person soon at Babylon.

Arrian reported (see below, p. 283) that, on Calanus falling ill and insisting, a pyre was prepared under the charge of Ptolemy, son of Lagus. A horse was provided but Calanus was too weak to mount it, and he was therefore carried in a litter to the pyre, where he lay down in the sight of the whole army (7.3.1–5). It is thus clear that Plutarch was not drawing on Chares or Onesicritus. To whom then do we turn?

A final clue is afforded by Calanus' greetings and his remark that he would see A soon at Babylon. Arrian mentioned this in another passage, at 7.18.6, which runs as follows:

Further, as regards Calanus, the Indian sophist, a story (λόγος) of some such sort has been recorded, that as he was going to his death on the pyre he greeted the other Companions but was unwilling to go up and greet A, for he said he would meet him and greet him at Babylon. His words were disregarded at the time, but later after A died at Babylon it came into the minds of his hearers that he had indeed been inspired to foretell the death of A.

Plutarch evidently was following the author of this *logos*, i.e. someone other than Ptolemy and Aristobulus.

The one remaining author whose description of the end of Calanus survives[4] is Diodorus at 17.107.1–6. He presented Calanus as a seventy-three-year-old who 'had reached the peak of wellbeing at the hands of nature and of fortune'. Illness led to the preparation of a pyre.

Calanus, following his own principles, mounted the pyre in complete confidence (τεθαρρηκότως) and died, consumed along with it in the flames. Of those present some judged him to be mad and others vainly boastful of his endurance, while certain persons (τινές) admired his courage and contempt for death. The king gave him a costly funeral. (17.107.6)

This brief account is compatible with that of Plutarch; for Calanus evidently did endure the flames stoically in Diodorus' account. In *THA* 71 I attributed this passage in Diodorus to Cleitarchus as source, partly because of the cynical judgement

---

[4] Arrian cited Nearchus as saying that in accordance with A's order the bugles sounded, the army raised the war-cry and the elephants trumpeted shrilly as in war in honour of Calanus (7.3.6). There is no indication here that Nearchus was followed by Plutarch.

with madness and conceit taking priority over courage. I am therefore inclined to see Cleitarchus as the source which Plutarch used for 69.6–8. At the same time he will be the source for the *logos* in Arrian that Calanus would soon meet and greet A at Babylon. It was characteristic of Cleitarchus to collect or invent portents and prophecies of ills to come (see *THA* 77). Then at the end of 70.1 Plutarch turned to Chares for the details of the drinking contest.

In 70.3 A has advanced to Susa. Plutarch crammed into this one section a series of important events:[5] the marriages of A and the leading Macedonians to Asian ladies, the formalisation as marriages of the liaisons of Macedonian soldiers with Asian women,[6] the lavishness of the wedding feast, 'at which they say 9,000 guests were each given a gold cup', and A's paying of the debts owed to (Asian) creditors, which totalled 130 talents short of 10,000 talents.[7] This compressed account is due to Plutarch himself, who summarised his reading in this way. The information under 'they say' is not mentioned elsewhere.[8] The source or sources are not discernible.

The account of Antigenes in 70.4–6 enrolling himself as a debtor and being found to be fraudulent had been told of Tarrias (probably Atarrias) in *Moralia* 339b–c, where Plutarch listed three Macedonians as men of superb courage but with a predilection for women and money – Tarrias, Antigenes and Philotas, son of Parmenio. There is a similar case in *Moralia* 339c–d and 180f–181a, where Antigenes feigned sick to follow a girl named Telesippa to Macedonia, and in the *Life* 41.9f., where the same story was told of Eurylochus. We must infer that Plutarch had found a more trustworthy source in the

---

[5] Plutarch was presumably aware that this *Life* was much longer than most, and he abbreviated for that reason and not because, as Hamilton *C* 195 held, 'he conspicuously fails to register enthusiasm for the marriages'. There is not enough evidence in Plutarch to support Hamilton's view that his source 'is probably Chares rather than Onesicritus'.

[6] This occurred at a separate ceremony according to Arr. 7.4.8.

[7] The figure is common to Diod. 17.109.2 'a little less than 10,000' and Curt. 10.2.10f., but the occasion was later in both authors.

[8] It may be inaccurate. Arrian said that the Macedonians numbered more than 10,000 (7.4.8), but nothing is said of a dinner. One wonders if the figure 9,000 has been taken from the dinner at Opis (Arr. 7.11.9).

meantime, and that he decided in favour of Antigenes[9] for the episode of debt and Eurylochus for the episode of sickness. There is no clue to his sources.

The subject of chapter 71 is the mutiny at Opis, which Plutarch placed between the payment of the army's debts at Susa and the death of Hephaestion at Ecbatana.[10] The antecedent event is the arrival of 'the 30,000 boys whom he left behind while they were being trained and learning'. The reference is to the boys at 47.6 who were 'to learn Greek letters and to be trained in Macedonian weapons'.[11] Their arrival and performance delighted A but filled the Macedonians with discontent and fear, for they thought he would pay less attention to themselves. Plutarch passes at once to the mutiny, whereas in Arrian's history there was a gap of several weeks. It is obvious that Plutarch was being economical with words and mentioning only salient points.

His account of the mutiny is relatively brief. In particular he did not include any speeches, whether to the Macedonians or the Persians. It was enough for him to say that A in his anger poured much abuse on the Macedonians. Other differences from the account of Arrian may be noted.

(1) 'When A was sending the weak and maimed men down to the [Mediterranean] coast (καταπέμποντος) the Macedonians said that it was an outrage' etc. The present tense, not the aorist tense, is used here, implying contemporary events – the men already selected being now sent off and the other soldiers saying it was an outrage. In Arrian's account A summoned the Macedonians to an Assembly and told them in advance what he intended to do (7.8.1). On the other hand, Diodorus provided an interval between 'the release of the oldest of the citizens[12] from the expedition' and the Assembly; and in that

---

[9] As Berve II 41f. maintains, this Antigenes was not the later commander of the Silvershields.

[10] Hamilton *C* 197 'Plutarch places the mutiny at Susa' is inaccurate. In the *Life* Plutarch is not giving an itinerary but mentions occasional points *en route* – here Susa at 70.3 and Ecbatana at 72.1. Events mentioned between 70.3 and 71.9 happened in the interim between the two places.

[11] On these boys see H*RP* 278f.

[12] For the significance of this expression see Hammond *MS* 64.

interval he recorded the payment of the released soldiers' debts (17.109.1f.). Since the sequence of events here is so different from that in Plutarch, we can exclude the source of Diodorus, who was probably Diyllus (*THA* 72f.), from consideration as a source used by Plutarch. Justin, however, is closer to Plutarch. Writing in his most concise manner Justin followed the payment of the army's debts with these cryptic sentences: 'Dimissis veteranis exercitum iunioribus supplet. Sed retenti veteranorum discessum aegre ferentes missionem et ipsi flagitabant' (12.11.4f.). 'Veterans having been despatched A filled up the army with younger men' – these being presumably 'the 30,000 boys' of Plutarch – 'but those who had been kept back took the departure of the veterans ill and were demanding that they too should be sent [home].' Thus the source of Justin, who was probably Cleitarchus (*THA* 106), may well be the source followed here by Plutarch.

(2) Plutarch reported more of what the soldiers had to say than Arrian did. In particular he had them say to A that 'he should count them all as useless and go ahead with these young war-dancers (πυρριχισταί) and win for himself the inhabited earth' (τὴν οἰκουμένην). The mention of world-conquest was typical of Cleitarchus. Justin too gave a sentence or two to the soldiers' complaints and taunts, including a reference to 'his father Ammon', a subject dear to Cleitarchus[13] and mentioned also in Arrian 7.8.3.

(3) A discharged the Macedonians (ἀπελάσας),[14] entrusted to Persians the duties of guarding himself (τὰς φυλακάς) and formed from them bodyguards and chamberlains (ῥαβδοφόρους). Plutarch here restricted the deployment of Persians to the men of the Guards[15] and the Court. Arrian had Persians deployed in all Macedonian units (7.11.3). Justin, however, had A say that he would entrust to the Persians 'custodiam corporis', and in consequence he selected 1,000 young men to form the special guards ('in numerum satellitum') and intro-

---

[13] See, for instance, Diod. 17.51.2f., of which the source was Cleitarchus (*THA* 44).
[14] This word recalls the last word in the speech of A, ἄπιτε (Arr. 7.10.7).
[15] For the various formations of Guards see H*VG*.

duced a detachment of Persian troops trained in Macedonian drill into his army. The emphasis here is as in Plutarch.

(4) Plutarch described the emotions and the desperation of the Macedonian soldiers at considerably greater length than either Arrian or Justin. The timing is different in Plutarch and in Arrian. When the Macedonians saw what A was doing, they went 'without their weapons and wearing tunics only' (ἄνοπλοι καὶ μονοχίτωνες) and begged for mercy, but A refused to see them until the third day thereafter (71.6–8); but in Arrian 7.11.4f. the soldiers came armed and threw down their weapons in supplication and were received at once by A. Justin is too brief for any comparison in detail.

The conclusion to be drawn from these differences is that Plutarch based his version in chapter 71 on the account of Cleitarchus, which had been used earlier by Trogus. The record was set straight later by Arrian, who chose to follow Ptolemy and Aristobulus (see below, p. 291).

2. The deaths of Hephaestion and Alexander (72–6)

Drinking played a part in the deaths of both Hephaestion and A in Plutarch's account. At 72.2 Hephaestion was already ill with a fever and had been put on a strict diet by his doctor, Glaucus; but while the latter was absent Hephaestion, 'a young man[16] and a military type as he was, devoured a boiled chicken, drank down a mighty beaker of chilled wine, was taken poorly and a little later died'. We may compare this account with two other versions. According to Diodorus 17.110.7, A engaged 'in continuous drinking with his Friends and in the course of it Hephaestion, having indulged in intemperate drunkenness, was taken ill and departed this life'. According to Arrian 7.14.1, A engaged

in drinking with his Companions, and at this time Hephaestion fell sick in body, and it was already on the seventh day of his illness – this being the day, they say,[17] when the stadium was full for the boys' athletic event –

[16] In fact Hephaestion was in his early thirties, and he held the highest position under the king in Asia. Only a Greek writer would have called Hephaestion young, νέος.

[17] Arrian drew this detail from a source other than Ptolemy and/or Aristobulus. I see

that A on hearing that Hephaestion was poorly hastened to him but found him no longer alive.[18]

Plutarch was not following Arrian's source or sources, namely Ptolemy and/or Aristobulus, since Hephaestion's illness was not associated by Arrian with Hephaestion drinking. Nor was he following the source of Diodorus, namely Diyllus in my opinion (*THA* 73), since the drinking by Hephaestion preceded his illness. Plutarch gave a more hostile account, in that Hephaestion, being already ill, disobeyed the doctor, over-ate and over-drank, and paid for it with his death.

The death of A was described in similar terms by Diodorus and Justin. During a revel with Medius 'A filled himself up with much unmixed wine to celebrate the death of Heracles, downed a mighty beakerful, suddenly shrieked as if pierced by a weapon and was carried out half-alive' (Diod. 17.117.1f.). 'A accepted a beaker, and in the middle of drinking it he cried out suddenly as if pierced by a weapon and was carried out half-alive' (Just. 12.13.8f.). The common source of these two writers was Cleitarchus, as Hamilton asserted without question (*C* lix and 208f.),[19] and as I maintained with arguments (*THA* 77f. and 108f.). The form of the story and the attitude towards the Macedonian leader are so similar to those which Plutarch deployed in his account of Hephaestion's death, that we can conclude with confidence that Plutarch too was drawing on Cleitarchus.

In 75.4f. we see that Plutarch had before him Cleitarchus' account of A's collapse.

At the request of Medius A went to revel with him, and after drinking there throughout the next day he began to be feverish, neither through drinking down a beaker of Heracles nor through being suddenly crippled with pain in the back as if struck with a spear – but that is what some thought they

---

no reason to suppose that the subject intended for 'they say' was these two writers, as Brunt *L* II 248 n. 1 suggested. Diod. 17.110.7, Plu. 72.1 and Arr. 7.14.1 all placed Hephaestion's illness within a period of festival.

[18] This dramatic finale resembles that of Darius, whom A just failed to find alive in the accounts of Justin and Curtius, of which Cleitarchus was in my opinion the common source (*THA* 101 and 133).

[19] Plutarch here attacks the dramatic version of A's illness given by Cleitarchus.

should write, fabricating (πλάσαντες)[20] as it were a tragical and pathetic finale to a great drama.

The explanation of 'the beaker of Heracles' is apparent from Diodorus' fuller version of Cleitarchus' account; for the beaker was in honour of Heracles in that version.[21] It was at 'neither through drinking down a beaker' that Plutarch changed from Cleitarchus to Aristobulus and then to the *Ephemerides*.

The next question is whether there are grounds for supposing that Plutarch was following Cleitarchus for the passages which intervene between 72.2 and 75.5. I subdivide the description of A's grief as follows.

(1) 'At once A ordered the clipping of all horses and mules as a sign of mourning, and he removed the battlements of the cities round about ... and he banned all flute-playing and music-making in the army for a long time, until a response came from Ammon, ordering him to honour Hephaestion and sacrifice to him as a hero' (72.3).

According to Arrian there were various accounts of A's grief (7.14.2). In one of them A cut off his own hair 'over the corpse'; and this Arrian regarded as not unlikely, because A emulated Achilles who had cut his hair over the corpse of Patroclus (*Iliad* 23.141–52). The clipping of the horses and the mules belonged probably to that same account; for when Pelopidas was killed the Thessalians cut their own hair and that of their horses (Plu. *Pelop.* 33.2), no doubt in emulation of their own heroic ancestor, Achilles. Arrian remarked that accounts of A's grief were designed to be to A's credit or to A's discredit.[22] In his *Life of Pelopidas* 34.2 Plutarch gave his verdict on A's demonstration of grief at the death of Hephaestion. 'A not only clipped the horses and the mules, but he also removed the battlements from the walls, so that the cities

---

[20] See Hamilton *C* 209 and Mossman 91. Plutarch is dismissing the story as false.

[21] The death of Heracles was celebrated annually at this time. There is irony in the fact that A considered himself a rival to Heracles and that he was killed by 'a Heracles-beaker' on the anniversary.

[22] Arr. 7.14.3, making it clear that the accounts were generally fictitious. He gave what he regarded as historical facts at 7.14.8–10.

might seem to be mourning ... but that was a despot's order and the actions were carried out under strong compulsion ... a parade of barbaric bombast, extravagance and conceit.' In this connection Plutarch associated A with Dionysius, the tyrant of Syracuse. At 72.5 he recorded as an example of such extravagance the expenditure of 10,000 talents which A intended to lay out for the funerary monuments.

The consultation of the oracle of Ammon links 72.3 with 75.3, where A 'ended his period of mourning on receiving from the god the responses about Hephaestion'.[23] It seems likely that Plutarch was following the same source at 75.3.

When we consider the nature of Plutarch's source for this account, we see that it was a hostile source, as in 72.2. On the negative side we can exclude Ptolemy and/or Aristobulus, who were not hostile to A. We can also dismiss the source of Diodorus and Justin, because they both gave 12,000 talents instead of the 10,000 talents of Plutarch, and they both had Hephaestion worshipped 'as a god' (17.115.5f. and 12.12.12). I have argued that their common source was Ephippus, *On the End of Alexander and Hephaestion* (*FGrH* 126; see *THA* 75 and 108). Arrian was aware of all these variants (7.14.7 and 15.8). On the positive side Cleitarchus is the most likely source of Plutarch; for Cleitarchus was hostile to A, emphasised the connection of A with Achilles (*THA* 64f., 109, 128), and represented A as a despot, comparable to the Great King of Persia. He would have known too that Hephaestion was worshipped as a hero at Athens[24] and elsewhere in Greece.

(2) 'A crucified the wretched doctor' (72.3). Plutarch made this act particularly repulsive, because he had reported the absence of the doctor during Hephaestion's over-indulgence and had pinned the blame on Hephaestion for having disobeyed the doctor's orders. Arrian noted that some writers said A hanged the doctor, Glaucias (Plutarch named him as Glaucus), 'some for prescribing a wrong drug, others for having looked on in person while Hephaestion filled himself up

---

[23] Correctly dated by Plutarch, because Arrian reported the arrival of envoys from Ammon shortly before A's illness (7.23.6 and 7.24.1).

[24] Hyperides, *Epit.* 21, and Habicht 28f., 236f. and 272.

with wine' (7.14.4), It is evident that Plutarch's source had his own subtle variants, which portrayed A in a worse light. Once again, the source may be Cleitarchus.

(3) 'Making war a relief from mourning, A went out as if on a manhunt with his hounds and overwhelmed the tribe of Cossaeans, massacring all of them from youth upwards. This was called an offering to Hephaestion as a hero' (72.4, ἐναγισμός). That Plutarch was incorrect about the massacre is certain; for Arrian reported that A reduced the Cossaeans and then founded cities for them, his sources being Ptolemy and/or Aristobulus and Nearchus (7.15.1–3, mentioning Ptolemy, and *Ind.* 40.7, following Nearchus), and Diodorus wrote of the Cossaeans submitting, being granted peace, and having cities founded by A (17.111.4–6), where his source was in my opinion Diyllus (*THA* 74). Neither Arrian nor Diodorus connected the campaign with any offering to Hephaestion. That idea was perhaps inspired by Achilles' sacrifice of twelve Trojan youths at the cremation of Patroclus (*Iliad* 23.175).[25] Here too Cleitarchus is a likely source; for he delighted in representing A as a merciless hunter, indulging in massacre, taking Achilles as his model but far exceeding Achilles in the scale of destruction.

Plutarch's emphasis on gross extravagance led him into a rather pointless digression (72.5–8) – pointless because A rejected the proposal of Stasicrates to sculpt Mt Athos into a gigantic likeness of A, as in *Moralia* 335c–e. The fact that it is pointless suggests that it came from a source other than that which he was using before and after the digression, and I see no means of determining who it was.[26]

The next narrative step came at 73.1 with the arrival of Nearchus, who had sailed 'through the great sea' to the Euphrates, his meeting with A who was advancing towards Babylon, and his report to A that some Chaldaeans had met him and advised A to keep away from Babylon. The idea

[25] Cf. Mossman 91.
[26] The grandiose plan appeared later in Vitruvius 2.1 p. 31,7, and in Eustathius on the *Iliad* 14.229 p. 980 R, but with different names – Deinocrates and Diocles – for the planner.

that Nearchus' famous voyage through the great sea, i.e. the Ocean, was to terminate at the Euphrates was common to Diodorus and Curtius; for in Diodorus 17.104.3 Nearchus while still on the Indus was ordered to meet A in the estuary of the Euphrates, and this order was repeated at Salmus (17.107.1), and a similar order appeared in Curtius at 10.1.16. I argued in *THA* 71 and 156 that the common source of Diodorus and Curtius was probably Cleitarchus. If I am correct, then Plutarch was following Cleitarchus at 73.1. Arrian's account was different; for the meeting between Nearchus' fleet and A took place on the Pasitigris (Arr. 7.5.6 and 7.7.1; *Ind.* 41.5–8). His account is to be preferred, since it came from Ptolemy and/or Aristobulus and Nearchus himself.

Why did the Chaldaeans report to Nearchus and not to A? The answer is provided by Diodorus 17.112.3, 'the leader of the Chaldaeans, one Belephantes ... did not dare to address the king in his terror ... but spoke to Nearchus'. On the other hand, Arrian reported that 'the Chaldaeans took A aside from his Companions and begged him to halt his march to Babylon' (7.16.5). It seems that Plutarch's source had represented A as a terrifying despot, and that this was in line with the ruthless hunting of the Cossaei in 72.4. The source, then, may still be Cleitarchus. 'A paid no heed but proceeded on his way', wrote Plutarch, thus closing the episode. Since other accounts in Diodorus (17.112.4f.), Justin (12.13.3–6) and Arrian (7.16f.) made A try to conform with the request of the Chaldaeans but in the end enter Babylon (see below, p. 300), it is evident that Plutarch simply stated the end-result, A's entry into Babylon.

Plutarch passed next to omens foreshadowing the death of A. These, he wrote, were 'many and disturbed A' (73.6). He cited a couple: crows mauling one another and some falling at his feet as he was entering Babylon, and a domesticated donkey kicking to death the finest and largest of the lions which A was feeding (73.2 and 6).[27] Diodorus too said that 'many paradoxical omens and portents occurred' (17.116.1; resuming 114.5). In my opinion the source Diodorus was following at

[27] Large numbers of animals were kept, no doubt for the Royal Hunt.

that point was Cleitarchus (*THA* 76f.), and the two omens
Plutarch gave at 73.2 and 6 were worthy companions of those
Cleitarchus recorded before the fall of Thebes (Diod. 17.10.2–
5; see *THA* 15 and 26). Plutarch recorded also two omens,
which unlike the two I have cited were reported also by other
writers. I consider each separately.

(1) 'When information was laid against Apollodorus, the
commandant of Babylon, that he had had a victim sacrificed
[to learn] about A, A summoned the diviner, Peithagoras, who
did not deny the affair. A asked how the sacrifice had turned
out. On his saying that the liver had no lobe, A remarked:
"Alas, it's a powerful omen." He did not do Peithagoras
any wrong' (73.3–5). Appian and Arrian both wrote of this
omen. According to Appian, *B.C.* 2.21 (152), Apollodorus was
afraid of A and Hephaestion, and his diviner, Peithagoras,
interpreted the omen of the lobeless liver to mean imminent
death for both. When Hephaestion died, Apollodorus was
afraid that there might be some conspiracy against A, and
so he reported the divination to A, who smiled and asked
Peithagoras what the portent meant. On his reply that it meant
a fatality, A smiled again and commended Apollodorus for his
loyalty and the diviner for his frank speech. It is obvious that
the source of Plutarch was different from the source followed
by Appian. The account of Appian was a shorter version of
what Arrian wrote somewhat later about this affair (17.18.1–4).
Their common source was Aristobulus, whom Arrian cited
as his authority.[28] Plutarch, then, used a source other than
Aristobulus, and in that source he found a hostile approach to
A, who was represented as having been approached by informers. This is compatible with Cleitarchus still being
Plutarch's source.

(2) The second omen occurred when A had stripped for a
game of ball with the young ball-players who were part of his
entourage (cf. 39.5). He was about to dress, when the young
men saw a man seated on the royal throne, silent and wearing
the diadem and the robes of the king (73.7). Diodorus had

---

[28] So too Hamilton *C* 203; cf. G. Wirth in *Historia* 13 (1964) 209f.

A anointing himself with oil when a man, unnoticed by the guards, reached the throne inside the palace and put on A's clothes (17.116.2). Arrian, citing Aristobulus as his authority, had A allocating reinforcements from the Mediterranean and Persian troops to units of the army; and in the course of that operation his empty throne was occupied by a man (7.24.1f.). It seems that each writer followed a different source.[29]

To continue with Plutarch's account, the man was asked who he was.

For long speechless and with difficulty collecting his senses, he gave his name as Dionysius and his race as Messenian. He said he had been brought from the coast on some charge and had been in chains for a long time, but just then Sarapis, standing over him, loosed the chains and led him to this spot with the order that he should take the dress and the diadem, sit down and keep quiet. (73. 8–9)

According to Diodorus A asked the man, but the man made no answer at all (17.116.4). According to Arrian, citing Aristobulus, A ordered that the man be tortured in case he had acted under orders as part of a plot (7.24.3). Again we see that each author had his own separate source.

Plutarch went on to say that he disposed of the man as the diviners ordered (i.e. had him killed). Diodorus reported that A killed the man in accordance with the judgement of the diviners.[30] Arrian did not say what happened to the man in the end.

In my analysis in *THA* 76f. I noted that the climax of Diodorus' account in which A was angry with the Greek philosophers who had persuaded him to disregard the warning of the Chaldaeans and enter Babylon referred back to 17.112.5, a passage ascribed to Diyllus. It is thus probable that Diodorus followed Diyllus for this episode. The much more sensational version of Plutarch with the mysterious silence of the man, his origin in Greece and the miracle worked by Sarapis (like the loosening of Dionysus' chains in *Bacchae*) is certainly appropriate to Cleitarchus.

---

[29] Even in such details as there being guards at the palace in Diodorus' account and there being eunuchs near the throne in Aristobulus' version.

[30] See Hamilton *C* 204 for the suggestion that the man was a 'scapegoat'.

In 74.2–6 Plutarch engaged in a digression which ran far beyond the life of A and had an appendage in 77.2–4. In 74 after the episode of the man occupying the royal throne Plutarch had A suspicious of his Friends and in particular of Antipater and his sons, Iolaus the cupbearer-in-chief and Cassander. In 77.2–4 Iolaus was said by Olympias to have administered poison to A, and Antipater was said by Hagnothemis to have planned the poisoning with Aristotle; and we learn elsewhere that Cassander was said to have brought the poison from Macedonia to Babylon. In the digression Cassander, having come recently (νεωστί) to Babylon, laughed at barbarians doing obeisance to A and had his head bashed against a wall by A. A rather trivial conversation between the two men is recounted, and the point is made that Cassander had a terrible fear of A even when Cassander was ruler of Greece. We shall discuss the source of 74.4–6 when we come to 77.2–4 (below, p. 147).

In 75.1 Plutarch resumed 74.1, A being fearful and apprehensive of the gods in both passages; and now A became obsessed with superstitious dread (δεισιδαιμονία), which Plutarch deplored. In 75.2 A was cheered by the oracular response concerning Hephaestion (from Ammon) and ended his period of mourning for him. Sacrifices, drinking-parties and a feast for Nearchus and company were followed by A taking a bath, which usually preceded his going to bed, but at the request of Medius he went to him to engage in a revel. There after drinking all the next day he began to have a fever (75.3–5). Diodorus was brief: after a further omen, when a swimmer put on A's diadem, the diviners were urging A to make magnificent sacrifices to the gods with all speed but he was invited to go to Medius for a revel (17.117.1) (and did so), the implication being that A failed to make the sacrifices.[31] The source of Diodorus on my analysis was Cleitarchus (*THA* 77). Plutarch, then, was not following Cleitarchus here. Arrian's order of events in 7.24 is close to that of Plutarch: first the man on the throne, then sacrifices to win good results

---

[31] The same motif occurred at 50.7 before the death of Cleitus, a passage we ascribed to Cleitarchus (above, pp. 89–92).

(for Nearchus' next voyage) – some sacrifices being as a result of the oracular response (from Ammon) – then feasting for the Friends (no doubt including Nearchus) with drinking late into the night, and finally, as 'some have written', A wanted to retire to bed but was invited to revel with Medius. In view of this closeness it seems that Plutarch in 75.3f. and Arrian in 7.24.4 were using the same source. It was evidently Aristobulus in Plutarch's case; for, as we have seen above (p. 138), Plutarch turned within this chapter from Cleitarchus to Aristobulus. In Arrian's account, then, Aristobulus was one of the 'some who have written'.

To summarise our conclusions for 72–5, the main source was Cleitarchus, demonstrably in some parts, probably in others and compatibly in others. The passages within 72–5, where Plutarch followed a source other than Cleitarchus, were the proposal to sculpt Mt Athos, the digression on Antipater and Cassander, and the final events leading to his illness with the citation of Aristobulus[32] at the end of 75.

In 76 Plutarch reported 'what is written about the illness in the *Ephemerides*'. We shall discuss his report when we come to that of Arrian on the *Ephemerides* (below, p. 306).

3. A tailpiece (77): suspicion of poisoning

In 77.2 Plutarch said that suspicion of poisoning did not arise in the five years after the death of A, and that 'in the sixth year [317] they say acting upon information Olympias put many to death and scattered the remains of Iolaus' corpse, since he poured the poison [into A's cup]'. Here Olympias and her partisans were clearly the source of the allegation that A was poisoned. A different version appeared in 75.3f.: Aristotle was the prime mover, he discovered and provided the poison – icy water from the Styx, stored in a donkey's hoof – and

---

[32] On the extent of the use of Aristobulus I am closer to the view of Jacoby in *FGrH* 139 F 59 than to that of Tarn 41 n. 5. Hamilton *C* 209 held that Aristobulus was combating the view that A's death was due to excessive drinking; but this is not stated or indeed implied, because Aristobulus had A drinking all day – no doubt in a social manner – and then, when 'madly feverish and thirsty', drinking wine 'exceedingly' (σφόδρα, which goes with πιεῖν, *pace* Perrin).

he instigated Antipater to do the deed (i.e. using his sons
Cassander and Iolaus). Those who gave this account 'say that
one Hagnothemis told the tale on hearing it from Antigonus
the king', i.e. Antigonus Monophthalmus. Thus both versions
originated in the years of conflict after Antipater's death in
319, when Olympias was at odds with Antigonus and with
Cassander. Each version was designed to win support from the
Macedonians rather than from any Greek states. It seems that
Olympias started the propaganda war, and that her accusation
of Antipater and his sons gained some credence in Macedonia.
Antigonus countered by shifting the responsibility onto
Aristotle, the Greek tutor of A, plausibly enough in the eyes
of the Macedonians who believed Callisthenes had inspired
the attempt of the Pages to murder A, and who supposed his
uncle Aristotle would plan to avenge his death.

The first version has survived in Diodorus 17.118.1f., Justin
12.14.1–9, Curtius 10.14–17 and other writers.[33] Diodorus
and Curtius made the point that the power of Antipater and
then of Cassander was such that the poisoning was a matter of
'rumor' (Curt. 10.10.18), and that 'many authors did not dare
to write about the poisoning' (Diod. 17.118.2). Thus the original publication in writing of the charges against Antipater's
family was issued late, probably after Cassander's death in
297.[34] At that time the most accepted historian was Hieronymus of Cardia, and it is certain that Diodorus drew upon him
for book 19.[35] In that book, after describing how Philip
Arrhidaeus and Eurydice were destroyed by Olympias,
Diodorus wrote that 'Olympias killed Nicanor, Cassander's
brother, and demolished the tomb of Iollas, avenging the death
of Alexander, as she said', and that she slaughtered a hundred
leading Macedonians (19.11.8). Plutarch might have been referring to Hieronymus as one of those who 'say that Olympias

---

[33] See Hamilton C 214f. for references.
[34] The phrase of Diodorus 'many authors did not dare' should not be taken to imply
that some authors did dare to publish the accusation; for other reasons may have
been advanced for not publishing, and Curtius' use of the word 'rumor' supports Plutarch's mention of the five years which passed without any suspicion of
poisoning.
[35] See HM III 94–8.

killed many persons and scattered the remains of Iolaus' corpse'. But it is clear that writers other than Hieronymus were responsible for the more detailed and sensational accounts, which are reflected in the works of Diodorus, Curtius and Justin but not in that of Plutarch.

The second version, promulgated by Hagnothemis, who is otherwise unknown, left fewer echoes. Arrian noted points from a variety of accounts (7.27), the first being that the poison for A was sent by Antipater, that it was devised by Aristotle, who was afraid of A because of Callisthenes, and that Antipater's son, Cassander, brought it (to Babylon). It is probable that both versions were incorporated in Satyrus, *Life of Alexander*, which we have suggested that Plutarch used in connection with the death of Philip (above, pp. 10–13). Plutarch may have used Satyrus here.

At this point we have to turn back to 74.2–6, which we noted as a digression (above, p. 144). There the clashes between A and Cassander at Babylon were reported, the presence of men denouncing Antipater was mentioned, and Cassander's defence of his father was ridiculed by A, who said that Cassander had derived his arguments from the sophistic tricks of Aristotle (74.2–4). All this would have been grist to the mill of Satyrus, who attributed the poisoning of A to Antipater and his sons. I suggest, then, that Plutarch drew on Satyrus, *Life of Alexander*, for 74.2–4 and 77.3f. Since Satyrus wrote after the death of Cassander, he might well have included the picturesque detail of Cassander's ineradicable fear of A, which figures in 74.6.

In 77.5 Plutarch recorded the view held by most writers that the story of poisoning was entirely a fabrication (ὅλως ... πεπλάσθαι). He cited as no small proof of their view the fact that A's corpse showed no effects of poisoning and in fact remained pure and fresh for many days.[36] Curtius made the same statement about the condition of A's corpse (he defined Plutarch's many days as seven days), but he warned his reader

---

[36] This was possible if A died from *Malaria tropica*; for death may have occurred considerably later than was thought at the time. See AG^2 304 n. 174.

that he reported rather than believed it (10.10.9–12). We cannot define their source or sources.

In 77.6 Roxane's pregnancy and her prestige with the Macedonians were mentioned, but mainly to cast blame upon Perdiccas, who was 'at once in the position of greatest power'. The charges against Perdiccas are that he was aware of and 'acted with' Roxane in murdering Stateira, whom A had married, and her sister, Drypetis, whom Hephaestion had married, and that he dragged Arrhidaeus around like a puppet of monarchy[37] – Arrhidaeus being king as Philip III. A note on Arrhidaeus was appended to the effect that he was the son of Philip 'by an ignoble, common woman' called Philinna,[38] and that he was not *compos mentis* as the result of a physical illness, which was not spontaneous. 'Indeed they say that in his boyhood he was clearly of a charming and not undistinguished disposition but then he was wrecked by Olympias using drugs and his mind was destroyed.'

Here the text ends. Because the next *Life*, that of Caesar, seems to lack its opening part, it has been suggested that part of the text was lost.[39] If so, it is anyone's guess how Plutarch brought this work to its end. In fact, he had already passed beyond the death of A, and anything more that he had written could only have prolonged this disappointing tailpiece. It seems that Plutarch was enthralled by the propaganda which had been issued by the opponents of Olympias and Perdiccas in the civil war of 321 and had probably been proclaimed by Hagnothemis on the instructions of Antigonus Monophthalmus.[40] Whether or not Plutarch was hinting at Hagnothemis and Antigonus in his phrase 'they say' (77.8), he warned his reader that he did not vouch for the truth of their statements about Philip III.

[37] Or literally as someone playing a mute part in a play; see Hamilton *C* 217, citing Plu. *Moralia* 791c with the manuscript reading.

[38] She was said to have been a dancing-girl in Athen. 578a, citing Ptolemy, *History of Philopator* (*FHG* 3.168), and also a prostitute (Just. 9.8.2 and 13.2.11). In the case of Justin 9.8.2 I argued in *THA* 90–3 that Justin's source was Cleitarchus.

[39] See Hamilton *C* 217.

[40] Hagnothemis was probably a close friend of Antigonus rather than a writer. For an example of Antigonus' technique see Diod. 19.61.1f. and *HM* III 148.

9

ATTRIBUTIONS AND DEDUCTIONS

1. Attributions

The attributions which we have suggested for the chapters which are based on a narrative sequence are as follows:

2.2	Love match of Philip and Olympias	Satyrus
2.3–6	Dreams and omens	Eratosthenes etc.
3.5–9	Birth of A and omens	Timaeus, Hegesias
4.8–6.8	Boyhood and Bucephalus	Marsyas Macedon
9.5–10	Quarrel with Philip	Satyrus
9.11–10.5	Demaratus, Pixodarus	Satyrus
10.6f.	Olympias and Philip's death	Satyrus
11	Balkans and Thebes	Cleitarchus
12	Timoclea	Aristobulus
13	Athens, A's remorse	Cleitarchus
14.1–5	Diogenes	Onesicritus
14.6f.	Delphi	Cleitarchus
14.8f.	Portents	Aristobulus
15.1–3	A's forces	Aristobulus, Onesicritus, Duris etc.
15.3–7	A's gifts to Friends	Cleitarchus
16	The River Granicus	Aristobulus and another
17–20.4	Courses open to A and Darius	Cleitarchus, Letter, 'Many historians', Menander, Aristobulus
20.1–9	Issus	Aristobulus, Chares, Letter
20.10–21.4 and 24.1–3	Darius' family	Cleitarchus
24.4–mid–5	Advance to Tyre	—
24.5–9, 25.1–3	Omens	Aristobulus, Cleitarchus, Chares
24.10–14	Antilebanon	Chares
25.4f.	Gaza	Aristobulus
25.6–26.2	Spoils	Onesicritus etc.
26.3–7	'Pharos' dream	Satyrus via Heracleides Lembus
26.8–10	Barley at Alexandria	Cleitarchus
26.11–27.9	Siwa	Cleitarchus, Callisthenes, Herodotus
29.1–6	Festivals in Phoenicia	Chares
29.7–9	Darius' letter and envoys	—
30	Darius on Stateira's death	Cleitarchus

31.1–5	A mock battle	Cleitarchus, Eratosthenes
31.6–32.3	Pre-Gaugamela	Cleitarchus
32.4–7,		
33.1–11	Gaugamela	Cleitarchus, Callisthenes etc.
32.8–12	A's armour and Bucephalus	Chares
34	A and the Greeks	Cleitarchus
35–6	Naphtha	Cleitarchus, Theophrastus, Dinon etc.
37.1f.	Lycian guide	Cleitarchus
37.3	A's order	*Ephemerides* or Letter
37.4–7	A at Susa	Cleitarchus, another
38	A at Persepolis	Cleitarchus versus Aristobulus, others
42.5–43.7	Pursuit, deaths of Darius and Bessus	Cleitarchus
44.1f.	Caspian Sea	? Cleitarchus or Aristobulus
44.3–5	Theft of Bucephalus	Marsyas Macedon
45.1–3	A's Asian dress	Eratosthenes
45.4–6	Macedonians admire A	Aristobulus
46	Amazon Queen	Cleitarchus, Letter, many named
47.1–4	A persuades Macedonians	Cleitarchus
47.5–12	A and Asians	Aristobulus
48–49.7	Philotas suspected	Aristobulus
49.8–15	Philotas, Parmenio, Antipater	Plutarch's choice of items
50–52.7	Cleitus	Aristobulus
52.8–55.1	Callisthenes	Hermippus (53.3–54.2), Chares
55.2–8	Pages' Conspiracy	Plutarch's choice, 2 Letters
55.9	Death of Callisthenes	Aristobulus, Ptolemy, Chares etc.
56	Death of Demaratus	—
57.1f.	Burning of baggage	Aristobulus
57.4	Omen of A's successor	? Satyrus
57.5–9	Spring of oil	Aristobulus, Letter, another
59.1–4	Taxiles	Onesicritus
59.5–8	Indian mercenaries, philosophers	Cleitarchus
60.1–11	Battle of Hydaspes	Letters, Onesicritus
60.12–14	Porus' elephant and reply	Chares
60.15f.	Lands of Porus and Philip	Onesicritus
61.1f.	Bucephalus	Onesicritus, 'most' including Cleitarchus and Chares
61.3	Peritas	Sotion
62	Army turns back	Eratosthenes
63	City of Malli	Aristobulus
64	Interrogation of Gymnosophists	Megasthenes
65.1–3	Onesicritus and philosophers	Onesicritus
65.4–8	Philosophers' questions	—
66.1f.	Indus estuary	Aristobulus
66.3–7	A to Gedrosia	Cleitarchus
67	Revel in Carmania	Cleitarchus

67.8	Bagoas	Dicaearchus
68.1–5	Confused narrative	Plutarch's composition
68.6–7	A and some satraps	—
69.1	Bounty to Persian women	Ctesias
69.2f.	Ochus and Cyrus' Tomb	—
69.4–5	Inscription on the Tomb	Aristus
69.6–8	Death of Calanus	Cleitarchus
70.1f.	Death of drinkers	Chares
70.3	Susa weddings and feasts	Plutarch's composition
70.4–6	Antigenes	—
71	Opis	Cleitarchus
72.1–5	Mourning for Hephaestion	Cleitarchus
72.5–8	Athos	—
73–74.1	Omens near Babylon	Cleitarchus
74.2–6	A and Cassander	Satyrus
75.1	Resumes 74.1	Cleitarchus
75.2–4,6	Onset of illness	Aristobulus
75.5	Beaker of Heracles	Cleitarchus
76–77.1	Illness and death of A	*Ephemerides*
77.2–8	Poison and conflict	Satyrus

In this summary I have written 'Aristobulus', whereas in my analysis I had 'Aristobulus and/or Ptolemy'. That occurred in reference to 20.1, 2, 4 and 6 (advice of Amyntas to Darius), 24.5 (A's dream of Heracles at Tyre), 25.4f. (omen at Gaza), 48–49.7 (part of the Philotas episode), and 57.1f. (burning of baggage). In these cases the probability is that Aristobulus rather than Ptolemy was being followed by Plutarch, because we know that he made extensive use of Aristobulus.

2. Deductions for the narrative passages

The writing of ancient history was not regarded by Greek and Roman authors as a combination of research into primary sources (original documents, inscriptions, archaeological data etc.) and of exposition in a literary style. The general attitude was that that research had been done at the time by contemporary and near-contemporary writers, of whom there had been a plethora during the life and after the death of A. Where the writer of what had become ancient history exercised his originality was in choosing which of the earlier accounts he would adopt to be the backbone of his own work. Once that choice was made, he tailored the chosen version (or versions if he was following more than one account) to fit his own approach and to accord to some extent with his own style. What he finally produced was his own composition. There was no expectation that he would name the author (or authors) of the chosen version (or versions). Indeed Arrian was almost unique in doing so for his *Anabasis Alexandrou*.[1] However, when the writer found himself at odds with his chosen version (or versions) and offered instead of or alongside it a point from another account, he was apt to name that account or the author of it. We have seen many examples of this practice in our analysis of the narrative passages. A notable one, because it is common to Plutarch and Arrian, is the naming of the *Ephemerides* – an account which neither author was using for his main narrative – and it was named to offset the widely held view that A had been poisoned.

'Accounts of A differ one from another', wrote Arrian, 'and there is no one about whom more persons have written and with a wider degree of disagreement.' How far was Plutarch familiar with those accounts? Many of them were available for purchase, when he was writing the *Life*, probably in the decade A.D. 100–10; for we learn from Aulus Gellius (*c*. 130–80) that he saw 'bundles of books for sale' ('fasces, librorum venalium') at Brundisium and amongst them the works of Ctesias, Onesicritus and Hegesias – three authors to whom Plutarch referred in the *Life*.[2] State and city libraries were well stocked.[3] When Diodorus was in Alexandria in Egypt, he consulted and based his account of the Red Sea on 'the Royal Records in Alexandria' (3.38.1), i.e. on what some authors called the *Ephemerides* of the King.[4] One of those records was

---

[1] This practice was not limited to the Alexander-histories. Diodorus did not continually name Hieronymus as his source for the period after A, nor did Livy continually name Polybius as his source in what we call Livy's Polybian books.

[2] Gellius 9.4.1–3 = *FGrH* 134 T 12.

[3] Plu. *Demosth.* 2.1 mentioned the facilities which were available in cities of some size.

[4] B. Bommelaer in the Budé edition of Diod. III p. xvii 'il est donc difficile d'écarter totalement l'idée d'une consultation personnelle des archives par Diodore'. It would have been absurd for Diodorus to have written that he had consulted the Records

the *Royal Ephemerides* of Alexander, on which Strattis of
Olynthus wrote a lengthy commentary, probably at Alexandria (*FGrH* 118 T 1). There were, no doubt, copies of those
Ephemerides elsewhere, because they were of great interest.
Even Strattis' commentary was not a single version; for fragments of a copy of it dating to the second century B.C. have
been found in Egypt.[5] Plutarch certainly read very widely
indeed in both general history and in local history of the Greek
and Roman periods.[6] Thus where Plutarch cites an author by
name the probability is that he had direct knowledge of that
author's work.

What authors did writers choose? Diodorus, writing a universal history and making A his centrepiece, followed a competent Hellenistic historian, Diyllus of Athens, for a straight-
forward factual account, and he adopted a sensational writer,
Cleitarchus, to highlight the major incidents (see *THA* 50 and
79); then he added an occasional item from elsewhere, such as
the funeral of Hephaestion from Ephippus. Of course, he did
not name Diyllus and Cleitarchus; for what he had taken had
become Diodorus' own narrative. Next, we infer from an
analysis of Justin's epitome that Trogus chose Cleitarchus and
Satyrus, both lively writers, for his main narrative of A, and
he occasionally drew on several other writers, such as Dinon
(*THA* 114 and 163). Curtius read very widely in Greek and
Latin literature and composed his own speeches and some
other passages out of his head; but like the others, he had to
follow one narrative, and he therefore chose Cleitarchus for
Macedonian affairs and Diyllus for Greek affairs. He drew
also for incidents on Aristobulus, Onesicritus, Hegesias and
Timagenes, and probably on Chares and Marsyas Macedon,
and others besides (*THA* 162f.). Curtius did not give the
names of his narrative sources; for the narrative was very
much his own. It was when he disagreed with Cleitarchus

---

if none such had existed at Alexandria; and particularly foolish if the local scholars
had never seen him in the Library. The contrary view, however, was advanced by
W. Peremans in *Historia* 16 (1967) 432ff.

[5] See H*PF*.

[6] For the extent of his reading see Stadter *P* 133.

that he named him as the author of an untrue statement
(9.5.21) and of another statement which was at least exaggerated (9.8.15). Plutarch differed from these three predecessors
in that he was writing a biography and they had written
histories, albeit dominated by A but including Greek affairs.
Even so he needed a main narrative source or sources, and
we have identified them as principally Cleitarchus and sometimes Aristobulus. In addition he drew on many authors for
incidents.

Plutarch's method in composing his main narrative may be
illustrated by a study of chapters 11 to 13 (from A's accession
to the aftermath of Thebes' destruction). The author whom he
followed for 11 and 13 was, as we have seen, Cleitarchus,
and something of Cleitarchus' florid style and sensationalism
reaches us in Plutarch's version. Chapter 12, being the story
of Timoclea and A, was very different in style and in tone.
Plutarch's writing here was restrained and artistic, especially
in the rhythms, which varied from iambic and spondaic runs
to occasional tribrachs (συγγενόμενος, δεδεμένη, μεγαλόφ-
ρων). The story is so narrated that the rape of Timoclea at the
start of chapter 12 is a climax to the atrocities of chapter 11,
and the clemency of A at the end leads on to other acts of
clemency in chapter 13. Thus Plutarch has certainly reshaped
this story to fit the context in the *Life*.[7]

In this case we can see what the story was like when it
was not in this context. For in *Mulierum Virtutes* 24 (*Mor.*
259d–260d) Plutarch described the episode as a self-standing
example of a woman's courage, and it was this version (not
that in the *Life*) which was adopted and abbreviated by
Polyaenus[8] for his list of women's courageous acts (8.40). The
order of narration was different, and there were differences of
detail: Theagenes fighting at Chaeronea is at the start (it came
at the end in the *Life*), he shouts 'pursue to Macedonia', the
rapist is a Macedonian officer named Alexander (a Thracian
in the *Life*), Timoclea is helped by maidservants (she is alone

[7] So Stadter *P* 114 it 'has been made a part of the continuous narrative'.
[8] The comparison is made by Stadter *P* for all the instances of such courage in the
list of Polyaenus.

in the *Life*), A had ordered no killing of Thebans, and A let all related to her go free (her children in the *Life*). This version was undoubtedly closer to the original account than that in the *Life*, for which, as P. A. Stadter remarked, 'Plutarch reshaped his source's account in accord with the context in which he wished to place it and his own remarkable narrative skill.'[9]

Neither in the *Life* nor in the *Mulierum Virtutes* did Plutarch name the source of the Timoclea story, which had become his own story and which could be told in different ways by him. It was purely incidentally that he referred to 'what Aristobulus wrote about Timoclea' (*Mor.* 1093c), and thus revealed that he had taken the story from Aristobulus. Equally Plutarch did not name the source from which he derived the material of chapters 11 and 13. Indeed throughout the *Life* he named the source of a narrative passage only twice: Chares for 24.10–14 (a foray into the Antilebanon) and the *Ephemerides* for 76 (the illness of A). He was probably uneasy about the historicity of Chares' episode, and he wanted the authority of the *Ephemerides* to support his denial of the rumour that A had been poisoned. Once this method of composition for the narrative passages is realised, we can dismiss as unsound the supposition that Plutarch did not use Cleitarchus because he cited him only twice and that for minor points in the *Life*.[10]

We turn next to the practice of Plutarch in providing the names of sources in the *Life*. As we have said, he did so not for the backbone of the narrative but for occasional additions and for points of difference from his main source. We may take as an example the narrative sections which ran from the capture of Darius' family to the enemy in flight at Gaugamela (20.10 sporadically to 33). The main source of this narrative was Cleitarchus, as we have seen. At 21.9 the main narrative is concerned with A's continence towards the Persian women except in the case of Barsine, with whom alone he had inter-

---

[9] Stadter *P* 139. See also 114 'in *Mul. Virt.* 24 he preserved the fuller dimensions and the style of his original'.

[10] A common supposition, e.g. in Stadter *P* 113 n. 291 'it is furthermore most unlikely that Plutarch could have used Cleitarchus [in the *Life*] in any case; he cites him only twice and in neither case directly'.

course 'at the urging of Parmenio, as Aristobulus says'. This advice was evidently not mentioned by Cleitarchus. Plutarch added it and named his authority. At 27.3 the narrative tells of crows leading the laggards by daylight on the way to Siwa. 'Most surprising of all, as Callisthenes says, they summoned the stragglers by night and put them on track by their cawings.' This night-time cawing was an addition to Cleitarchus' narration of marvels. At 31.5 the victor in the single combat was rewarded by A with twelve villages and permission to wear Persian dress. 'That, at any rate, is what Eratosthenes has recorded.' Here Plutarch justified what may have seemed an unlikely form of reward by citing Eratosthenes, an expert on the nature of Persian dress.

At 33.1 the narrative had A lead his men into battle, he holding his lance in his left hand and appealing to the gods with his right hand. The addition comes: 'as Callisthenes says, praying that if he was really descended from Zeus the gods should defend and strengthen the Greeks'. This was an addition to the preliminaries which Cleitarchus had provided. At 33.10, when A had answered Parmenio's request for help and Darius thus had a clear start for his flight, Plutarch reported that Parmenio was generally blamed for having been 'sluggish and incompetent'. He gave alternative explanations: 'either old age was already weakening his audacity somewhat, or the authority and the massiveness, as Callisthenes says, of A's power made him sullen and resentful'. Here the order of words (which I have preserved from the Greek text) makes it clear that the first alternative was in the narrative source and the second alternative was cited from Callisthenes.[11]

When this practice by Plutarch is appreciated, there are no grounds for supposing that the source used by Plutarch for the treatment of the Persian women was Aristobulus.[12] Rather,

---

[11] Parmenio was killed two and a half years before Callisthenes was arrested. Within that time Callisthenes may well have put out a report such as this at the request of A. Hamilton C 90 translated ὄγκον as 'arrogance'; but one cannot see Callisthenes offending A with such a derogatory sense of the word.

[12] As for instance in Hamilton C 54 'Plutarch here certainly follows the version of Aristobulus'.

the citation of Aristobulus by name shows that the main source was not Aristobulus. The same holds for the other three citations. Eratosthenes was not the source of the single combat,[13] and Callisthenes was not the source either of the march to Siwa[14] and the reception by the priest, or of the preliminaries to and the opening of the Battle of Gaugamela,[15] or of the criticism of Parmenio on the grounds of old age.

3. *Ephemerides* and *Epistolai*

One narrative source used by both Plutarch and Arrian was the *Ephemerides* (76.1 and 77.1) or *Royal Ephemerides* (7.25.1, 26.1 and 26.2).[16] This source was treated like any other in that Plutarch and Arrian tailored its account to fit their own requirements and their own styles.[17] Plutarch concentrated on 'the course of the illness' (τὰ περὶ τὴν νόσον); and he went on to report the entry of the soldiers after A became speechless and the names of two Companions sleeping in the temple of Sarapis. Arrian did not limit his account to the course of the illness; he therefore reported more of A's dealings with others, and he named more of the Companions who slept in the temple of Sarapis. This selection was in accord with the writers' claims, Plutarch that he was writing a biography (1.1–3) and Arrian that he was giving a true record of events (*Preface*; cf. 6.11.2). In regard to style Plutarch and Arrian were poles apart. Each moulded to his own style the material which he had adopted from the *Ephemerides*. For example, Plutarch used finite tenses, especially the graphic imperfect indicative tense, and he avoided hiatus except with the definite article. Arrian put the material into the accusative and infinitive throughout 7.25, varied his method in 7.26, and used much

---

[13] Jacoby printed the whole chapter of Plutarch as F 29 of Eratosthenes (*FGrH* 241).

[14] Jacoby in *FGrH* 124 F 14 printed 27.3 as well as 27.4 as a fragment of Callisthenes.

[15] See a discussion of Callisthenes as a possible source in 'The Battle of Gaugamela' by A. M. Devine in *The Ancient World* 13 (1986) 87–9.

[16] See H*RJ*.

[17] In H*RJ* 145 I argued that their accounts were both from the same passage in the *Ephemerides*. See further below, p. 307.

hiatus in both sections and in particular violent hiatus[18] (e.g. Μηδίῳ αὐτόν, κἀκεῖ αὖθις, πλοῦ αὖθις). Neither of them was quoting verbatim, αὐτοῖς ὀνόμασι. When Plutarch said that most of what he had written was κατὰ λέξιν (77.1), he indicated that he had used most of the original phraseology and had put the rest in his own words. Each was a conscious stylist. When Arrian wrote of Homer immortalising Achilles and of his own endeavour to make A famous (1.12.1–5), he was laying claim himself to the highest stylistic excellence.

Another source of material was *Epistolai*. Ancient writers were aware that there existed both genuine letters and fictional letters, the latter being a recognised literary form. The King's Letters were sometimes inscribed for public viewing (some survive, e.g. in *Arch. Eph.* 1934–5.117). Some genuine letters in Alexander-histories were derived from the *Royal Ephemerides*, in which the Chief Secretary had recorded at the time letters both from and to the king (as we learn for A from Plutarch's *Life of Eumenes* 2.3) and details of diplomatic negotiations (e.g. Polyaen. 4.6.2 for an Antigonus). A letter concerning drainage work in the Copaïs area from a Greek engineer to A, mentioned casually by Strabo (407), was no doubt genuine and came from the *Ephemerides*. Arrian cited a letter from Darius to A and a letter from A to Darius,[19] which he certainly regarded as genuine. He reported the first in a paraphrased summary (2.14.1–3), and the second *in extenso* but not necessarily verbatim. A letter, allegedly from Olympias to A, which was mentioned by Diodorus in a passage where he was following Cleitarchus (17.32.1; see *THA* 41), was fictional. It warned A to beware of Alexander Lyncestes and probably also of his doctor Philip, and it was said by Diodorus to have led to the arrest of the former.[20]

---

[18] For the effect of this stylistic feature see D. H. *De Comp. Verb.* 12 and my remarks in *CQ* 2 (1952) 129.

[19] There is no reason to question the genuineness of these letters. Bosworth *C* 232f. thinks that Arrian's source may have been Callisthenes and not 'the archives', i.e. the *Ephemerides*. Yet Arrian's declared sources were not Callisthenes but Ptolemy and Aristobulus, and he did not cite the two letters as *legomena*. See below, p. 222.

[20] See Goukowsky 189 and my arguments in *THA* 41f.

Plutarch mentioned more than thirty such *Epistolai*, which he evidently thought to be genuine. They were used mainly in the reflective passages to exemplify A's personal qualities. We shall consider here only those cited in the narrative passages. A letter addressed by A to Craterus, Attalus and Alcetas concerning the confession of the Pages (55.6) is genuine, since a forger would not have known that these three officers were involved in a separate operation at that time,[21] and it probably carries with it the second letter on this subject, addressed by A to Antipater (55.7).[22] Then a letter from A to Antipater, in which A regarded the spring of oil as a good omen (57.8), was mentioned casually by Athenaeus (42f); it is generally regarded as genuine,[23] because one cannot see any motive for a forgery. On the same grounds one may accept as genuine A's letter to Antipater specifying privileges for returning veterans in Macedonia (71.8). Moreover, this letter was evidently that carried by Craterus, containing 'written orders', of which a copy was found in the *Royal Journal* and discussed by the Army Assembly at Babylon[24] (Diod. 18.4.1f.).

I have argued for the genuineness of the letter in which A 'himself' (37.3 αὐτός) mentioned the reason for ordering the killing of 'those who were being caught' in the operation at the Persian Gates (see *AG*[2] 167f.).[25] The order will have been recorded in the *Royal Journal*. Plutarch did not say to whom A was writing, but it may well have been to Antipater; for he seems to have kept Antipater well posted by letter, for instance on meeting the Scythian king (46.3) and on persuading a section of the Macedonian army to proceed further (47.3), both being letters which may well be genuine.[26] From this

---

[21] So Hamilton *L* 15f. and 18; Hamilton *C* lx; and see above, p. 98.
[22] Hamilton *L* 16 inclined towards acceptance; I am more positive on p. 99 above.
[23] Hamilton *L* 16f. and above, p. 103.
[24] This point was not noted by Hamilton *L* 18, whose verdict was *non liquet*. See *HM* III 20 for A's orders to Craterus and *AG*[2] 281ff. for the genuineness of these orders.
[25] See above, p. 71, where I argue that Hamilton *L* 14 misapplied the letter to Persepolis, in which context he thought it to be 'doubtful' as regards authenticity.
[26] Hamilton *L* 14 seems to regard the first as genuine and the second as an open question. He noted that Curtius was aware of this letter at 6.4.1; for the words of the soldiers 'iubentium quocumque vellet ducere' are echoed in those of Plutarch ὅποι βούλεται τῆς οἰκουμένης ἄγειν. See above, p. 80.

last letter Plutarch cited 'almost verbatim' (σχεδὸν αὐτοῖς ὀνόμασιν). He reported another letter from A to Antipater about the Battle of Issus, in order to correct a statement by Chares (20.9). Similarly a letter from A to Olympias about the responses A received at Siwa was cited as a corrective of the statements of 'most writers' (27.8). Both these letters may be accepted as genuine.[27]

A letter from Darius and A's reply to it (29.7–9) coincide so well with the report of these negotiations in Arrian 2.25.1–3 that the contents of the letters may be accepted as genuine. However, Plutarch misapplied them to a later time (see above p. 62); thus he derived them not from Ptolemy and/or Aristobulus but from his narrative source who set the date, perhaps Cleitarchus (see above, p. 64).[28] Two other letters seem to have been included in narratives which Plutarch was adopting: one from A to Leonidas which accompanied a gift of incense (25.8), and the other from Parmenio to A at the time of his illness at Tarsus (19.5). The author of the first narrative was most probably Onesicritus. The narrative in Plutarch is remarkable for supposedly verbatim citations of Leonidas' words to A as a boy and of A's words in the letter. Presumably Onesicritus saw this letter; for it would hardly have been included in the *Ephemerides*.[29] Parmenio's letter 'from camp' (19.5), where he will have been commanding the army in the absence of A, was historical in itself, but it was set in a sensational narrative which emanated from Cleitarchus (see above, p. 48).[30] At 34.2 Plutarch mentioned A writing to the Greeks (of Asia and some islands) and to the Plataeans after the

---

[27] Hamilton *L* 13 seemed to see no good reason to doubt the authenticity of these two letters.

[28] The letters derived from Ptolemy and/or Aristobulus were in my opinion genuine. The confused accounts of the negotiations are outlined in *THA* 99f. Hamilton *L* 13 saw no good reason for doubting the authenticity of Plutarch's letters from Darius and from A, and in *C* 77 he suggested that Plutarch made 'direct use of Callisthenes'. He refers there to earlier literature.

[29] See above, p. 58. Hamilton *L* 13 found it 'impossible to say whether ... genuine or not'.

[30] The Alexander-historians apart from Diodorus record the sending of a letter. Hamilton *L* 13 'Plutarch has taken the whole incident, including Parmenio's letter, from the historical source which he is following at this point.'

victory at Gaugamela. It seems that he took this from his narrative source, probably Cleitarchus (see above, pp. 66–70), rather than from any letters.[31]

Finally we turn to the account of the Battle of the Hydaspes, which Plutarch introduced with the following words. 'Of the action with Porus A himself has written in the letters; for he says' etc., what follows being in the accusative and infinitive (60.1 αὐτὸς ἐν ταῖς ἐπιστολαῖς ... γέγραφε; cf. 60.11 αὐτὸς ἐν ταῖς ἐπιστολαῖς). The expression with the plural 'in the letters' is significant. It was used otherwise only at 17.8: 'A himself says in the letters' (αὐτὸς ... ἐν ταῖς ἐπιστολαῖς). All other passages in Plutarch mentioned a letter in the singular.[32] Thus Plutarch referred at 60.1 and 11 and at 17.8 (concerning his march in Pamphylia) to a collection of letters which he called 'the letters'. Such collections certainly existed, not only of A's letters but also of Antipater's letters, and there is no doubt that many of them were fictional.[33] As I have argued (above p. 44), the account of the Battle of the Hydaspes based on this collection is fictitious. The letter at 17.8 was cited from the collection by Plutarch in order to deny the miraculous interpretation of A's passage along the coast of Pamphylia; it is uncertain whether that letter is genuine or not.[34]

It seems, then, that the majority of the letters mentioned by Plutarch in the narrative passages were authentic and only a few were fictitious. They were included sometimes for their intrinsic interest (e.g. negotiations of Darius with A), and sometimes to correct or challenge a report which figured in Plutarch's main source (e.g. in Pamphylia and at Siwa). He found some of these letters in his narrative source (e.g. on A's

---

[31] The letter to the Plataeans was followed later by a proclamation at the Olympic Games of 328 which Plutarch mentioned in *Arist.* 11.9. Hamilton *L* 14 'more probably Plutarch is following a historical source'.

[32] When he used the plurals γράμματα and ἐπιστολαί in the *Life* (e.g. 39.8 and 42.1), he meant more than one epistle.

[33] See Hamilton *L* 10f. He mentioned that Athenaeus and Hesychius used αἱ ἐπιστολαί for a collection of letters.

[34] Hamilton *L* 12 did not reach a decision. However, he misunderstood the content of the letter (see p. 46 n. 5). Plutarch at 17.6 had referred to 'many of the historians' suggesting a divine intervention; see Hamilton *C* 44 for references and below, p. 313.

illness at Tarsus), three only in a collection or collections (in Pamphylia and at the Hydaspes), and the remainder in his own wide reading. The ultimate source of most of them was no doubt the *Royal Journal of Alexander*, which Plutarch read for the final illness of A and may therefore have read for other purposes. It may be that many letters had been excerpted from the *Royal Journal* by commentators such as Strattis, and that they reached Plutarch via such commentaries.

Our conclusions concerning the method of Plutarch in composing his narrative passages are simple. Plutarch chose one account out of many for a single run of narrative, selected from that account the appropriate material and then reduced it to the dimensions which he required for his biography. Finally he cast it into his own form and style, and the resulting version of events was his own creation.[35] As a general rule he did not name the chosen account which had been the basis of his own version. On the other hand, if he found in another account a piece of information which had not been in the chosen account or was at variance with it, then he might add it to his own version, and in doing so he tended to name that other account (e.g. a Letter or a phrase of Callisthenes). In the course of the next chapter we shall consider why he chose the accounts of certain historians for the basis of his narrative sections. He attached special importance to what he judged to be genuine original documents, the Letters and the *Ephemerides*; and in that judgement we have seen that he was usually right.

---

[35] In chapter 68 Plutarch seems to have written out of his own head instead of adapting a narrative account. The result was incoherence and some confusion. Chapters 74.2–6 and 77.6–8 are little better, because Plutarch was drawing on an anecdotal life of A written by Satyrus.

PART TWO

10

PLUTARCH'S REFLECTIVE PASSAGES AND ALEXANDER'S PERSONALITY

1. Natural endowment and formative factors until the accession of Alexander

In his Introduction Plutarch maintained that the personality of such a man as Alexander or Caesar may be revealed by 'a small incident, a saying or a joke' rather than by a great battle-narrative (1.2). Plutarch should therefore be allowed to 'enter into the indicators of a man's soul (εἰς τὰ τῆς ψυχῆς σημεῖα) and thereby to characterise his life'. Where he was acting on this principle in this *Life*, I have called the passages 'the reflective passages' in contrast to 'the narrative passages'.

The key to Plutarch's characterisation of Alexander's life is provided in chapter 4.1–7. He assumed, as Pindar and many Greek writers had done, that a man's natural endowment (φυά or φύσις), both physical and mental,[1] was the basis of his development. He therefore began his study of A by commenting on A's physique. He took as his sources the statues of Lysippus, the paintings of Apelles and the *Memoirs* of Aristoxenus,[2] which he read directly (ἀνέγνωμεν). This Aristoxenus was ten years or so older than A, joined the school of Aristotle and wrote 'Lives' of some philosophers;

---

[1] Pindar, *O.* 2.86 σοφὸς ὁ πολλὰ εἰδὼς φυᾷ coupled poetic inspiration and physical prowess as due to natural endowment. See C. Gill, 'The question of character-development: Plutarch and Tacitus', *CQ* 33 (1983) 473ff. for Plutarch's views on φύσις.

[2] See Wardman 102 and Hamilton *C* 11.

and his idea of the body being 'tuned' by the soul may have influenced Plutarch in his approach to A.

According to Plutarch A was remarkable for the poise of his neck, the liquidity of his eyes, the fairness of his skin, the ruddiness of his face and particularly of his chest, and the very pleasant aroma of his body (εὐωδία), which imbued his clothing. Plutarch attributed these characteristics 'perhaps' to A's bodily heat; for 'the temperament of his body was hot-blooded and fiery' (πυρώδης). It was this heat which generated the pleasant aroma, 'as Theophrastus supposes'.[3] It was probably from Theophrastus that Plutarch derived his analogy that the hot sun, acting on moist decaying matter, produced the finest perfumes (i.e. in Arabia). 'The bodily heat, so it seems (ὡς ἔοικε), made A both fond of drink and passionate' (4.7 ποτικὸν καὶ θυμοειδῆ). Here we see one aspect of the interaction between body and soul (the latter including one's mind), which underlay Plutarch's theory of personality.

The other aspect of the interaction was illustrated by a description of A as a boy (4.8–11). He had in his mentality a sense of restraint (σωφροσύνη) which enabled him to resist the pull 'of bodily pleasures', despite the fact that he was otherwise 'violent and exceedingly impetuous' (ῥαγδαῖον ... καὶ φερόμενον σφοδρῶς). And he also had a 'desire for honour' (φιλοτιμία) beyond his years, and this desire made him serious in mind and 'magnanimous in spirit' (μεγαλόψυχον). (These were among the mental qualities which were to be seen 'tuning' such bodily urges as his sexual desires at 21.10f. and 22.6.)[4]

Plutarch then turned to anecdotes which illustrated A's physical and mental qualities. His love of honour for himself was not unbridled, like that of Philip, but selective, so that, when being swift of foot he was urged by other boys to compete at the Olympic Games, he replied 'Yes, if I am to have

---

[3] Theophrastus wrote a treatise *De Odoribus*; see Wardman 102 and Hamilton *C* 12 for possible passages in Theophrastus' works. Plutarch made the same points about A in *Mor.* 623e.

[4] These two qualities σωφροσύνη and μεγαλοψυχία were associated with self-control, ἐγκράτεια, in the reported speech of the eunuch to Darius at 30.10.

kings as competitors.' Plutarch did not enlarge here on this cryptic reply; but in *Moralia* 179d it was Philip who urged A to compete and received that answer, and in *Moralia* 331b A showed his bent for philosophy by saying that defeat in an open competition would be defeat of a king by commoners. Thus Plutarch used the same anecdote here to illustrate a different point. And he went on to mention A's aversion to the rougher form of athletics, such as boxing and the pancration, and his delight in competitions of drama, music, recitation, hunting and duelling with sticks. In 5.1–3 Plutarch illustrated A's serious-mindedness and desire to do great things (μεγα-λοπραγμοσύνην) by the story of the Persian envoys being questioned by the boy A (above, p. 20), and by A's fears that Philip's triumphs would leave no opening for A to show his excellence and win glory. He would rather inherit a kingdom which offered not wealth, luxury and enjoyment but struggles, wars and ambitious prospects (5.6). That wish was fulfilled at A's accession when the kingdom was the centre of discontents, enmities and dangers (11.1).

Education was another factor in developing one's natural endowment into an adult personality. Plutarch therefore commented on the qualities of two among many teachers[5] of A – Leonidas and Lysimachus (both were to appear later in the *Life*). Then the story of Bucephalus illustrated A's passionate nature (6.3 περιπαθοῦντος) and his courage at a young age (above, pp. 21f.). The secondary education of A, in whom Philip saw 'a nature (φύσιν) resistant to any form of compulsion (δυσκίνητον) but capable of being led by reason to appropriate action', was entrusted to Aristotle (in 342 B.C. when A became fourteen). The subjects of instruction were a matter of Plutarch's own speculation (ἔοικε) and of inference from a letter of A to Aristotle, quoted from 'a copy' (ἀντίγραφον), and Aristotle's summarised reply – both now regarded as not authentic.[6] Plutarch also thought (δοκεῖ μοι) that A's love of medical theory and of actual healing was due mainly to Aristotle,

---

[5] See Berve I 4 for the names of others.
[6] See Hamilton *C* 19, giving references.

and he looked forward to the concern which A was to show
for the illness of his friends in his letters (as in 41.7). A's love
of literary scholarship and of reading was illustrated by the
Iliad of the Casket (defined in 26.1f.), the text of which had
been revised by Aristotle, and by a list of the books, mainly of
poetry, which were sent by Harpalus to A in Asia. Although
A's affection for Aristotle declined later, his zest for philosophy, innate by nature (ἐμπεφυκώς) and cultivated from the
outset, continued unabated, as was seen from his dealings with
Anaxarchus, Xenocrates, Dandamis and Calanus.

The discharge of the duties laid upon him as regent at the
age of sixteen and at the Battle of Chaeronea[7] at the age of
eighteen won for him the exceeding love of his father (9.4).
However, quarrels ensued between them. Plutarch drew upon
the unsatisfactory work of Satyrus for highly-coloured examples of these quarrels in 9.5–14 and in 10.1–5 (see above, pp.
7–13). He was not prepared to give his own approval to the
report that A had connived in the planned assassination of
Philip (10.6–8).[8]

Thus, although Plutarch had formed a general opinion of
A's personality in his earlier writings in *Moralia* and in his
preliminary reading, he took great trouble at the start of the
Life to define the natural endowment of A in body and mind.
He relied mainly on his own theories of physiognomy and
especially on A's bodily heat as one of the controlling
humours. He drew on his own observation, the *Memoirs* of
Aristoxenus and the ideas of Theophrastus. He chose anecdotes and incidents which supported his own preconceptions,
and he no doubt shaped the narrative to produce the desired
effects. His source for A's boyhood was, we have argued,
Marsyas Macedon, an exact contemporary of A and later
a capable commander – a good choice; and he referred to
Onesicritus for a point about the keeping of the *Iliad* in a
casket under A's pillow. Then Plutarch seems to have relied on
his own reading and knowledge of philosophy to estimate the

---

[7] Plutarch was probably relying on his memory; and he expressed his hesitation about
A being the first to charge the Theban Sacred Band (λέγεται πρῶτος ἐνσεῖσαι).
[8] See above, pp. 8–11.

influence of Aristotle on A. He may well have been shown the Nymphaeum at Mieza[9] and he mentioned 'A's oak' by his home-town Chaeronea. The stories which he took from Satyrus illustrated A's hot blood, passionate nature and fondness of drink, and in the Pixodarus affair A's φιλοτιμία, which demanded that he should have first place after his father. Whatever Plutarch thought of Olympias, he hesitated to think A capable of conniving in parricide.

2. Victories of 335–333 and Alexander's self-mastery (11–23)

Plutarch wrote narrative passages not for their own sake but as illustrations of A's personality in action. He drew therefore on the accounts which seemed best to fit the parameters of A's personality as he had described it in 1–10, but he modified them in his own version for his own purpose. Thus in 11–13 he drew on Cleitarchus for A's impetuosity and speed, his 'most savage and most dismal act' (13.2, the sack of Thebes), the passionate anger which he sated as lions do, and his policy of *Schrecklichkeit* in Greece. Because Cleitarchus was used also by Diodorus (17.8.2–14.4) and Justin (11.3f.),[10] we can see that Plutarch reduced the emphasis on anger and introduced into his version A's 'daring and greatness of mind' (11.4 τολμῇ καὶ μεγαλοφροσύνῃ), gratifying of his allies (11.11), remorse and clemency. Even so, Plutarch wanted to show A in a less terrifying light; so he drew on Aristobulus for the story of Timoclea and A's humane treatment of her and her children.

Plutarch packed a variety of episodes and anecdotes into 14–15. He adopted Onesicritus' account of A's visit to Diogenes and the saying of A 'Indeed, were I not Alexander, I would be Diogenes', in order to illustrate A's love of philosophy. He took from Cleitarchus the stories of A's impetuous violence at Delphi (βίᾳ ... τῆς σπουδῆς) and his excessive gratifying of his friends. Plutarch saw the latter as a further

---

[9] Rediscovered in this century and shown to members of the First Symposium on Ancient Macedonia in 1968.
[10] *THA* 13–16 and 26; 95.

example of A's 'impetuosity and mental preparedness' (ὁρμῇ καὶ παρασκευῇ διανοίας).[11] He obtained from Aristobulus two anecdotes which illustrated A's desire for glory (14.9 and 15.9).

For the Battle of the River Granicus Plutarch drew on Aristobulus, probably because Aristobulus provided two sayings of A and concentrated more on A's actions in the battle than Ptolemy did. A showed here above all his 'mental preparedness' in acting at once and in contradiction to his advisers (as he had done at 11.3f.), his daring impetuosity (16.3 ἐμβάλλει ... ἔδοξε μανικῶς καὶ πρὸς ἀπόνοιαν μᾶλλον ἢ γνώμῃ στρατηγεῖν) and his acting in passion rather than in calculation when he was the first to charge at the Greek mercenaries (16.14 θυμῷ μᾶλλον ἢ λογισμῷ). After the victory A's desire for honour prompted the wording of the inscription on the spoils (16.17 φιλοτιμοτάτην ἐπιγραφήν). Plutarch drew on Aristobulus for the description of the Battle of Issus (20.1–9), because Aristobulus had the anecdote of Amyntas, 'familiar with A's nature', declaring 'Alexander will march against you, indeed is almost already on the march' and represented A as eager to engage (σπεύδων ἀπαντῆσαι). It seems likely that Plutarch himself introduced the figure of Fortune favouring A (20.5 τῇ συντυχίᾳ; 20.7 ἡ τύχη πάρεσχεν), because he had written on the Fortune of A in *Moralia*.

The intervening narrative, 17–19, is far from consecutive. A managed to restrain his impetuosity (17.3) and was encouraged by a prophetic tablet to follow the slower course of conquering the coastal area first. As he passed along the Pamphylian coast Plutarch mentioned the statements of many historians that the sea gave way before him, and he then cited a letter of A which made no such marvel of it (17.8).[12] Plutarch preferred to write of a drunken after-dinner spree by A, in which A put garlands on the statue of a distinguished local philosopher;[13] for this illustrated Plutarch's regard for a

---

[11] Perrin omitted διανοίας altogether. 'Mental preparedness' was one reason for it being difficult to deflect A from his purpose.

[12] See above, p. 46.

[13] See Hamilton *C* 45 for this philosopher, Theodectes.

piece of fun (παιδιά τις) as an indication of personality (1.2), and A's regard for philosophy and Aristotle. The treatment of A by Philip the doctor was described in such a way as to stress A's goodwill towards and trust in the doctor (19.7).

At 20.12f. Plutarch told the story of A bathing in Darius' gold-fitted bathroom and saying in jest to his Companions: 'This is what it was to be king, it seems.'[14] Thus A mocked Darius' priorities and showed his own disregard for luxury. A's courtesy to the royal ladies is praiseworthy but puzzling because the wife of Darius, 'it is said', was the most beautiful of all royal women and her daughters were equally lovely. Yet A kept his hands off them. Plutarch advanced his own explanation: A, as it seems, reckoned it more kingly to be master of himself than to be master of the women (21.7). Nor was A lacking in the sexual urge; for he said in jest that Persian women were torments to the eyes and yet he passed them by, parading by contrast his own self-mastery and restraint (ἀντεπιδεικνύμενος ... ἐγκρατείας καὶ σωφροσύνης).

A's resistance to luxury in the bathroom and the charms of the captive ladies prompted Plutarch to write a reflective passage, 22–3. He began with letters by and to A which were in his judgement genuine. The first exchange showed a Macedonian officer forwarding an offer of two pretty boys for sale, and A reprimanding the officer and ordering him to get rid of the procurer. The second exchange was on the same subject and had the same result. Then A wrote to Parmenio with an order to execute, if they were found guilty, two Macedonian soldiers who were reported to have raped the women of two mercenary soldiers. This was a matter of military discipline. But in his letter to Parmenio A wrote this phrase (κατὰ λέξιν): 'So far from having seen Darius' wife or desired to see her, it will be found that I have not allowed anyone to speak of her beauty.'[15] Indeed A used to say that sleep and sex made him conscious of his being a mortal (22.6).

Having demonstrated A's restraint in sexual matters, both

---

[14] See above, p. 51.
[15] Because Plutarch accepted this letter as genuine, he had not included a visit by A and Hephaestion to the royal ladies (see above, p. 52).

heterosexual and homosexual, Plutarch went on to other forms of self-mastery. In conversation with the Carian Queen, Ada, A rejected her offer of lavish titbits and quoted his tutor's precepts: the best preparation for breakfast was a night-march, and for dinner a light breakfast. And he went on to say that this tutor, Leonidas, used to check in his wardrobe that there was nothing luxurious or special which had been sent by his mother. Next, 'he was less given to wine than he was thought to be' because of the long time he spent over each glass, in conversation when he had leisure; for nothing distracted him when he had a job in hand. Plutarch then gave a specimen leisure-day: sacrifice to the gods on rising, breakfast sitting, daylight hours spent in hunting, judging, arranging a matter of war, or reading. If he was on a leisurely march, he would practise archery[16] or mounting and dismounting from a chariot in motion. Often for sport he used to hunt foxes and birds, 'as can be gathered from the *Ephemerides*'. Dinner at nightfall was well served and well provided, and he prolonged the drinking for conversation, 'as has been said' (23.6). After the drinking he bathed and slept, sometimes until midday, sometimes until the evening (23.8). In 23.7 there was a digression about A, when he was drinking, becoming over-boastful and letting himself be 'ridden' by his flatterers, which annoyed the better guests.

Plutarch then went back to the subject of titbits, only to say that A gave them all away to his Companions and kept none for himself. But his dinners were magnificent. The cost rose with his military successes to 10,000 drachmae both for a dinner he provided and for a dinner to which he was invited.

What were the sources of this reflective passage? In 22–23.2 Plutarch seems to be drawing on letters and incidents which he had already mentioned in the *Moralia*. Thus the offer of the pretty boys and the reprimand occurred in *Mor*. 333a (but only one boy) and 1099d. The saying on sleep and sex being signs of A's mortality was explained in *Mor*. 65f and 717f.[17]

---

[16] Probably for use in hunting birds and deer, since A did not carry a bow in battle.
[17] At *Mor*. 65f 'A said that he did not believe those who proclaimed him to be a god in the matter of sleep especially and sexual intercourse.'

The conversation with Queen Ada was mentioned thrice but without the appendage of Leonidas at *Mor.* 127b, 180a and 1099c. Then the moderate use of wine was part of a discussion at *Mor.* 337f and 623e. One may conclude that Plutarch was writing here either from his own memory or after consultation of the *Moralia*. The only letter in chapter 22 which did not figure in the *Moralia* was that to Parmenio. As there are other instances of execution for breaches of discipline in A's army,[18] there is no reason to regard this letter as unhistorical.

Chapter 23.3–6 and 8 is not an echo of the *Moralia*, nor of any writing by anyone else. Plutarch must have turned to a different source. At 23.4 he named his source as the *Ephemerides*. Commentators seem to have thought that Plutarch obtained from the *Ephemerides* only the hunting of foxes and birds;[19] but it is much more likely that Plutarch went to that source in constructing this typical leisure-day. I suggest, then, that 23.3–6 and 23.8 all came from the *Ephemerides*. This suggestion is much strengthened by the fact that Philinus was cited by Plutarch in *Mor.* 623f as having obtained from the *Ephemerides* the information that after drinking A slept all day and sometimes the next day as well. There is no doubt that Plutarch and his contemporary Philinus had access to a copy of Alexander's *Ephemerides*.[20]

In 23.7 the comment on A's boastfulness and the influence of the flatterers may have resulted from Plutarch's reading of some account of the conversation between A and Cleitus;[21] but boastfulness and flatterers were not reported in his own account in 50–1. The flatterers were named as active only after the killing of Cleitus, at 53.1. In 23.10 the limit on expenditure for a dinner makes no sense unless one knows how many

[18] Even a Page was executed by Philip II for disobeying an order to stay under arms (Aelian, *V.H.* 14.48), and a Companion disobeying orders was killed by Alexander (*PA* 57.3).

[19] It would certainly be odd if this was all that Plutarch found in the *Ephemerides* which he considered worthy of mention about A's daily round.

[20] So too later writers such as Athenaeus, who confirmed at 434b that such bouts of sleep were shown in the *Ephemerides*, and Aelian, *V.H.* 3.23, who claimed to report A's drinking and sleeping from the *Ephemerides*.

[21] Such is the account which was transmitted by Curt. 8.1.22–5 (boasting) and Arr. 4.8.3 (flatterers).

guests were to be entertained. That information was supplied by Ephippus (*FGrH* 126) F 2, namely 60 or 70 guests. It is probable that Plutarch had read Ephippus but did not trouble to mention the matter of guests.

3. Divine birth (28) and excessive generosity to friends (39–42)

In chapters 24–7 Plutarch had less to add in illustration of A's personality. He chose Chares' story of A risking his own life to save that of his ageing tutor, Lysimachus; stressed the trust and the affection A had for his favourite diviner, Aristander (25.2); and told the anecdote of A's generosity to his teacher, Leonidas.[22] A's love of poetry and learning appeared in his placing of the *Iliad* as the most precious of all his possessions in the Casket (26.1f.). A's faith in omens and dreams as indications of the gods' wishes and purposes is never questioned throughout the *Life*, and in these chapters it is conspicuous in the preliminaries to the siege of Tyre, on the day of its fall, during the siege of Gaza, before and during the founding of Alexandria, and especially during the journey to Siwa. Indeed Plutarch was as confident as A himself was that 'the aids which coincided with his difficulties came from the god' (i.e. from Ammon), and that the responses of the oracle were inspired by Ammon. What those responses were was another matter. Plutarch gave first the report of 'most writers' about A's questions and the answers of Ammon's priest. But honesty led him to mention the Letter to Olympias in which 'A himself says that the prophecies that had been made were not to be divulged; but on his return he would tell them to her alone' (27.8). Plutarch reported also the saying of 'some' that a silly slip in pronunciation by the priest led to the story that A was addressed as 'the son of Zeus by the god' (i.e. by Ammon).[23] These varied versions naturally raised the question whether A

---

[22] This anecdote was mentioned earlier by Pliny, *N.H.* 12.62; it figures also in *Mor.* 179e–f.

[23] The story offsets the statement of A to his mother that there were prophecies (μαντεῖαι). The moral of the story is that it was due to a mistake that A was supposed to be a son of Zeus. For a different view see Hamilton *C* 73.

was born of man or god, the question which he was to tackle in the reflective passage (28).

Before he did so, Plutarch introduced a *legomenon*:

A is said to have listened to Psammon in Egypt, the philosopher, and to have accepted this particularly of his utterances, that all men are subject to the kingship of god, since the ruling and controlling force in each [man] is of god (θεῖον). But A himself is said to hold and express a more philosophical belief on this matter, that while the god is the common father of all men he adopts as his own the best men.

Since Psammon is so named as a spokesman of Ammon, 'the god' to whom Psammon referred was Ammon, a deity very familiar as 'Zeus Ammon' to the Greeks and especially to the Macedonians, who worshipped him at the oracular shrine of Aphytis in Chalcidice.[24] The idea of 'Zeus the King' ruling over the world was nothing new; indeed A had chosen to portray on his coins Zeus the King in such a way as to suggest that he was the same as the Belus (Ba'al) of the Asians.[25] That the ruling force in each of us is some form of spirit or soul, and that this is the divine element in each of us was a widespread idea from the time of Pythagoras in the Greek world and a fundamental idea in Egypt. While A accepted this belief, he is said to have improved on it by making the best of men particularly the children of the god – not in terms of physical paternity but metaphorically.[26] To see 'excellence' (ἀρετή) in men without distinction of race was certainly characteristic of A. The source of this *legomenon* is unknown.

As compared with the teaching of Psammon, Plutarch's reflections in chapter 28 are disappointing. 'A dealt haughtily with the barbarians and behaved like someone fully persuaded of his origin and begetting from god'; and it was in this connection that he represented A as using the belief in his divinity (τῇ δόξῃ τῆς θειότητος) as a means of 'enslaving the others' (i.e. the barbarians).[27] 'With the Greeks he made a god of

[24] See *HM* II 180 and 192.
[25] *AG*² 158f.
[26] In *Mor.* 180d 'Zeus is the father of all by nature (φύσει) and makes the best his own.'
[27] At 28.6 τοὺς ἄλλους picks up the distinction made at the start of the chapter. Perrin mistranslates as 'others', and Hamilton *C* 75 does not bring out the point.

himself with moderation and rather sparingly.' Plutarch gave examples which did indeed show A treating the idea lightly and humorously. The sources of two of them are known. When wounded by an arrow and in great pain, A quoted a line of the *Iliad* about ichor flowing in the veins of gods and remarked that in his own case it was blood, not ichor. Athenaeus gave the earlier part of the story as coming from Aristobulus (251a).[28] The other concerned a clap of thunder and A being asked by Anaxarchus whether, as the son of Zeus, he could do likewise. To that question A replied with a laugh that he had no wish so to frighten his friends. And A then referred to an earlier remark of Anaxarchus about A supplying at dinner a dish of fish and not a dish of satraps' heads, the implication being that there was no point in making the effort of conquest if one then ate a humble dish of fish. This second example was given also by Athenaeus (250f), citing Satyrus as his source.[29] It is evident that Plutarch obtained these passages from his reading of Aristobulus and Satyrus. After recounting these two examples Plutarch concluded that 'in view of what has been said A did not suffer in any way nor was he in a deluded state' (28.6 τετυφωμένος).

There was, however, one exception to this light treatment of the idea of being a god, which Plutarch cited: 'except that in writing to Athenians about Samos he says: "I would not have given you a free and famous city: you hold it after receiving it from him who was then in control and is being called my father" – meaning Philip' (28.2). This letter has been a subject

[28] Plutarch gave the same account in *Mor*. 180e and 341b, but in the latter passage with the addition that A was speaking to his flatterers (πρὸς τοὺς κόλακας εἶπεν). Athenaeus told the anecdote to illustrate the behaviour of flatterers, Dioxippus citing this line of Homer to A. These are evidently two parts of the same anecdote, in which Dioxippus cited the line in flattery and A responded with the line in mockery. This was suggested by Tarn 358 n. 5. The story was told differently as a criticism of A by Callisthenes (Seneca, *Suas*. 1.5) and by Anaxarchus (D. L. 9.60). See Hamilton *C* 74, who remarked that 'Tarn is doubtless right.' Brunt in *CQ* 24 (1974) 68, who did not mention the views of Tarn and Hamilton, supposed that Athenaeus had erred in naming as his source 'Aristobulus'; but Brunt did not say what name would have been more to his liking.

[29] Athenaeus cites 'Satyrus in the *Lives*', of which one was evidently that of Alexander.

of much controversy.[30] Plutarch did not provide a historical context. It seems that Athenians had written to A, saying that he had granted them Samos, i.e. had confirmed their possession of it, and that A replied that Philip made the grant, i.e. in the settlement after the Battle of Chaeronea, and that he himself would not have done so. The only attested period of such negotiations was in 324–323 B.C. Yet Plutarch's next sentence began 'But later A was wounded by an arrow', such a wound being attested at Massaga in 327. The natural conclusion is that the negotiations occurred in 334–332, when A had dealings with the islands off the coast of Asia.

Did Plutarch misunderstand the letter? The Athenians

---

[30] The text is as follows. ἐγὼ μὲν οὐκ ἂν, φησίν, ὑμῖν ἐλευθέραν πόλιν ἔδωκα καὶ ἔνδοξον ἔχετε δὲ αὐτὴν λαβόντες παρὰ τοῦ τότε κυρίου καὶ πατρὸς ἐμοῦ προσαγορευομένου. Perrin translated thus: 'I cannot have given you that free and illustrious city; for ye received it from him who was then your master and was called my father, meaning Philip.' 'Cannot' is clearly wrong, and to say to Athenians 'Philip was your master' was untrue and would have been most undiplomatic. Hamilton in *CQ* 3 (1953) 151 n. 2 translated as follows. 'I would not have given you that free and illustrious city but you have it as a gift from its former master, my "so-called" father, meaning Philip.' This translation assumes that Philip had become 'master of Samos' before the settlement; but Philip did not go anywhere near that island in the years before the battle of Chaeronea.

The diction of A's letter to Athenians has to be studied in relation to other Macedonian documents of the period. In A's letter ἔδωκα is used exactly as in two inscriptions of 335–334 B.C. within Macedonia (see my article in *CQ* 38 (1988) 384f.) and in an edict of 319 B.C. by Philip III Arrhidaeus in Diod. 18.56.7 Σάμον δὲ δίδομεν Ἀθηναίοις, ἐπειδὴ καὶ Φίλιππος ἔδωκεν ὁ πατήρ. The use of κύριος in A's letter is paralleled by A's words in his letter to Darius ἐμοῦ τῆς Ἀσίας ἁπάσης κυρίου ὄντος (Arr. 2.14.8; cf. 2.14.9 κυρίῳ ὄντι) and in his dedication of spoils at Lindus after the battle of Gaugamela (*FGrH* 532 F 1.38 κύριος γενόμενος τᾶς Ἀσίας). In A's letter I take it that τότε goes only with κυρίου, and the meaning is that Philip was then in control of Greek affairs. To refer to Philip as 'my father' is not surprising; for A did so in his letter to Darius (Arr. 2.14.5 τὸν ἐμὸν πατέρα), and Philip III did the same in 319 B.C. (Φίλιππος ἔδωκεν ὁ πατήρ; cf. Diod. 18.56.2 Φίλιππος ὁ ἡμέτερος πατήρ). I see no point in Philip being called A's father (πατρὸς ἐμοῦ προσαγορευομένου) in 338 B.C., when A was relatively unimportant. He was evidently being called so in the negotiations of 334–332 B.C. by Athenians, who hoped A would be reluctant to change his father's decision about Samos.

These analogies show either that the letter is genuine and is to be explained in terms of Macedonian terminology, as I have suggested, or that it was forged by someone conversant with Macedonian terminology of that time. Earlier literature on the subject is well summarised by Hamilton in *CQ* 3 (1953) 151–7. He himself concluded that the letter was genuine, but in my opinion he misunderstood the meaning of the letter.

would probably have said 'Philip your father made the grant', implying that the son would not undo his father's grant; and it would then be reasonable for A to reply that 'The man you call my father may have done so but I would not have.' What Plutarch apparently read into the phrase is 'Philip is being called my father but is not so, since Ammon is my father.' Such an inference is far from justified. My view is with those who regard the letter as not genuine, or who think that, if genuine, it was misinterpreted by Plutarch. Finally it is odd that, if A did parade a divine origin for himself to the Greeks, this letter is the best – apparently the only – evidence that Plutarch could produce.

In the narrative passages which follow Plutarch illustrated A's devotion to an actor friend, Thessalus, and his generosity in paying a fine which Athens had laid on the winning actor – a generosity far exceeded when A gave ten talents to an actor who inserted a request for that amount into a comedy (29.4–6). Here Plutarch repeated what he had mentioned in *Moralia* 334e. Next, the death of Darius' wife led to Darius' praise for A's self-mastery, restraint and great-mindedness (30.10f. σωφροσύνη, ἐγκράτεια, μεγαλοψυχία). For the Battle of Gaugamela Plutarch chose to follow the colourful account by Cleitarchus, in which A refused to steal victory by night despite the recommendation of Parmenio (31.12), whether he acted in youthful bravado or far-sighted policy. There was praise for A's greatness in his calm calculation and confidence in the planning (32.4), for the terror he inspired in action (33.6), and for his forbearance with the inefficient Parmenio (33.11). After the battle he sought honour for himself (φιλοτιμούμενος)[31] in paying tributes to some of the Greeks who had fought against Persia in 480–479; 'so much was A respectful of all excellence (ἅπασαν ἀρετήν), and so much a guardian and a kinsman of noble deeds'.

[31] I take it that the participle here is absolute (the meaning being comparable to that at 16.17 fin. above) and πρὸς τοὺς Ἕλληνας goes with ἔγραψε (as at 29.9 πρὸς τὸν Δαρεῖον ἔγραψεν), the Greeks here being contrasted with the Plataeans in particular. Perrin and Hamilton *C* 91 took πρὸς τοὺς Ἕλληνας with φιλοτιμούμενος (Perrin translating 'being desirous of honour among the Greeks').

There is nothing indicative of A's personality until his arrival in Persepolis, where a mob of people had pushed their way into the palace and overturned the statue of Xerxes. A addressed the statue. 'Are we to pass on as you lie there because of the expedition against the Greeks, or are we to raise you up because of your other high-mindedness and excellence?' (37.5 μεγαλοφροσύνην καὶ ἀρετήν). After a long time in silence, communing with himself, he finally passed on. The point of the story is that A attached more importance to Xerxes' crimes against Greece than to all his merits in Asia. It was perhaps told originally in order to explain A's action in burning the palace of Xerxes ἀπὸ γνώμης 'deliberately, as others say' (28.8). But Plutarch preferred to follow Cleitarchus in attributing the burning of the palace to an Athenian prostitute and to A leading a band of revellers behind her.

In a long reflective passage, 39–42.4, Plutarch began by enlarging on the munificence of A, on which he had already touched (15.3–6, 23.9f. and 29.5f.). The first two anecdotes (39.2f.) are not told elsewhere. Next Plutarch alludes to a letter, in which A told Phocion that he would not be treated as a friend if he rejected A's favours.[32] For this the full story was given by Plutarch in the *Life of Phocion* (18.1–4), and mention of it occurred in *Mor.* 188c. Two anecdotes follow. One names a young ball-player as Serapion; the story is too trivial probably to have been invented, and we know from 73.7 and Athen. 19a that A did play ball with a team of young men. The other names Proteas. He was mentioned by Athenaeus 129a as a son of Lanice, A's nurse, and as a boon-companion of A in drinking. Both anecdotes may be true. Plutarch then cites a letter of Olympias in which she chides A for so enriching others and depriving himself. She wrote often to this effect, said Plutarch; but as he adds that A kept her letters secret (ἀπόρρητα) it is not clear how such letters survived for Plutarch to see and read. He reinforced his statement about their secrecy by saying that A put his ring on Hephaestion's lips, when Hephaestion

---

[32] Hamilton *L* 14 reached no decision about the authority of this and the other two letters in chapters 39, 41 and 42.

happened to be reading with A one of her letters (39.8) – an incident previously mentioned in *Mor.* 180d, 332f and 340a. He was generous in sending presents to Olympias, and he was gentle but firm with her meddling in his practical affairs. When Antipater wrote a long letter criticising her, A commented: 'Antipater does not realise that one of my mother's tears wipes out ten thousand letters' (39.13). To leading men he was particularly generous, as Plutarch showed by supplying anecdotes concerning a son of Mazaeus and the gift of a mansion to Parmenio, and by mentioning a letter in which he ordered Antipater to have bodyguards. No doubt A was exceedingly generous to those he trusted.

In 40 A is represented as chiding gently but logically those of his Companions who indulged themselves in vulgar extravagance – Hagnon, Leonnatus and Philotas being named as such. On the other hand, A engaged even more energetically in military and hunting expeditions and risked his life, for instance, in despatching a great lion (with his spear). Plutarch provided an anecdote about that event, and noted that Craterus dedicated at Delphi a group of bronzes which showed the lion, the dogs, the king engaging the lion, and himself coming to help.[33] The artists were Lysippus and Leochares. In 41 the practice of A in courting danger and in urging the others to do likewise led them to become intolerant of him and even to speak ill of him. At first (ἐν ἀρχῇ) he bore this mildly, and he showed to them the marks of great goodwill and respect. Plutarch then gave a number of examples. These were drawn from letters to Peucestas, Hephaestion and doctors who treated Peucestas and Craterus, and from a dream which led A to sacrifice and to urge Craterus (who was sick) to sacrifice for recovery. When his boyhood friend Harpalus absconded with treasure in 333,[34] A distrusted those who informed him and put them in chains. Plutarch completed his list with a story which he had narrated twice in *Mor.* 180f and 339c. Then he

---

[33] The actual dedication was made by Craterus' son after his father's death; see Hamilton *C* 107.

[34] If this had been the second time Harpalus absconded, A would hardly have arrested the informers; see Hamilton *C* 109.

had named A's friend as Antigenes of Pellene, but here he called him Eurylochus of Aegae. However, the name of the prostitute with whom the friend was in love was the same in all versions, Telesippa. Perhaps Plutarch took trouble to check on the man's name for the *Life*.

In 42 Plutarch expressed surprise that A found time to write so many letters to the Friends. He cited three such letters, which were concerned with the slaves owned by Seleucus, Craterus and Megabyzus. As a judge, 'he is said' to have kept one ear free for the defendant's case 'at first' (ἐν ἀρχῇ). But later he was made harsh by the numerous prosecutions, since the many that were true led him towards accepting those that were false. In particular, when he was maligned, he abandoned reason and was harsh and inexorable, because indeed he loved his own glory above life and kingship. Here we have a pointer towards the later deterioration of A.

4. Gradual changes in personality

In the second part of the *Life* Plutarch let the narrative take control and he made reflective comments *en passant*. Although the *leitmotif* was a change in A for the worse in some respects, he was anxious to give a proper place to A's continuing fine qualities. He illustrated A's self-mastery and great-mindedness (42.10 ἐγκράτειαν καὶ μεγαλοψυχίαν) in giving back the water which was offered to him when all were overcome with thirst. The story was told of several places.[35] Plutarch chose to include it in the pursuit of Darius. It was followed by the picture of Darius on the verge of death praying that the gods would reward A for his decency towards the royal family (43.4 ἐπιεικείας). The theft of Bucephalus, reported here rather than earlier, showed A at his most merciful; for he not only pardoned but even rewarded the thieves[36] when they returned the horse unharmed (44.5 φιλανθρώπως). The change to

---

[35] Curt. 7.5.10–12 in Sogdiana; Arrian 6.26.1–3 in Gedrosia; Polyaenus without a location; and Frontinus, *Strat.* 1.7.7 on the way to Siwa. The accounts vary also in detail.

[36] A feature not in the versions of Curt. 6.5.20, Diod. 17.76.8 and Arr. 5.19.6.

which Plutarch attached great importance was the adoption by A of Asian dress and the wish of A to receive obeisance (προσκύνησις). When this change began, Plutarch offered two explanations (45.1–3):

Either A wished to associate himself with the local customs because common custom and common race are a great step towards the civilising of mankind. Or this was a furtive attempt to introduce obeisance for the Macedonians, as they were gradually accustoming themselves to put up with his changing mode of life.

These were not presented as exclusive alternatives. Plutarch implemented both explanations as his narrative proceeded.

The first explanation was developed when Plutarch came to report the training of 30,000 Asian boys (in 330) and the marriage with Roxane (in 327).

In his mode of life A was making himself still more like the local peoples, and he was bringing them (reading ἐκείνους) closer to Macedonian customs, thinking that he would stabilise the situation rather by goodwill than by force through an intermingling and partnership with them, at a time when he was about to march far away. (47.5)

Here Plutarch was repeating in more measured terms the praise he had expressed in *Moralia* 329f–330e for A 'the philosopher' envisaging 'for all men concord and peace and partnership'.[37] The barbarians saw A's marriage with Roxane as an example of such partnership (τῇ κοινωνίᾳ), loved A exceedingly and respected him for his restraint (47.8 σωφρονέστατος), in that, passionately in love though he was, he waited to marry Roxane legally. His power of conciliation was shown too in his dealings with Hephaestion and Craterus, although Hephaestion sympathised with the change in A's mode of life and Craterus clung to old Macedonian ways.

Plutarch came next to the affairs of Philotas, Cleitus, the Pages and Callisthenes. He was no doubt familiar with the many varying accounts, and it seems that he composed his own versions therefrom, except that he adopted Aristobulus' descriptions of the early suspicion of Philotas and of the

---

[37] Although Plutarch wrote in the *Moralia* of the Alexander-cities and of the spread of Greek education into remote parts of Asia, he was content in the *Life* to leave the matter at the philosophical level.

Cleitus affair. He never mentioned the Assembly of Macedonians, except in a letter of A to Antipater, and he attributed all decisions to A alone. A appeared in a favourable light at first; for he disbelieved the accusations which were made against Philotas in Egypt, and he gave important commands to Philotas and Parmenio. But in 330 A is represented as opening his ears to the arguments of Philotas' enemies, receiving '10,000 false accusations' (μυρίας διαβολάς), and taunting Philotas for uttering cries under torture. The killing of Parmenio followed. These aspects 'made A an object of fear to many of the Friends' (49.14).[38]

The rift between A and the older Friends was made manifest in the account of the Cleitus affair, and it was widened when the younger Friends sided with A and insulted Cleitus. A had lost that power of reconciling the old and the young which he had shown in dealing with Craterus and Hephaestion. The grounds of the rift were represented by Plutarch as in part charges of cowardice and mainly the policy of A in promoting Persians and in adopting Persian ways himself (51.2 and 5). The disaster was predestined, given the wilfulness of Cleitus (50.9 and 51.5). There was hearty drinking (50.8 πότου νεανικοῦ) and both men were flushed with liquor, but these were attendant circumstances, not the cause. Plutarch thus exonerated A from any charge of murder but not from adopting a policy which split the Friends.

The remorse of A was alleviated by Aristander, who said the fate of Cleitus was predestined,[39] and by Anaxarchus, who suggested that the king, like Zeus, was above the law, thus rendering A's character 'in many ways more conceited and more lawless' (52.7 χαυνότερον καὶ παρανομώτερον). The rift with the Friends was seen again in the matter of obeisance. A's attempt to introduce it was frustrated by Callisthenes, who thus 'saved the Greeks from a great disgrace and A from a

[38] Plutarch did not discuss the question whether Philotas was guilty of treason or innocent; he simply said that the reason for Philotas not informing A was 'unclear' (49.5 ἄδηλον). Plutarch's concern was with A's personality and its effect on others. He blamed the flatterers in *Mor.* 65d.

[39] This was the view of Aristobulus, which Plutarch was following in 50.1–7; see above, p. 93.

greater disgrace' (54.3).[40] But Callisthenes 'destroyed himself' thereby. For the flatterers of A made accusations, and when the Pages' Conspiracy was discovered the false charges gained verisimilitude.[41] Here Plutarch was less interested in Callisthenes' innocence or guilt than in the deterioration of A under the influence of the flatterers. 'He was now regarded with fear and he was inexorable in punishing those who offended him' (57.3).

As a military commander A was still his old self. 'In his ambition to overcome fortune by daring and force by valour (ἀρετῇ) he thought that nothing was insuperable for the confident and nothing was secure for those who lacked daring' (58.2). He grieved for the loss of a young man killed in action and for the deaths of Bucephalus and a dog he had trained. He showed gentleness and courtesy to Acouphis (πρᾳότητα καὶ φιλανθρωπίαν),[42] outdid Taxiles in generosity, and gave gifts in the end to the Indian philosophers. When he had to turn back at the river Hyphasis, he was overcome with despondency and anger (62.5 δυσθυμίας καὶ ὀργῆς), but he showed all his courage at the city of the Malli. The only 'stain' on his military record was the killing of the Indian mercenaries, after he had granted them a truce (59.7).

During the return from India A and his Companions engaged in drunken revels day and night, and once when A was drunk he kissed his beloved Bagoas passionately in public (67.8). Plutarch concerned himself more with A's drunkenness than with pederasty, which his source, Dicaearchus, had made into the moral of the story (Athen. 603a–b φιλόπαις ... ἐκμανῶς).[43] Then Plutarch told a story about Antigenes, which he had told of Tarrias in Moralia 339b–c – presumably

---

[40] Although Plutarch had praised A's Asian policy in the Moralia, he regarded obeisance as shameful for any Greek even to contemplate.

[41] Perrin translated διαβάλλω and its derivatives as 'accuse' at 49.10 and 55.3, but the word has the connotation of accusing falsely.

[42] Following Hamilton C 161.

[43] Plutarch had already mentioned A's disgust at being asked to obtain pretty boys for his sexual pleasure at 22.1–3. If we discount the difference in the moral they drew, the versions of Plutarch and Athenaeus are so close that a common source is to be presumed, namely Dicaearchus, a pupil of Aristotle. See Hamilton C 180 and for a different view E. Badian in CQ 8 (1958) 156.

now correcting himself: the story showed A being lenient to a very brave man for a peccadillo (70.6). The mutiny at Opis was attributed to the Macedonians' fear that A was paying more attention to his 30,000 Asian boys than to themselves. A was angry and abusive to the Macedonians, and he persisted in promoting the Persians, until the Macedonians were humbled and he wept with them over a reconciliation (71.8).

Qualities which A had once had and now lacked were moderation and self-mastery. The change was clear in Plutarch's account of his mourning for Hephaestion. He showed a complete 'lack of reason' (72.3 οὐδενὶ λογισμῷ). He demanded the clipping of the manes and tails of all horses and mules and the dismantling of all battlements, crucified 'the wretched doctor', massacred the young Cossaeans, and intended to spend a colossal sum on a grandiose funerary monument. He became suspicious of his Friends. He who had been a cause of terror to them, was now afraid of them, particularly of Antipater. He lost his temper with Cassander and treated him with brutality. His faith in the favour of the gods who had carried him from triumph to triumph weakened, as the diviners interpreted omen after omen as presaging disaster for him personally. He became 'down-hearted and as regards the gods despondent' (74.1 ἠθύμει καὶ δύσελπις ἦν πρὸς τὸ θεῖον). Finally, giving in to the signs of the gods, he became so bewildered and terrified in mind, that he interpreted anything unusual or out-of-the-way as a portentous sign. Priests sacrificing, purifying and prophesying filled the palace. Pious though he was, Plutarch saw that A was the victim of nonsensical superstition and panic fears (75.2).[44]

Relief came only with the announcement from Ammon's oracle, that Hephaestion should be honoured as a hero (72.3 and 75.3). He engaged again in sacrifices and drinking parties. Cleitarchus, whom Plutarch had been following as his main source, went on to complete the religious and moral disintegration of A by having him cap a night and day of continual drinking with 'a bowl of Heracles', whereupon he suffered

---

[44] Plutarch condemned superstition roundly in his essay *De Superstitione*.

a seizure and later died. Plutarch, however, preferred the view of Aristobulus, that the fever was not due to excessive drinking, and the day-by-day account of the illness in the *Ephemerides*.[45]

5. Attributions and deductions about Alexander's personality

In the reflective passages Plutarch relied a good deal on his own memory of what he had written in *Moralia* and in other chapters of the *Life*. However, he drew also on particular sources as follows:

(1) 4.1–8	A's endowment	Statues, paintings, Aristoxenus, Theophrastus	
(2) 21.5–23.10	self-mastery	Aristobulus (21.9), Letters, *Ephemerides* (23.3–6 and 8)	
(3) 28	divine birth	Aristobulus (28.3), Letter, Satyrus (28.4f.)	
(4) 39–42.4	generosity	Letters	

In (1) Plutarch put before the reader the main features of A's personality as Plutarch saw them. He did this at the outset, and not, as in a modern biography, at the end. The main features may be described as a passionate nature, a fondness for drink, a tendency to violence, an excessive impetuosity, a serious, indeed philosophical mind, a sense of restraint, a desire to do great things, and a desire to be honoured, while he was high-principled (μεγαλόψυχος) and difficult to deflect (δυσκίνητος). The first four of these features were basic in that they stemmed from an innate 'high bodily heat' – what we might describe literally, as well as metaphorically, as 'an unusually hot blood' and 'an unusually hot temper'. In (2) Plutarch showed that A's sense of restraint was in control of his sexual urges, his appetite for food and drink, and any desire to be inactive; this sense of restraint led here to self-mastery. In (3) Plutarch considered how far A's mind was affected by the report that he was of divine birth. The conclu-

---

[45] Rather different views of Plutarch's portrayal of A are to be found in Hamilton C lxii-lxvi, e.g. 'in general the Life is apologetic in tone', and in Tarn 296–309, e.g. 'Plutarch being quite inconsistent'.

sion was that A was not affected at all in his relations with Greeks and Macedonians, and that he used such a belief as a means of subjecting the barbarians. In (4) A's consideration for and generosity to others were carried almost to excess, and as a judge he made a point of reserving one ear to listen to the defendant stating his case.

Why did Plutarch place these reflective passages where he did in the narrative? Any answer must be tentative. In my opinion he wrote (1) as the backcloth to the boyhood and young manhood of A, so that the reader could see the interplay of the elements of A's personality in these formative years: the serious mind questioning the Persian envoys, the longing for fame when overshadowed by his father, the impetuous daring with Bucephalus, the philosophical mind developed by Aristotle and others, the drunken quarrel with Attalus and Philip, the hurt pride in the Pixodarus affair, the lion-like rage at Thebes, the mercy for Timoclea, the violence at Delphi, the impetuosity at the River Granicus, the passionate attack on the Greek mercenaries, the drunken revel at Phaselis, and the trust in his doctor at Tarsus. Up to this point we are seeing the elements in A's personality pulling in different directions.

In (2) the high principles of A and especially his self-mastery are displayed, and in the ensuing narrative they continue to be dominant. During this period of well-balanced maturity A was the happy recipient of dreams and omens, sent from the gods, which foreshadowed success after success, and in the journey to Siwa he received help from the gods which matched each difficulty (27.1). Perhaps A was thereby justified in his belief that 'the god' adopted as his own the best among men. Plutarch interrupted his narrative with (3) in which he showed that the balance of A's mind was not affected at all by a belief in a divine origin. The period of well-balanced maturity continued until the end of the Greek part of the campaign, the capture of Persepolis. Plutarch represented the burning of Xerxes' palace there as the act of the Greek girl, Thaïs, in which the Companions urged A to take part and which delighted the Macedonians. They were all of one mind then.

In (4) Plutarch wrote of the generosity and the consideration which A showed to common soldiers as well as to the Companions. The examples extended over the career of A in Asia. They showed A as the successful and unselfish leader of men. But in the latter part of (4) Plutarch struck a new note. 'In the beginning', i.e. up to the burning of Xerxes' palace, A heard a man's defence when he was accused. 'Later' he believed false accusations and became harsh. 'At first' he took it mildly if anyone spoke ill of him; but later, if this happened, he went out of his mind and became cruel and inexorable (41.2 and 42.4). Plutarch was looking forward – and directing us to look forward – to A's treatment of Philotas and Cleitus, and then to his hatred of Callisthenes. Thus at the end of (4) Plutarch marked a great divide.

In the ensuing narrative, although Plutarch praised A's ideas about relations with the barbarians, he drew attention to the cracks in A's personality which were revealed in his treatment of the Companions and the Macedonians. His attempt to introduce obeisance by the Companions was utterly disgraceful (54.3) and alienated the older and the better Companions. He became an object of fear to his associates and to the whole army (57.3), for he was inexorable. Passionate anger was mastering his judgement. He was more conceited and lawless, he lost his sense of proportion in his mourning for Hephaestion, and he suspected his Companions of disloyalty. As his hot blood took control of his personality, he engaged more in drinking-bouts. But the most sinister development was A's fear of adverse omens and portents, his yielding to superstition, and his panic fear and bewilderment.

To the modern historian there is a great deal that is unsatisfactory in Plutarch's analysis and protrayal of A's personality. We do not regard an infant's natural endowment, such as unusually hot blood, as a powerful element in the development of the adult personality. Plutarch chose to keep in separate compartments A's treatment of his Greek and Macedonian associates and troops on the one hand, and his policy towards the barbarians on the other hand; but A's determination to found and govern a kingdom of Asia meant that he had to co-ordinate his policies and his attitudes towards both groups of peoples. Plutarch was unduly influenced by the contemporary view that monarchical power corrupts the monarch and converts even a generous personality into a conceited, lawless and inexorable tyrant. His picture of a deteriorating A was certainly overdrawn. But Plutarch had access to more information than we do. He had more understanding of the religious beliefs of the time. And he was honest in believing what he wrote. Inevitably the worth of much of the *Life* depends on the value of his various sources. We shall assess some of them in the last section of the final chapter.

PART THREE

ARRIAN'S SOURCES FOR THE
ANABASIS ALEXANDROU

11

THE METHODOLOGY OF ARRIAN:
PREFACE AND 1.1–10

1. The *Preface*

When the writings of Ptolemy, son of Lagus, and Aristobulus, son of Aristobulus, are both in agreement concerning A, son of Philip, I am recording them as completely true (ὡς πάντῃ ἀληϑῆ). When their writings are not in agreement, I make my choice and I record of their writings that which appears to me more credible (πιστότερα) and at the same time more worth reporting (ἀξιαφηγητότερα). (*Preface* 1)

To be told at the start what Arrian intends to do is like a breath of fresh air to the source-critic. But we need to add some explanatory comments. Arrian was not intending to copy a writing of either author; for he was writing on a different scale, with a different aim, and in his own distinctive literary style. Rather, he was to select from the two accounts of these authors those facts and those interpretations which were common to both and interested him. When his two authors differed about the same event, he would choose whichever account seemed to him 'more credible'. When one of the authors described some events (say in a battle) and the other described other events, Arrian would choose whichever events seemed to him 'more worth reporting'.

It is important also to note what Arrian is not going to do. For instance, he does not say that he will tell his reader when his two authors differ; or that he will name the author whose account he chooses, when they do differ. And he does not say

189

on what principles he will judge an account of an event in either or both of his authors to be worth reporting. Thus we are to a great extent dependent on the judgement which he exercises.

'There are also some statements by others which I have recorded about Alexander but only as "what are said" (ὡς λεγόμενα μόνον), because they too seemed to me worth reporting (ἀξιαφήγητα) and not completely incredible (οὐ πάντῃ ἄπιστα)' (*Preface* 3).

This sentence was carefully composed to contrast with the opening sentence of the *Preface*. There he used the present tense ἀναγράφω for his regular practice; here he used the aorist tense to signify the occasional exception. There he records the agreed reports of Ptolemy and Aristobulus ὡς πάντῃ ἀληθῆ; here he recorded the other accounts ὡς λεγόμενα μόνον, 'as only said to be so'. The antithesis of πάντῃ ἀληθῆ there and οὐ πάντῃ ἄπιστα here, with a hiatus for emphasis in each case, is deliberate. As often, Arrian echoes Herodotus; for Herodotus had said 'I ought to say what is said (ἐγὼ δὲ ὀφείλω λέγειν τὰ λεγόμενα), yet I am not entirely obliged to believe it' (7.152.3). On some occasions Arrian went beyond his promise and recorded as a *legomenon* something which he did regard as incredible. The most notable instances were at 7.27. Then Arrian explained why he had included them. 'Let these matters be recorded by me rather in order that I may not be thought to be unaware that they are said (*legomena*) than because they are credible enough to report (ὡς πιστὰ ἐς ἀφήγησιν).'

Because Arrian was including two kinds of information – what he derived from Ptolemy and/or Aristobulus, and *legomena* from other authors – he made use of a stylistic device in order to make the distinction clear to his reader. The former material appeared normally in finite narrative tenses, and the latter was introduced by some word of 'saying', followed normally by ὅτι or by the accusative and infinitive construction. This practice was not announced by Arrian. It operated from the first word of his text at 1.1.1 λέγεται followed by the accusative and infinitive, and then, when A crossed the river

Nestus at 1.1.5, the narrative tenses began and continued until
1.2.7, when he mentioned a statement by Ptolemy alone. In
order to make it clear that the material of the narrative tenses
came from his two authors Arrian introduced it at 1.1.5 with
the phrase λέγουσιν ὅτι, 'they say that', 'they' being the
authors he has just named in the *Preface*, Ptolemy and
Aristobulus.

2. The sources for Alexander in Greece and the Balkans (1.1–10)

Arrian began with a *legomenon* (λέγεται) because he took his
information not from Ptolemy and Aristobulus but from unnamed sources. In 1.1.1–5 he supplied in the accusative and
infinitive a brief account of events from A's accession to spring
335 B.C. It was sketchy, in that it omitted for instance A's election as *archon* of Thessaly and his dealings with the Amphi-
ctyonic Council, and it was inaccurate in that some states
other than those within the Peloponnese were represented at
the meeting of the Council of the Greeks of the Common
Peace. But Arrian was concerning himself only with the events
which led to the planning of 'the expedition to Asia' (1.1.3 ἐν
παρασκευῇ εἶναι τοῦ ἐς τὴν Ἀσίαν στόλου); for that was the
meaning of his title, *Anabasis Alexandrou*.[1]

One aspect of that preparation was the campaign in the
Balkans, as Arrian explained that A did not think it right to
leave the Illyrians and the Triballians behind him during his
(projected) expedition so far from home, unless they were
thoroughly humbled (1.1.4). In the next section Arrian begins
to use Ptolemy and Aristobulus: 'they say that on the tenth
day after crossing the river Nestus he arrived at Mt Haemus'
(λέγουσιν ὅτι δεκαταῖος ἀφίκετο). The narrative from this
point to 1.10.6 is a detailed, uniform report of military and

---

[1] *Anabasis* meant an expedition up from the coast. Arrian chose the title in imitation
of Xenophon's *Anabasis Kyrou*. In Arrian's case the *Anabasis* began strictly with
the march from the Asiatic coast of the Hellespont at 1.12.6. At that point in his
text Arrian added a second prefatory passage (1.12.2–5) and referred then to
Xenophon's *Anabasis*. The strong hiatus in the phrase of 1.1.3 emphasises the
preparation for the *anabasis*.

diplomatic events. It is entirely different from the sketchy summary of 1.1.1–4. We see here the change from a *legomenon* to a narrative based on the accounts of Ptolemy and Aristobulus, all in accordance with Arrian's promise in his *Preface*. This change was noted by Brunt *L* I 4, when he appended a note to λέγεται at 1.1.1 as follows. 'The "tale" is not from the "vulgate",[2] but rather what all tell; §1–3 summarize well-known facts ... §4 – ch. 6 at end give a seamless narrative in which direct speech replaces indirect at the end of 1.1.5, presumably from Ptolemy/Aristobulus.'

A different view has been expressed by Bosworth *C* 45f. He argued that Arrian 'may have begun (at λέγεται) with Aristobulus and switched to Ptolemy for the Danubian campaign'. As regards λέγεται at 1.1.1 and λέγουσιν at 1.1.5 Bosworth commented: 'Initially Arrian does not present the narrative on his own authority but gives the received tradition (λέγεται, λέγουσιν).' These explanations, while inconsistent with one another,[3] are completely at variance with Arrian's stated method. Of the narrative of the Balkan campaign Bosworth *C* 51 wrote that 'it is probable that the entire campaign narrative is taken directly from Ptolemy, who is avowedly Arrian's principal source'. Once again Bosworth is at variance with Arrian, who stated that he would be following both authors. Further, the preference for Ptolemy, which Bosworth avows, is not stated by Arrian in his *Preface*, and it is, as Stadter says, not to be inferred from later mentions of Ptolemy.[4]

---

[2] 'Vulgate' is an umbrella-term used to include the writings of Diodorus, Justin and Curtius – and sometimes *PA* also – on the assumption that they derived their information from a common source, usually identified as Cleitarchus. Pearson, for instance, attributed all of Arrian's *legomena* to 'the vulgate, as we now call it', and Brunt *L* often does so. I have argued in *THA* that this is a loose and misleading term, because these three authors – and even more so Plutarch – did not confine themselves to a single source. The term is therefore not used by me. See below, p. 332.

[3] Unless Bosworth equated Aristobulus with 'the received tradition', for which we should turn rather to a fuller account, such as that of Diod. 17.3f., based on Diyllus (*THA* 35). However, in *AA* 39f. he seems to suppose that λέγουσιν did refer to 'his sources', i.e. to Ptolemy and Aristobulus, but he went on to say that 'the whole narrative was based on a single source' a case of having it both ways.

[4] Stadter 71f. 'some scholars have incorrectly taken certain statements as expressing a preference for Ptolemy, misunderstanding their context' and 'as regularly in Arrian's citations, the two writers are given equal treatment'.

The importance of understanding Arrian's method was emphasised by Stadter, whose book was published in the same year as Bosworth's *Commentary*. 'In his preface Arrian makes their agreement [that of Ptolemy and Aristobulus] the foundation of his narrative, and in fact he frequently cites the two authors together for a fact, usually against the vulgate' (70). Thus Stadter saw Arrian's accounts of the Balkan campaign and the capture of Thebes as samples of 'the excellence of Arrian's own method of presenting Alexander' and 'of Arrian's narrative technique' (91–3). While Stadter clearly thought of Ptolemy and Aristobulus being Arrian's sources for these events, he included in a list of *legomena* (on p. 73) the statement that from crossing the Nestus 'it took ten days for the army to reach Mount Haemus (1.1.5)', whereas I carry the *legomenon* down to A reaching the frontier of Macedonia before he came to the river Nestus.

Finally, the account of the Balkan campaign is peculiar to Arrian, since no more than a note of it was recorded by Diodorus (17.8.1, based on Diyllus according to *THA* 31 and 51), Trogus (Just. 11.1.6 and 2.4, following Cleitarchus according to *THA* 94f. and 113) and Plutarch (P*A* 11.5, following Cleitarchus; above, p. 25). The account was not due to Callisthenes, who was first employed by A to publicise the campaign of A and the Greeks in Asia, primarily for a Greek readership. The details of the account stem from a participant in the campaign, who was certainly at times an eyewitness. Thus we have to look to the participants in A's campaigns whom Arrian named in his *Preface*. He chose Ptolemy and Aristobulus precisely because they had campaigned with A (συνεστράτευσε βασιλεῖ 'Αλεξάνδρῳ).[5]

Within the narrative there were two comments by Arrian. At 1.2.7 'Ptolemy says that of the Macedonians themselves eleven cavalrymen were killed and about forty infantrymen', and at 1.8.1 'Ptolemy, son of Lagus, says that Perdiccas ... did not await A's signal for the battle ... but himself first attacked the palisade.' Arrian made these comments on the principle

---

[5] I had already argued that this was so in my article on the Balkan campaign in *JHS* 94 (1974) 77.

which he had laid down in the *Preface*: where Ptolemy and Aristobulus differed, Arrian gave the 'more credible' version – the difference being either that each gave a different version (e.g. number of casualties)[6] or that one mentioned an event and the other did not (e.g. Aristobulus may not have mentioned the initiative of Perdiccas). He provided a *legomenon* at 1.9.10, which occurred within a report of the Allies' decisions in the accusative and infinitive. In order to mark it off from these accusative and infinitives Arrian wrote: 'they say that A preserved the house of the poet Pindar' etc. (λέγουσιν ὅτι διεφύλαξεν). Thus Arrian's adherence to his declared method is a further reason for supposing that Arrian was here following his two main authors, Ptolemy and Aristobulus.

We know from accounts by authors other than Arrian that Ptolemy was probably the author behind Arrian at two points. For the exchange of remarks between A and the Celts by the Danube at 1.4.7f. had appeared earlier in Strabo 301–2; and Strabo had cited Ptolemy, son of Lagus, as his source. After the fall of Thebes A demanded the surrender by Athens of nine orators and generals whom Arrian named at 1.10.4; this list is best explained as coming from Ptolemy (see below, p. 209). Next, Plutarch mentioned that during the Illyrian campaign A was struck on the neck by a club, the word being ὕπερος (*Mor.* 327a). This rare word was used by Plutarch again in describing A's wounds at the city of the Malli (*PA* 63.9 ὑπέρῳ κατὰ τοῦ τραχήλου), a passage which we have ascribed to Aristobulus as source (above, p. 117). The probability, then, is that Aristobulus was also Plutarch's source for A's wound in the Illyrian campaign. During the Balkan campaign 'a longing (πόθος)

---

[6] Brunt *L* 1 12 n. 2, 'Pt. is perhaps cited because Arrian felt that such precise figures needed justification', is inconsistent with Arrian's declared purpose. Indeed 'about forty' is not precise. As we shall see, Arrian went on to report many figures of Macedonian casualties without citing Ptolemy by name. Bosworth *C* 60, 'Arrian specifies the source probably because of their disproportionate smallness compared with the Triballian losses', is no better, because similarly disproportionate losses were given for other engagements without the naming of a source. In *AA* 40 Bosworth deduced from this mention of casualties that 'the whole narrative' came from 'a single source'; but Arrian limits his citation of Ptolemy to one sentence, and the significance of the *Preface* is that Arrian was using the accounts of both Ptolemy and Aristobulus and that on this point he found Ptolemy 'more credible'.

seized A to go beyond the river' (1.3.5, the Danube). This longing was mentioned as πόθος also in 2.3.1, 3.1.5, 3.3.1, 4.28.4, 5.2.5, 7.1.1, 7.2.2, 7.16.2 and *Ind.* 20.1, the last being cited from Nearchus; and as 'ingens cupido' in Curtius 4.7.8 and 'cupido' in 4.8.3, 7.11.4 and 9.2.12. The argument of V. Ehrenberg, that the mentions of πόθος in the *Anabasis* were derived from Aristobulus, is probably correct.[7] I shall accept it in what follows. Consequently, we have independent evidence that Ptolemy and Aristobulus probably wrote detailed accounts of the Balkan campaign.

3. An evaluation of the sources used by Arrian in 1.1–10

In order to calculate the times within which Ptolemy and Aristobulus were writing, we need to consider Cleitarchus first. He published a voluminous work, *On Alexander*, in more than twelve books, which appeared in instalments between approximately 320 and 295.[8] In one of his later books, when he was living in Egypt and courted the favour of Ptolemy as king, he included Ptolemy among those who had saved the life of A at the city of the Malli in 326/5.[9] We learn from Curtius that Ptolemy denied in his own writing that he had been there at the time (9.5.21, 'ipse ... tradidit memoriae'). It is obvious that Cleitarchus wrote first, hoping to please Ptolemy by including him among the heroes. For if Ptolemy had been writing before Cleitarchus, why did Ptolemy trouble to say that he was not at the city of the Malli? And if Cleitarchus had written after Ptolemy, why did he contradict Ptolemy and suggest Ptolemy had been lying? After all, Ptolemy was a leading officer in 326/5, and Cleitarchus was not even a participant in

---

[7] V. Ehrenberg, *Alexander and the Greeks* (Blackwell, 1938) 52ff. It is not the phrasing which matters, for it is common enough, but the idea that such a longing seized A. See Brunt *L* 1 469f. and Bosworth *C* 62.

[8] I am following Goukowsky xx-xxiii, who reviewed the earlier literature and reached well-argued conclusions. The date 320 is appropriate to the evidence of Pliny, *N.H.* 3.57, who placed the works of Cleitarchus between Theopompus, *Philippica* and Theophrastus, *C.P.*, the latter being dated to 314 by Pliny.

[9] Curt. 9.5.21 has Cleitarchus report 'Ptolemaeum huic pugnae adfuisse' in a context where 'the fight' was that of A and his aides inside the city. In *AA* 81 Bosworth is misleading when he translates 'huic pugnae' as 'at this siege'.

the campaign. The conclusion is beyond doubt that Ptolemy wrote after Cleitarchus and so after approximately 300–295.[10]

Aristobulus wrote some time after 301, because he mentioned the Battle of Ipsus of that year (Arr. 7.18.5). In reporting the capture of Bessus in 329 Aristobulus said that Bessus was taken by Persian leaders first to Ptolemy and then to A (Ar. 3.30.5). However, in the accounts of Diodorus 17.83.8 and Curtius 7.5.26, which were derived from Cleitarchus (*THA* 61 and 140f.), there was no mention of Ptolemy. If Cleitarchus had written after Aristobulus, he would certainly have taken from Aristobulus the mention of Ptolemy, in order to please his patron. Thus we may conclude that Cleitarchus published a fairly late book of his history within the five years 300–295, and that Aristobulus published his version of the events of 329 some time after *c.* 300–295. Thus in relation to Cleitarchus Aristobulus is in much the same position as Ptolemy.

The relationship between Aristobulus and Ptolemy is shown in the reporting of the same incident of 329. Aristobulus had Spitamenes, Dataphernes and their associates take Bessus as a captive to Ptolemy and then hand him over to A. We learn this from Arrian 3.30.5. However, Arrian gave at considerable length in 3.29.6–30.5 the account not of Aristobulus but of Ptolemy, in which Ptolemy in command of some 7,000 men captured Bessus, while Spitamenes and Dataphernes withdrew, and Ptolemy then brought Bessus to A. Arrian, of course, chose the account of Ptolemy, because he was confident (and he had the full account before him) that it was the true one. In particular Arrian must have realised that Ptolemy would not have lied about the matter when there were so many eyewitnesses at the time – 7,000 men of named units on the expedition with Ptolemy and the rest of the army seeing Ptolemy hand over Bessus to A[11] – and some of them will still

---

[10] Fränkel, for instance (295), held that Cleitarchus had not read Ptolemy's history. See *THA* 83 and 156, where some cases of Aristobulus correcting Cleitarchus are adduced.

[11] Unlike Arrian, Bosworth *C* 377 chose the account of Aristobulus; but he did not consider what witnesses there had been of Ptolemy's actions.

have been alive when Ptolemy was writing. Who wrote first? If Ptolemy had written first, Aristobulus would not have denied the actions of Ptolemy by saying that Spitamenes and company had captured Bessus and brought him to Ptolemy and then to A. It follows, then, that Aristobulus wrote first, and he did so without consulting Ptolemy.

A similar conclusion is reached if we turn to reports of casualties on the Macedonian side at the Battle of the Granicus. Aristobulus reported 34 casualties 'in all' (P*A* 16.15 τοὺς πάντας), of whom he said 9 were infantrymen. Ptolemy, however, put the losses at 25 cavalrymen in the initial assault, over 60 other cavalrymen and up to 30 infantrymen (Arr. 1.16.4). Arrian, knowing both accounts, chose that of Ptolemy, because he thought it to be correct, as it clearly was when we remember that the infantrymen fought both against the Persian cavalry at the river-bank and against the 20,000 Greek mercenaries later. If Aristobulus had written after Ptolemy, he would not have reduced Ptolemy's figures to such a tiny number 'in all'.[12] Thus Aristobulus published his account of that battle before Ptolemy did so.

As Pearson said, 'it is generally agreed that he [Ptolemy] wrote towards the end of his long life, perhaps even only a year or two before his death in 283'.[13] On my calculations, as he wrote after Aristobulus and we need to leave several years for Aristobulus to write and publish his history, it is enough to split the difference and accord *c.* 295–289 to Aristobulus and *c.* 288–283 to Ptolemy.[14] This division suits the statement that Aristobulus said he started his work in his eighty-fifth year

---

[12] Brunt *L* 1 68 n. 3, 'probably he [Plutarch] did not include any non-Macedonians', seems to have missed the words 'in all' in Plutarch and the fact that there were very few non-Macedonian infantry in this battle (see *AG*[2] 76 for the numbers). Bosworth *C* 125 seems to overlook the fight against the Greek mercenaries, in which according to Plutarch most of the Macedonian killed and wounded fell fighting against desperate men (P*A* 16.14). On the statues of the 25 cavalrymen and not of the infantrymen see Hamilton *C* 42, *contra* Bosworth *C* 125. I agree with Hamilton that the mistake was made 'doubtless' by Plutarch, since Aristobulus must have visited Dium from his residence at Cassandrea, just across the Thermaic Gulf.

[13] Pearson *LHA* 193; so Goukowsky xxxi 'vers 285'.

[14] For different views see E. Badian in *Gnomon* 33 (1961) 665f. and R. M. Errington in *CQ* 19 (1969) 233–42.

(Lucian, *Macr.* 22 = *FGrH* 139 T 3); for if he was 45 years old at the start of the campaign in 334, he would have been in his eighty-fifth year *c.* 294.

4. The Balkan campaign

Now that we have sorted out the order in which Cleitarchus, Aristobulus and Ptolemy wrote, and now that we know that Callisthenes and Cleitarchus did not write about the Balkan campaign, we can take Arrian's account of the Balkan campaign as an uncontaminated example of Arrian's technique in drawing on his two chosen authors. The peculiar features of Arrian's account in 1.1.5 to 1.6.11 may be summarised as follows. He was drawing on a day-by-day narrative.[15] For he expressed distances and intervals between events in terms of days: 10 days from crossing the Nestus to reaching Mt Haemus (1.1.5), three days from crossing the Lyginus river to the Danube (1.2.1 and 1.3.1), and three days between A escaping through the Wolf's Pass and returning through it (1.6.9). He dated events within a single day (1.4.5; 1.5.8), or on 'the next day' (1.5.5; 1.5.8). Thus Aristobulus or Ptolemy or both were drawing on a full day-to-day diary of events. However, since the citing of days is not continuous but intermittent, we see that Arrian certainly and his source or sources probably were abbreviating drastically.

The geographical detail is considerable, and to anyone who knows the ground it is adequate. Thus A marched from Amphipolis into 'the Thrace of the so-called republican Thracians, keeping Philippoupolis[16] and Mt Orbelus on his left' (1.5.5), i.e. through the Rupel Pass and then north-eastwards through Mt Pirin.[17] This route was distinguished from the coastal route eastwards from Amphipolis (which A followed in spring 334) by Arrian's description of A 'passing Mt Pangaeum in the direction of Abdera and Maronea' (1.11.3

---

[15] See my article in *JHS* 94 (1974) 77f. and in general U. Wilcken, 'Hypomnematismoi', *Philologus* 53 (1894) 112f.

[16] Retaining the reading of Codex H, and not the reading Φιλίππους πόλιν, as in the Loeb edition.

[17] See H*SPA* 456 and for Mt Orbelus *HM* I 198f.

παρήμειβε τὸ Πάγγαιον ὄρος).[18] In the same way the vivid descriptions of the operations at Pelium fit the ground precisely (1.5.6 and 12; 1.6.5–8).[19]

The military detail is very full. The infantry are the Guard,[20] the Hypaspists, the Phalanx with its brigades (τὰς τάξεις), the Agrianians, the Archers, the Slingers, the Artillery (αἱ μηχαναί), and the draught-animals (τὰ ὑποζύγια),[21] and the cavalry are the Bodyguards (οἱ σωματοφύλακες),[22] 'the Companions with A', the horsemen from Bottiaea and from Amphipolis, the horsemen from Upper Macedonia, and the light-armed cavalry. The Slingers and the Cavalry of Upper Macedonia were not mentioned later by Arrian; for they were part of the forces left with Antipater in Macedonia.[23] It should be noted as a striking omission that the numbers of men in any regular unit were not stated by Arrian, presumably because he did not find them in his source. The names of some officers were reported: two commanders of Phalanx brigades (1.6.9), four officers responsible for transporting loot (1.2.1 and 1.4.5), three commanders of Cavalry formations (1.2.5), a commander of a Phalanx group (1.4.2), and a commander of a foraging group (1.5.9). Patronymics were not supplied by Arrian; but they must have figured in the original source, in order to avoid confusion, for instance between the two officers

[18] Bosworth C 54, published in the same year as H*SPA* and *AG*² 46, accepted the Loeb text and supposed that A took the coastal route, crossed the Nestus near its mouth, and proceeded via Xanthi to Mt Rhodope. He did not observe that Arrian described that coastal route as one 'passing Mt Pangaeum' (1.11.3) and not Mt Orbelus at all, as indeed anyone travelling from Amphipolis to Kavalla sees. Bosworth repeated the mistake in *CE* 29.

[19] See my geographical study in *JHS* 94 (1974) 77ff. with plates x and xi. Topography is an exact and exacting form of scholarship. Nothing is gained by vague remarks such as 'the whole action could have taken place in the Lyncestian plain' (Bosworth C 70) and 'Arrian's topographical data are too vague to support an identification' (*CE* 31). It is Bosworth who is vague, and Arrian who gives full topographical details, to which the Lyncestian plain (below Florina) offers no parallels. See further my comments in *HM* III 41 on the lack of topographical investigation in the proposals of Papazoglou *CBT* map, Bosworth in *Studies Edson* 87–97 and *M–G* 75–84, and T. K. Sarantes in *Anc. Mac.* III 247ff.

[20] This is the Royal Infantry Guard, not the Royal Brigade of Hypaspists. See H*VG* 4f. and 9.

[21] As distinct from pack-animals (ἀχθοφόρα); see H*AT* 27.

[22] H*VG* 10.

[23] These cavalrymen were the *asthippoi* of Diod. 19.29.2; see H*CU*.

called Philotas at 1.2.1 and 1.2.5. But the central figure throughout the narrative was A himself – figuring often as 'himself'
(e.g. 1.6.7 twice αὐτός). In particular the orders issued by A
were reported meticulously, even when they were pointless in
the sense that they were not fulfilled (1.6.5f.; 1.6.10; cf. 1.1.11f.
A's intended action not fulfilled). The citations of orders were
extremely frequent, namely fifteen times between 1.1.8 and
1.6.10.[24] Some figures were reported: enemy losses in round
numbers (1.1.13; 1.2.7), prisoners taken (few, 1.1.13; 1.2.7;
not a few, 1.6.10), enemy forces in round numbers (1.3.5),
own numbers only of special detachments (1.3.6; 1.5.10; 1.6.1;
1.6.6), casualties of 'Macedonians themselves' only once (1.2.7:
11 cavalry, about 40 infantry, 'says Ptolemy'), and own force
safe and sound (1.1.10; 1.4.5; 1.6.6).

Ptolemy and Aristobulus were not highly placed officers
in 335 B.C. Indeed Ptolemy, as a contemporary of A, was a
junior cavalryman, and Aristobulus 'never appears in a military capacity.'[25] They could not possibly have known all A's
orders at the time, let alone those which were unfulfilled. If
either or both had kept a personal diary – very unlikely on
such a campaign – the details in the narrative were not what an
individual would have written down. The alternative, a precise
memory of such details, can be ruled out immediately; for the
interval of time was some fifty years, and if I may judge from
my own experience with a similar interval since 1941, one
remembers personal matters and not the orders of General
Freiberg, the names of other commanders and the figures of
losses on either side.

The only explanation is that Ptolemy and/or Aristobulus
had access to the official Diary of A, for which we may use the
term 'Journal', as a translation of the Greek name 'Ephemerides', meaning day-by-day records. The Journal was the
record day-by-day of the King's orders, actions, dispositions,
letters, negotiations and so on, as we can see from citations

---

[24] Arrian varied the word for issuing an order: κελεύω (1.1.11; 1.2.4; 1.4.2; 1.5.3;
1.6.4; 1.6.6; 1.6.8), παραγγέλλω (1.1.8; 1.6.1), προστάσσω (1.2.5; 1.6.10) and
σημαίνω (1.6.2). In *Tactica* 32 Arrian gave examples of such orders as were
implicit in the account of the drill at Pelium (1.6.1f., where Brunt's 'difficult
formations' is presumably a slip for 'different formations').

[25] Berve II 330 'Altersgenosse Al's' and Pearson *LHA* 151.

and references to the *Journals* of A and of his successors.[26] We can thus understand why A's orders – even unfulfilled ones – were reported in Arrian's account; why the numbers of men in regular units were omitted altogether,[27] but numbers of men in special detachments were provided; why names of officers in positions of responsibility were supplied; why numbers of one's own casualties (even of wounded men in major battles) and even the absence of casualties were noted; why distances and intervals between events were given in terms of days; and why topographical details were recorded so carefully[28] (e.g. round Pelium).

In 1985 W. Clarysse and G. Schepens published fragments of a papyrus which in their opinion came from a historical narrative of A's campaign in the Balkans.[29] If so, the narrative was very much more detailed than that even of Arrian. In 1987 I showed that the fragments came from a copy of Strattis' *Five books on The Journal of Alexander*, i.e. a commentary on points in A's *Journal*, that citations from the *Journal* could be distinguished from the comments, and that it was indeed concerned with A's Balkan campaign.[30] From the papyrus fragments we see that the *Journal* recorded A's disposition of troops for the defence of the north-west frontier of Macedonia; A's appointment of 'Corragus, son of [M]en[oitas]' (vel sim.) in command of the defence-force; A's prescription of special stakes for fortifying a camp and of some signalling system; places on A's geographical route, namely Eordaea, Elimea, River Skios (a tributary of the Danube) and a stream of which the name is not complete; A's appointment of 'Philotas [Parme]nionos' to command a task force; and mention of himself as just 'he himself' (αὐτός). Thus there is a striking similarity to the outstanding features of Arrian's narrative of the Balkan campaign. The conclusion is certain, that the ulti-

---

[26] See H*RJ* 131.

[27] They were of course familiar to A, and he had no need to specify them in his *Journal*.

[28] Whatever the other skills of A, he had a brilliant understanding of topography. The importance which A attached to recording topographical detail is apparent from a fragment of Callisthenes (*FGrH* 124 F 35); for he certainly controlled what Callisthenes wrote.

[29] In *Chr. Eg.* 60 (1985) 30–47.

[30] H*PF*.

mate source of Arrian's account of the Balkan campaign was the *Journal of Alexander*.

To return to Ptolemy and Aristobulus, which of them used the *Journal of A*? Arrian gave the first clue when he attributed to Ptolemy the number of Macedonian casualties as eleven cavalrymen and around forty infantrymen (1.2.7). Thus, since the original source of that information was the *Journal*, Ptolemy was using the *Journal*. There is also a clue which derives from the history of A's *Journal*. Just after A's death in 323 Perdiccas took over A's *Journal* in Babylon (Diod. 18.4.2); but when A's orders were either fulfilled or negated, the *Journal* will have been associated with the corpse and the insignia of A. Early in 321 the corpse was taken not to Macedonia, where Aristobulus lived at the time of his writing, but to Egypt (Diod. 18.27.2f.). There Ptolemy had the *Journal* under his own hand. After the death of Ptolemy the *Journal* itself or a copy of it was no doubt placed in the Library at Alexandria. Strattis, an Olynthian,[31] probably wrote his commentary on the *Journal* in Alexandria around the middle of the third century B.C.; and Eratosthenes, the Librarian at that time, read reports of A's couriers on distances, which were preserved in the Archive of A at Alexandria.[32] Diodorus consulted the Journals of the Kings there towards the end of the Roman Republic (Diod. 3.38.1).[33]

Finally, how dependable was the *Journal of A*? In 1954 Pearson maintained that the *Journal* which ancient writers cited as the *Journal of A* 'was not a genuine document but a literary production, a faked or fictitious diary'.[34] In 1987 Badian overtrumped Pearson by proposing that there were several 'fictitious' versions.[35] Whether one or several, a genuine *Journal* was circulating also, as Pearson and Badian admitted. Because the genuine *Journal* recorded genuine events,

---

[31] This worried Pearson *LHA* 260 with n. 92, but see H*RJ* 142 for men calling themselves citizens of Olynthus a century after the destruction of the city.

[32] See H*RJ* 137–40 on this matter.

[33] For the history of A's *Journal* and consultations of it see H*RJ* and *Historia* 40 (1991) 382f.

[34] In *Historia* 3 (1954/55) 429ff. The quotation is from *LHA* 260.

[35] In *Zu Alexander der G.* 1 (Amsterdam, 1987) 605ff., edited by W. Will and J. Heinrichs. Brunt *L* 1 xxv expressed a similar view.

it could not be displaced by a fake *Journal* reporting faked events until the contemporary witnesses of those events had passed away. Realising this, Pearson dated the first circulation of his supposed 'faked diary' to some time after the lifetime of anyone born before 348 B.C., i.e. after *c.* 258.[36] By then, of course, A's genuine *Journal* had been in existence since its completion in 323 B.C. How could a faked one displace so well-known and authenticated a *Journal*? Who would go to the immense labour of composing a faked *Journal* with entries covering the 4,500 days or so of A's action-packed life? And to whose benefit? These are but a few of the arguments which I have advanced against the views of Pearson and Badian. My conclusion is that there was only one *Journal of A*, that it was genuine, and that there never was a 'faked *Journal of A*'.[37]

How reliable was the *Journal*? Ancient writers for whom the full *Journal* was available – whereas we can judge only from a few fragments – took its statements to be correct. We may name those whose names have survived: Strattis, Eratosthenes, Patrocles, Philinus, Plutarch, Athenaeus and Aelian, in addition to Arrian. They were right to do so. For the *Journal* was written not for publication in each King's lifetime but as a record for the King's own use. Thus the plans which were entered in the *Journal* on A's instruction in the first part of 323 B.C. were not published at the time. They became known only when Perdiccas reported them to the Assembly of the Macedones at Babylon. Similarly, the report of the discussion which A and his senior officers (ἡγεμόνες) held about promotions to fill vacant positions of command was confidential and certainly not to be made public (P*A* 76.5, cited from the *Ephemerides*). The record had to be accurate; for the king had to refer to specific orders he had issued, letters he had written and received, diplomatic negotiations, judicial verdicts and so on.[38] When A wished to publicise his actions for propaganda

---

[36] See further H*RJ* 135f.
[37] I have argued the case fully in *AG*² 1f., 57f. and *passim* (see *Royal Journal* in the index of *AG*²), H*RJ* and H*AAJ*.
[38] See H*RJ* 130–2 for the contents of such Journals.

purposes, he employed a Greek writer, Callisthenes, to publish the versions of events which A wished the world to receive.

Did Ptolemy change what was in the *Journal* in order to promote his own image or damage that of others? When Cleitarchus wrote that Ptolemy was one of those who had saved A's life at the city of the Malli, Ptolemy could have substituted his name for one in the *Journal*. But he did not do so; instead he wrote in his own history that Cleitarchus was mistaken and that he, Ptolemy, was on a separate mission at the time. Thus he did not tamper with the *Journal* in this crucial instance. Did he or others change, for instance, the record of A's drinking habits in the *Journal*? We know from Plutarch and Arrian that the *Journal* recorded the events of the King's days and nights, and therefore his drinking-parties and his sleeping for very long hours. Pearson thought these to be an indication that the *Journal* was a forgery; for he wrote that such behaviour by A 'would certainly be described less bluntly in an official document'.[39] Here he imports his own moral standards, and he assumes tacitly that the *Journal* was for publication as the 'official' version. In fact, the citation of these reports from the *Journal* is an indication that the *Journal* was not altered either in the original or in citation. Lastly, we have Arrian's own expressed opinion in the *Preface*, based on a full reading of the works of Ptolemy and Aristobulus and a comparison of them with the works of many others, that they were more worthy of trust, were participants in the campaigning of A, and were not influenced by any hope of gain or constrained by any form of compulsion to write anything but the truth. In addition, wrote Arrian, 'it was more shaming for Ptolemy as a king to lie than for anyone else'. This is still true for a head of state.[40]

Our conclusion, then, is that the bulk of Arrian's account is derived ultimately from a totally reliable unbiassed record of factual matters. It therefore provides the fundamental basis for any understanding of A's career. This view is not that of

---

[39] *LHA* 260.

[40] A made this point (Arr. 7.5.2); and most heads of state have agreed with A, even in modern times.

some recent writers. It has been maintained that the *Journal* was merely an account of the King's 'private life' ('Privatleben-journal'), that it was compiled only for the King's last years, and that it gave 'an account which deliberately selected facts to suggest a specific interpretation'. As regards Ptolemy drawing on the *Journal* for his history of A, the view has even been expressed that 'there is no evidence that a court diary was systematically used by Ptolemy'.[41]

5. The Theban campaign

In 1.7.1–8.8 the narrative continues with the same marked features. Days are noted: 'seventh day to Pelinna', 'sixth day to border of Boeotia', 'the next day' (1.7.5; 1.7.1; 1.7.9). Geographical details are provided: for A's march from Pelium to Thebes (1.7.5, mentioning Eordaea, Parauaea, Tymphaea and Elimeotis; and from Pelinna via 'The Gates', i.e. Thermopylae, to Onchestus);[42] for A's camps (1.7.7; 1.7.9; 1.8.1); for actions at Thebes the precinct of Iolaus, the gates for Eleutherae and Athens, the Cadmea, the Heracleum, the Ampheum, and the Agora. Some officers are named: Amyntas and Timolaus of the Macedonian garrison;[43] Perdiccas and 'Amyntas, son of Andromenes',[44] as brigade-commanders; and A himself 'appearing now here, now there' in the fighting inside the city. A's all-important order was reported (1.8.3, ἐσήμηνεν). Macedonian units were some light-armed (probably including Slingers),

---

[41] See, for instance, R. M. Errington in *Gnomon* 7 (1984) 780; W. Will, *Alexander der Grosse* (Stuttgart, 1986) 14; Bosworth *C* 23f. and *CE* (1988) 299.

[42] For this march see H*MAT*. Having placed the battle of Pelium well inside Macedonia, Bosworth made no sense of the pursuit 'to the mountains of the Taulantii' (*C* 73) or of A passing by the heights of Parauaea and Tymphaea (*C* 76). The route which he proposed for A's army from Lyncus to Pelinna in Thessaly is absurd: from Lyncus towards Kozani, Siatista Pass, Grevena, Upper Peneus, Pelinna; for the direct route is easy – Lyncus, Kozani, Volustana Pass, Pelinna. He even placed Pelinna west of Trikkala. See H*A* map 12. In *CE* 31f. Bosworth moved farther east in placing Pelium 'close to ... Edessa' but still made A march through the Siatista Pass.

[43] Bosworth *C* 74 rightly dismissed the suggestion of Niebuhr that these men were not Macedonians but Thebans.

[44] In the original source there was presumably a patronymic also for the Amyntas of the garrison; and consequently for other officers, as in the papyrus fragments of Strattis, *Five Books on the Journal of A*.

Archers, two phalanx-brigades named after their commanders, the Agrianians, the Infantry Guard 'of the Macedonians',
the Royal Hypaspists,[45] the Hypaspists. Seventy casualties of
one unit – the Archers – in the initial fighting were reported
and their commander was named (1.8.4).[46] The military account is very clear, and the action is seen entirely from the
Macedonian viewpoint. It is evident that much of this detail
was derived from the *Journal of Alexander* by Ptolemy.

In 1.9.1–8 the calamity suffered by Thebes in the action (the
decision to enslave the survivors came later, at 1.9.9) was compared to the calamities suffered in the past by Greek states –
Athens in Sicily, Athens at Aegospotami, Sparta at Leuctra
and at Mantinea, Sparta when Epaminondas and his allies
invaded Laconia, the massacre of those captured in Plataea (in
427 B.C.), the destruction of Melos and of Scione. What concerned the writer was the shock felt at the time 'not a bit less
by the other Greeks than by those who took part in the action'
(1.9.1 αὐτοὺς τοὺς μετασχόντας τοῦ ἔργου). The passage thus
seems to have been written by someone who was present on
the Macedonian side at the time; for he stressed the sharpness
of the action, the unexpectedness of the victory, and the capture 'with so little trouble (1.9.6 οὐ ξὺν πόνῳ) of the foremost
city-state in military power and prestige in the Greek world'.[47]

[45] Bosworth *C* 81 accepted Schmieder's emendation of the original text τὰ δὲ
ἀγήματα καὶ τοὺς ὑπασπιστάς to τὸ δὲ ἄγημά τε καὶ τοὺς ὑπασπιστάς, where τε
is misplaced. This led him and others before him to find 1.8.4 τὸ ἄγημα τὸ τῶν
Μακεδόνων καὶ τοὺς ὑπασπιστὰς τοὺς βασιλικούς confusing, to say the least.
The MS reading should be retained. See H*VG* for the two Infantry Guards here
and elsewhere, one being of Pezhetairoi and the other of Hypaspists.

[46] The mention of a few officers in the *Journal* may be compared to a mention in
dispatches in the British Army. That of Perdiccas is particularly interesting, as his
initiative made the rapid capture of Thebes possible. In the gallant action he was
severely wounded, recovered to command a Brigade of the Phalanx at the River
Granicus (1.14.2) and was promoted Somatophylax by 330 B.C. (Curt. 6.8.17).
That Ptolemy named Perdiccas as acting without an order from A was due not to
any dislike Ptolemy had of Perdiccas but to its being included in the *Journal*. The
idea that it was connected with the Council's decision to raze Thebes is most
far-fetched. See my remarks in *THA* 166f. with references to R. M. Errington in
CQ 19 (1969) 237; Brunt *L* I 35; Bosworth *EH* 22 (1976) 14 and *C* 80f. See also
below, p. 330.

[47] By Greek city-state standards of siegecraft Thebes was impregnable and could
have been reduced only by blockade over several years. That Thebes fell in an hour
or two was incredible to a city-state Greek.

The choice of source being Ptolemy and/or Aristobulus, we should opt for Aristobulus, who, having been on the Balkan campaign, as we have seen, was in the Macedonian army which captured Thebes. As a Greek of Phocis,[48] which had suffered so much from Thebes in the Third Sacred War and its aftermath, he went on to explain the slaughter of man, woman and child in the city 'by Phocians,[49] Plataeans, and the other Boeotians' (1.8.8) as being 'such as [you would expect] from peoples of the same race who were pursuing feuds of long standing' (1.9.6). The expression 'of the same race' contrasts their responsibility with that of the Macedonians (cf. 1.8.8).

In 1.9.6 the fall of Thebes was explained as due to 'the wrath of god' (μῆνιν τὴν ἀπὸ τοῦ θείου) in retribution for her past sins of an 'un-Hellenic' nature: siding with Persia, breaking the Thirty Years treaty, destroying Plataea where the Hellenes had repelled Persia, and their vote for the destruction of Athens in 404 B.C. The viewpoint is that of a Greek rather than of a Macedonian. The belief is appropriate to Aristobulus, who believed in the wrath of god and in omens foreshadowing retribution in the Cleitus episode (above, pp. 90–3). But in this case Arrian introduced a *legomenon* (ἐλέγετο) for the prior indications of the impending disaster 'from the divine power' (1.9.8 ἀπὸ τοῦ θείου). We shall discuss this *legomenon* together with the next one at 1.9.10.

In 1.9.9 Arrian reported the decision of 'the allies', i.e. of the Council of the Greeks of the Common Peace, in an abbreviated form. 'A entrusted it to the allies who participated in the action to manage the matter of Thebes' (τὰ κατὰ τὰς Θήβας διαθεῖναι).[50] In other words he left it to them to make the proposals which were in fact carried: to garrison the Cadmea,

---

[48] See Pearson *LHA* 151. An inscription of the middle of the third century B.C. named 'a son of Aristobulus, a Phocian living in Cassandrea', and we know from Plu. *Demosth.* 23 and Athen. 43d that Aristobulus lived in Cassandrea. So the identification is highly probable.

[49] It is interesting that the Phocians were listed first. They were not mentioned by Diodorus at 17.13.5, who named Thespians, Plataeans and Orchomenians as fighting inside Thebes; his account was based on Cleitarchus in my analysis in *THA* 13ff. and 26f.

[50] For the meaning of διαθεῖναι compare Thuc. 6.15.4 κράτιστα διαθέντι τὰ τοῦ πολέμου.

raze the city, distribute secular territory among the allies, enslave the surviving Thebans with a few exceptions, and rebuild
Orchomenus and Plataea as fortified cities. Here Arrian abbreviated to the point of obscurity[51] the account of his source,
whom I take to have been Aristobulus still. He added a *legomenon*: 'they say that A preserved the house and the descen-
dants of Pindar the poet out of respect' (αἰδοῖ τῇ Πινδάρου).

We have a clue to the source of the first *legomenon*. Diodorus
reported 'certain utterances by diviners and signs from gods'
which had foreshadowed disaster for Thebes (17.10.2–6). The
author whom Diodorus followed for the Theban episode was
without doubt Cleitarchus (*THA* 13–16 and 26f.). Some of the
signs were reported also by Aelian, *V.H.* 12.57, who may
also have drawn on Cleitarchus. The second *legomenon*, illu-
strating A's respect for Pindar, occurred also in P*A* 11.12, a
passage in which Plutarch was drawing on Cleitarchus (see
above, p. 27). As regards this *legomenon* Brunt added a note:
' "vulgate", unless "they" are Pt. and Ar.'; and Bosworth *C* 91
'the λέγουσιν does not necessarily mean that Arrian derived
the story from his subsidiary sources; Aristobulus, or even
Ptolemy, is a possibility'. Herein they show no respect for
Arrian's declaration in the *Preface*. It is perfectly clear in
1.9.10 that the *legomenon* applied not to the other exceptions
which were made by the Council of the Greeks of the Common
Peace but only to Pindar. The source or sources which Arrian
was following for the other exceptions, namely on his declaration Ptolemy and/or Aristobulus, were not the source of the
legomenon.

In 1.10 Arrian described the reactions of the other Greeks
when the disastrous collapse of Thebes (τῶν Θηβαίων τὸ
πάθος, resuming the πάθος of 1.9.1, not the decision by the
Council of the Greeks of the Common Peace to raze the city
etc.) was reported to them. These reactions are described from
the Macedonian point of view: men favourable towards A
being reinstated in Elis, the individual tribes of the Aetolian

[51] See Bosworth *C* 89f.

League sending embassies, the Athenian Assembly congratulating A on his safe return from the Balkans and his punishment of Thebes, and sending ten envoys to A who were chosen because they were known to be most favourable towards A. The reply of A was 'kindly' (φιλανθρώπως) and he wrote a letter (ἐπιστολήν, the normal Macedonian expression) in which he demanded the surrender of nine named Athenians. Arrian cited, evidently from the letter since he used the accusative and infinitive construction, A's charges of their responsibility for Athens' sufferings at Chaeronea and for her offences against Philip and himself at Philip's death, and of their guilt in the revolt – a guilt which was equal to that of the Theban revolutionaries.[52] No doubt A's letter was recorded at the time in the *Journal*. There too a report of the second Athenian embassy was later added, in which Athens asked A to relent.[53] A did so, except for his order that of the named Athenians Charidemus was to be exiled. Reasons for A's leniency were 'perhaps his eagerness (σπουδῇ) to undertake the expedition to Asia, and perhaps his respect for the city, since he did not wish to leave any ill will among the Greeks when he would be away' (οὐδὲν ὕποπτον).[54]

Of A's two main sources for this chapter it is clear that he was drawing on Ptolemy, for two reasons. Ptolemy alone had access to the *Journal* in which the content of A's letter was recorded. The list of names for the nine Athenians has been explained as due to Arrian having followed the list reported by Ptolemy (Brunt *L* 1.44 n. 3). If this is so, Arrian's list of names is to be accepted as historical, in preference to the list in Plu. *Demosth.* 23.4.

My conclusions may be summarised conveniently as follows:

---

[52] A similar summary of a letter of A in the accusative and infinitive is in Arr. 2.25.3.

[53] That such letters were recorded in A's time is clear from Plu. *Eum.* 2.3; an Antigonus was able to study earlier records of diplomatic negotiations in Journals (Polyaen. 4.6.2). See H*RJ* 130f.

[54] Bosworth *C* 96 finds Arrian's expression 'inept' and thinks A should have 'humbled Athens as he had Thebes'; but A, like Philip, did everything possible not to humble and alienate Athens, largely because he wanted her as a naval power on his side or at least neutral.

1.1.1–5	sources of this *legomenon* unknown, but not Ptolemy + Aristobulus
1.1.5–1.6.11	Ptolemy + Aristobulus (Ptolemy preferred at 1.2.7; Aristobulus probably at 1.3.5)
1.7.1.–1.8.8	Ptolemy + Aristobulus (Ptolemy specifically for 1.8.1, and Aristobulus probably for 1.8.8)
1.9.1–8	Aristobulus
1.9.9f.	Ptolemy and/or Aristobulus
1.10.1–6	Ptolemy
Legomena: 1.9.8	Cleitarchus
1.9.10	Cleitarchus

These conclusions differ widely, for instance, from those of Bosworth. He suggested the following as sources: for 1.1.1–5 Aristobulus; 1.1.5 Ptolemy; 1.7 Ptolemy (*C* 79); 1.8 'no doubt' Ptolemy; 1.9.1–5 Arrian himself; 1.9.6–8 Aristobulus; and for 1.10 Ptolemy at 1.10.4–6 (*C* 95 and 96). Arrian said he would be following Ptolemy and Aristobulus when in agreement. Bosworth makes him use only one at a time in 1.1–10. As regards the *legomena* he attributed 1.1.1–5 to Aristobulus; and 1.9.10 to 'Aristobulus, or even Ptolemy' as 'a possibility' (*C* 91). Thus he makes Arrian belie himself after saying in the *Preface* that his *legomena* are drawn from sources other than Ptolemy and Aristobulus. He did not note 1.9.8 as a *legomenon*. With regard to Cleitarchus Bosworth has written in *AA* 93 'there is no indication that Arrian used the work of Cleitarchus'. Yet Bosworth believes still in 'the vulgate' and in Cleitarchus as the chief source of it (*CE* 297). How could Arrian have failed to use Cleitarchus before making his not infrequent criticisms of 'the vulgate tradition'?[55]

---

[55] See my review of Bosworth *AA* in *CR* 39 (1989) 22 and that of A. M. Devine in *CP* 85 (1990) 322, who found Bosworth's view on this matter 'passing strange'.

12

FROM MACEDONIA TO THE TANAÏS
(ARRIAN 1.11 TO 4.4)

1. Macedonia to Gordium (1.11 to 2.3)

The narrative here is marked by the same characteristics as the earlier narrative. These characteristics on my interpretation were derived from the *Journal of A* through Ptolemy as an intermediary. I list them in the same order.

(1) Dating of events by days. There are thirteen instances, which range from 'the first day' of the siege of Halicarnassus to the '20 days' from Macedonia to Sestus (1.20.4 and 1.11.5). We learn also that A recorded the units specified each day for special duty (1.14.6) and for the positioning each day within the phalanx of the brigades, which were named each after its commanding officer (1.28.3; cf. 5.13.4). The record of each day's standard orders[1] lived on in the *Journal*.

(2) Topographical detail. The short descriptions of Aspendus and Telmissus (1.27.1 and 5f.) are useful, and the details which are given for the scene of the Battle of the River Granicus make a reconstruction possible, if one visits the ground and allows for changes in the courses of the two rivers since antiquity.[2] Distances were normally recorded in stades (e.g. 1.17.4). They were measured by A's surveyors, *bematistai*, and the length of each day's march was called a *stathmos*. The records of these *stathmoi* were kept in his Archive.[3] When the *bematistai* were absent, as in the foray north of the Danube, a rough measurement was given, namely as a 'parasang' – a term familiarised by Xenophon in his *Anabasis* (1.4.4). As a Greek writer

---

[1] Such orders were issued daily in the Welch Regiment in 1940, when I was serving in it.

[2] See *HGR*, and E. Badian and C. Foss in *Anc. Mac.* 2 (1977) 271–93 and 495–502.

[3] I use this term to describe papers kept together with the *Journal of A*, such as the letters mentioned in Plu. *Eum.* 2.3. For the *stathmoi* see Pearson *LHA* 137 and my comments in H*RJ* 137ff.

with more pretensions to literary style, Aristobulus may be preferred rather than Ptolemy as the source of the word, which would have been pedantic in the prose of Arrian's day.[4]

(3) Routes taken by the army. That from Macedonia (probably from Amphaxitis) to Sestus was carefully defined (1.11.3–5). Arrian reported two routes from Phaselis to Perge: one through the mountains on a road which the Thracian troops made, and the other along the shore, which was rendered practicable only by a strong offshore wind (1.26.1). When he was in Caria, A sent part of the army under Parmenio to Sardis and thence to Gordium (1.24.3 and 1.29.3), and A himself followed the coast at first and then went inland via Celaenae. The route of Parmenio was not described at all; that of A was described place by place. The siting of A's camp was recorded on six occasions.

(4) Numbers of forces. The total on setting out from Macedonia was given as 'not much more than 30,000 infantry and over 5,000 cavalry' (1.11.3). These figures are different from those of Anaximenes (*FGrH* 72 F 29), Callisthenes (124 F 35) and Aristobulus (139 F 4), but they agree with those of Ptolemy (138 F 4), who reported in round figures 30,000 infantry and 5,000 cavalry. Thus Arrian followed Ptolemy in this instance.[5] The numbers of men in the regular units were not given by Arrian, but the numbers of those in special forces and also in reinforcements from Europe were given (e.g. 1.18.1, 1.29.3 and 1.29.4). Persian losses were recorded in round numbers (1.16.2; 1.22.7; 1.28.7) and some distinguished men among them were named (1.16.3; 1.20.10).

A's own losses at the River Granicus were reported in detail as 25 cavalrymen at the first onset (bronze statues of them being set up at Dium), over 60 other cavalrymen and up to 30 infantrymen (1.16.4). Since Aristobulus gave different figures (*PA* 16.15; see above, p. 36), Arrian took these figures not from him but from Ptolemy. It will be recalled that Arrian quoted Ptolemy as his authority for the first citation of Mace-

---

[4] However, Bosworth *C* 63 attributed 'this single aberration' to 'a piece of deliberate antiquarianism' by Arrian.

[5] So Brunt *L* 1 lxix 'it is evident that Arrian adopted Ptolemy's figures.'

donian losses at 1.2.7, distinguishing cavalry and infantry as here. Arrian mentioned a number of things for the first time with the tacit assumption that his reader would supply them later: for instance, the burial of his dead with their arms and other marks of honour, the remission of taxes etc. to their parents and children, the visit to the wounded, the listening to their stories, and the burying of the Persian commanders, all after the Battle of the River Granicus (1.16.5f.). Accordingly, it seems that Arrian intended us to understand from 1.2.7 that citations of Macedonian losses would be taken thereafter from Ptolemy, i.e. ultimately from the *Journal of A*. This is made practically certain when we note the report of casualties at Halicarnassus as 16 dead and 300 wounded (1.20.10). It is evident that when A visited the wounded his aides kept a count, and the number was included in the *Journal of A*.[6] None of the earlier casualty lists, which have survived in literature or on stone, included the wounded. Arrian mentioned among the 40 dead three leading men by name and 'other Macedonians of repute' – these last were evidently named in Arrian's source but Arrian selected three of them (1.22.7; only one at 1.28.8). This information came evidently from Ptolemy, who derived it from the *Journal*.

In the naming of units Arrian was inconsistent. For instance, the terms used in the order of battle at 1.14.1–3 differed from those in the narrative. Thus 'the Agrianians the javelin-men' appeared in the order of battle; previously they had been simply 'the Agrianians'.[7] A force of light cavalry was called 'the Lancers' in the order of battle (σαρισσοφόροι) but 'the Scouts' at 1.12.7 and 1.14.6 (πρόδρομοι). The Hypaspists were called 'of the Companions' in the order of battle, but elsewhere just the Hypaspists. The addition no doubt was made in order to show that they, like the men of the pikemen-phalanx, were members of the King's Companionate.[8] The Brigades of the phalanx were called 'phalanges' in the order of

---

[6] See HCR 58 and 61.

[7] At 1.27.8 Arrian's expression 'the brigades of the javelin-men' referred to the Agrianes.

[8] Of the pikemen some were called *pezhetairoi* 'Footmen-companions' (1.28.3) and others *asthetairoi* 'Townsmen-companions' (e.g. 2.23.2).

battle, but elsewhere simply 'brigades' (τάξεις, e.g. at 1.15.4).
The explanation of the variations is probably that as Arrian
was using Ptolemy and Aristobulus he took one term from one
and another term for the same thing from the other.

Again, terms such as 'chiliarches' (commander of a thousand, i.e. of a brigade of Hypaspists) and 'hipparchia' (an
aggregate of squadrons of Companion Cavalry) are to be
similarly explained (at 1.22.7 and 1.24.3). They are not to be
interpreted as erroneous anachronisms made by Arrian or his
source.[9] So too the personal retinue of A in battle was described in more than one way. The seven Somatophylakes
were called 'the King's Somatophylakes' at 1.21.4, and 'those
around A' were 'the Companions around A' at 1.6.5.

Orders issued by A numbered twenty-one between 1.11.1
and 2.3.8, some being relatively trivial such as the order that
Lysippus be employed to make the statues of the 25 Companion Cavalrymen at Dium (1.16.4) or that the siege-engines
were to be moved on to Tralles (1.23.6). In this category I
include what we should call appointments to administrative
positions (e.g. at 1.29.3). The persons responsible for carrying out some of the orders were named, e.g. for taking over
Priapus (1.12.7), Dascylium (1.17.2) and Sardis (1.17.4). If
such a person failed, the order as recorded in the *Journal* could
be cited against him (e.g. 6.27.1, Apollophanes).

The naming of officers by Arrian is as in the earlier chapters,
i.e. occasionally those in command of some regular units (e.g.
in the order of battle at 1.14.1–3) and frequently those in command of special task-forces (e.g. Ptolemaeus, son of Seleucus,
at 1.23.6; 1.24.1; 1.29.4). Parmenio was named frequently
among the latter (1.14.1; 1.17.2; 1.18.1; 1.24.3; 1.29.3). Within
this section, 1.11 to 2.3, some forty-eight officers (including
deserters but not patronymics) were named, several in connection with special orders. Since a considerable number of
patronymics were recorded by Arrian, it is evident that his
source did so regularly. The details in this category were such
that neither Ptolemy nor Aristobulus could have held them in

---

[9] As suggested for 'the hipparchy' by Brunt in *JHS* 83 (1963) 29 and Bosworth *C* 155.
Griffith in *JHS* 83 (1963) 70f. was of my opinion in this matter.

their memory for some fifty years. The names and the duties were no doubt taken by Ptolemy from the *Journal of A*.

The spotlight was on A, except at the beginning of book 2. 'Himself' appears very frequently (e.g. at 1.17.3 and 5), and he is at the centre of the account of the Battle of the River Granicus, both in its preliminaries (1.13.6–14.3) and in the action itself (1.14.6f. and 15.6–8). When we compared the account of Plutarch with that of Arrian about A's personal combat (P*A* 16.7–11 and Arr. 1.15.6–8), we noted some differences in points of detail (above, p. 35); and we may add, for instance, A breaking his lance on striking Rhoesaces and then taking to his sword in Plutarch's account, whereas according to Arrian A broke his lance earlier, asked a 'groom' of the King's retinue[10] for a replacement, obtained one from Demaratus and later went on to attack Rhoesaces. Thus Arrian was correcting Plutarch, and he did so presumably because Arrian knew he had a more accurate source (as in the recording of the casualties on the Macedonian side). I have argued above (p. 36) that the best explanation is that Plutarch was drawing on Aristobulus, and that Arrian, while drawing on both Ptolemy and Aristobulus, chose to follow Ptolemy on some matters of detail, because he knew that Ptolemy had derived them from the *Journal of A*.

The naval side of the campaign has sometimes not been clarified, for instance, by Brunt *L* 1 453: 'In 334 A had 160 ships (1.11.6) ... Diod. 17.17.2 ... 60, which may be amended to 160; Just. 11.6.2 has 182, presumably in error.' In my opinion the numbers were correct. The (Greek) fleet of 160 triremes and many merchant ships transported 'the cavalry and most of the infantry' from Sestus to Abydus (Arr. 1.11.6), Parmenio being appointed to take charge. A and the rest of the infantry sailed from Elaeus to the Troad (ibid.) in the (Macedonian) fleet of 60 ships (Diod. 17.17.2), of which 22 were triremes and 38 were evidently penteconters and triaconters if we take Justin's figure to refer to the total number of triremes (11.6.2). At 1.18.4 Nicanor brought forward 'the Greek fleet' (τὸ

---

[10] For this 'groom' (ἀναβολεύς, lit. 'mounter') see H*RP* 268; *contra* Berve II 58 and Bosworth *C* 122.

Ἑλληνικὸν ναυτικόν; cf. 1.19.7) and anchored 'with 160 ships' at Lade; and it was this Greek fleet which A disbanded, partly because its numerous contingents had not practised together as a fleet (1.18.7). Up to this point Arrian may have taken his figures from Ptolemy, who had drawn on the *Journal of A*.

We learn only from Diodorus that A kept a few ships, which included 'the twenty Athenian allied ships',[11] for the transport of the siege-engines (17.22.5), and that these siege-engines and food supplies were taken by sea to Halicarnassus (17.24.1). The source of Diodorus was probably Diyllus (*THA* 38f.). In any case, since the fleet was not in immediate contact with A, it did not figure, it seems, in Ptolemy's source, i.e. the *Journal of A*. On the other hand, when the siege-engines were sent from Halicarnassus inland to Tralles, no doubt for Parmenio to transport[12] to Gordium, the order to that effect was noted in Arrian 1.23.6, drawing probably on Ptolemy, who had taken the order from the *Journal*.

Other items in Arrian's account which may have come ultimately from the *Journal* were reports of negotiations, whether by letter (1.18.4) or by envoys (1.19.1; 1.24.5; 1.26.2f.; 1.27.3f.; 1.28.1; 1.29.2; 1.29.5). For we know that such reports were included in the Journals of Hellenistic kings.[13]

Arrian reported a number of *legomena* within 1.11 to 2.3. The most striking instances were in the Troad. The narrative tenses brought A to Elaeus (at the south-east tip of the Chersonese), and there he sacrificed to Protesilaus (1.11.5). Then at 1.11.6 'the general story prevails' (ὁ πλείων λόγος κατέχει) was followed by the accusative and infinitive construction with further mentions *en passant* of 'they say' (λέγουσι) and 'the story holds' (λόγος κατέχει) down to 1.11.8. At 1.12.1 a narrative tense reappeared, and a lacuna in the text followed. After the lacuna 'the story' took over again (οἱ δέ sc. λέγουσι;

---

[11] The correct term νῆες συμμαχίδες in accordance with the alliance which had been made between the Greeks of the Common Peace and the Macedonians (3.24.5), represented sometimes by their king (e.g. 2.2.2); see Curt. 3.1.20 'ex foedere naves sociis imperatae'. See *HM* 3.571–9.

[12] Parmenio had been sent to Tralles earlier (1.18.1), and he had 'the waggons' (1.24.3), which were necessary for transporting heavy gear; see *HAT* 29.

[13] See *HRJ* 130f.

λέγουσιν ὅτι; ὡς λόγος). The narrative tenses resumed at
1.12.6. As Arrian had stated in the *Preface*, the narrative
tenses marked an account which was derived from Ptolemy
and/or Aristobulus. When he said 'the general story prevails',
he did not necessarily exclude either Ptolemy or Aristobulus
as sharing in that story, as we see at 3.3.6 'Aristobulus and
the general story prevails in this case.' Other authors who
contributed to the general story may have been Callisthenes,
Cleitarchus, Marsyas, Onesicritus etc., but Arrian did not
name any of them. Frequent comparisons were made no
doubt with the crossing of the Greeks for the Trojan War and
the crossing of Xerxes for the war against the Greeks.

Elsewhere Arrian used such simple expressions as 'others
say' (1.11.1; 1.12.1), 'it is said' (1.12.10) and 'as a story goes'
(1.16.3). The first of these *legomena* appeared also in Diodorus
17.16.3f., a passage for which I suggested Diyllus as source
(*THA* 31 and 51), and there is no particular parallel for the
others. At 2.3.7 Arrian contrasted the *legomenon* of some that
A cut the Gordian knot with his sword (οἱ μὲν λέγουσιν) with
the statement of Aristobulus that A removed the yoke-pin and
detached the yoke from the pole (Ἀριστόβουλος δὲ λέγει).
The cutting with a sword was reported in Justin 11.7.16 and in
Curtius 3.1.14–19. In *THA* 97 and 120 I considered that different sources were probably used by Trogus and by Curtius, and
that one of those sources was Cleitarchus.[14] Plutarch had
already reported both methods of undoing the knot, and he
had attributed the second one to Aristobulus (*PA* 18.4; see
above, p. 47, where I held that Plutarch had read Cleitarchus).

Arrian made two interjections of his own. Thus on the
subject of the Gordian knot he remarked 'I cannot state confidently the way in which A dealt with the knot.' His uncertainty
is probably to be explained by the fact that Ptolemy either did
not say how the knot was overcome or did not give the same
explanation as Aristobulus or 'some' others did.[15] We see
from this example that Arrian was extremely scrupulous in

---

[14] Jacoby in *FGrH* 2 D 511 attributed the story of the cutting of the Gordian knot to
Cleitarchus.
[15] Bosworth *C* 187 came to a different conclusion, namely that 'Ptolemy did give the
sword story in some form.'

assessing the truth of what he narrated. At 1.12.2–5 Arrian asserted that he was 'not unworthy' to celebrate the deeds of A even as Homer had celebrated those of Achilles. He gave his own estimate of A: 'there is no one among Greeks and barbarians who has performed so many deeds on such a scale, both in numbers and in greatness,' as A (1.12.4). In this honest statement so early in his work Arrian informed his reader of his own attitude towards his subject.[16]

Since Arrian marked his own interjections so clearly, it is evident that all the rest of the account in 1.11 to 2.3 came from Ptolemy and/or Aristobulus. Thus it was one or other, or both, who reported A's attitude to omens at 1.18.7–9, 1.20.1 and 1.25.8, to thunder (1.17.6; ἐκ θεοῦ and 2.3.8 ἐξ οὐρανοῦ ... τοῖς θεοῖς) and to the timely wind in Pamphylia, which A and his retinue interpreted as 'not without divine direction' (1.26.2 οὐκ ἄνευ τοῦ θείου).[17] In the same way singly or together they were responsible for the dialogue between Parmenio and A over the action to be taken at the River Granicus (1.13.2–7) and in facing the Persian fleet (1.18.6–9),[18] and for the report of A's consultation of his Companions about Alexander, son of Aëropus (1.25).[19]

The Persian naval offensive of 333 (2.1f.) was described from the Persian point of view and not with reference to orders given by A. Thus it was not based at all on references in the

---

[16] This passage has been called 'the second Preface', but it arose naturally enough from A congratulating Achilles on the account of Achilles' deeds by Homer. See Stadter 61ff.

[17] Strabo 666f. described the two routes – over the mountain and along the coast (as in Arr. 1.26.1) – and attributed A's success in using the latter route to his trusting in 'fortune' (τῇ τύχῃ). Strabo reported the passage along the coast as lasting all day with water up to the men's navels, whereas Arrian reckoned it 'easy and speedy' as compared with the arduous route over the mountain, which he called 'circuitous and steep'.

[18] That Parmenio as the senior general and as second-in-command should exchange views with A was most sensible, and this may well have been standard practice. A report of their views was also an artistic way of representing the issues at stake. It was a recognised technique of Greek historians from Herodotus onwards. There is no attempt to denigrate Parmenio; for his policies of caution at the River Granicus and of some form of attack at sea were both tenable.

[19] Such consultation was normal, as we see in the case of Philotas (Curt. 6.8.1–15). The different account of Diodorus (17.32.1–2) came probably from Cleitarchus; see THA 41f.

Journal of A. Ptolemy and Aristobulus must have acquired the information from Greek islanders and from Greeks in the Persian navy, and of the two Aristobulus may have taken more interest in this campaign in Greek waters than Ptolemy. The account is well-informed both on sea-routes (e.g. 2.1.2), and on the treaty-relationships of Greek cities with Alexander (2.1.4), with Alexander and the Greeks (of the Common Peace) (1.2.3) and with Darius (2.1.4 and 2.2.2).[20] However, it was in an abbreviated form. Thus it is not stated that the Macedonian fleet, as opposed to the Greek fleet, had not been disbanded and was holding the Hellespont, and that A sent large sums of money to two Macedonian officers there (Amphoterus and Hegelochus) and to Antipater and Greek officers of the Common Peace, who were to reassemble the Greek fleet (Curt. 3.1.19f.). Arrian's account reported only the delay involved in reassembling a fleet (1.2.3) and the bold and successful action of Proteas, a Macedonian officer acting under the orders of Antipater (1.2.4f.).

2. Ancyra to Memphis (2.4–3.5)

Those features of Arrian's narrative which were due ultimately to Ptolemy's use of the *Journal of A* are again conspicuous in this section. On ten occasions events were dated by days (e.g. 3.1.1, the march to Egypt in six days). Orders issued by A were reported fourteen times. Geographical details were provided with precision for A's marches in Cilicia, the Battle of Issus,[21] the sieges of Tyre and Gaza, and the expedition to Siwa. Distances were given in stades and *stathmoi* (e.g. 2.26.1 and 2.6.1), and some measurements were given in feet (e.g. 2.27.3). The military information was extremely full. Within this section no fewer than 56 officers were named, often with their patronymic and generally with a statement of each's respon-

---

[20] See my account in *HM* III 70f. and for the treaties 72f. with 73 n. 1, where I discuss views advanced by Badian, Bosworth and Brunt.

[21] Arrian gave a clue to a change in the shape of the coast since antiquity; see *AG*[2] 98ff. with photographs in the first edition as figs. 23–8, and the important fragment of Callisthenes in Plb. 12.17.5.

sibility. The regular Macedonian and other units were named time and again, and a few for the first time: the squadron of Companion Cavalry 'from Anthemous', the squadron called 'Leugaia', and a brigade of *asthetairoi* (2.9.3 and 2.23.2). The Infantry Guard was distinguished from 'the Hypaspists whom Nicanor, son of Parmenio, commanded' (2.8.3).[22] The numbers of men in these regular units were not specified. On eight occasions we are told which units A selected for special missions under his personal command. The centre of the military narrative was held by A, especially in the sieges of Tyre and Gaza (e.g. 2.23.4 and 2.27.1); and it was sufficient to write just 'himself' (αὐτός) on ten occasions (e.g. 2.4.3–6). Due credit was given to Parmenio for carrying out special missions (2.4.3; 2.5.1; 2.8.4; 2.11.10; 2.15.1); but no details were given of Parmenio's orders or actions, even when he was commanding the entire left wing during the Battle of Issus (2.8.4). Much of this detailed information could not have been carried in the memory of either Ptolemy or Aristobulus.

Numbers of enemy forces and of enemy losses were given in round figures (e.g. at Issus 2.8.5–7; 2.11.8; 2.13.1f.; and at Tyre 2.24.4f.). Losses on the Macedonian side were reported sometimes for single groups (2.10.7 Ptolemaeus and 120 phalangites; 2.24.4 Admetus and 20 Hypaspists). The total loss in the Battle of Issus was not stated. The omission is best explained as an oversight by Arrian. For Curtius gave the loss as 32 infantry, 150 cavalry and 504 wounded (3.11.27),[23] figures which in my opinion came ultimately from the *Journal*; moreover, Curtius' figure for the Persian losses was the same as that of Arrian (2.11.8), who certainly owed his figures for losses within single groups to the *Journal of A*.[24] The total of 'the Macedonians' lost at Tyre was given by Arrian as '400 or so'

---

[22] This Guard is that of 1.8.4. In the Battle of Issus A led it in the initial dash through the river-bed (2.10.3 ἐπὶ τοῦ δεξιοῦ τεταγμένος δρόμῳ resuming 2.8.3 ἐπὶ τοῦ δεξιοῦ κέρως). The river-bed was not suitable for a dash by cavalry, which has often been proposed (e.g. recently by A. M. Devine in *The Ancient World* 12 (1985) 52 'slowly and painfully'). See n. 73 in *AG²* 292.

[23] See H*CR* 58 with n. 12, rejecting additions to the text as in the Loeb edition.

[24] Such a record was needed by A in order to arrange for replacements; see H*CR* 59.

(2.24.4), a figure probably derived from the *Journal*, in which losses of allied troops were, I imagine, not recorded.[25]

Two speeches by A were reported by Arrian. The first, which was delivered to a meeting of Commanders before the Battle of Issus, was reported in the accusative and infinitive (2.7.3–9), but it was interrupted by a *legomenon* in a narrative tense (2.7.8f. λέγεται). If we interpret this unusual juxtaposition in the light of Arrian's *Preface*, we conclude that Arrian took the report from his usual sources – Ptolemy and/or Aristobulus – and the *legomenon* from a source or sources other than them. Thus he believed the reported speech to be true and the *legomenon* to be 'worth reporting and not altogether incredible'. The second speech, which was delivered to a meeting of Companions and Commanders when the Tyrians had refused to admit A, was given by Arrian in direct speech (2.17, introduced by ἔλεξεν ὧδε). When the narrative was resumed, 'in saying these things he was persuading them' (18.3 ταῦτα λέγων ... ἔπειθεν) and 'since these things won the day, he decided to build a mole' (18.3). The difference in the methods of reporting the two speeches is significant. The first speech consisted of a summary of the points which Arrian took from the version given by Ptolemy and/or Aristobulus, and Arrian felt free to interpose a *legomenon*. The second speech was a report *in extenso* but not verbatim (for Arrian imposed his own style) of a speech, the text of which he read in Ptolemy and/or Aristobulus. How could such a speech have survived? The answer is the same as we shall propose shortly for the letter of A to Darius (2.14.4 introduced by ἔχει ὧδε and resumed by ταῦτ' ἐπέστειλεν), and as we shall give for the report of the *Royal Journal* at 7.25 (introduced by ὧδε ἔχουσιν): either Arrian saw them *in extenso* in the account of Ptolemy, who used the *Journal*, or Arrian himself read them in the *Journal*, as was the case at 7.25. I am now excluding Aristo-

---

[25] At the first mention of casualties at 1.2.7, which came from Ptolemy and on my interpretation ultimately from A's *Journal*, casualties of non-Macedonian troops in A's army were excluded by the words 'of Macedonians themselves'. Brunt *L* I 13 omitted αὐτῶν in his translation despite its emphatic position, and Bosworth did not comment on it.

bulus from consideration, because I do not think that anyone could have remembered such a speech *in extenso* or verbatim after an interval of some forty years.[26]

Within this section Arrian gave reports of embassies: of Paphlagonians at 2.4.1;[27] of Darius at 2.14 and at 2.25; of many from Greece at 3.5.1; and of Carthaginians at Tyre at 2.24.5. We know from Polyaenus that detailed reports of embassies were recorded in the *Journal* of an Antigonus (4.6.2), and it is reasonable to expect that this was so in the *Journal of A.* The most illuminating is the report of Darius' first embassy and of A's reply. The letter from Darius which the envoys delivered was summarised by Arrian in reported speech (2.14.2 ἐδήλου δὲ ἡ ἐπιστολή). On the other hand, A's letter in reply was recorded by Arrian in direct speech (2.14.4, introduced by ἔχει ὧδε). Thus we have an exact parallel to Arrian's different methods of reporting the two speeches of A. Our deduction is the same: Arrian summarised the content of Darius' letter which he read either in the account of Ptolemy or in the *Journal*, and he put in his own style the actual letter of A, which he read either in Ptolemy or in the *Journal*.[28]

Both A and Arrian believed in divine manifestations. Thus A's dream of Heracles welcoming him into Tyre, both in itself and as interpreted by Aristander, was said to have been 'something divine' (καί τι καὶ θεῖον); and the dream contributed to A's decision to lay siege to the city (2.18.1). Then as A was sacrificing outside Gaza, a stone was dropped on his head by a bird of prey. The interpretation by Aristander was taken seriously and was believed by A to have been confirmed in the

[26] A summary of previous views about these two speeches is given by Bosworth *C* 204 and 238. He himself held that in the first speech the section before the *legomenon* was derived from Arrian's 'main source, most probably Ptolemy'; and that as regards the second speech 'Arrian found in his sources a speech in favour of conquering the Levant and turned it into a set piece before Tyre'. In my opinion the speech is anchored historically to the occasion by Arrian, and the phrases of introduction and resumption indicate that it is an authentic account of what A said. So also Atkinson 271.

[27] Arrian mentioned an agreement but not its terms. He was no doubt abbreviating the narratives of Ptolemy and Aristobulus, as at 2.4.2 where the 'country beyond the Halys' was presumably defined in that narrative.

[28] See *AG²* 113 and n. 79, with references to other views, to which add Bosworth *C* 227f.

event (2.26.4 and 2.27.1f.). On the way to Siwa there was much rain, which was attributed to divine intervention (3.3.4 ἐς τὸ θεῖον), and the same was said of snakes or crows guiding A to his destination (3.3.4–6). On this occasion Arrian added his own belief in the first person: 'I can state confidently that some divine power helped A' (3.3.6). This addition shows us that the expressions of belief in the narrative were in the source or sources.

The preliminaries to the Battle of Issus provided another instance of divine power. When Darius left his favourable position at Sochi through his own wishful thinking and the advice of flatterers (2.6.4f.), 'some superhuman power chanced' (2.6.6 καί τι καὶ δαιμόνιον τυχόν)[29] to lead him into the very place where his huge forces were unavailing and victory was granted 'easily' to A. 'For it already had to be that the Persians would lose the rule of Asia to the Macedonians, just as the Medes had lost it to the Persians, and the Assyrians still earlier to the Medes' (2.6.7). As we see from Arrian's statements in the *Preface* and from his practice at 3.3.6, the belief in a form of divine chance or predestination was expressed by Ptolemy and/or Aristobulus and was taken over by Arrian.[30] 'The god' played a similar role in the speech of A (2.7.3).

Naval affairs within this section were narrated only when they impinged on A. Thus ships which had carried mercenaries to join Darius at Sochi (2.2.1) were seized after the Battle of Issus by escaping mercenaries (2.13.3). In A's speech at 2.17 his understanding of the issues at sea was shown, and his forecast of the future was more far-sighted than it had been when he first enunciated the policy of defeating the Persian fleet on land (1.20.1). The naval side of the sieging of Tyre was described with admirable detail (e.g. 2.20.1–3) and with full understanding of oarsmanship (2.21.9). On the other hand, the progress of the naval war in the Aegean was not described when it was happening. It was made known after the event by

---

[29] The idea that circumstances which appeared to be due to mere chance (τύχη) were controlled by a divine power was not uncommon.

[30] Arrian did not interject any view of his own, such as for instance the view that the rule of Asia was taken from the Macedonians by the Romans.

Hegesippus, whose report to A in Egypt was summarised in 3.2.3–7. The explanation is no doubt that Ptolemy found this material in the *Journal of A*, and that neither he nor Aristobulus was concerned with the development of the war in the Aegean Sea.[31]

The illness of A at Tarsus was due to exhaustion according to Aristobulus, but 'others say' (οἱ δέ ... λέγουσι) that A swam in the river Cydnus of which the water was cold (2.4.7). The same two explanations were reported by Plutarch but without mentioning Aristobulus (P*A* 19.2, above p. 48). Arrian did not opt for one or the other explanation. Thereafter the narrative was expressed in the accusative and infinitive, which probably indicated to the reader that Arrian was drawing upon both Aristobulus and the 'others' for a narrative which was mainly a *legomenon*.[32] It was far less sensational than the account of Plutarch, for which we have suggested the source was Cleitarchus (above, p. 48). All we can say is that Cleitarchus was not among the 'others'. There are two other *legomena*, for which we cannot name the sources: one in the course of the reported speech by A (2.7.8f. λέγεται), and the other being that Darius had at the Battle of Issus 600,000 men (2.8.8), a figure given also by Plutarch (P*A* 18.6) and *POxy* 1798 (*FGrH* 148 F 44 col. ii).[33]

At 2.12.3 Arrian described A's reaction when he realised that the women of Darius' family were mourning. He introduced his account with the remark that 'certain of those who wrote of A's achievements say', and this was followed by the accusative and infinitive. Then at the end of this account he wrote: 'that is what Ptolemy and Aristobulus say' (2.12.6). He presumably indicated to the reader that these two were his main sources but not his only sources for the account so far.

---

[31] Curt. 4.5.14–22 gave a more detailed account in historical sequence, his source being probably Diyllus (see *THA* 128).

[32] Bosworth *C* 190 suggested including Ptolemy. However, if Ptolemy and Aristobulus had given the same version, Arrian would not have introduced his *legomenon*, or he would have named both authors as he did at 2.12.6.

[33] The nearest figure in our sources was 500,000. It was given by Diodorus, following Cleitarchus in my opinion (*THA* 41), for the size of the army which Darius mustered at Babylon, not for the army which fought at Issus, to which Greek mercenaries from the fleet and probably local forces had been added.

He turned next to an account of what was said to have happened on the following day – a *legomenon* (λόγος δὲ ἔχει), i.e. not in Ptolemy and/or Aristobulus – namely a visit to the ladies by A and Hephaestion. When the account ended, Arrian wrote: 'and this I have recorded neither as true nor as utterly incredible' (2.12.8 οὔτε ὡς ἀληθῆ οὔτε ὡς πάντη ἄπιστα, with strong hiatus for emphasis). The wording was deliberately reminiscent of the wording in the *Preface*, where Arrian said he would report matter from his two main sources, when in agreement, as πάντη ἀληθῆ, and *legomena* as οὐ πάντη ἄπιστα. Since he was keeping an open mind, Arrian gave his own reaction to the alternatives. If the visit did occur, Arrian approved of A's behaviour. If it did not, Arrian approved of the writers' belief that A would have spoken and acted so. The ultimate source of the *legomenon* was probably Cleitarchus; for it appeared also in Diodorus 17.37.5f. and Curtius 3.12.15–17, and in these passages I have argued that the common source was Cleitarchus (*THA* 19f. and 118). See also above, p. 52, where I considered Plutarch's version of the first part of Arrian's account and suggested that Plutarch's more picturesque details came ultimately from Cleitarchus. Arrian will have read both Cleitarchus and Plutarch, and he preferred to be guided primarily by Ptolemy and/or Aristobulus.

After describing the second offer which Darius made to A, Arrian reported a *legomenon* (2.25.2 λέγουσι), that Parmenio said in a council of the Companions that he would accept if he were A, and that A said he would have accepted if he had been Parmenio. This *legomenon* had been told already by Diodorus (17.54.3–5) and by Plutarch (*PA* 29.7f.; see above, p. 62), and in an expanded form by Curtius (4.11.10–14). In *THA* 45 and 122 I concluded that the common source of Diodorus and Curtius was Cleitarchus.[34] Arrian did not find that anecdote in either Ptolemy or Aristobulus.[35]

---

[34] So too Goukowsky 208f.; Atkinson 398 suggested that Callisthenes reported it and possibly invented it (but invention would have been most foolish at a time when so many companions had been present).

[35] Bosworth *C* 257 claimed of the *legomenon* that it did not 'mark a switch from main to subsidiary sources'. His claim is diametrically opposed to Arrian's stated method in his *Preface* and should be rejected. Plutarch dated the anecdote to summer 331; see above, p. 62.

At 3.2.1 Arrian introduced a *legomenon* with words which are reminiscent of those in the *Preface*: 'there is told also a story as follows, a story not incredible to me at least' (λέγεται ... λόγος, οὐκ ἄπιστος ἔμοιγε; and in the *Preface* οὐ πάντη ἄπιστα). Because the builders had no chalk to mark the layout of A's new city, Alexandria, they used barley-meal, and this led Aristander to regard it as an omen that the city would prosper in the fruits of the earth. An even shorter version had appeared in Strabo 792. But Plutarch (P*A* 26.8–10; see above, p. 59) and Curtius (4.8.6) added a flock of birds descending to devour the barley-meal, which seemed a bad omen but was favourably interpreted by the diviners. The ultimate source of this *legomenon* was probably Cleitarchus, as I argued in the case of Curtius (*THA* 123f.).[36] At 3.5.7 Arrian stated as a *legomenon* (λέγεται) that A gave positions of command in Egypt to several persons, because to entrust them to one man would have been dangerous. The source of this *legomenon* is not known.

This last *legomenon* was followed by an interjection by Arrian himself to the effect that in his opinion the Romans learnt from A to make special arrangements for Egypt (3.5.7 Ῥωμαῖοί μοι δοκοῦσι). Other interjections within this present section were marked equally clearly by Arrian. At 2.16.4–6, having distinguished the Tyrian Heracles from the Egyptian Heracles and the Greek Heracles in his narrative (i.e. drawing on Ptolemy and/or Aristobulus), Arrian said emphatically 'I think' (δοκῶ ἐγώ), that the Heracles worshipped at Tartessus[37] is the Tyrian Heracles and not the Greek Heracles, and he supported his view by drawing on his personal knowledge of Epirus (2.16.6 οἶδα δὲ ἐγώ)[38] in connection with the cattle

---

[36] See Hamilton *C* 68 for barley-meal being a symbol of abundant food; that no doubt was why it was used in this way in Macedonia (Curt. 4.8.6). Bosworth *C* 265 accepted the *legomenon* as coming from Arrian's subsidiary sources.

[37] Bosworth *C* 236 claimed that Arrian meant Gades and not Tartessus. Such a claim is strange, when we note that Arrian sensibly said Gades (Γάδειρα) when he meant Gades, at 3.30.9 and 7.1.2. The confusion seems to emanate from Bosworth rather than Arrian. At 2.16.4 'some pillars named after Heracles' were in Tartessus; thus they were not the famous pillars of Heracles of 5.26.2, which were those at Gades. Arrian had probably served in Spain and knew the country.

[38] He had lived in Epirus as a pupil of Epictetus.

of Geryones. For he reckoned it not unlikely that the king of
Epirus was called Geryones (οὐκ ἔξω τοῦ εἰκότος τίθεμαι). By
this repeated use of the first person Arrian marked out punctil-
iously the limits of his own interjection. The same is true of
2.24.6, where, after the capture of Tyre, A dedicated a sacred
Tyrian ship to Heracles, Arrian did not report the epigram
of dedication, for 'it was not worth recording' (οὐκ ἄξιον
μνήμης; cf. in the *Preface* ἀξιαφήγητα) 'and that is why I did
not think fit to report it' (ἐγὼ αὐτὸ ἀναγράψαι ἀπηξίωσα,
with hiatus for emphasis). At 3.3.6, after mentioning the
snakes or crows guiding A to Siwa, Arrian continued: 'that
some divine power helped him I can assert (αὐτῷ ἔχω
ἰσχυρίσασθαι, with hiatus), because probability also inclined
that way; but the exact truth of the account is lost through the
variations which the writers have provided in their versions'.

Within this section Arrian made mention of Aristobulus
alone at 2.4.7 (for the cause of A's illness at Tarsus) and
at 3.3.3 (for A's march, presumably from Alexandria, to
Paraetonium), no doubt because he found his reports different
from those of others. In connection with Ptolemy's mention
of snakes guiding A and Aristobulus' mention of crows having
that honour Arrian noted that Aristobulus was in agreement
with 'the general story' (3.3.6 ὁ πλείων λόγος). This is a good
example of his wide reading and open-mindedness. A further
difference between Ptolemy and Aristobulus was noted by
Arrian at 3.4.5: Aristobulus brought A to Egypt 'by the same
way back' (τὴν αὐτὴν ὀπίσω ὁδόν) 'but Ptolemy ... by a different way direct to Memphis'. Here the word 'back' (ὀπίσω)
recalled the matter of the snakes, according to Ptolemy, leading A to the oracle 'and back again' (3.3.5 καὶ ὀπίσω αὖθις,
with the usual hiatus), whereas Aristobulus had the crows
guide A only on the way to the oracle. Arrian was here most
accurate and precise.

At 2.11.8 Arrian made mention of Ptolemy alone as having
accompanied A in the cavalry pursuit at the Battle of Issus,
and as reporting that the cavalrymen crossed a gully on the
corpses of Persians. Evidently Aristobulus had not reported
this. Arrian mentioned the incident as particularly vivid. We

may compare his report of Persian infantrymen trampling others of their company to death in crossing the moat at Halicarnassus (1.22.5).[39]

3. Phoenicia to the Tanaïs (3.6 to 4.4)

Within this section there are twenty-five instances of dating of events and intervals by days (e.g. in the day-by-day pursuit of Darius, the twenty days' march from Babylon to Susa, and comparative dates at 3.19.4f.). Orders issued by A were reported for thirty-three occasions, those during the Battle of Gaugamela being of particular interest (3.13.12–14). No fewer than seventy-six officers (some being Persians appointed by A) were named, sometimes with a patronymic and usually with the duty of each defined. The military details are very full on the Macedonian side. The regular units keep recurring, but the number of men in any of them is never stated. On the other hand, a number was sometimes given for a special detachment (e.g. 3.17.2, 8,000 other infantry), and the units taken by A on special operations were named on ten occasions. All his actions on such operations were described. The actions of other commanders, e.g. of Parmenio, were not described, unless they impinged on A himself (e.g. 3.14 fin. and 15).[40]

It is evident that Arrian took military details from the accounts of both Ptolemy and Aristobulus, because he introduced some unusual terms: 'the Guard of the Hypaspists', previously 'the Royal Hypaspists' (3.11.9), 'the King's Squadrons', usually limited to the one Royal Sqadron (3.11.8), 'the

---

[39] Callisthenes had said that most Persians died in the gullies in the flight (Plb. 12.20.4). The account of Ptolemy, who was accompanying A at the time, has been questioned by some scholars. See the summary in Bosworth C 217. Brunt's translation of φάραγξ at 1.163 'a deep gully' has added to the confusion. In Plb. 12.20.4 Callisthenes called these gullies ἐκρήγματα and κοιλώματα, which meant hollowed out torrent-beds such as were caused by seasonal rains rather than gorges and ravines. Arrian had already stated at 2.11.3 that the Persian cavalrymen suffered heavy losses through riding over one another in their panic. It would be strange indeed if modern scholars knew better what happened then than two contemporaries, Ptolemy and Callisthenes.

[40] Even then very briefly. The description of Ptolemy's action in taking possession of Bessus and bringing him to A was an exception, no doubt because it was based on Ptolemy's account in his own history (3.29.7–30.3).

Grooms' (3.13.6), 'a tetrarchy of cavalry' (3.18.5), 'hipparchies of Companion Cavalry' (3.29.7), and 'the Bodyguards' in a context which seems to refer not to the seven Bodyguards of A but to the Royal Infantry Guardsmen (3.17.2 and 4.3.2).[41] An explanation of these terms was no doubt given by Arrian's sources and then omitted through abbreviation; for there are explanations of the 'Mounted Archers' becoming a regular unit (3.24.1), of 'Companies' being introduced into the organisation of the cavalry (3.16.11), and of two Hipparchs taking command of the Companion Cavalry (3.27.4). Of reinforcements from Macedonia the infantrymen were drafted into their 'national' brigades (3.16.11).[42] It is certain that the great bulk of this extremely detailed information came not from the memory of two old men (Ptolemy and Aristobulus) but ultimately from the *Journal of A*, kept at the time.

'The written order of battle of Darius' army was captured afterwards, as Aristobulus says' (3.11.3). It gave the disposition of the forces before the battle, and not on the day of battle, when the elephants, for instance, were not in the line but in camp (3.15.5).[43] It has sometimes been assumed that Aristobulus reproduced this order of battle in his own history, and that Arrian got his information from there.[44] Arrian did not say that. In fact, it is highly unlikely that the captured document stayed with Aristobulus. It is much more likely that it was included among A's papers, and that it became available to Ptolemy but not to Aristobulus. Arrian provided also some round numbers for Persian forces. We see that they were based on estimates, made e.g. by the Scouts (3.7.7)[45] and presumably recorded in the *Journal of A*. Enemy troops with Darius or other commanders were reported in round figures (e.g. 3.19.5 and 3.28.8), and their losses likewise (3.30.11; 4.4.8).

[41] See H*VG* 9f.

[42] This refers to the cantons of Upper Macedonia, each having its own 'tribe', and to the Macedones proper of Lower Macedonia; see Thuc. 2.99.6 ἐκράτησαν ... τῶν ἄλλων ἔθνων οἱ Μακεδόνες οὗτοι and *HM* I 438f.

[43] See *AG*² 141–3.

[44] Bosworth *C* 297, adding that the detailed description (of the battle) was 'presumably also taken from Aristobulus'; he gave references to earlier literature, to which add now A. M. Devine in *The Ancient World* 13 (1986) 100ff.

[45] Two reports were made; we may compare the report in 1.13.2.

The number of A's 'entire army' (3.12.5 ἡ πᾶσα στρατιά) was given as 7,000 cavalry and 40,000 infantry. These round figures came from Ptolemy and/or Aristobulus, and they were not drawn from the *Journal of A*, which would have recorded less imprecise numbers. 'About sixty of the Companions of A fell, and Hephaestion himself, Coenus and Menidas were wounded' in the head-on collision towards the end of the Battle of Gaugamela (3.15.2). Then during the very long pursuit up to 100 men 'of those with A' (Parmenio's cavalry went separately to capture the camp) lost their lives,[46] and over 1,000 cavalry mounts died, of which about half were of the Companion Cavalry (3.15.6). These details of losses were no doubt recorded in the *Journal of A*, who needed such information in order to make replacements (cf. 3.30.6).[47]

The king's own actions formed the centre of interest in Arrian's narrative, as no doubt in the *Journal*, and he is just 'himself' at times (4.3.2; 4.4.5 and 7). In a council of Commanders, when most urged a further advance, the advice of Parmenio to encamp and reconnoitre was accepted by A (3.9.3f.). A's speech to the same council after a reconnaissance was reported in the accusative and infinitive, being a summary of an original which Arrian had before him (3.9.5–8; 3.10.1 ταῦτα καὶ τοιαῦτα ἄλλα οὐ πολλά).[48] On eight occasions Arrian reported sacrifices conducted by A, often associated with a festival of games or of arts (e.g. 3.6.1). One was to Moon, Sun and Earth after the eclipse of the moon on the night of 20–1 September 331 (3.7.6), and Aristander's interpretation of its significance was recorded. When A hoped for favourable omens from a sacrifice, Aristander refused to alter the indications 'from the divine power' (4.4.3). These sacrifices were recorded in the *Journal of A*, as we see from 7.25.

---

[46] The phrase τῶν ἀμφ' Ἀλέξανδρον, wrongly translated in the Loeb edition as 'of Alexander's troops', resumed the phrase of 3.15.5 A ἀναπαύσας τοὺς ἀμφ' αὐτὸν ἱππέας. As so often it means 'the men with A', whether few or many (e.g. 3.21.2). For the terms 'men' and 'horses' in such circumstances see 3.21.6. Bosworth *C* 312 found the figure of a hundred men 'obviously ridiculous', because he followed the Loeb translation and thought it meant the total loss on the Macedonian side in the Battle of Gaugamela; so too A. M. Devine in *The Ancient World* 13 (1986) 107.

[47] See my comments in H*CR* 59.

[48] See above, p. 221, for similar reports of speeches.

The arrivals of five embassies were reported by Arrian. The two Athenian envoys were named and the entire crew of the sacred trireme *Paralus* were associated with them (3.6.2). Two embassies from Scythian groups came to A at the river 'Tanaïs': one from the 'Asiatic' side and the other from the 'European' side, since the 'Tanaïs' (here in fact the Syr-Darya) was thought to divide the two continents (4.1.1; 3.30.9). It is evident that the arrivals of the Scythians were recorded before new views were formed about the river by Polycleitus (*FGrH* 128 F 7), i.e. before probably A's last year.[49] The treatment of envoys sent from Greek states to Darius and captured by A is reported, and A's reasons for varying his treatment of them are given in terms of treaty-relationships obtaining at the time: those of Sinope had no part in 'the community of the Greeks', i.e. of the Common Peace (3.24.4 τοῦ κοινοῦ τῶν Ἑλλήνων); Greek mercenaries serving before 'the peace and alliance [of those Greeks] with the Macedonians'[50] were liberated (the others being retained, as at 3.23.8f. and 24.5), and envoys from Athens and Sparta were kept in custody, Sparta having been forced into membership of 'the community of the Greeks' more than a year earlier.

Arrian added to his abbreviation of accounts by Ptolemy and/or Aristobulus the following *legomena*. One concerned the cause of an eclipse (3.7.6 λόγος κατέχει). Then the total of Darius' forces at Gaugamela 'was said' to be 40,000 cavalry, a million infantry, 200 scythed chariots and a few elephants (3.8.6). The first two figures marry well with Diodorus' million men leaving Babylon, though differently divided (17.53.3, being 200,000 cavalry and 800,000 infantry), and Plutarch's million men 'coming down', i.e. from Babylon (P*A* 31.1). Their common source was probably Cleitarchus, whom I identified in the case of Diodorus (*THA* 25f.). This *legomenon* came then probably from Cleitarchus. On the evening before the battle 'they

---

[49] At 7.16.1 A regarded the Caspian as a 'sea' (θάλασσα). This was incompatible with the Syr-Darya being the upper Tanaïs. See Bosworth *C* 377f., citing Arist. *Meteor.* 350a24f., in which the Tanaïs was a side-stream of the Araxes, which rose in the Caucasus (Hindu-Kush).

[50] See *HM* III 571f. for the significance of this passage.

say that' (3.10.1 λέγουσιν ὅτι) Parmenio went to A's tent and advised a night attack, but as others were listening A replied that it was shameful to steal victory, and that he had to win openly without trickery. This *legomenon* had already appeared in a very extended form in Curtius 4.13.4–10, and in Plutarch (*PA* 31.10–14, Parmenio being accompanied by the older Companions). I have argued above, p. 38, that the history of Cleitarchus was the source of this story in Plutarch, and that should apply also to Curtius' version and to Arrian's *legomenon*. After the battle the Persian dead 'were said' to be 300,000 (3.15.6), a number which Arrian rightly distrusted; but it certainly was in the class of other Cleitarchan figures.[51] At 3.23.9 the Greek mercenaries who had stayed loyal to Darius 'were said to be up to 1,500', whereas the figure of 4,000 had been given by Curtius (5.8.3), whose source was probably Cleitarchus for the pursuit of Darius (*THA* 132 and 137); thus Arrian drew this *legomenon* from an author other than Ptolemy, Aristobulus and Cleitarchus. Finally, at 3.28.5 'they say' (λέγουσι) that Mt Taurus and other great mountains are part of the long range known as Mt Caucasus (the Hindu-Kush). Arrian introduced this *legomenon* to supplement and correct Aristobulus' description of Mt Caucasus as a single peak, higher than any other in Asia. He probably had Eratosthenes in mind as one of those 'who say'.[52]

Arrian continued to mark his own interjections clearly. Having described A's reply to Parmenio's proposal of a night attack as a mark of confidence rather than of arrogance – i.e. from Ptolemy and/or Aristobulus,[53] Arrian wrote: 'in my opinion at least (3.10.2 δοκεῖν δ' ἔμοιγε) A made a precise calculation on the following lines'. He then stated his case for A, and ended up by saying: 'I commend A' (3.10.4 ἐπαινῶ Ἀλέξανδρον). At 3.16.8 Arrian extended his use of the first person to his contemporaries in saying that the restored statues

---

[51] See *THA* 25 for examples.
[52] See Bosworth *C* 370.
[53] Not a comment by Arrian, as Brunt *L* I 255 n. 3 supposed, because ἐφαίνετο is a narrative tense and it precedes the words δοκεῖν δ' ἔμοιγε.

of Harmodius and Aristogeiton are placed at Athens in the Ceramicus, 'where we go up to the Acropolis' (3.16.8 ᾗ ἄνιμεν ἐς πόλιν).[54] At 3.18.12 Arrian sided with Parmenio against A over the burning of the Persian palace at Persepolis: 'It is my opinion too that A did not act sensibly in this at least, and that this was not a form of punishment of the Persians of long ago' (οὐδ' ἐμοὶ δοκεῖ).[55] Arrian repeated his disapproval in the first person at 6.30.1. At 4.4.9, with reference to the defeat of the Scythians and A's illness checking the pursuit, Arrian added his own comment: 'otherwise in my opinion they would all have been destroyed in their flight' (δοκοῦσιν ἄν μοι). Since Arrian was so meticulous in marking his own contributions to the history, it is inappropriate to postulate that Arrian was making his own personal 'verdict on Darius' at 3.22.2–6.[56] Both his declared method in the *Preface* and his practice throughout his history show that this was not so, and that the obituary on Darius was derived from Ptolemy and/or Aristobulus.

When he came to the trial of Philotas and its aftermath, Arrian named his two main sources. 'Ptolemy-and-Aristobulus say' (3.26.1 λέγει Πτολεμαῖος καὶ Ἀριστόβουλος) that Philotas had been under suspicion in Egypt.[57] These two authors were the subject of λέγουσι at 3.27.1, saying that the trial of Amyntas and his three brothers as accomplices of Philotas had occurred at the same time; and the account went on from there as a narrative based on Ptolemy and Aristobulus. On the other hand, Arrian cited Ptolemy alone for his account of the trial

---

[54] Bosworth *C* 317 discusses the topographical problem which arises from this passage. The Loeb text at 3.16.8 should be altered to read not τοῦ Εὐδανέμου but τῶν Εὐδανέμων. See D. M. Lewis in *CR* 24 (1974) 186.

[55] The burning of the palace is treated by Arrian as an act of deliberate policy by A, correctly because pillaging preceded the burning, as the excavators showed (see E. F. Schmidt, *Persepolis* (Chicago, 1953–7) I 75, 78, 79 and 157). Arrian no doubt knew of the story of Thaïs prompting A in a drunken revel to burn the palace (see above, pp. 72–4), but he did not deign to add it as a *legomenon*.

[56] 'The verdict on Darius is certainly Arrian's own' (Bosworth *C* 346). Thucydides started a long tradition when he wrote his notices of Pausanias and Themistocles, and there is no reason to suppose that Ptolemy and/or Aristobulus did not follow it in regard to Darius.

[57] For this episode in *PA* 48.4–49.2 see above, p. 84.

of Philotas and the execution of Parmenio, together with the possible reasons A may have had for carrying out the latter (3.26.2–4 τυχὸν μὲν ὅτι ... τυχὸν δ' ὅτι). Arrian presumably cited his sources here, because so many varying accounts of the trials were in existence. At 3.17.6 Ptolemy was named as his source for Sisigambis interceding on behalf of the Uxians. Presumably Aristobulus had not mentioned this incident.[58] Conversely, Aristobulus was cited, presumably when Ptolemy had been silent, for the capture of the Persian battle-order (3.11.3), the height and bareness of Mt Caucasus (3.28.5, i.e. the Hindu-Kush), the importance of silphium there and in Cyrene (3.28.6) and the native name for the Tanaïs (3.30.7).[59]

Some differences between his two main sources were noted. During the Sogdian revolt, when A attacked seven cities, 'Ptolemy says' that the seventh city was taken through surrender, and that the men of it were kept under guard until A left their country; but Aristobulus says that A took it by force and killed all who were caught in it (4.3.5). Arrian left this difference unresolved.[60] At 3.30.5, after giving Ptolemy's account as his narrative, in which Ptolemy brought Bessus 'naked, bound and wearing a wooden collar' to A, Arrian noted that Aristobulus said this was done by Spitamenes and Dataphernes and others. Arrian had already presented Ptolemy's account in 3.29.7–30.5 as the historical one.[61] Why he chose to mention

---

[58] This campaign in open country against the Uxian hillmen was different from the campaign against a high-ranking Persian commander holding a fortified city (Curt. 5.33.3–15). Goukowsky 219, Bosworth C 321f. and I in THA 130f. took this view. On my interpretation the Queen Mother Sisigambis appealed to A at the end of each campaign. Bosworth chose to have her appeal only once, namely at the end of the campaign in Curtius, and he then condemned Ptolemy for attaching it to the wrong campaign. This is unduly complicated and anyhow unnecessary. In THA 131 I suggested that the source of Curtius was Cleitarchus.

[59] Orxantes in Arrian's manuscripts, Orexartes in PA 45.6 and Iaxartes in Strabo 507.

[60] A comparison with Curt. 7.6.14–23 is difficult, because Arrian put the wounding of A at Cyropolis and Curtius put it at the city of the Memaceni. I suggested in THA 142 that Arrian was making use of both his main authors, and that Curtius used not Ptolemy but Aristobulus (and perhaps another writer).

[61] His reasons were no doubt that Ptolemy had described his own actions, and that Ptolemy did not tell lies (so in the Preface); contra Bosworth C 377. See THA 83 for the account in Diod. 17.83.7–9 being based on Cleitarchus' account, which had not even mentioned Ptolemy as a participant – a sure indication that Cleitarchus had published before Ptolemy began to write.

these two points of difference is not known. As he had indicated in his *Preface*, he was under no obligation to do anything more than incorporate in his narrative the version he
thought to be more credible and more worth reporting.

13

FROM THE TANAÏS TO THE INDUS VALLEY (ARRIAN 4.5–4.30)

1. From Scythian envoys to elephant hunts (4.5–4.30)

There are twelve instances of dating by days, sometimes day by day, sometimes of a duration in days, such as the crossing of the Hindu-Kush or the siege of a city (4.22.4 and 8). Measurements in stades are reported five times. Reports of or references to A's orders figure on nineteen occasions. At 4.6.2 the fear of officers if they should depart from A's orders was noted, and there were three passages in which it was reported that A's orders had been duly implemented (4.22.7; 4.24.6; 4.28.5). Some seventy officers or other followers of A were named, often with a definition of their position or function. The eight Pages who figured in the Conspiracy of the Pages were named with their patronymics; otherwise patronymics were rarely given by Arrian (I have not included the names of fathers among the seventy officers etc.). A dozen of those who opposed A or came into contact with him were named. Negotiations with embassies and through heralds were recorded seven times. The offers of the Scythian envoys and of Pharasmanes the Chorasmian, and the replies of A to them were given in considerable detail (4.15.1–6). We can best account for this mass of detailed information on the hypothesis that it was contained in the *Royal Journal* and that Ptolemy had access to it in writing his history. It was surely more than any participant could carry in his memory.

Whereas the actions of A himself in command of a task force were fully described by Arrian (e.g. 4.23.1–24.7) and he was often mentioned just as 'himself' (e.g. in 4.24–30), the actions of Craterus and those of Hephaestion and Perdiccas in charge of large task forces were mentioned only briefly. Thus at 4.22.1f. Craterus was sent with 600 Companion Cavalry and four phalanx-brigades against the rebels in Pareitacene, and the result was then appended, including a rebel Austanes 'brought to Alexander' and a note of barbarian casualties. At 4.23.5 Craterus was left to deal with the last rebel cities, and at 4.24.7 it was noted that he rejoined Alexander after carrying out his orders. So too Hephaestion and Perdiccas, in command of half the Companion Cavalry, half of the phalanx-brigades and all the mercenary cavalry, were given orders at 4.22.7 and had carried them out at 4.22.8, when they dealt with a further revolt; at 4.30.9 there was a back-reference to their bridging the Indus, which was mentioned because Alexander sent some newly-built ships to it. The best explanation of this disparity is that Ptolemy was drawing on the *Royal Journal* in which the king's own actions were narrated but those of other commanders were mentioned only when Alexander issued the orders and received a report of their fulfilment.

There are, however, in book 4 some detailed descriptions of actions in which A was not involved and which therefore came from other sources than ultimately from the *Royal Journal*. Thus the disaster near Samarcand and its aftermath were reported at length. The first part (4.5.2–6) was drawn from Ptolemy and Aristobulus in accordance with Arrian's usual method, and the second part was provided in two versions, one by implication from Ptolemy (4.5.7–9)[1] the other explicitly from Aristobulus (4.6.1f.). Another disaster occurred, when some Companion Cavalrymen, left behind as invalids at Zariaspa, together with some Pages and 80 mercenary cavalry, made a daring attack on Scythian raiders, but during their return were caught in an ambush and lost seven Companions and 60 of the mercenary cavalry (4.16.6f.). Two men were named: Aristonicus the harpist (Alexander dedicated at Delphi a bronze statue of him with his harp and his lance) and Peithon who was in charge of the court retinue (this including the

---

[1] Brunt *L* I 351 n. 2 stated that the passage beginning at 4.5.2 was 'clearly from Ptolemy'; but what Aristobulus described in 4.6.1f. was the destruction of the main body of Macedonians (τὸ πολὺ τῆς στρατιᾶς), and that corresponded with 4.5.7–9. See also my article 'The Macedonian defeat near Samarcand', *The Ancient World* 22 (1991) 41–7.

Pages).[2] Craterus took prompt action to avenge this disaster (4.17.1f.). There is a link between the accounts of the disasters in that numbers were supplied for the Scythian contingent at 4.5.4 and for the Massagetan contingent at 4.17.1, and attempts were made to explain the Macedonian failures (in the later episode because 'no one was commanding'). Arrian drew evidently on Ptolemy and Aristobulus.[3]

Other actions, in which Ptolemy was involved, were described at some length. For instance, at 4.24.1f. Arrian reported with the usual brevity the details of A's force, its capture of a city and its pursuit of the enemy. To this he appended an *aristeia* of Ptolemy and the conflict over the body of the local ruler (ὕπαρχος in 4.24.1 and 4.24.5), whom Ptolemy had killed in the course of the said pursuit. It is evident that Ptolemy added the incident from his memory to a short entry in the *Royal Journal*. Similar expansions or additions are to be observed at 4.24.8f., 4.25.2f. (as compared with the adjacent reports of A's group and Leonnatus' group) and 4.29.1–6.[4] That Ptolemy wrote at considerable length is clear from the citation of him by Arrian at 4.25.4 for the number of men and cattle which were captured.

Because Arrian followed his two main sources and went into considerable detail about some military actions, we find some unusual terms in this book. Thus at 4.4.6f. we have a hipparchy of mercenary cavalry and three hipparchies of the Companions; at 4.5.7 Caranus 'the hipparch', being in command of 800 mercenary cavalry (4.3.7, a passage based on Ptolemy); and at 4.24.1 about four hipparchies of Companions.[5] It is evident that A had reorganised his cavalry forces between the organisation after the death of Philotas

---

[2] See Berve II 68 no. 132 and 311 no. 622., and *Itin. Alex.* 43.

[3] Perhaps mainly from Ptolemy because the lack of a commander corresponds with the lack of a command at 4.5.7, a passage derived from him.

[4] As Brunt *L* 439 pointed out, Ptolemy recorded 'an implied criticism of himself' at 4.29.4.

[5] Excluding the Royal Squadron, and not including it as Brunt *L* I 59 supposed; for the text is clear in the matter: τῶν ἱππέων τὸ ἄγημα καὶ τῶν ἄλλων ἑταίρων ἐς τέσσαρας μάλιστα ἱππαρχίας.

(3.27.4) and his arrival at the river Tanaïs.[6] Of the infantry, when A took 700 of the Bodyguards and the Hypaspists and led them on a climb at night (4.30.3), the reference was evidently to the *agema* of the Macedones (1.8.4; see above p. 206) as contrasted with the Royal Hypaspist Guard (4.24.10);[7] there was mention of 'the Agrianians the thousand'[8] (4.25.6); there were 'two chiliarchies of the Archers' (4.24.10); and the commanders of some Hypaspist brigades were called 'chiliarchai' (4.30.6). For the assault on the rock Aornus A selected from some phalanx brigades 'the nimblest and at the same time best-armed men' (4.28.8).[9]

Macedonian casualties (to be inferred in part if we subtract the survivors at 4.6.2 from the total at 4.3.7; at 4.16.7, seven Companion Cavalrymen and 80 mercenary cavalrymen; 4.17.6, 25 cavalrymen and 12 infantrymen; at 4.19.2, 30 rock-climbers; at 4.27.4, 25 men; and at 4.23.3, wounding of A, Ptolemy and Leonnatus) were presumably recorded in the *Royal Journal*, from which Ptolemy obtained them. The first, however, we owe to Aristobulus,[10] and the last perhaps to Ptolemy himself. Enemy forces were given in round numbers, sometimes according to report (4.5.4; 4.17.4; 4.25.5; 4.26.1), and so too enemy losses (4.17.2; 4.17.6; 4.22.2; 4.26.4; 4.27.4). To the origin of these there is no specific clue.

2. Arrian's views on the episodes of Bessus, Cleitus and Callisthenes

Comments were made by Arrian himself on the fate of Bessus, the Cleitus episode, its aftermath, on Callisthenes and A, and

---

[6] See my comments in *CQ* 30 (1980) 465ff. and *AG²* 191f. with references to earlier writers on this subject. Caranus commanded a hipparchy of mercenary cavalry, such as that mentioned at 4.4.6.

[7] See in general H*VG*.

[8] These were perhaps a Royal Brigade of Agrianians, and there were other chiliarchies of Agrianians, as there were of Archers at this time.

[9] Such men had been selected and equipped for commando-type operations in 331–330. See *AG²* 165f.

[10] He had reported casualties at the Battle of the River Granicus according to P*A* 16.15 (incorrectly; see above, p. 35).

on the death of Callisthenes. As we shall see, Arrian was scrupulous in presenting his own comments in the first person, as he had done in previous books.

At 4.7.1–3 a series of items, ending with the mutilation of Bessus and the sending of him to Ecbatana for execution, was reported in the usual manner. The account was derived in accordance with Arrian's standard procedure from Ptolemy and Aristobulus, the former probably having used the *Royal Journal*. At 4.7.4 Arrian commented in the first person: 'I do not approve' (4.7.4, ἐγὼ οὔτε ... ἐπαινῶ with the emphatic hiatus). He expanded his disapproval to include also A's adoption of Median and Persian opulence, his regal life-style, and the wearing of Median dress and the Persian *kitaris*. Physical endurance (he continued), exalted birth and continued success in war – even beyond A's (for A did indeed intend to add Libya to Asia) – all were of no avail if a man reputedly of the greatest achievements should lack self-control. Arrian was drawing here on his own insights,[11] not upon any particular source.

Cleitus and Alexander (4.8.1–9.8)

Arrian then described the episode of Cleitus, 'although it happened a little later', because it was to show A lacking self-control and overcome by anger and drunkenness (4.9.1). The account is Arrian's own. That is emphasised by his use of the first person: 'I shall narrate' (4.8.1 ἀφηγήσομαι).[12] The narration itself was delivered in the accusative and infinitive, except at 4.8.8, where A shouted out (the exception being for vividness). But it was interrupted by *legomena* and interjections in finite tenses. Let us take these first.

(1) 'They say that he overlooked sacrificing to Dionysus but did sacrifice to the Dioscuri, it occurring to him for some reason to make the sacrifice to the Dioscuri.' (2) 'A had al-

---

[11] Arrian was mistaken in saying that A wore the *kitaris*; see *FGrH* 241 (Eratosthenes) F 30, P*A* 45.2 (above, p. 78), and Brunt *L* I 533.

[12] This important word is mistranslated and lost in Brunt *L* I 363, 'the story goes as follows'.

ready revolutionised the conduct of drinking-parties in a more barbaric direction.' (3) 'Some did not abstain from mentioning even Heracles in the drinking-party.' (4) 'I do not approve of Cleitus' speech; indeed amid such drunkenness I think it proper for a man to keep silence for his own part and not to commit the same error of flattery as the others did.' (5) 'Some say that on leaping up he snatched a spear from one of the Somato-phylakes, others that he snatched a pike from one of the guards (4.8.9 σάρισσαν), and Aristobulus says as follows.'

Of these *legomena* and interjections the substance of (1) is found in Plutarch's account (50.7; see above, p. 89). (2), i.e. drunkenness, was common to the accounts of Justin (12.6.2), Curtius (8.1.22; cf. 6.2.2) and less so Plutarch (50.8f.). (3) is not found elsewhere. (4) is suggested by Curtius (8.1.38 'omnibus inconsulte ac temere iactis'). (5) Curtius had A seize a pike from a Bodyguard ('rapta lancea ex manibus armigeri') but be disarmed, and then strike the fatal blow with a spear snatched from a guard ('vigili excubanti hasta ablata'), and Plutarch ended with A seizing a spear from a guard (51.9 λαβὼν παρά τινος τῶν δορυφόρων ... αἰχμήν). On this matter Aristo-bulus, as cited by Arrian, had A kill Cleitus with a pike (τῇ σαρίσσῃ). It is obvious that Arrian had read many accounts and drew on them in making these *legomena* and interjections.

Arrian cited in an abbreviated form the account of Aristo-bulus for the removal of Cleitus, his return alone and his death. He chose to do so, no doubt, because he thought that account 'more credible' for the reasons stated in the *Preface*. Nor was Arrian alone in this belief. For Plutarch had based his version on that of Aristobulus (see above, p. 93). Arrian's statement that Aristobulus did not mention the origin of the drunken behaviour is indeed confirmed by the fact that Plutarch did not report Cleitus' belittling of A's achievements (as in Arr. 4.8.5f.).[13]

Reverting now to Arrian's own narrative, we can see that he was giving his own version of the affair.[14] It is very well

---

[13] The reference is not general in regard to the drunkenness (ἡ παροινία) as Brunt *L* I 534f. suggested, but specifically to its origin ὅθεν μὲν ἡ παροινία ὡρμήθη.

[14] See above, p. 91.

written and highly dramatic. The words of A at 4.8.8 are of great importance in showing that A thought he was about to be seized and killed, as Darius had been.[15] Yet we do not know what source Arrian was using at that point. Finally, having cited Aristobulus as saying that Cleitus alone was at fault for the disaster (i.e. because he came back after being removed), Arrian gave his own verdict at 4.9.1. 'I blame Cleitus greatly for his insolence ... and I pity Alexander for his misfortune (τῆς συμφορᾶς as at 4.8.1);[16] for he showed himself to be subject to two evils, anger and drunkenness, to which a man of self-control should not surrender himself' (cf. 4.7.5).

'For the aftermath', Arrian continued, 'I commend Alexander for recognising at once what a dreadful thing he had done.' 'Some say he tried to kill himself with the pike' – this having been stated by Justin 12.6.8, Curtius 8.2.4 and Plutarch 51.11, the last drawing probably on Aristobulus (above, p. 92) – 'but most writers say otherwise, namely that A lay on his bed mourning for Cleitus and Lanice' – this occurring in Justin and Curtius but not in Plutarch. For three days A refused all food and drink and took no care of himself. Then some of the diviners chanted 'wrath from Dionysus' because A had failed to make sacrifice to Dionysus. This and persuasion by his friends brought A out of his depression. A similar explanation had been given by Plutarch, who was drawing on the account of Aristobulus (above, p. 93). In Arrian's version A sacrificed to Dionysus, 'since he too was not unwilling that the mishap (4.9.5 τὴν ξυμφοράν) should be attributed to wrath from heaven somewhat rather than to his own wickedness'. The next step in A's recovery was provided by Anaxarchus in the accounts of Plutarch and of Arrian. When Arrian introduced this step, he began with the phrase 'there are those who say'. One of them was Aristobulus (above, p. 94).

---

[15] These words provide an explanation for A trying to summon the Hypaspist Guard; see H*VG*.

[16] The phrase at 4.8.1 is mistranslated in Brunt *L* I 363 as 'the suffering it caused to Alexander'. The meaning of ἡ ξυμφορά is 'the accident' of Cleitus returning by himself and happening to meet A at that very moment, and so 'the mishap' or 'misfortune' of A in killing him. So too at 4.9.5.

Arrian interposed his own comments. 'I highly commend this attitude in A' (4.9.6). 'As I say, Anaxarchus did great harm to A in arguing ... that anything the king does is just' (4.9.8). Thus Arrian ended as he had started with the stress on his own personal narration and on his comments. All we can say about his sources is that they were numerous and included in particular Aristobulus, and that Arrian had selected from them to give his own version.[17]

Obeisance

At 4.9.9 Arrian turned to his next topic, that of obeisance. It is introduced by the expression 'report holds' (λόγος κατέχει), followed by the accusative and infinitive until the first sentence of 4.10.1. Thus Arrian was basing his account not just on his two main sources but upon the general run of the writings about A (as we may say, 'good, bad and indifferent'). In what follows we may detect therein Arrian's own preferences; for he linked A's demand for obeisance with A's opinion that his father was Ammon rather than Philip (as at 3.3.2), with A's admiration for Persian and Median ways, A's adoption of their dress for himself, and the changes in court ceremonial (as at 4.7.4f.), and with the abundance of flatterers (as at 4.8.3). The 'report' continues with Callisthenes disapproving of A's desire for obeisance.

Again Arrian comments in the first person: 'I myself go along with Callisthenes therein, but I think his behaviour was no longer reasonable, if what has been written is true, namely that he used to declare A's fame and share in divine stock depended on his own writings.'[18] (Oddly enough, Arrian him-

---

[17] The passage from 4.7.4 to 4.9.8 was discussed by Brunt *L* I 532ff. He employed the umbrella-term 'the vulgate', to which he attributed as source 4.8.1–8, 4.9.2–4 and 7ff. On p. 537 he seems to use 'the vulgate' to include even a contemporary writer such as Chares. For my objections to the term altogether see *THA* 1–3.

[18] Brunt *L* I 542 held that this was an allusion to Callisthenes' history of A. But the text at 4.10.1 does not support that interpretation: ἐκεῖνα δὲ οὐκέτι ἐπιεικῆ δοκῶ τοῦ Καλλισθένους, εἴπερ ἀληθῆ ξυγγέγραπται, ὅτι ... ἀπέφαινε. For if Callisthenes had so written, the question whether it was 'true' is nonsensical. The point Arrian is making is that someone else wrote to that effect, and the question then was whether Callisthenes did truly make such a declaration, presumably in conversation.

self had set out to make A's deeds known to men by his own writings at 1.12.4 fin.) He appended a *legomenon* by 'some', to the effect that Callisthenes had hinted Philotas should do away with A.

'Of Callisthenes' opposition to A over obeisance the following story holds' (4.10.5). Again Arrian is to follow the general tradition (as at 4.9.9). The story (λόγος) follows in the accusative and infinitive down to 4.12.2. It contains a long speech by Callisthenes in oratio recta (4.11.2–5), which is certainly unhistorical but well within the literary conventions of the period. The story ended with A telling the Macedonians to think no more of doing obeisance, and with the Persian courtiers performing obeisance to the amusement of Leonnatus.[19] Another 'story' which ended with Callisthenes saying he was 'poorer by a kiss'[20] is then given (4.12.3–5). As it appears also in Plutarch 54.4–6, it is evident that Plutarch and Arrian had a common source. Plutarch names him as Chares of Mitylene (above, p. 97).

Arrian then gave his own opinion on these incidents in the first person:

I do not approve at all of A's arrogance or of Callisthenes' stupidity. I say that anyone willing to wait on a king should behave properly and promote the king's cause. I regard as not unreasonable A's enmity with Callisthenes, and I infer that it was not difficult on that account for the detractors of Callisthenes to be believed, when they said he had a part in the Pages' Conspiracy, some indeed claiming that he incited them to make the plot.

To summarise our conclusions for the passage from 4.9.9 to 4.12.7, Arrian was not following his usual procedure, namely preferring the agreed views of Ptolemy and Aristobulus. Instead, he was basing his account on the general tradition, which no doubt included reports by Ptolemy and Aristobulus but also by many others. Arrian made his subjective selection. He then was in a position to state his own personal views, and he did so emphatically. One report which Arrian certainly did use was that of Chares concerning the banquet at which the staging of obeisance by some Macedonians led to the *bon mot*

---

[19] Another such story was told of Polyperchon in Curt. 8.5.22–4.
[20] See above, p. 96 for this story with some differences in detail in P*A* 54.4–6.

of Callisthenes 'I'll go away the poorer by a kiss.' Otherwise we cannot name Arrian's sources, nor can we exclude any.[21]

The Pages' Conspiracy and the end of Callisthenes

Arrian introduced the subject with a summary of the institution of the Pages. Curtius had written a similar introduction. If they had a common source, it cannot be named. On the other hand, we can say that Ptolemy and Aristobulus would have described this institution earlier in their histories, and that they can be excluded from Arrian's immediate sources.

One of the Pages, Hermolaus, as a student of philosophy, was known to cultivate the company of Callisthenes. 'About him [the] story holds' that he was punished by A etc., and the story unfolds in indirect speech up to the point when some Pages planned to set upon A while he was sleeping (4.13.2–4). Two versions are then reported to explain why the plan failed. 'Some say A drank spontaneously until daybreak, but Aristobulus wrote as follows', his story being that a Syrian clairvoyante, 'possessed of a divine spirit', told him to return to the drinking-party, and that A regarded this as a sign from heaven and obeyed. Arrian leaves it open for his reader to choose.

The next phase was narrated by Arrian mainly in vivid present tenses (4.13.7). The informer named the conspirators, who confessed under torture and named some others. Two versions are then reported. Aristobulus said, and Ptolemy was in agreement, that the conspirators stated that Callisthenes had 'incited them to the deed of daring'. (Arrian had prepared the ground for this view at 4.12.7, where he said that detractors of Callisthenes made such an allegation.) Most writers said otherwise, namely that A already hated Callisthenes and readily believed circumstantial evidence. 'Some have actually recorded the following also', namely the substance of Hermolaus' speech at the trial by the Macedones and the stoning of Hermolaus and the others under arrest (4.14.2f.).

Here too Arrian has given us the story as he found it in

---

[21] See Brunt L I 538–42 for a discussion of the passage on obeisance with references to earlier literature.

the general tradition. He had clearly read not only his main sources (for at 4.14.3 he remarked that they were 'entirely trustworthy in their narratives') but also a variety of authors, and he has left us to judge between alternative versions at critical points. His remark at 4.12.7 may have been intended to make us look at Aristobulus and Ptolemy as 'detractors of Callisthenes' and so not as dependable witnesses. He thought it appropriate to repeat the list of Hermolaus' points against A: Philotas unjustly executed, Parmenio and the others even more unjustly killed, Cleitus murdered in a drunken fit, the Median dress, the obeisance-plan not yet abandoned, and the drinking and sleeping habits of A. In view of all that, Hermolaus claimed, no free man could tolerate such conduct any longer, and therefore he had sought to liberate himself and his countrymen from such abuse. Most of this had already been written by Curtius at much greater length (8.7.1, 4–6, 12–14), and no doubt by many writers before Curtius.[22]

For the fate of Callisthenes Arrian cited the different versions of Aristobulus and Ptolemy. 'Thus even those who were entirely trustworthy in their narratives and were with A at that time failed to agree in their accounts of well-known events within their cognisance' (4.14.4). It may be noted that Plutarch had already given the version of Aristobulus as that of 'some' writers, and that of Ptolemy as 'of others', and he had added a fuller account by Chares, which Arrian chose not to repeat (PA 55.9; above, p. 99). Thus for the Conspiracy of the Pages and its aftermath Arrian gave a narrative which he himself compiled from various sources and principally from Aristobulus and Ptolemy for actual events. He was careful to inform his reader of varying versions, and he left his reader to make the final judgements, as in the case of Cleitus.

Looking back, I think, over these events recorded in 4.9.9 to 4.14.3, Arrian wrote as follows at 4.14.4: 'About these very

---

[22] It is most unlikely that Hermolaus would have been permitted to make such an attack on A in the trial, and that if he did so it was recorded at the time. No historical value should be attached, for instance, to the statement that obeisance 'had not yet been abandoned' in spring 327 B.C. According to the narrative at 4.12.1 A had abandoned obeisance for Macedonians.

matters[23] many varying accounts have been narrated in differing ways, but as far as I am concerned let what I have written be sufficient'. He had given the account which he considered the more probable, and he had hedged parts of it by providing some of the variant versions on which a reader could form a judgement for himself. One may be tempted to censure him for departing from his stated method of following Ptolemy and Aristobulus. But the departure was justified. In most of the *Anabasis* Arrian was recording factual events. In these chapters, however, where the events themselves were uncertain, the centre of interest was in the personality of A, and the question constantly arose: was he justified in what he did? Arrian was wise to leave the answer to his readers.[24]

[23] Mistranslated in Brunt *L* 1 387 'of the same events'. The text is ὑπὲρ τούτων αὐτῶν, not ὑπὲρ τῶν αὐτῶν.

[24] For a discussion of the Pages' Conspiracy see Brunt *L* 1 542–4, again using the umbrella-term 'the vulgate' and attributing to it 4.13.1–4 and 14.2. See above, pp. 97–100 for the versions of Curtius and Plutarch.

14

ADVANCE FROM NYSA AND RETURN TO THE HYDASPES (ARRIAN 5.1–29)

1. Nysa, the crossing of the Indus and the geography of 'India'

In the latter part of book 4 Arrian had described the fighting in the mountainous region between the Cophen and the Indus, and he ended the book with A approaching the Indus (he crossed it at 5.4.3). Arrian opened book 5 with an episode which must have occurred while A was still in the mountainous region, namely his treatment of the sacred city, Nysa.[1] He reserved it for this place in his history, because he thought it to be particularly relevant to A's decision to cross the Indus and proceed into 'India'.

In this region between the Cophen and the Indus which A invaded they say that there is also a city Nysa founded as a colony, that it was a foundation of Dionysus, and that Dionysus founded Nysa, when he subjugated the Indians, whoever this Dionysus was, and whenever and whence he campaigned against the Indians.

Thus Arrian began with a typical *legomenon*: 'they say', which was repeated in the form λόγος at 5.1.2 and λέγεται at 5.2.3 and followed by the accusative and infinitive.[2] But in what followed, he used two forms of exposition: a historical narrative sometimes with vivid present indicative tenses, and the *legomenon* in the accusative and infinitive. Thus at 5.1.3 'When A approached Nysa, the Nysaeans send out to him their leading man' etc., and in the next sentence with the accusative and infinitive we have to supply 'it is said' that 'the envoys came to A's tent' etc. The first form of exposition recurred in the last sentence of 5.2.1f., in 5.2.4, and in the first sentence of 5.2.5,

---

[1] Strabo 698 placed Nysa between the two rivers.
[2] Brunt *L* II 440 thought that the opening words of 5.1.1 'point to a change of source'. The word λέγουσι indicated that this was certainly so.

and the second form of exposition – including two speeches in *oratio recta* by Acouphis – was used for the other sections.

Such moving to and from narrative tenses to the accusative and infinitive is unusual in the *Anabasis*. Yet the purpose is clear enough. Arrian wanted to mark the narrative facts, which he derived in his usual way from Ptolemy and Aristobulus, and thus to keep them apart from the *legomenon* associated with those facts.[3] Thus we have in the narrative sections items typical of what Ptolemy had probably taken from the *Royal Journal*: the envoys' request, A's grant of freedom to the settlers of Nysa, and his demands in the way of military service, and his final orders to Acouphis.[4] We have also A's delight and his desire to believe that Dionysus had founded Nysa, which is the sort of insight that Aristobulus was wont to report. The next narrative item, the longing ($\pi\acute{o}\vartheta o\varsigma$) which overcame A to visit the memorials of Dionysus on the sacred mountain, was derived probably from Aristobulus. He may have been the source also of the explanation of A's delight, namely the thought that the Macedonians would not refuse to join him in still further labours in rivalry with Dionysus (5.2.1).

On the other hand the *legomenon*, although it contained matter on which Ptolemy and Aristobulus must have touched,[5] was derived in the main from another source or sources. It is sensational, graphic, with A sitting still dusty, helmeted and spear in hand when the envoys entered his tent, and inventive

---

[3] In his discussion in *L* II 435–42 Brunt noted what he called 'a mixture of direct speech and indirect'; but he explained it as 'probably under the influence of Eratosthenes' scepticism', and he concluded that 'the narrative is consecutive throughout'. He suggested 'Aristobulus alone' as Arrian's source and thus saw 5.1.1–5.3.4 as a single narrative. Pearson *LHA* 217 with n. 20, on the other hand, saw 'the whole Nysa episode' as a *legomenon*, derived from neither Ptolemy nor Aristobulus. Hamilton *C* 161, 'Arrian relates this incident as a *logos*', appears to share the opinion of Pearson.

[4] The ending of the service of the Nysaean cavalrymen was noted at 6.2.3, where the narrative was derived from Ptolemy and/or Aristobulus.

[5] It is important to keep closely to Arrian's declaration in the *Preface*, that matters written up by others (i.e. others than his main sources) were recorded as *legomena* by himself. He did not say that such matters were not to be found at all in the histories of those main authors, Ptolemy and Aristobulus.

in the two speeches by Acouphis, which cannot have been recorded at the time or remembered verbatim. It continues in the same vein with A and his picked troops wreathed and serenading Dionysus. Then comes an added *legomenon*: 'some have recorded this too', that many distinguished Macedonians were possessed by the god Dionysus (5.2.7). Similar scenes of Dionysiac revelry had been recorded by Justin (12.7.6–8) and Curtius (8.10.11–18), apparently using a common source,[6] who was probably Cleitarchus (see *THA* 104, 148 and 186 n. 39). If that is so, it seems that Arrian drew on Cleitarchus for some of the Dionysiac scene.[7]

We must also consider *PA* 58.6–9 in this connection. The points of similarity between Plutarch's account and Arrian's *legomenon* concern the Acouphis episode, which did not occur in Justin and Curtius. When envoys came to A, they were amazed to find him 'fully armed and unkempt'[8] (58.7), as in Arrian 5.1.4; A made Acouphis the ruler (58.9), as in Arrian 5.2.2; A demanded the surrender to him of 'the hundred best men' (58.9), as in Arrian 5.2.2; whereupon Acouphis laughed, as in Arrian 5.2.3. Each author had his own separate frills and responses. But the similarities indicated that Plutarch and Arrian were following the same source for the Acouphis part of the *legomenon*. That source, however, was not used by Curtius, who has nothing about Acouphis; thus if Curtius did follow Cleitarchus, Plutarch and Arrian were following not Cleitarchus but someone else. A likely candidate is Chares of Mitylene, who gave the Indian name of the wine-making god (*FGrH* 125 F 17), evidently in reference to the god at Nysa. For Chares was cited more than once by Plutarch as his source.

Arrian made his own comments clear by using the first

---

[6] Both authors have the citizens surrender (Just. 12.7.6 'non repugnantibus', Curt. 8.10.11 'se dedidere'), Liber founding Nysa, A taking 'the army' up the sacred mountain, and the army being in a Bacchic frenzy and incapable of defending itself. Both authors turned next to Daedala.

[7] Not for all of it, because Arrian had A take not the army (as in the accounts of Justin and Curtius) but the Companion Cavalry and the Infantry Guard (5.2.5 τῷ πεζικῷ ἀγήματι, an unusual term in the *Anabasis*).

[8] See Hamilton *C* 161 on the meanings which have been suggested for ἀθεράπευτος.

person at 5.1.2, 5.3.1 and 5.3.4. Although he could not decide
the origin of this Dionysus and was surprised at Dionysus'
unique use of military force[9] against Indians, he refused to be
hypercritical of a story in which divinity was involved and
which was therefore not wholly incredible (5.1.2, ἐπειδὰν τὸ
θεῖόν τις προσθῇ τῷ λόγῳ, οὐ πάντῃ ἄπιστα φαίνεται; note
the use of hiatus). At 5.3.1 he objected to the hypercritical
spirit of Eratosthenes as regards both the wanderings of
Dionysus and the Macedonian beliefs that Prometheus and
Heracles had been in these parts before them. He concluded
that it was up to his readers to decide whether they accepted
the story of the Macedonians being in a Dionysiac frenzy
on the mountain (5.3.1), and that the beliefs mentioned by
Eratosthenes should also be left 'in the middle', i.e. undecided
as far as Arrian was concerned (5.3.4).[10] Here we see Arrian's
capacity for religious faith, his personal honesty, and his willingness to let the final judgement lie with his readers. For the
modern historian the important matter is that Ptolemy and
Aristobulus as the sources behind Arrian 5.2.1 reported that
A wanted the wanderings of Dionysus and his founding of
Nysa to be credible, so that (ὡς for ὥστε, as e.g. at 5.15.4)
he and his Macedonians would have already gone as far as
and would now go farther than Dionysus,[11] and so that the
Macedonians would not refuse to go with him (5.2.1).

At 5.5.6 Arrian resumed the normal form of his narrative,
following Ptolemy and/or Aristobulus as his sources. Taxiles
had already been reported as bringing gifts to A (4.22.6); now
he is reported as bringing more gifts, which included animals
for sacrifice by the army. Athletic and equestrian games were
held on the west bank and the omens of the sacrifice were
favourable. At dawn next day A and his army crossed the river
Indus 'into the land of the Indians' (5.4.3 ἐς τῶν Ἰνδῶν τὴν
γῆν).[12] It was as decisive for them as the crossing of the

---

[9] Just. 12.7.6 had the same idea in his phrase 'militiam ... dei'.

[10] These were ancient controversies as we see from Strabo 688, citing Megasthenes
and Eratosthenes as the protagonists.

[11] See the latest discussion in Brunt *L* II 435–42.

[12] The fact that some Indians were reported to be fighting in the country west of
the river is not, as Brunt *L* II 449 suggested, inconsistent with the geographical

Hellespont had been; for they believed that they were entering the last province of the continent of 'Asia' (Arr. 4.15.6), and they were committing themselves to the conquest of 'India'. A's hopes that the Macedonians would go forward in rivalry with Dionysus (5.2.1) were thus fulfilled.

At 5.4.1f. Arrian made a digression on the rivers of 'India' and compared them with other great rivers. He presumably followed his usual main authors, Ptolemy and Aristobulus; and later, at 5.20.8, Arrian cited Ptolemy as describing the size of the Acesines 'alone', 15 stades wide with rapids and great, sharp rocks, which caused casualties to the Macedonians crossing the river on boats and rafts, and we know from Strabo 692 that Aristobulus commented on the Acesines in flood. Ptolemy and Aristobulus knew from A's exploratory voyages down the Indus into the Ocean that it had two mouths (5.4.2).[13] Arrian then provided figures for the maximum and the minimum width of the Indus from the account of Ctesias, a Greek doctor at the Persian court, who wrote on India at the end of the fourth century B.C. He added the sensible proviso 'if anyone thinks Ctesias a competent witness'.[14] That proviso was one reason for Arrian saying in the first person that his own report on the Indus was beyond dispute.

division being at the river Indus. The Indians west of the river (4.22.6 τοὺς ἐπὶ τάδε τοῦ Ἰνδοῦ) were more warlike than the other barbarians of the region (4.25.3 τοὺς ἄλλους τοὺς ταύτῃ βαρβάρους); and there were Indian mercenaries, employed by the barbarians, who had come 'from the further Indians', i.e. from those east of the river (4.26.1 τοῖς ἐκ τῶν πρόσω Ἰνδῶν). Such Indians outside 'India', whether settlers or mercenaries, were like Greeks settled or serving in Asia. Pliny, N.H. 6.78 gave the Kabul river as an alternative frontier for his own time, not for that of A. See also Arr. Ind. 2.5.

[13] Brunt L II 13 n. 1, Arrian 'was unaware that by his time the Indus had seven outlets', assumes that Arrian was writing to describe not A's knowledge of the Indus but Arrian's own knowledge of contemporary geography in the second century A.D. That surely was not Arrian's intention.

[14] It has to be borne in mind that there was no simple method of measuring the width of an unbridged river in spate. Arrian was aware of that; so he gave at 5.20.10 such measurements for the Indus as what 'seem to be' (δοκεῖ ... εἶναι). Brunt L II 450 held that Arrian cited Ctesias from Eratosthenes 'presumably'. This can hardly be so. Arrian's proviso implies for me that Arrian based his poor judgement of Ctesias on having read him, and in the next section, where he mentioned far-fetched stories current before A's expedition, he was surely referring to Ctesias, Indica. It seems to me almost inconceivable that Arrian would fail to read that work.

A further digression followed. Arrian warned his reader that he was not going to repeat the marvellous tales and ridiculous lies about India, many of which were proved false by A and his Macedonians. Since the chief writer about India before their time was Ctesias, Arrian was referring chiefly to his tall stories. The contemporaries of A who denounced them as false were no doubt Ptolemy, Aristobulus and Nearchus. In particular they regarded the Indians as the noblest fighters of all the then inhabitants of Asia (5.4.4; cf. 4.25.3 and 27.3). Arrian himself, using the first person, confessed he could not profitably compare the Indian fighters with their predecessors in Asia – the Persians and the Scythians of the time of Cyrus. He then announced that he would in the future write a monograph on India, but that he would record now only what appeared relevant to A's achievements (5.5.2). What follows is not drawn from his main sources but is explicitly his own material, culled in part from Megasthenes and Eratosthenes, whom he cited by name at 5.6.2, and his main emphasis was on the huge size of 'India'.

The next digression is on the bridging of rivers. 'Aristobulus and Ptolemy whom I chiefly follow (5.7.1, οἷς μάλιστα ἐγὼ ἕπομαι) do not say how the Indus was bridged.' He mentioned Persian bridging methods, and he then described the Roman technique. Alexander, he thought, might have used a similar technique to that of the Romans. After this spate of reflections and digressions A resumed his normal narrative at 5.8.2.

2. From the Indus to the Hyphasis and the return (5.8.2–29.5)

This narrative has the standard characteristics of the earlier narratives which were derived from Arrian's main sources, Ptolemy and/or Aristobulus. Intervals were recorded by days (5.22.3f., 28.2 and 3). Acts of sacrifice, sometimes together with games or festivals, were reported on five occasions. On six occasions envoys came to A with propositions or gifts. A batch of arrivals at A's headquarters is sometimes reported (e.g. 5.20.5–7). Macedonian forces were described by the names of individual units, of which the strength was not reported, and round numbers were given for Indian allied troops (e.g. 5.11.3). Unusually (but cf. 1.3.6) totals were stated for the cavalry and infantry which landed with A on the east bank of the Hydaspes; that was probably due to Ptolemy himself, who as one of A's Bodyguards at the time was in a position to know. Troops sent with Hephaestion on a special mission were specified by units only (5.21.5). Numbers and sizes of cities and of villages in the territory of the Glauganicae (or Glausae) were stated at the time when A handed them over to Porus (5.20.4); it was probably an example of a record of such conquests which was regularly kept. Enemy casualties were reported in round figures at 5.15.2, 18.2, and 24.3, 5 and 7, numbers of waggons and horses being given. A's casualties were more specific. Of the 6,000 infantry who crossed with A (5.14.1) some 80 were killed, and of the cavalry ten mounted archers of those who began the action (i.e. at 5.16.4), about 20 Companion Cavalrymen and 200 other cavalrymen (5.18.3). The siege of Sangala cost A nearly 100 killed and over 1,200 wounded, the officers among the latter including Lysimachus the Bodyguard (5.24.5). Twenty-one officers holding command-posts and nine leading Indians were named, usually with a definition of their position and duties. The remarkably detailed information[15] which we have mentioned cannot have been held in the memory alone of Ptolemy and/or Aristobulus.

Orders issued by A were reported on seventeen occasions. Two of these were given in *oratio recta*, being thus direct citations. At 5.11.4 the first part of A's orders to Craterus was given in brief, and the second part in direct speech.

And if Porus should take part of his army and lead it against me, and if a part and the elephants remain behind in camp, do you indeed even so stay

---

[15] Its specific nature is sometimes misunderstood. For instance, at 5.13.1 Arrian said that the Bodyguards Ptolemy, Perdiccas and Lysimachus embarked with A on a triaconter to cross the Hydaspes. Brunt *L* II 38 n. 1, commenting on this passage, asked 'why does Arrian not name the other Bodyguards?' The answer is that only these three of the Bodyguards were with A, and that the other four had other duties at that moment. Brunt also asked why Arrian mentioned Seleucus being a king later and not Lysimachus; the answer is that Arrian had just mentioned Lysimachus as a Bodyguard.

in your position. But if Porus takes with him all the elephants against me and some part of the rest of his army remains in camp, do you cross at speed. For it is only the elephants (he said) which make it impossible to disembark horses. The rest of his army is easily dealt with.

The other order was issued by A to Ptolemy and to other officers commanding units for an operation during the night.

You, on observing that they are breaking out at this point, are to stop them yourself with your force from going further, and order the trumpeter to give the signal. And you, commanding officers, when the signal is given, proceed each with his own force to the scene of uproar, wherever the trumpet may summon you. I shall not be absent myself from the action. (5.23.7)

A record of A's orders verbatim was certainly kept in the *Royal Journal*,[16] and it was presumably from there that Ptolemy cited them.

A himself – often just αὐτός – is the centre of attention (e.g. 5.12.2f.; 13.1f.; 20.2 and 8). When the army was divided into detachments, detailed description was given only of the force with A. Thus in the Battle of the Hydaspes there were apparently three detachments which were posted each at a point on the west bank between A's crossing-place and the camp of Craterus, and their commanders were ordered by A to cross progressively, as soon as they should see the Indians engaged in battle (5.12.2). However, we are not told whether or when they did cross, detachment by detachment. There is simply a note at the end that 'they kept crossing as they saw A winning brilliantly', and that being fresh they added impetus to the pursuit (5.18.1). The best explanation for all these features of the narrative is that they were obtained by Ptolemy from the record in the *Royal Journal*.

That Arrian was in general following his two main sources is clear from the fact that he noted some differences between their versions or named one rather than the other. Thus Aris-

---

[16] See H*RJ* 131. The first condition in the order to Craterus did not eventuate (as for instance in an order at 1.6.5). A historian who was merely recording events would not have mentioned that condition, but Ptolemy was concerned with A's generalship and he was basing his account on A's orders, which in my opinion he was able to read in the *Royal Journal*.

tobulus had Porus' son arrive with 60 chariots before A's last crossing from the island, whereas Ptolemy had him arrive with 120 chariots and 2,000 cavalry only after A's men had already crossed from the island (5.14.3 and 6). Arrian noted that Aristobulus and Ptolemy differed in their naming of an Indian tribe (5.20.2). He preferred Ptolemy to Aristobulus in the matter of Porus' son's troops and action (5.14.4 ὅτῳ καὶ ἐγὼ ξυμφέρομαι), no doubt mainly because Ptolemy was accompanying A at the time, but also because Arrian judged his account superior in 'probability' (5.14.5f. εἰκός). He then reported Ptolemy's account of the defeat of the young Porus in the accusative and infinitive (5.15.1f.). Even in its abbreviated form the description has a vividness which was due to Ptolemy's participation in the action.[17] Similarly, Ptolemy's account of the casualties in the crossing of the swollen Acesines has the vividness of the eyewitness (5.20.8f.). Another indication that Arrian was drawing on both Ptolemy and Aristobulus for military matters is to be seen in the naming of Macedonian infantry brigades usually as τάξεις but occasionally as φάλαγγες[18] (at 5.20.3 and 5.21.5, as at 1.14.2f.), and in the description of the Hypaspist Guard as τοὺς ὑπασπιστὰς τοὺς βασιλικούς alongside the Royal Infantry Guard, τὸ ἄγημα τὸ βασιλικόν (5.13.4).[19]

Finally, although Arrian did not say so, the detailed account of Ptolemy's part in the night operation during the siege of Sangala was evidently taken from Ptolemy's history and not from that of Aristobulus (5.23.7–24.3). So too it was Ptolemy,

---

[17] So too in the main battle at 5.16.1, where A gave his infantry a breather, and in describing the elephants throughout the battle. In *AG*[2] 210 and especially 215f. I adduced reasons for regarding Ptolemy as A's main source for the battle. So too in the latest study by A. M. Devine in *The Classical World* 16 (1987) 94 'the better part of the narrative must derive from Ptolemy'. The tactical terms in the narrative are as much due to Arrian's practice as to Ptolemy's account.

[18] In *Harv. Stud. CP* 81 (1977) 249 and in *C* 118 A. B. Bosworth maintained that the term was used by Aristobulus; but if so it was probably used also by Ptolemy, since it is unlikely that two terms were in use for an infantry brigade in 326 B.C. It is more likely that in the *Anabasis* Arrian used τάξις as he did in his *Tactica*, and that he occasionally and inconsistently let φάλαγξ stand as the original Macedonian term. He used it also in archaising passages in his *Ectaxis contra Alanos* (5, 6 and 15).

[19] See H*VG*.

and by implication not Aristobulus, who reported that A sacrificed on the bank of the Hyphasis and that the omens were unfavourable for crossing (5.28.4).

It is, however, certain that Arrian had read other detailed accounts. At 5.14.4 he noted that 'others say' a battle took place where A made his crossing and that A was wounded. Then too it was alleged that the war-horse Bucephalus was killed there (5.14.4). As we have seen (above, p. 111), that was the version given by Cleitarchus and by Chares. Whereas Arrian's obituary for Bucephalus at 5.19.4–6 was drawn from Ptolemy and/or Aristobulus in his usual manner, he noted as a *legomenon* that the horse was given a different colour in accounts by 'others' (5.19.5). One of those 'others' was Onesicritus, who started the romantic idea that Bucephalus was born in the same year as A, and that he was therefore thirty years old at the time of his death; for Arrian also gave that improbable age (5.19.5; see above, p. 23). The description of Porus fighting, though wounded, and of A asking Porus what he wanted was based as usual on Ptolemy and/or Aristobulus; and it seems that one or both saw the remarkable cuirass of Porus (5.18.5 ὡς ὕστερον καταμαθεῖν θεωμένοις ἦν).[20] But the reply of Porus and A's response were given in direct speech as a *legomenon* (5.19.2 λόγος ὅτι). Both the reply and the response were similar in P*A* 60.14 and thrice in the *Moralia*, where I suggested that Chares may well have been the source (above, p. 109). Chares may have been one of the contributors to Arrian's *logos*.

When Arrian was expressing his own opinion, he made it clear by using the first person. He did so at 5.14.4, 5.19.6, and 5.20.2. Also at 5.14.5f. he wrote 'I go along with' Ptolemy (καὶ ἐγὼ ξυμφέρομαι), and he gave his reasons for doing so.[21] When he had, he resumed the citation of Ptolemy's account (λέγει). This had been his practice in previous books. Once it

---

[20] Ptolemy and Aristobulus will also have seen Porus and noticed how tall he was; see above, p. 107, for different reports on the matter.

[21] They are conveyed in the sentence beginning οὐδὲ γὰρ εἰκός. Brunt *L* II 43 n. 4 noted that this was 'the comment of Arrian'; he was refuting the view of Jacoby in *FGrH*.

is appreciated that Arrian always marked his own interjections and expressions of opinion with the use of the first person, we can be confident that Arrian did not write the speeches of A and Coenus at 5.25.3–26.8 and 5.27.2–9.[22] Rather, in accordance with Arrian's declared method, they were based upon speeches in his declared sources, Ptolemy and/or Aristobulus. Because the speeches were delivered at the council of officers who were in command of units, they were certainly heard by Ptolemy, who as a Bodyguard was in attendance on A. Aristobulus was probably not present; but he could have learned from others at the time and later what had been said. It is to be expected that Arrian relied more on Ptolemy than on Aristobulus, but not to the exclusion of the latter.

There is nothing in A's speech which is inconsistent with A's previous actions. He addressed the officers as 'Macedonians and allies' (cf. 2.17.1 and 3.9.3), for he was treating some Indians as allies,[23] and he bestowed lands on them as 'allies' (5.25.6 and 28.3). He claimed to be in control of the Cappadocians (cf. 2.4.2) and 'Hellenic Libya', being the lands of Cyrene (cf. Diod. 17.49.3 and Curt. 4.7.9; and Arr. 7.9.8), and to have driven the Scythians 'as far as to the desert' (cf. 4.4.8, and 4.6.5 with the same phrase). The belief in the speech that the Hyrcanian (Caspian) Sea was part of the outer Ocean had been expressed at 3.29.2 and 5.5.4. A claimed that he would in the future show to the Macedonians and the allies that the outer Ocean ran from the Caspian Sea to the Indian Gulf and thence via the Persian Gulf and the south of 'Libya' to the Pillars of Heracles (the Straits of Gibraltar). This claim was consistent with his (and Aristotle's) concept of the world at the time of the speech.[24] His references to the deeds of Heracles and Dionysus and to the Macedonians' advance beyond Nysa and their capture of the rock of Aornus were inspired by the

---

[22] On the other hand Brunt *L* II 533, after an interesting discussion of the speeches in Arrian, *Anabasis*, seems to come to the opposite conclusion: 'this is an epideictic display by Arrian and the same is then probably true of the speeches at the Beas' (Hyphasis).

[23] This was probably true of the communities in Asia which A had declared free, e.g. the Lydians who sent troops to serve in the East.

[24] See *AG*² 174ff. and fig. 17.

actions which had been reported in Arrian 4.27.2–4 and 5.2.1. Thus there is nothing inappropriate or anachronistic in the content of the speech,[25] and the sentiments expressed by A are certainly in character.

Arrian introduced the speech with the words 'he spoke thus' (ἔλεξεν ὧδε), and at the end he wrote 'saying these and suchlike things' (5.27.1 ταῦτα καὶ τοιαῦτα εἰπόντος). Thus he assured his reader that he was reproducing the main substance of A's speech, not of course verbatim or *in toto* or in the original style (for Arrian was writing in his own literary style). When he turned to the speech of Coenus, he used rather different terms: at 5.27.1 'he spoke such as follows' (ἔλεξε τοιάδε) and at 5.28.1 'saying suchlike things' (τοιαῦτα).[26] Here Arrian – and probably his sources before him – was less confident of keeping close to what had actually been said. The substance of Coenus' speech is again entirely appropriate,[27] when we allow for some rhetorical exaggeration. The unwillingness of Greek mercenaries to be settled in Alexander's cities in Bactria and Sogdiana was no secret at the time. The suggestion that A might wish to campaign in the area of the Black Sea or to Carthage and beyond was entirely reasonable, since A had already declared his interest in the Black Sea in the reply to Pharasmanes (4.15.5f.), and since Carthaginian envoys had been in Tyre when it fell (2.24.5). The tone of the speech is particularly interesting; for it shows the manner in which a Field Marshal addressed the King as his Commander-in-Chief. I conclude that this speech too was based on speeches incorporated in their histories by Ptolemy and Aristobulus, and that

---

[25] Brunt *L* II 532 held that Arrian erred in having Thessalians sent home from Bactra. The last Thessalians were sent back at 3.29.5 when they were still west of the River Oxus and probably in Bactria (5.29.1).

[26] Brunt *L* II 530 referred to passages in Xenophon, *Anabasis*, as analogies; but those he cited at 1.3.2 and 7, 1.3.9 and 13, and 2.5.3 and 15 resumed the speeches with ταῦτα or τοσαῦτα alone.

[27] Tarn 287–90 argued that Coenus was not at the Hyphasis, because he had been left behind at the Acesines (5.20.1); but Tarn failed to notice that Coenus had been ordered to supervise the crossing of the Acesines and the conveying of supplies to A by the rearguard of the army. Tarn labelled the speech 'a very late composition, a mere piece of patchwork'. Brunt *L* II 530ff. rejected Tarn's case as 'typically learned sophistry'.

Ptolemy was in a better position than Aristobulus to record the substance of Coenus' arguments.

The reaction of the audience – uproar and even tears – was reported, rather surprisingly, in the accusative and infinitive without any governing verb (5.28.1). A's own reaction was then conveyed in a narrative tense, and he spoke to a second meeting of the same officers, the substance of his speech being reported briefly in *oratio obliqua*. Then the accusative and infinitive construction without any governing verb occurred again, this time recording A's withdrawal into his tent and his hopes that there would be a change of heart. Next, 'Ptolemy says that A sacrificed' etc., and the narrative concluded with a vivid present as A made a public declaration that he was turning back. Why did Arrian twice use this unusual accusative and infinitive construction without any governing verb? On my interpretation Arrian was, as usual, drawing on Ptolemy and/or Aristobulus. In those two unusual sentences Arrian presumably intended to convey to his reader that he was not fully confident in the veracity of what was being reported, even though he found the material in his two main sources. At 5.28.4 he cited Ptolemy as his authority for A's sacrifice 'with a view to crossing' (ἐπὶ τῇ διαβάσει), because it had not been mentioned by Aristobulus and because it was thought by Arrian to be of importance.[28]

---

[28] See the discussion by Brunt *L* II 531f. and his conclusion that 'Ptolemy was used here for the first time and only recorded that A decided to turn back after and because of the sign of divine will, without even hinting that the army was not prepared to go further.' During the delay everyone in the army knew that the Macedonians were unwilling to go ahead. Ptolemy would have been most foolish to omit A's staying in his tent for three days and the reasons for his anger.

15

FROM THE HYDASPES TO PERSEPOLIS
(ARRIAN 6.1–30)

1. General features of the narrative

The narrative in this book has the features which characterised the earlier books. Thus orders issued by A were reported on twenty-eight occasions, and it was noted in the case of Apollophanes that A's order had not been obeyed (6.27.1). Progress by water and on land was reported in terms of days fourteen times. Distances were recorded in stades eight times; of these some were estimates of river-widths (6.4.2; 6.14.5; and 6.18.5). During the campaigns in the Indus valley and on the return to Persia the army was often divided into three or four groups, each of which operated separately. Detailed description was provided only for the group which was accompanying A (e.g. at 6.2.2). Often it was only the departure and then the return to A of other groups that were recorded (e.g. the forces of Craterus and Hephaestion at 6.4.1 and 6.5.5; Craterus at 6.17.3 and 6.27.3; and Peithon at 6.17.4 and 6.20.1). In the narrative A was the centre of all activity. It was enough to refer to him simply as 'himself', αὐτός, on at least seven occasions (e.g. 6.20.2–5). Events which occurred elsewhere were not described in their own context, but they figured simply in the reports which were made to A, on some six occasions (e.g. 6.17.1 and 6.27.4). The only reasonable explanation of these features of the narrative is that Arrian was deriving his account ultimately from the *Royal Journal*. For it is inconceivable that his two immediate sources, Ptolemy and Aristobulus, could have retained in their memory such diverse and detailed matters.

2. The start of the voyage down river at 6.1–5

Jacoby maintained that Arrian's source in 6.1–5 was Nearchus (*FGrH* II B 467). Brunt thought that Jacoby's theory was open to question. In his opinion the similarities between the accounts of the start in Arrian, *Anabasis*, and in Arrian, *Indica* 18f., could be equally well explained by supposing that 'Ptolemy and Nearchus reported the facts accurately' (*L* II 446). 'It seems unlikely', he wrote, 'that Arrian used the same source [viz. Nearchus] for two accounts of the same transactions, which are indeed sometimes complementary but sometimes divergent.' In practice, however, Brunt attributed the central part at least of 6.1 to Nearchus as source (*L* II 101 n. 2).

If, unlike them, we pay attention to what Arrian himself told us about his sources, we see our way clearly. At 5.5.2 Arrian had said that in regard to India he intended to relate in the *Anabasis* only what he considered relevant to A's activities (ὅσον ἐς τὰ Ἀλεξάνδρου ἔργα ἀποχρῶν ἐφαίνετο), and that in a future work (this was to be the *Indica*) he would provide a general description in accordance with reports by Nearchus, Megasthenes and Eratosthenes. In his *Preface* he had told us that his main sources in the *Anabasis* were Ptolemy and Aristobulus. If Arrian is to be believed – and we must remember that his contemporaries had access to the full works of all these authors and could check on his use of those works, whereas Jacoby and others rely only on sparse fragments – Arrian's sources for *Anabasis* 6.1–5 were Ptolemy and Aristobulus, and for *Indica* Nearchus, Megasthenes and Eratosthenes. Of his two sources for the *Anabasis* he added in regard to the number of the ships at the start: 'I am following Ptolemy, son of Lagus, most' (6.2.4 ᾧ μάλιστα ἐγὼ ἕπομαι, with an emphatic ἐγώ), i.e. more than but not to the exclusion of Aristobulus.[1]

In the opening chapter Arrian described the development of A's views about the Indus and its tributaries. There were two stages, which were contrasted:[2] the earlier one (πρότερον μέν γε) that the Indus was the upper Nile and flowed into the inner

---

[1] Arrian probably named Ptolemy here, because he knew that some authors had given different figures.

[2] The translation and the punctuation of Brunt *L* II 101–2 are bad. He takes πρότερον with ἰδών ('he had already seen crocodiles') instead of with ἔδοξεν, and he therefore misses the contrast of πρότερον μέν γε with ἐπεὶ μέντοι at 6.1.5.

sea (the Mediterranean), and the later informed one (ἐπεὶ μέντοι ἀτρεκέστερον) that the Indus flowed into 'the Great Sea'. In reporting the earlier, incorrect view Arrian used the narrative tense 'he thought' (ἔδοξεν), and he followed on with the accusative and infinitive construction from 6.1.2 to the first sentence of 6.1.4. It seems probable that Arrian was drawing here on Aristobulus, and that he implied by his use of the accusative and infinitive that he did not have complete confidence in Aristobulus' version.[3] Within this description of A's views Arrian mentioned a letter of A to Olympias. Having inferred from the crocodiles in the Indus and the Egyptian-type beans on the banks of the Acesines[4] that the Nile rose in India, A wrote to Olympias among other matters that he thought he had found the sources of the Nile, 'basing his deduction over so important a subject on small, indeed trivial points' (6.1.4). This sarcastic comment was made not by Arrian himself, since he was scrupulous in using the first person whenever he made an interjection himself, but by Arrian's source, namely Aristobulus on my interpretation. When he was better informed, 'A cancelled what he had written about the Nile in the letter to his mother' (6.1.5, ἀφελεῖν).

This letter, or rather two letters to Olympias, since the cancellation was presumably done in a later letter,[5] is of considerable interest. Aristobulus presumably did not read A's letters to Olympias at the time of their writing. He had access to them later, either when Olympias was keeping them in Macedonia, or after her death, when they passed into the possession of Cassander and Thessalonice.[6] Aristobulus evidently regarded them as authentic; and so too did Arrian. This

---

[3] Brunt *L* II 101 translated 'it is reported that' as his explanation of the accusative-and-infinitive construction.

[4] These two observations were no doubt made by most of the army and were reported by most historians; for Strabo noted at 696 that Nearchus reported A's observations and A's deductions, and at 707 that Aristobulus commented on the crocodiles of the Indus being like those of the Nile.

[5] Brunt *L* II 103 n. 2, 'Nearchus' report of a draft letter', assumed that there was only one letter; but A reached the Acesines (5.20.8) some months before his return to the Hydaspes, when he obtained more dependable information (6.1.5).

[6] Aristobulus was living at Cassandrea, when he was writing his history.

conclusion is of importance when we consider other letters attributed to A.

At 6.1.6 Arrian returned to the use of the narrative tense: 'the *hyperesiai* for the ships were made up for him from those men of Phoenicia, Cyprus, Caria and Egypt who were following along with the army' (τῶν ξυνεπομένων τῇ στρατιᾷ). The term ὑπηρεσίαι was probably technical; for in the corresponding passage in *Indica* Arrian contrasted the *hyperesiai* with the oarsmen (18.1). Indeed, in the fourth century B.C. it meant, as J. S. Morrison has demonstrated,[7] the group of 'specialists', i.e. coxes, boatswains, carpenters, petty officers etc., whereas most men could be oarsmen if need be on a river-boat running with the stream. A recruited such specialists in part from the camp-followers (also in *Indica* 18.1 ὅσοι ... εἴποντο ἐν τῇ ἄνω στρατηλασίη).[8] Whereas Arrian did not mention oarsmen in *Anabasis* 6.1.6, he later specified probably as oarsmen 'Islanders, Ionians and Hellespontine Greeks serving in the army' who had an interest in nautical matters (*Ind.* 18.2), while he omitted from the non-Greeks the Carians whom he had mentioned in the *Anabasis*. The differences are attributable to the change of source from Ptolemy-Aristobulus to Nearchus. The same explanation is to be advanced for the difference in the number of boats: 'not much short of 2,000, including old ones plying on the rivers', in *Anab.* 6.2.4, and 'in all 800' in *Ind.* 19.7 (both Diod. 7.95.5 and Curt. 9.3.22 wrote of 1,000 in all); for in *Ind.* 19.7 the vessels mentioned were of standard types such as grain-carriers but not native craft.[9]

Before embarking on his ship A made a formal enthronement of Porus in the presence of the Companions and some Indian envoys. The number of cities in the realm of Porus was reported, no doubt from a record in A's archive, as at 5.20.4

---

[7] In *JHS* 104 (1984) 55.

[8] The Greek phrases are clear in each case. I see nothing in favour of Brunt's suggestion in *L* II 518f. that these men had been summoned from the Mediterranean Sea and had travelled 'under escort of reinforcements'. The camp-followers provided many services as well as a market.

[9] Brunt *L* II 519 made unconvincing attempts to harmonise the figures. There is no need since Arrian made no attempt. He reported what his sources recorded and left others to decide which figure was correct.

(see above, p. 254). The names of the units accompanying A on the voyage were given, but not the number of men. That was usual in the *Anabasis*. But in *Ind.* 19.2 the number was given as 8,000 men, the units were named but with the omission of the Agrianians, and 'the so-called Companion cavalry' appeared instead of 'the Royal Cavalry Guard'. The difference is due to the sources: Ptolemy probably in *Anabasis*, and Nearchus in *Indica*. Ptolemy was presumably correct, since a very large number of horse-transporters would have been needed for the Companion Cavalry who numbered some 4,000,[10] and since some squadrons of first-class cavalry were needed by the three groups which were to march by land.[11] The appointment of Nearchus as admiral was noted, and then that of Onesicritus as cox of A's ship; and it was remarked that Onesicritus lied in this matter also, writing that he was not cox but admiral. I attribute the remark to Ptolemy–Aristobulus and not to Arrian, who would have marked his own interjection with the use of the first person.[12]

The details about A's sacrifices came ultimately from the *Royal Journal*, as we see from 7.25.2, 3, 4 twice, 5 twice, and 6. The vivid description of the bugle sounding, the ships starting and the Indians chanting on the banks was derived from Ptolemy–Aristobulus; and it was they who had the precedent of Dionysus in mind (6.3.4–5). The account of the stages of the voyage downstream and the movements of the groups on land has a fullness which was due ultimately to the use of the *Royal Journal* by Ptolemy, and a vividness which we owe probably to Ptolemy, who was with A as a Bodyguard until he was given a separate command at 6.5.6.

3. The campaign against the Malli (6.6–13)

The account falls into two parts: the swift attacks on the Malli in 6.6–8, and the capture of their strongest city, during which

---

[10] See *AG*[2] 191.
[11] The inclusion of all the Companion Cavalry by Nearchus was necessary to make up his total of 8,000 men; for the Hypaspists numbered 3,000 and the Archers were usually 1,000 strong.
[12] I differ here from Brown *Ones.* 8 'Arrian upbraids him'.

A was severely wounded, in 6.9–13. The first part may be compared with the corresponding narratives of Diodorus at 17.98.1–4 and of Curtius 9.4.15–29, both of whom omitted the opening phases and then drew on a sensational, inaccurate account, of which the source was Cleitarchus (see *THA* 65 and 153) . On the other hand, Arrian's narrative of the swift attacks is both full and impressive. The strategic purpose of the moves which were made by A's own group and by as many as five other groups under separate commanders is carefully explained at 6.4.3, 6.5.4 and 6, 6.6.3, 6.8.3, and in retrospect at 6.11.3. The units commanded by A and by others were named, but the total numbers were not provided; and Macedonian casualties were mentioned once, 'up to twenty-five' during a withdrawal (6.7.4). The round numbers which were reported for the strength of the enemy and for enemy losses at 6.8.6, 6.6.5 and 6.7.6 were clearly estimates. The timings and the distances of A's own marches were stated with precision (6.6.2). There are many vivid details, such as A being seen alone on the wall to the shame of the Macedonians, and the exceptional courage of the Indians (6.7.5–6).

As we know from Arrian's preface, the account was based on Ptolemy and/or Aristobulus. We can narrow the source down to Ptolemy in this case. For Ptolemy was particularly expert in military matters, he was a Bodyguard accompanying A on the campaign, and he commanded one group for one episode (6.5.6). The characteristics of Arrian's narrative which we have summarised are indeed typical of Ptolemy's writing. A detail supports the identification. Some of the phalanx-brigades in A's army were named *asthetairoi* and others *pezhetairoi* by Arrian alone of the Alexander-historians and by Arrian very rarely.[13] Who noted this differentiation, which was a matter of interest only to the Macedonians? At 4.23.1 and at 5.22.6 Arrian mentioned 'the brigades of the *asthetairoi*' and in the ensuing operations the presence of Ptolemy, at 4.23.3 and 5.23.7. In these cases it is clear that Arrian was following the account of Ptolemy. The next in-

---

[13] See Bosworth *C* 251f., Brunt *L* I lxxix n. 99 and Hammond *MS* 148ff.

stance occurs here, at 6.6.1. The last example of the *asthetairoi* in action is at 6.21.3, against the Arabitae, when Ptolemy as a Bodyguard was presumably with A.[14] There is only one mention of *pezhetairoi* brigades in action, at 1.28.3,[15] during the attack on Sagalassus, a passage which has unusually full military detail and which mentioned the Macedonian losses as 'about twenty' and the enemy losses 'up to 500'. From these instances we may infer with confidence that Ptolemy was the author who wrote of the *asthetairoi* and the *pezhetairoi*. The two terms occurred together in the account of the aftermath of the mutiny at Opis (7.11.3), a passage which we may now attribute to Ptolemy as source (see also below, p. 290).

The campaign was presumably described in more detail by Ptolemy than by Arrian. For we may assume that Ptolemy specified which troops were allocated to each commander, as well as those accompanying A. Yet Arrian named only those taken by A on each occasion and those entrusted once to Perdiccas (6.6.4). Abbreviation may explain a mistake in Arrian's account, in which the mounted archers were placed contemporaneously in two separate groups. The alternative is that a copyist introduced the error at 6.5.5.[16]

The campaign culminated in the attack on the strongest city in the land of the Malli (6.8.7). During it A commanded 'one part' and Perdiccas 'the other part' of the army (6.9.1). Arrian is here abbreviating; for we may assume that the original

---

[14] Curt. 9.10.6 reported Ptolemy being in command of some light-armed troops in the land of the Oreitae.

[15] Mistranslated by Robson *L* I 115 as 'the territorial foot'. At 5.22.6 Brunt *L* II read τῶν πεζεταίρων in the text and gave the translation 'of the *asthetairoi*'.

[16] The mounted archers were correctly allotted to A's group at 6.6.1 where τε ... καί marked off the units of infantry and then the units of cavalry, and where the expression 'all the mounted archers' can be paralleled by the same expression at 6.21.3. In both passages the mounted archers were part of a swift-moving force. On the other hand, at 6.5.5 the mounted archers were said to be accompanying the elephants and Polyperchon's infantry brigade – a slow-moving force which followed the river-bank. Here the mounted archers are out of place; for instance at 6.2.2 the 200 or so elephants were escorted by 'the largest and heaviest part of the army' (τὸ πλεῖστόν τε καὶ κράτιστον τῆς στρατιᾶς), and in Curt 9.3.24 they went with the baggage-train. Brunt *L* II 113 n. 2 commented on 6.5.5 'here, or in 6.6.1, the mounted javelin-men must be meant'; but the mounted javelin-men were as useful as the mounted archers in swift attacks (e.g. at 6.17.4) and would not have been moving with the elephants.

account specified the troops – only infantry – in each part; for we learn later that the Hypaspists were being led by A in the final assault (6.9.4).[17] Where A and his men attacked, the enemy abandoned the walls and fled to the citadel. A's men then broke down a small gate and pursued towards the citadel. Meanwhile the men with Perdiccas, supposing that the fighting was over, when the walls opposite them were no longer defended, lagged behind. However, A's men began the assault. A thought his Macedonians were slow in bringing the ladders. He seized a ladder from one of them, set it up himself, and 'was climbing up, huddled under his shield' (6.9.3).

The brilliant narrative which follows owes much to the artistry of Arrian, who used vivid present and imperfect tenses and hiatus to excellent effect, but the clarity in the sequence of events is derived from an account to which participants in the action contributed. The author of that account was, as in general, either Ptolemy or Aristobulus. Ptolemy was cited twice with reference to A's wounds. When A was first struck in the chest, 'breath as well as blood issued from the wound'. The only witnesses to that were Peucestas and Leonnatus; the third man, Abreas, was already dead. A then fainted. For 'the breath and blood' Arrian cited Ptolemy (6.10.2), who evidently learnt it from Peucestas or Leonnatus. In the narrative A received that wound only. Arrian said later that according to some A was also struck on the helmet with a club and became dizzy, but that Ptolemy said there was only the one wound (6.11.7). Thus Ptolemy's account was being followed by Arrian in his narrative. There is also the negative evidence that Aristobulus reported a blow with a club (Plu. *Mor.* 341c). Moreover, we have shown above (p. 117) that in *Alex.* 63.3–13 Plutarch was following the version of Aristobulus. In fact Plutarch's account differed from that of Arrian in many points: e.g. at the end Plutarch had A put on his cloak and show himself to the Macedonians outside his door, whereas Arrian concluded with A coming by boat, then riding his horse, and

[17]   As in the final assault at Tyre (2.23.4 and 24.2).

finally walking, and with the soldiers garlanding him with the flowers which India produced at that time (6.13.3).

According to Arrian Ptolemy wrote, evidently in his account of this episode, that he himself 'was not even present' but was commanding another force in action elsewhere (6.11.8). He based his account then on what he learnt from the participants. In particular A must have told him why he had jumped down from the wall into the citadel, what thoughts had been in his mind, and how he had fought on his own (6.6.5–6). Ptolemy must have gathered from other officers what the state of mind of the men in the camp was when they thought that A was dead, and even when A sent a letter saying that he would come to the camp (6.12). Arrian closed his account with a citation from Nearchus, who said that A was pained by criticism of his conduct which had been that not of a commander but of a soldier, and that A was delighted with the remark of an elderly Boeotian soldier who told him 'action is a man's task, Alexander' (6.13.4–5). In citing Nearchus Arrian indicated that he was no longer following his main sources. He added his own interjection, marked as usual by the first person: 'it seems to me that A knew the criticisms to be true'; and he went on to censure A for yielding to the pleasure of personal combat.

In the middle of his account Arrian introduced a digression of his own, summarised with the first person at 6.11.8 ἀναγεγράφθω μοι. It arose from variant accounts of the way in which the arrowhead was extracted from A's chest, some saying the extracter was a doctor (so Curt. 9.5.25–8),[18] others Perdiccas (6.11.1). As one of the variants was clearly false, Arrian went on to list some other false reports. He introduced them with the phrase 'the entire *logos* maintains' (6.11.3 ὁ πᾶς λόγος κατέχει) i.e. the tradition of all authors except Ptolemy and/or Aristobulus (see above, p. 116). The falsehoods were

---

[18] Curtius remarked that the doctors had to be careful in cutting the wooden shaft above the arrowhead (9.5.22). Plutarch said it was difficult to saw off the shaft at P*A* 63.11, a passage where he followed the account of Aristobulus (see above, pp. 117f.). Curtius may well have read Aristobulus' account.

that the action occurred among the Oxydracae, that the final battle against Darius was at Arbela, which was according to some writers 600 stades from Gaugamela and according to others 500 stades, and that not Leonnatus and Abreas but others were named as defending A during the action. 'I rate as the greatest error of those who wrote the history of A' the statement by some that Ptolemy climbed up the ladder after A and Peucestas, held the shield over A, and on that account was called 'Saviour' (6.11.8 Σωτήρ).

As usual, Arrian did not name the authors of the variants and the *legomena*. On my interpretation of P*A* 63 Aristobulus wrote about the extraction of the arrowhead and its size, and he must have committed himself to one of the variants. Arrian let both stand presumably because Ptolemy either was silent on this matter or took a different view from that of Aristobulus. As regards the Oxydracae Curtius placed the action in one of their towns (9.4.26), the source of Curtius being Cleitarchus (see *THA* 153f.); Diodorus 17.98.1 and Justin 12.9.3f. were vague but probably drew also on Cleitarchus and had the same location in mind as Curtius (see *THA* 65 and 105).[19] The placing of the great battle not at Gaugamela, where Ptolemy and Aristobulus put it, but at Arbela can be traced through Strabo 737 to 'the Macedones' and through Strabo 814 to Callisthenes – no doubt on the authority of A who named a nearby hill 'Victory Hill' (Strabo 737 fin. Νικατόριον). The battle took its name from Arbela in Diodorus 17.53.4 and 17.61.3 and in Curtius 4.9.9 and 6.1.21; both authors were following Cleitarchus (*THA* 44, 20 with 27 and 64; and 100).[20] Those falsely said to have been with A when he was wounded were in the surviving accounts Timaeus and Aristonoüs (Curt. 9.5.15), Ptolemy and Limnaeus (Plu. *Mor.* 327b and 344d), and Limnaeus (P*A* 63.7). Curtius drew

---

[19] Strabo 701 placed the action among the Malli. Brunt *L* II 460 held that Strabo drew on Aristobulus in this passage.

[20] The error was not very great because A pursued as far as Arbela (3.15.5). Arrian himself used the common term 'at Arbela' for the flight of Darius at 3.22.4, as Bosworth *C* 34 noted, and Strabo 737 mentioned both Gaugamela and Arbela as the scene of the victory.

probably on Cleitarchus for Timaeus and Aristonoüs, because he stated that Cleitarchus had mentioned Ptolemy as being present at the battle. Plutarch obtained the name of Ptolemy presumably from Cleitarchus, and that of Limnaeus probably from Aristobulus (see above, p. 117).

Arrian made the final comment that Ptolemy himself wrote (6.11.8 ἀναγέγραφεν, i.e. in his own history) that he was not present in the action when A was wounded. This point had already been made by Curtius at 9.5.21, in refuting the accounts of Cleitarchus and Timagenes (the latter writing at the end of the Roman Republic) that Ptolemy had been present. The explanation of Ptolemy recording his non-presence, because he was correcting the lie of Cleitarchus, had been clearly provided by Curtius, and Arrian implied as much at 6.11.8 but without naming Cleitarchus. The passages are important in proving that Cleitarchus had already published this part of his history before Ptolemy wrote his own comment.[21]

4. From the city of the Malli to Persepolis (6.14–30)

After the fall of the city 'the remaining Malli' sent envoys, and the officials of the Oxydracae, together with 150 leading personalities, came from their cities and regions to A to discuss the terms of their surrender. The arguments of the Oxydracae were summarised by Arrian. They included a reference to Dionysus in India and to a report that A was of divine origin (6.14.2 Ἀλέξανδρον ἀπὸ θεοῦ γενέσθαι a variant reading being ἀπὸ θεῶν), and an offer of hostages. A replied demanding 1,000 leading men to serve as hostages or, at his discretion, in his armed forces. The Oxydracae complied, and added 500 chariots with their drivers. A sent back the hostages and kept the chariots. Neither the arguments nor the terms of 'the still surviving Malli' were reported by Arrian. It is obvious that Arrian was abbreviating a fuller account in which the dealings with the Malli were described, and even in the account of the

---

[21] Tarn's arguments to the contrary (26f.) are unconvincing.

Oxydracae there was no assessment of the tribute which they said they were willing to pay (6.14.2).

Because A was dealing with civilised, organised communities in the lands east of the Indus ('India'), he entered into diplomatic negotiations very frequently. They were reported succinctly by Arrian (omitting those with Nysa which were the subject of a *legomenon*): with Taxiles (4.22.6; 5.3.5f.); Abisares (5.8.3; 5.20.5; 5.29.4f.); Doxareus (5.8.3); republican Indians (5.20.6); the bad Porus (5.20.5; 5.21.3); the Ossadians (6.15.2); Musicanus (6.15.6f.); Sambus (6.16.4); and the ruler of Pattala (6.17.2f.). Occasionally some terms or some gifts were mentioned. In addition there were reports simply that a people 'came over by agreement' (e.g. προσεχώρησαν ὁμολογίᾳ at 5.22.4; ὁμολογίαις at 6.4.2), the terms not being stated. The impression is that Arrian had before him a considerably fuller account.

The sources on which Arrian drew were Ptolemy and/or Aristobulus. It was not possible for either of them to have kept in his memory a record of all these negotiations, especially if the record was accompanied by such arguments as the Oxydracae advanced. Nor would they have figured in any personal diary. The ultimate source was an official record, namely the *Royal Journal*; for we know from Polyaenus 4.6.2 that negotiations with embassies were reported there.[22] We conclude, then, that Arrian's source in these cases was Ptolemy, who had given in his own history a fuller account based on the *Royal Journal*, and that Arrian abbreviated it drastically.

The descent downstream to the 'Great Sea' was described very concisely. The despatch of task forces was carefully noted, ten of them between 6.15.1 and 6.20.1, sometimes with their troops defined (e.g. 6.17.3), and rarely with the return reported (6.20.1). The addition of ships and the repair of damaged ships figured at 6.14.4, 6.15.1 and 4, 6.18.4f., and 6.19.3. Founding of a new city (6.15.2), building of fortifications, construction of harbours and docks, details of sacrifices and measurements

[22] See H*RJ* 130 and 132.

272

of widths of the Indus[23] and then of its delta seem to be drawn from a fuller account which derived its information from the *Royal Journal*. We owe probably to one or other, if not to both Ptolemy and Aristobulus, the prominence of Ammon in A's religious beliefs (6.19.4 on two occasions), and the preservation of what A 'used to say' on the subject (ἔφασκεν). When A reached the Great Sea, he sailed out 'to observe, as he was saying, if land rose up somewhere from the deep' (6.19.5).

Arrian wrote little about the Indians. Brahmans were first mentioned as holding a city and fighting to the end (6.7.4–6), and then as philosophers responsible for a revolt (6.16.5).[24] The account which he was following probably described their views, for Arrian said at 6.16.5 that he would defer an explanation until he was writing his *Indica*. The admiration which A felt for the city and the territory of Musicanus was mentioned, but A's reasons which were no doubt stated in the original account were not provided. The peasants near Pattala were persuaded to return to their fields (6.17.6; cf. 1.17.1 and 6.22.2), and A arranged for wells to be dug so that land could become habitable (6.18.1). Abbreviation by Arrian led to confusion at 6.20.4.[25]

A was already planning the voyage which he hoped would reach the Persian Gulf (6.19.5). He chose the point of departure, had wells dug along the coast, gathered four months' supply of grain for the fleet (and probably some for the army too), and fixed the time for the fleet to set out with favourable winds (6.21.2). The operations of A, who started earlier than Nearchus as admiral of the fleet, were described in the usual

---

[23] This subject interested Arrian particularly. He expressed his own opinion, as usual in the first person, at 6.14.5 οὐκ ἀπιστῶ. The records of A's surveyors were kept in the King's Archive; see H*RJ* 137ff.

[24] Nearchus was probably typical of A and his staff in distinguishing between Brahman councillors and Brahman philosophers (Strabo 716 fin.); for at home Plato and others were political advisers as well as philosophers.

[25] A, having sailed down the eastern branch of the Indus at the delta, decided that the western branch's outlet (τὴν ἐπὶ τάδε ... ἐκβολήν) would be better for Nearchus. In order to prepare for his voyage, A dug wells westwards from the western outlet. In abbreviating the original account Arrian has left A's route obscure; see H*SPA* 469, which Brunt *L* II 161 n. 3 seems to have partly misunderstood.

manner. To provide for the fleet he had wells dug (6.21.3), and he ordered Leonnatus, whom he left behind in Ora in command of 'all the Agrianians, some of his archers and cavalry, and Greek mercenary infantry and cavalry to await the passage of the fleet along that coast' (6.22.3). Rejoined by forces under Hephaestion, which had been building a new city, A went through the Gedrosian desert 'by a difficult route, devoid of supplies and often of water'. He was eager to follow the coast, discover what harbours there were, provide water by digging wells, make dumps of stores and arrange anchorages for the fleet; but he was compelled to move at night and farther inland (6.23.1). Even so he sent some cavalry to the coast to reconnoitre, and when he found supplies of food he sent them to the coast for the fleet on three occasions, despite the fact that his first attempt failed through the soldiers breaking the seals and distributing the food to those most in need (6.23.4–6). Sixty days after leaving Ora A reached the Gedrosian palace at Pura (6.24.1). He rested his army there (6.27.1). Between 6.24.1 and 6.27.1 Arrian back-tracked with a description of sufferings and losses in the Gedrosian desert.

The reason for Arrian completing his account and then back-tracking is that he drew first on his chosen authors, Ptolemy and Aristobulus. It was probably Ptolemy who insisted on the strategic purpose of A, namely to make provision wherever possible for the fleet. Arrian cited Aristobulus for a description of flora and fauna in the desert area just before entering the Gedrosian desert (6.22.4–8). Neither author seems to have mentioned any particular loss of life among the troops; for at 6.28.3 Arrian cited Aristobulus again, to the effect that later A sacrificed 'in thanksgiving for the preservation of the army through Gedrosia' (τῆς κατ' Ἰνδῶν νίκης καὶ ὑπὲρ τῆς στρατιᾶς ὅτι ἀπεσώθη ἐκ Γαδρωσίων).[26] On the other hand in back-tracking Arrian drew his material from writers other than Ptolemy and Aristobulus. They were introduced at 6.24.1 as 'the majority of those writing histories of A', and what they said was regarded as legomena (λέγουσιν οἱ πολλοί).

---

[26] Strabo 686, 'how majestic that A saved his army too with victory through the same peoples and places', may have been drawing on Nearchus.

The *legomena* were reported at first in the accusative and infinitive, from 6.24.1 to 5, and then an explanation for the length of the marches was appended in finite past tenses (in the latter part of 5 and in 6). Thereafter Arrian continued with finite tenses, although he was still reporting *legomena*: the killing of the draught-animals, the breaking up of the waggons, and the lack of transport for the sick or exhausted – 'few out of many were saved' (6.25.3 fin.). A flash flood killed 'most of the women and children of those following the army', i.e. of the camp-followers (6.25.5).[27] Stories about men dying from over-drinking water, of A pitching camp some way from a waterpoint and of A refusing water and pouring it out in the sight of his men were told of this march. They were in fact floating tales, applied to different places, e.g. Sogdiana by Curtius (7.5.15), Parapamisadae by 'certain writers' (6.26.1), Choarene by Plutarch P*A* 42.7 (see above, p. 75), and Sogdiana by Curtius 7.5.10–12, while Polyaenus 4.3.25 did not name a place. Frontinus located A's refusal of water on the way to Siwa (*Strat.* 1.7.7).[28]

The *legomenon* that 'a great part of the army was destroyed' (6.24.4) and 'few out of many were saved' came probably from Cleitarchus; for the same idea appeared in Diodorus 17.105.6 'many dying for lack of food' and 8 'A lost many of the soldiers', a passage ascribed to Cleitarchus on my analysis in *THA* 69f., and in P*A* 66.4 'A lost a multitude of people', probably based on Cleitarchus (see above, pp. 124f.). The starvation, the killing of draught animals, the lack of transport for the dying, 'who almost outnumbered the living', and the curses of the abandoned appeared in the rhetorical account of Curtius 9.10.11–16, again probably inspired by Cleitarchus (*THA* 156). The closest similarities[29] appeared in Strabo 722, who did not

---

[27] Brunt *L* II 177 mistranslated γύναια καὶ παιδάρια τὰ πολλὰ τῶν ἑπομένων τῇ στρατιᾷ as 'most of the women and children following the army', for which he would have to delete τῶν and read ἑπόμενα. The point is important. For the women and children of the soldiers had evidently been sent with Craterus on the safe route through Arachosia. It was the families and animals of the camp-followers which were drowned in the flood (the Phoenicians had draught-animals at 6.22.4f.). So too at 6.23.4 those who were starving were camp-followers, who accompanied the army at their own risk.

[28] See Hamilton *C* 113.

[29] The similarities include loss of draught-animals, sand-banks, long marches, camp-

name his source or sources, but we should include Cleitarchus among them.

To those who reported such unmitigated disaster A had committed a grave error of judgement. 'The majority of historians say' that A took this route not because he was unaware of its difficulty, but because no one had ever yet survived with an army on that route, so he heard, except for Semiramis in her flight from India and Cyrus on his way to India, and even they according to local reports survived respectively with twenty and with seven soldiers only. These reports, the historians say, inspired A to engage in rivalry with Semiramis and Cyrus[30] (6.24.3). The idea that A wanted to rival these two was introduced by Strabo into his account of the appalling sufferings of A's men (722 init.). That such stories about Semiramis and Cyrus were current at the time is not in doubt. The question is how far A was influenced by them.

Arrian went on to cite what Nearchus had said: 'it was for the sake of that [the rivalry with Semiramis and Cyrus] and at the same time so as to provide for the fleet what was necessary from close at hand that A took that route'. Strabo had already quoted Nearchus for the first part of the statement; and Strabo contrasted the few survivors accompanying Semiramis and Cyrus with 'the majestic achievement of A in bringing his army victoriously through the same peoples and places' (686). He had reported the second part but without naming Nearchus at 721: 'A being at most 500 stades from the sea, in order also to equip the coast with what was needed for the fleet, and often marching beside the sea despite the difficulties of its rough shores.' He probably took this also from Nearchus, whom he cited soon afterwards.

To sum up, Ptolemy and/or Aristobulus reported that A went on a difficult route in order to provide for the fleet, and that despite being forced to go inland he sent supplies to the

---

ing at a distance from a waterpoint, men exhausted and overpowered by sleep, a flash flood at night, and the loss of the King's equipment.

[30] Brunt *L* II 173 n. 2, 'Arrian obscures the fact that Nearchus said this (S. xv 1, 5)', is puzzling; for τούτων τε οὖν ἕνεκα refers to rivalry with Cyrus and Semiramis, and in the same sentence Arrian was citing Nearchus.

coast and a cavalry force conducted a reconnaissance along the coast. They did not mention any army losses; but they described the troops distributing looted food to 'those who were most oppressed by starvation' – evidently not soldiers but camp-followers. Nearchus gave a more complicated account. A did not know how difficult the route would be (6.24.2, Nearchus being alone in saying this).[31] A took that route in order to provide for the fleet (6.24.3). A was actuated by rivalry with Semiramis and Cyrus (ibid.). We do not know whether Nearchus said anything about losses in the desert; but it seems from Strabo 686 that Nearchus stressed A's success. Finally, 'the majority of the historians who wrote of A's deeds' held that A was aware of the difficulties but chose to go that way in rivalry with Semiramis and Cyrus. The result was appalling, 'few out of many' being saved. These writers either played down or denied A's intention to provide for the fleet.

Arrian left his readers to make their own choice. He commented in the first person favourably on A's 'endurance and generalship' in pouring out the water which was offered to him (6.26.3). And he went on in the next section to narrate an episode which was to A's credit, namely that, when the guides failed, A found the way to the coast and to water in the shingle (6.26.4f.) The author from whom Arrian took this episode is unknown, except that it was neither of his main sources, Ptolemy and Aristobulus.[32]

On resuming his narrative at 6.27.1 Arrian mentioned incidents which were reported to A: Apollophanes' neglect of his orders and his demotion,[33] and the murder of the satrap Philip

---

[31] Strabo, for instance, wrote 'they say that A acted in rivalry, although he knew of the difficulties' (722, εἰδότα τὰς ἀπορίας).

[32] This episode was reported at the same place in the sequence of events by Strabo (722 fin.). At 6.23.3, a passage based on Ptolemy and/or Aristobulus, Thoas reported to A that the aborigines got water by digging in the shingle by the sea. At 6.26.5, when A found water in this way, the implication seems to be that it was his discovery; if so, Arrian was following a different writer.

[33] In fact Apollophanes had been killed (*Ind.* 23.5). The demotion was presumably recorded in the *Royal Journal* at the time of the adverse report, and came via Ptolemy into Arrian's narrative. The death would have been reported at a later date and recorded then. Brunt *L* II 507, 'the supersession of Apollophanes was unjust', together with II 182 n. 2, seems to assume that Apollophanes' complete neglect of matters he had been ordered to carry out (6.27.1) was with reference

in India. A's acts, his letter to Eudamus, the arrival of Craterus and Pharismanes, the execution of Cleander and Sitalces and later of Heracon, and the provision of draught-animals to replace losses – all these were derived ultimately from entries in the *Royal Journal*, transmitted by Ptolemy and selected by Arrian. The comment that the execution of three officers assured A's subjects that he would not tolerate misgovernment was made not by Arrian, who used the first person to mark his own interjections, but by Ptolemy and/or Aristobulus.

There follows a *legomenon* 'not recorded by Ptolemy or Aristobulus or by any other author that one might judge capable of true reporting in such matters' (6.28.2). It was the story of A and his Companions holding a drunken revel in Carmania as a form of triumph in imitation of Dionysus. This story was told by Plutarch (P*A* 67.1–6) and by Curtius (9.10.24–8), both drawing probably on Cleitarchus (see above, p. 125 and *THA* 156). Arrian expressed his own conviction that this *legomenon* was not credible (6.28.2 μοι ὡς οὐ πιστά).[34] On the other hand, he cited Aristobulus for the thank-offering for 'the victory over the Indians and on behalf of the army that it was delivered safe from Gedrosia' (6.28.3), for a festival and for the enrolment of Peucestas in the Bodyguards. He reported from Aristobulus the names, patronymics and local citizenships of the seven Bodyguards – the standard number hitherto – and A's reasons for adding Peucestas.

Next, the arrival of Nearchus and A's orders for the next voyage were reported briefly, since Arrian proposed to cover that voyage in his future work, the *Indica* (6.18.5–7), and the orders to Hephaestion to proceed with the main army in the direction of Persis were stated. A set off with a mobile force to Pasargadae. There some acts of misconduct which had occurred during his absence were dealt with.[35] These items were

only to sending supplies forward to A. Until we know what A's orders had been, we are in no position to say whether the demotion was justified or not. Reports of Apollophanes' failings will have reached A on his way from Gedrosia to Carmania together with reports about Philip's death in India (6.27.2).

[34] Most scholars agree with this opinion; see Hamilton *C* 185. For Arrian the authority of Ptolemy and Aristobulus independently was decisive.

[35] The reports of misconduct in Media and the persons involved came to A in Carmania from Media (6.26.3).

evidently taken by Arrian from Ptolemy, who had drawn on the *Royal Journal*. Arrian then cited Aristobulus for the desecration of the Tomb of Cyrus at Pasargadae, for a description of it, and for the repair being entrusted to Aristobulus. When he reached Persepolis, A repented of his destruction of 'the palace' (this no doubt according to Ptolemy and/or Aristobulus). Arrian referred back in the first person to his own disapproval of the destruction (at 3.18.12). Orxines was executed for misconduct as satrap of Persis, and Peucestas was appointed in his place. According to Arrian at 6.28.3, citing Aristobulus, A had decided on this appointment already in Carmania, no doubt because a report of Orxines' behaviour had reached him.[36] The reasons for choosing Peucestas and the gratification of the Persians were reported, no doubt from Ptolemy and/or Aristobulus.

---

[36] Brunt *L* II 199 held that, when A in Carmania decided to appoint Peucestas satrap of Persis (6.28.3), he could not have known of charges against Orxines, the then satrap. This is incorrect. Reports about Orxines could well have reached A there, just as reports did from Media (6.27.3 ἐνταῦθα). Charges against the officers in Media were laid 'both by the army and by the natives' (6.27.4). In Orxines' case the army may well have sent reports of charges to A in Carmania; the charges made by Persians were heard at Persepolis (6.30.2). Arrian did not say what the charges were. It is unwise to assume that they included robbing the Tomb of Cyrus; for Strabo 730 stated clearly that 'the robbery was the work of thieves and not of the satrap', and the passage in Curt. 10.1.33–7 is worthless. See Tarn 321 and E. Badian in *CQ* 8 (1958) 147ff. for varying opinions.

16

THE LAST YEAR OF ALEXANDER'S LIFE
(7.1–30)

1. Events in Persis (7.1–7.6)

Book 7 opens with the 'longing' of A, who has reached Pasargadae and Persepolis, 'to sail down the Euphrates and the Tigris into the Persian Sea'. Normally a 'longing' is followed immediately by action, for instance in crossing the Danube or marching to Siwa (1.3.5 and 3.3.1), but this is not so in book 7. Numerous affairs took place at Susa, and only when they were completed did A 'sail down towards the sea' at 7.7.1. The separation of the 'longing' from the action becomes understandable, when we consider the special needs of the last book. Arrian planned to end his work with the death of A and with an appreciation of A. There were, however, matters which would have to be treated in advance, such as A's plans for the future, his attitude to philosophy, his pursuit of fame, and his policy towards the Asians. For the final appreciation would become disjointed if it had to include digressions on these matters. Instead, Arrian attached discussion of these matters to narrative points in his text.

Thus Arrian used the 'longing' as a peg on which to hang some *legomena* and some personal interjections. The source from which he derived the sentence about the 'longing' was Ptolemy and/or Aristobulus in accordance with his declared practice, and in this case probably Aristobulus.[1] The *legomena*, coming from other authors, were judged by Arrian to be 'not completely incredible' (see above, p. 190). 'Some have recorded this too, that A was intending (ἐπενόει) to circumnavigate most of Arabia' and the supposed southern fringe of 'Libya' (i.e. Africa) as far as Gadeira (Cadiz), and to subjugate 'Libya' and Carthage. This the first part of the *legomenon* had

---

[1] See above, p. 195, for the probability that Arrian derived mentions of A's 'longing' from Aristobulus.

been touched on earlier. At 5.26.2, when A addressed his senior officers at the Hyphasis river, he had looked ahead to the future: 'from the Persian Gulf to Libya our fleet will carry out the circumnavigation as far as the Pillars of Heracles' (Straits of Gibraltar). He was expressing a distant hope in which he assumed that the Greek concept of the earth's shape at the time was correct (see above, p. 258). Arrian made this hope into a definite intention in one of his own interjections: for he wrote at 4.7.5, when condemning A for failure to control his excesses, 'he was indeed intending (ἐπενόει) to circumnavigate and add Libya to Asia'.[2] Such a circumnavigation was, of course, quite separate from a Mediterranean campaign conducted from the west along the north African coast. It figured elsewhere only in P*A* 68.1, a passage of which the author is unknown (see above, p. 127). In conclusion, we can say only that the idea of circumnavigation had been a commonplace in Greek thought since the report by Herodotus (4.42), that A used it in speaking to his officers, and that Arrian attributed this intention to A as an example of excessive ambition, indeed almost of delusion.

In the next part of this *legomenon* it was said that A wished to outdo the self-styled 'Great Kings' by conquering the whole of Asia plus Africa – a somewhat puerile idea, again of unknown source, and indicative of overweening ambition in A. Arrian then went on to another *legomenon*: 'from there [i.e. from Africa] some [say] A was intending (ἐπενόει) to sail into the Black Sea up to Scythia and the Maeotic Lake [Sea of Azov], and others [say] to Sicily and the Iapygian promontory [the heel of Italy], for he was somewhat disturbed by the great rise of the name of Rome'. The former saying was no doubt inspired by A's response to the offer of Pharasmanes, reported by Arrian from his main sources at 4.15.6, and the latter by authors who wished to exaggerate the power of early Rome.[3] They are clearly of no historical value.

---

[2] This is Arrian's own view, as Hamilton *C* 187, 'he appears to give his own opinion', noted.

[3] Brunt *L* II 501, 'the last point betrays the lateness of Arrian's vulgate source', seems to refer to all the items in 7.1.2f. But Arrian's οἱ δέ, οἱ μέν and οἱ δέ shows that he drew on several sources. The lateness applied only to the last item.

Having reported so many ideas, Arrian felt obliged to express his own view, as usual emphasised by the use of the first person (7.1.4 ἐγώ ... οὔτε ἔχω), namely that he could not conclude what sort of thoughts were in A's mind, except that his intentions were neither small nor trivial – 'that I think I can asseverate' (αὐτὸς ἄν μοι δοκῶ ἰσχυρίσασθαι). He reckoned that, whatever conquest A might make, he would never stop but always seek a further goal in competition with himself, if with no one else. Arrian then quoted with approval the *legomenon* (λέγουσιν) of the Indian sophists saying that no one possesses more ground than is allotted to one's corpse (7.1.5f.).[4] This might have been enough to show Arrian's disapproval of A's outlook, but two further incidents were then adduced to drive the point home.

(1) A's visit to Diogenes, and Diogenes' reply, that all Diogenes needed was for A and his fellows to stand away from the sunlight, were recounted briefly. Since Arrian was reporting the visit as an historical event (i.e. in 336 B.C.), he was drawing on his main sources, here probably on Aristobulus rather than on Ptolemy. The addition, that 'A is said to have admired Diogenes',[5] just as he praised the Indian sophists, may well have come from Onesicritus, who was probably the source of Plutarch's version in which A admired Diogenes (P*A* 14.1–5 θαυμάσαι; see above, p. 28). Arrian's point here is that A admired the better course (i.e. of the philosophers) but that his actions were to the contrary; 'for he was terribly dominated by glory' (7.2.2 ἐκ δόξης γὰρ δεινῶς ἐκρατεῖτο). (2) When A reached Taxila (in 326 B.C.) a 'longing' seized him to have one of the Indian naked philosophers accompany him on the campaign, because he admired their endurance. All refused except Calanus. Here Arrian drew evidently on Aristobulus rather than Ptolemy.[6] The grounds of their leader's refusal was the subject of a *legomenon* (7.2.3 λέγεται). Arrian's source here

---

[4] The source is unknown. Brunt *L* II 204 n. 2 referred his reader to Appendix xx, but he did not discuss the passage there.

[5] The word θαυμάσαι is mistranslated as 'expressed surprise' in Brunt *L* II 205. The argument is that A 'admired' (7.2.2 ἐθαύμασε) and praised (ἐπήνεσε) the philosophers, but that he acted in a contrary manner (τἀναντία οἷς ἐπήνεσε).

[6] We know from Strabo 714 that Aristobulus wrote of the sophists at Taxila.

was evidently Onesicritus; for he was cited by Strabo 715 init. as the author of a long account with a piece of the leader's speech, and he was followed also by Plutarch (P*A* 65.1–4; see above p. 119).[7] Arrian gave Megasthenes as the authority for the description of Calanus by his fellow-philosophers as lacking in self-control (7.2.4).

The temptation to describe the spectacular suicide of Calanus was irresistible. As Arrian wrote naively, 'it had to be told in the history of Alexander'. Numerous writers had treated the subject. Accounts by Nearchus, Onesicritus, Chares, Strabo, Diodorus and Plutarch[8] have survived in fragments or in short versions,[9] and many others, such as that by Cleitarchus, have perished. In tackling this stock episode Arrian made it clear that he had consulted many accounts: 'some say' this and 'others say' that (7.3.2), 'the Indians say' (7.3.3), 'Nearchus says' (7.3.6), and in ending his own account 'that and such as that is what competent men have written on the subject of Calanus the Indian' (7.6.6). We can say that Arrian did not follow Onesicritus and Chares who had Calanus 'throw himself' (ῥίψας ἑαυτόν) into the fire, but did follow the line of Strabo and Plutarch that Calanus lay down decorously on the pyre; but we cannot name the authors that he did follow individually. The final result was an artistic amalgam of his own creation, and the moral he drew was that the human will is 'strong and invincible'.[10]

At 7.4.1 Arrian resumed his narrative which was based on Ptolemy and/or Aristobulus, and he took from them the explanation of the readiness of some satraps to misgovern. Abulites, satrap of Susiane, was arrested for misgovernment, and he was killed together with his son. 'Many other offences had been committed.' The explanation that those in control of 'the spear-won lands' reckoned on A not returning was pro-

---

[7] The name of the leader in Arr. 7.2.2 and P*A* 65 is Dandamis and in Strabo 715 fin. Mandamis; that in Strabo may well have been due to corruption in transmission.

[8] See above, pp. 130–3, where comparisons were drawn and the source of Plutarch was discussed.

[9] Nearchus (*FGrH* 133 F 4 = Arr. 7.3.6), Onesicritus (134 F 17 and F 18), Chares (125 F 19a), Diod. (17.107) and P*A* 69.6–9.

[10] On the other hand Diod. 17.107.5 showed a cynicism which was probably due to his source, Cleitarchus (see *THA* 71).

vided by Ptolemy and/or Aristobulus.[11] A *legomenon*, taken from another source or sources, followed: 'A became at that time quicker to trust the accusations as being indeed utterly plausible,[12] and quicker to punish heavily those who were convicted even of light offences, because he thought that in the same state of mind they might commit great crimes.' The source of this *legomenon* is not known.

The account of the weddings – 'up to eighty' – of A and his leading Macedonians to 'the noblest daughters of the Persians and the Medes' at Susa was derived as a piece of narrative from Ptolemy and/or Aristobulus. Since Ptolemy was one of the bridegrooms, Arrian's version of 'the Persian rite' is to be regarded as authentic.[13] The only difference between the account of Ptolemy and that of Aristobulus which Arrian noted was the mention by Aristobulus of the second bride taken by A on this occasion.[14] Either or both were responsible for the comment that the communal wedding was thought to be 'democratic and Companionable', if one may play on the term 'Companion' (7.4.3 δημοτικόν τε καὶ φιλέταιρον).

[11] A was punishing his officials for their abuse of his subjects, as was made clear at 6.27.4f., and not for rebellion, for which Arrian used the appropriate terms νεωτερισμός and ἀπόστασις as at 6.29.13. Plutarch gave a different account of Abulites' offence and of his punishment (see above, p. 128). The reading of the codices ἐπεμελεῖτο should be kept as in the Teubner text and not as in the Loeb text, because Abulites alone was the governor.

[12] Brunt *L* II 211 mistranslated ὡς πιθανοῖς δὴ ἐν παντὶ οὖσι 'as if they were reliable in all circumstances'. See L–S–J⁹ for the meanings of πιθανός and ἐν παντί (s.v. πᾶς D 4).

[13] Differences in other accounts are slight. The elder daughter of Darius was named not as in Arrian 'Barsine' but 'Stateira' in Diod. 7.107.6, Just. 12.10.10, Plu. *Mor.* 338d and *PA* 70.3. The number of brides was put at 90 by Aelian *V.H.* 8.7, at 92 by Chares (*FGrH* 125 F 4) and at 100 by Plutarch (*Mor.* 329b). A was the bridegroom of only one bride in Plu. *Mor.* 329e (μιᾶς νύμφιος); Arrian named a Bactrian princess but called the brides collectively 'daughters of Persians and Medes'; Diodorus called them 'Persians'; and Justin 'of all races' ('ex omnibus gentibus'). The explanation is that Asians when contrasted with Greeks and Macedonians were often called 'Persians', a politer term than 'barbaroi'. Chares (*FGrH* 125 F 4) in a verbatim quotation dated the weddings 'after A overcame Darius' (i.e. *c.* 330 B.C.) and Justin placed them in Babylon before the mutiny (i.e. in 324 B.C.). Diodorus, Plutarch and Arrian were in agreement in placing the weddings at Susa (in 324 B.C.).

[14] Tarn II 333 misunderstood Arrian's method, when he said that the list of brides 'is from Ptolemy' because Aristobulus is cited for A's second bride. The list was given no doubt by both authors, and Arrian simply noted one point of disagreement between his main sources (as in the *Preface* ὅσα δὲ οὐ τὰ αὐτά).

In 7.4.8–5.6 Arrian gave from his main sources a short account of the registration of marriages between Macedonian soldiers and Asian women, the paying by A of Macedonian soldiers' debts to Asian creditors, and the honouring of officers and men for distinguished service. The saying of A that truth was the basis of trust between himself and his men affords an important insight into his personality. The naming of Peucestas and Leonnatus as the saviours of A at the city of the Malli is consistent with the narrative of that event in 6.10.2, where Arrian drew on Ptolemy (see above, p. 268). In an aside Arrian informed his reader that Nearchus had already arrived at Susa (7.5.6).[15] There is one legomenon (7.5.3 λέγεται), that the payment of the soldiers' debts at Susa amounted to 20,000 talents. The only other author who gave that figure – Justin 12.11.1–3 – put the payment of the debts of 'all' just after the weddings in his narrative, but he gave the location as Babylon and connected the event with the return of Macedonian 'veterans' to Macedonia.[16] The confusion was no doubt due to Justin himself, in abbreviating the account of Trogus, and the passage does not enable us to name the author of Arrian's legomenon.

The beginning of 7.6 is to be translated as follows.

The satraps too came to him: they brought some 30,000 boys, already attaining manhood – boys of the same age from birth – from both the newly-founded cities and the rest of the spear-won territory. Alexander called them Epigoni (Successors). They were equipped with Macedonian weapons and they were practised in the arts of war in the Macedonian manner.[17]

---

15 Brunt L II 211 n. 1, 'Arrian neglects to record the junction with Nearchus', seems to overlook this statement at 7.5.6.

16 In THA 106f. I suggested that Justin here was probably following Cleitarchus. Other accounts are as follows. Diodorus described the payment of 'a little less than 10,000 talents' at Opis to meet the debts of Macedonians selected for return to Macedonia (17.109.2); Curtius reported the payment of 9,870 talents at Opis to meet the debts of 'all soldiers' there (10.2.9–11); and Plutarch said that A paid at Susa after the banquet for the Macedonians married to Asian women the sum of 9,870 talents to their creditors (PA 70.3). It may be that A paid debts on two occasions, the first after the wedding banquet being a sum of 20,000 talents, and the second after arranging the return of Macedonians to Macedonia being a sum of 9,870 talents. The two payments then became confused in the ancient accounts as well as in some modern comments.

17 Brunt L II 217 translates οἱ σατράπαι οἱ ἐκ τῶν πόλεών τε ... παῖδας ... ἐς

This passage, derived from his main sources, was followed by a *legomenon* (7.6.2 λέγονται), to the effect that the Macedonians were distressed, supposing that A was planning everything to dispense with the need of them which he had had in the past. This idea had been expressed in the account of Diodorus (17.108.3): 'A created this unit, consisting of a single homogeneous age-group of the Persians, and being capable of opposing the Macedonian phalanx' (ἀντίταγμα γενέσθαι τῇ Μακεδονικῇ φάλαγγι; cf. 11.67.5 of mercenaries being an ἀντίταγμα to citizen forces, and Plu. *Cleom.* 23.1 of men armed to be an ἀντίταγμα to the Whiteshields of Antigonus). In *THA* 72 I argued that Diyllus lay here behind Diodorus; he may well be the source used by Arrian in this part of the *legomenon*. The next part states that no small pain was caused among the Macedonians by seeing A in Median dress and by the use of the Persian rite in the weddings[18] – a rite displeasing to some even of the bridegrooms, although they had been greatly honoured by being on the same level as the king. There is no clue to the identity of the author used here by Arrian.

At 7.6.3 Arrian returned to his main sources for a list of Macedonian grievances: Peucestas dressing and speaking as a Persian with A delighting in Peucestas going native; the enrolment of Asians in various ways in A's cavalry forces;[19] and the arming of some of them with Macedonian lances. 'All these points were paining the Macedonians, who supposed A was going utterly native in policy and putting Macedonian customs and the Macedonians themselves in a dishonourable position' (7.6.5).

τρισμυρίους ἄγοντες as 'the satraps from the new towns'. But the satraps were not placed in the seventy or so new towns as a rule (indeed Tarn 247 held that this was rarely intended), and what was of interest was not the residences of the satraps but the origins of 30,000 young soldiers. Then his translation of κεκοσμημένους ... ὅπλοις as 'dressed in Macedonian dress' is not supported by any meaning of ὅπλα in L–S–J⁹. He might have been guided by Diod. 17.108.2 πανοπλίαις κεκοσμημένοι in the same context.

18 The emphasis is on the Persian rite and it balances the Median dress; it is not on the racially mixed marriages which had been normalised for some 10,000 Macedonian soldiers and were common enough in the royal family.

19 See my article in *JHS* 103 (1983) 139–44 for the details of the enrolment and for the text of the passage which has been a matter of some dispute.

2. The Persian Gulf, the mutiny and the settlement at Opis

At 7.7.1 Arrian resumed the first sentence of the book, in which A had longed to visit the Persian Sea. The orders which A now issued for doing so are in the usual vein of the narrative deriving from Arrian's main sources (7.7.1 κελεύει); for the forces of Hephaestion are not itemised, whereas those of A are, the information coming ultimately from the *Royal Journal* in my opinion. He took on board the Hypaspists and the *agema*, these two corresponding to the Hypaspists and the Pezhetairoi at 7.2.1; for the infantry *agema* was called sometimes the Pezhetairoi (as at 7.2.1) and at other times the *agema* of the Macedones (as at 1.8.4).[20] An account of the river-systems in Mesopotamia is given next. It is not in past narrative tenses but in present tenses.[21] Thus Arrian is addressing his contemporary readers, and the conditions which he describes are those which obtained in Mesopotamia in his time. They were well known as a result of Trajan's campaigns, in which Arrian may have served as a *tribunus militum*.[22] At 7.6.6 Arrian resumed in past tenses the narrative based on his main sources. A's voyages and actions included the removal of Persian dams from the Tigris, and his saying was reported, that such devices were not appropriate to those who possess military supremacy (as he now did).[23]

The voyage ended at Opis, where A convened an assembly of the Macedonians. Arrian's account of what followed was derived from Ptolemy and/or Aristobulus. It is clear and vivid.

---

[20] See H*VG*.

[21] The same change from past narrative tenses to present tenses occurred at 6.14.4f. There Arrian gave his own description of some tributaries of the Indus, and he marked his own contribution by writing οὐκ ἀπιστῶ with regard to the width of the Indus.

[22] See *CAH* 11 (1936) 244–7 for the importance of the rivers in the campaigns of Trajan, in which it was suggested by Stadter 9 that Arrian took part. It seems more likely that Arrian drew on his own knowledge than that he was drawing on an account by Eratosthenes (Brunt *L* II 223 n. 1). When Arrian wrote of the Acesines, he cited his source, Ptolemy (5.20.8).

[23] This seems a preferable translation of the sentence at 7.7.7 Ἀλέξανδρος δὲ οὐκ ἔφη τῶν κρατούντων τοῖς ὅπλοις τὰ τοιαῦτα σοφίσματα, and Arrian went on to say that A accordingly did not consider this (form of) safeguard advantageous for himself. Brunt *L* II 225 translated 'Alexander, however, said that the contrivances of this kind were the work of men lacking military supremacy.'

It brings out the misjudgement of A by the use of δῆθεν when he thought his speech would please the Macedonians (7.8.2), and it suggests that their annoyance at his speech was not unreasonable (οὐκ ἀλόγως ... ἠχθέσθησαν). Thus Ptolemy and/or Aristobulus were not uncritical of the King. After the arrest of the agitators 'A spoke thus' (ἔλεξεν ὧδε), and the speech was summarised at 7.11.1 'That is what he said' (ταῦτα εἰπών). These words indicate that Arrian was presenting the speech as that actually delivered by A. Moreover, in accordance with his own declared method he was deriving the substance of the speech from Ptolemy and/or Aristobulus, even as he derived the substance of the narrative from them. The actual diction, of course, was Arrian's own both in the narrative and in the speech; for he was writing in an archaising Attic style,[24] which had not been used by his sources. But the contents of the speech were taken from his sources. How much did they know? On the occasion of the speech Ptolemy was standing beside the King as one of his Bodyguards (they accompanied A when he departed from the assembly at 7.10.11), and Aristobulus was no doubt in the crowd of soldiers. These two and others could have recalled the substance of the speech, which must have been as memorable as a speech of Winston Churchill at a time of crisis. There is also the probability that the speech or a summary of its contents was recorded after the event in the *Royal Journal*,[25] even as the events certainly were. Thus there is every reason to suppose that what Arrian has reported in his own words and style conveys to us the substance of A's speech at Opis.

Philip and A were famous as powerful, persuasive orators (Diod. 16.3.1 τῇ τοῦ λόγου δεινότητι, and 16.4.3 οἰκείοις λόγοις, 17.4.9 λόγοις ἐπιεικέσι). Indeed they had to be in

---

[24] For this style and the high praise accorded to it by Photius see Bosworth *C* 34f. Echoes of Xenophon in particular are typical of Arrian's writing; for Arrian adopted him 'as a model of style' (Stadter 166). Bosworth *AA* 104f. has noted the debt of Arrian to Xenophon in the phrasing of A's speech at Opis. As we have seen, Arrian made good use of hiatus. He did so in this speech, e.g. in the sentences at the start and at the end.

[25] Ptolemy II checked each day that 'all that he had said and done' was correctly recorded in his *Journal*; see H*RJ* 132 with n. 13.

their direct dealings with numerous Assemblies of their time (Diod. 16.3.1 ἐν συνεχέσιν ἐκκλησίαις; 17.108.3 πολλάκις ἐν ταῖς ἐκκλησίαις).[26] That the speech in Arrian 7.9f. is very oratorical by our standards is thus a sign of its genuineness. There is certainly considerable exaggeration. For instance, the dramatic revolution in the way of life which Philip was said by A to have brought about was portrayed as if it was universal, whereas it took place mainly in Eordaea and Upper Macedonia.[27] If one demands pedantic accuracy in such a speech and analyses it word by word, there appears to be one misstatement: 'as you returned to Susa, you desert him and depart' (7.10.7). At 7.8.1 it was assumed that the main body of the army under the command of Hephaestion had marched from Susa via the shore of the Persian Gulf (7.7.1) and a camp inland by the Tigris (7.7.6) to a city farther up the Tigris, Opis (7.7.6); so one might have expected 'Opis' and not 'Susa' in 7.10.7, and it was at Opis that the mutiny occurred (7.8.1). But to replace Susa with Opis, as has been suggested,[28] is not enough; for since the army had not been to Opis previously, the word 'you returned' has to be changed also. There is, however, no need to call the text in question if one takes the phrase in its context, which is as follows. When the soldiers reach Macedonia they are to tell the folks at home (7.10.5

---

[26] See H.*SPA* 462f. and Hammond *MS* 58–61 and 167f. for the evidence from inscriptions and literary texts which reveal the activities of the Assembly of Macedones. This evidence is sometimes overlooked, for instance recently by E. M. Anson in *Historia* 39 (1990) in writing of the evolution of the Assembly.

[27] Exaggerations have been suggested in the mention of Macedonia paying tribute to Athens (but see Hammond *MS* 88), in A being appointed ἡγεμὼν αὐτοκράτωρ (but see Diod. 16.89.3 and 17.4.9), in A inheriting debts amounting to 500 talents (but see Curt. 10.2.24), and in A making the same marriages as his Macedonians (but some 10,000 had made these marriages). The translation of ἐμοῦ ἄγοντος as 'under my command' in Brunt *L* II 235 could suggest that A was lying because of the disaster near Bukhara; but the correct translation is 'when I was leading' (see L–S–J⁹ ἄγω II 2), i.e. in action. See Brunt's notes for some of these points, pp. 228–37.

[28] For instance by Bosworth in *AA* 107, Susa 'has obtruded into the speech in place of Opis'. Brunt commented in *L* II 236 n. 7 'Arrian presupposes the accuracy of the vulgate, contradicting his narrative', but he did not quote any example of Arrian preferring a *legomenon* to an account of events by his main sources, Ptolemy and/or Aristobulus. It is unlikely that Arrian would be so stupid as to 'contradict his narrative' a few sections before (7.8.1).

οἴκοι ἀπαγγείλατε) that after all their victories and travels ending with the fleet sailing round from India to Persia (7.10.7) they deserted their king. The place of this desertion which they are to name is not Opis, a little-known place to the stay-at-home Macedonians, but Susa, known to all and sundry. I therefore regard the text as correct in the sense that that was what A said.[29]

The narrative of what happened thereafter, 7.11.1–12.3, was taken from Ptolemy and/or Aristobulus. There was, however, a *legomenon* at 7.11.9, where the number of guests at the banquet, their pouring of 'one libation' (i.e. of reconciliation) and their singing of a victory song were mentioned. 'This *logos* prevails', wrote Arrian, i.e. it is the general tradition; but Arrian does not vouch for it as certain, because he did not find its content in his main sources.

A few points in the narrative invite comment. Ptolemy as a Macedonian commander is more likely than Aristobulus to have given the names of the Persian units which were to be formed in place of the Macedonian ones at 7.11.3: a Persian infantry *agema* corresponding to the infantry *agema* of Macedones (as at 1.8.4), Persian *pezhetairoi* and *asthetairoi* corresponding to the phalanx brigades, a Persian brigade (τάξις) of Silvershields[30] corresponding to the Royal Brigade of Hypaspists (as at 1.8.4), a Persian Companion Cavalry and a

---

[29] It should be noted that of recent writers Brunt in *L* II 532f. regarded the speech as 'an epideictic display by Arrian', containing 'exaggerations and absurdities ... unlikely to have been fathered on him [A] by a well-informed writer, either Ptolemy or Aristobulus'. Bosworth took a more extreme view, in *AA* 108, for instance, concerning the revolution brought about by Philip (7.9.2): 'as it stands, it [this passage] is an absurdity' and later 'wildly inaccurate'. As regards its origin 'there is a simple answer. It is based on a passage in the *Indike*' (7.2–7). Arrian, were he alive, might easily accuse Bosworth of absurdity; for the *Anabasis* was written before the *Indica* (see 5.5.1), and a passage in *Anabasis* could have been based on a passage in the *Indica* only by a feat of clairvoyance. That argument is topsy-turvy. Nor is it likely, when one reads *Indica* 7.2–7, that Arrian – as inventor of the speech – would attribute to Philip's Macedonians in 359 B.C. the primitive habits of the Indian aborigines. Neither Brunt nor Bosworth concerns himself with Arrian's declared method in his *Preface* when considering this speech and that at the Hyphasis. Of earlier writers F. R. Wüst in *Historia* 2 (1953/54) 177–88, argued that the speech was not in any way authentic; Brunt thought 'not all his objections ... well-founded'. This is not the place to discuss them.

[30] For the name being given in India see *AG*[2] 222 with the ancient references. The word τάξις was the technical term for a brigade.

Persian Royal Cavalry *agema*. The Persian Silvershields were in fact formed and served (Diodorus used the older name 'Hypaspists' at 17.110.1). They numbered 1,000 men (Just. 12.12.3),[31] as did the Royal Brigade of Hypaspists.

The words of Callines and the reply of A, which together sealed the reconciliation of A and his Macedonians, were introduced differently by Arrian: the former at the beginning by 'he said suchlike things' (7.11.6 τοιαῦτα εἶπεν) and the latter at the end by 'that is what he said' (ταῦτα εἰπόντα). The difference, no doubt inherited from Ptolemy and/or Aristobulus, indicated that the exact words of Callines were not known, but the exact words of A were known. In the banquet of reconciliation 'Persians' at 7.11.9 was used to include other Asians (τῶν ἄλλων ἐθνῶν of 7.11.8), just as Bactrian brides had been included under the general term 'Persian and Median girls' at 7.4.6.[32] When he arranged for the Asian wives of returning Macedonians to stay in Asia with their children, he said he would himself be in charge of their upbringing 'in the Macedonian manner both in other respects and in preparation for military service' (7.12.2). This is the earliest mention of a specifically Macedonian system of education for Macedonian boys, paid for by the King (representing the state) and including military training, not just for the Royal Pages but for the children of ordinary Macedonian soldiers.[33] He undertook also to bring these Macedonian boys to Macedonia on their reaching manhood. The comment that his undertakings for them were 'uncertain and indeterminate' (ἀστάθμητα καὶ ἀτέκμαρτα) was inspired not by distrust of A's intentions but by the knowledge that his death was to intervene before they reached manhood.

Craterus was to command the returning Macedonians. He was to take over the duties of Antipater in Macedonia, Thrace and Thessaly and in regard to 'the freedom of the Greeks', i.e.

---

[31] They figured as a Palace Guard of 'Persian Apple-bearers' on the tablets attached to A's funerary car in Diod. 18.27.1.

[32] See n. 14 above.

[33] For the importance of A in the history of state education see my article in *Historia* 39 (1990) 275–9.

the Greek League, which as a free community of states was in alliance with Macedonia;[34] and Antipater was to bring out a force of Macedonians in the prime of life. The appointment of Craterus gave rise to a rumour which was put into circulation by persons 'who were eager to distinguish themselves by expounding the purposes of the King's affairs, all the more so when those affairs were secret,[35] and who put their faith less in the true interpretation than in the baser interpretation to which speculation and their own malice lead them' (7.12.5). This narrative and this description of the rumour-mongers, being in the past narrative tenses, was taken from Ptolemy and/or Aristobulus. The rumour was that the removal of Antipater was due to A having given in to the slanders which his mother had expressed. A possible explanation was then put forward, this too being derived from Ptolemy and/or Aristobulus. In the course of it reference was made to the contents of letters written by Antipater and by Olympias about one another to A – another example of one or other or of both Ptolemy and Aristobulus having access to these letters (see above, p. 263). 'Yet there was no report of any single act or word on A's part which might have led anyone to conclude that Antipater was not as much to A's liking as he had always been.' A lacuna in the text then intervenes.

3. Media to Babylon (13–19)

It has been estimated that the lacuna corresponds to two pages of Loeb Greek text.[36] The topics in it included the advance from Opis to Ecbatana (7.14.1), the flight of Harpalus, and

---

[34] 'The freedom of the Greeks' was not a reference to the liberation of Greek cities in Asia, as Brunt's note recommending section 39 of his Introduction in *L* I li would seem to suggest, but to the members of the Greek League. When A set off for Asia in 334 B.C., he entrusted to Antipater the conduct of affairs concerning 'Macedonia and the Greeks' (1.11.3), i.e. the Greeks of the Greek League. For the alliance see 3.24.5 and *HM* III 571ff.

[35] The orders to Craterus were of course secret. They, in part at least, were written orders (Diod. 18.4.1), which became known only after A's death and were discussed by the Assembly of Macedones. A's arrangements were then changed; see Arr. *Succ.* 1b (Dexippus) 3, edd. A. G Roos and G. Wirth.

[36] See Brunt *L* II 506.

some dispute between Hephaestion and Eumenes. When the text resumes, we may have the end of a *legomenon*, since the construction is the accusative and infinitive. It reports a reconciliation between Hephaestion and Eumenes, the former unwillingly, the latter willingly.³⁷ A definite *legomenon* follows: A is said (λέγεται) to have seen the stud-farm of the Persian kings and to have found 'not many more than 50,000 mares, where in the past (πάλαι) there had been up to 150,000'. A similar statement had been made by Diodorus at 17.110.6: 'in the past (τὸ παλαιόν), they said, 160,000 mares used to graze, but at A's visit only 60,000 were counted'. It is most probable that the two passages came from a common source. In *THA* 73 I argued that the likely source of Diodorus in chapter 110 was Diyllus. Thus Arrian may have drawn on Diyllus for this *legomenon*. In the course of the *legomenon* Arrian referred to Herodotus for the name of these horses, Nesaean.³⁸

Another *legomenon* follows at 7.13.2. They say (λέγουσιν) that Atropates, the satrap of Media, gave A a hundred women and told him they were 'of the Amazons'. Of those who state this some say (οἱ δὲ λέγουσιν) that the women had small right breasts and left them exposed in battle. (Returning to the main *legomenon*) A sent the women away and informed the queen that he would come to beget children with her. 'Neither Aristobulus nor Ptolemy nor any other writer who is competent in such matters has recorded this.' Plutarch had already named the writers who dismissed the Amazon story as fiction: Aristobulus, Ptolemy, Chares, Anticleides, Philip of Theangela in Caria and three others of whom nothing else is known. And he named those who reported a meeting of A and the queen as Cleitarchus, Polycleitus, Onesicritus, Antigenes and Ister (*PA* 46; see above, p. 81). It appears from the order of the names that Cleitarchus started that particular hare; and this appear-

³⁷ This reconciliation was probably that mentioned in Plu. *Eum.* 2.1, when A took Eumenes' side and censured Hephaestion. Arrian at 7.14.9 referred back to this quarrel.
³⁸ Hdt. 3.106.2 and 7.40.2–4, confused with Nysa by C. B. Welles in the Loeb edition of Diodorus, vol. VIII p. 443 n. 4. Brunt *L* II 247 n. 2 and 557 'perhaps from Aristobulus' overlooks the statement of Arrian in *Preface* 3 that *legomena* are from authors other than Ptolemy and Aristobulus.

ance is strengthened by Strabo 505 naming for the visit of the queen to A Cleitarchus, whom he considered 'not worthwhile' on the geography of the supposed habitat of the Amazons (491). On my interpretation in *THA* 59, 102 and 135 it was Cleitarchus who inspired the versions in Diodorus 17.77.1–3, Justin 12.3.3–7 and Curtius 6.5.24–32. Arrian then expressed his own opinion (δοκῶ ὅτι), to the effect that Amazons did exist in mythical times but not in historical times,[39] and that, if Atropates produced a hundred women, he had them dressed up to look like Amazons.

The next event in the narrative drawn from Ptolemy and/or Aristobulus was the celebration of some 'good event' (mentioned perhaps in the lacuna) with a festival of athletics and the arts and with drinking parties for A and the Companions.[40] Hephaestion fell ill and died on the seventh day – they say (λέγουσι) that the stadium was full, for the boys' athletic competition was on that day – and on the news that Hephaestion was in a bad state A hastened to him but did not find him alive. It is difficult to see why Arrian mentioned the circumstances in the stadium; perhaps he has abbreviated a longer passage in which these circumstances delayed A, and he stated not as a *legomenon* but as a fact that it was the day of the boys' competition.[41] Of A's mourning, although all agreed it was great, 'various accounts were written'. Arrian then made a digression in which he analysed some accounts and expressed his own opinion of some of them, as usual marking his own contribution by the use of the first person (7.14.3 μοι δοκοῦσιν;

[39] The division was noted by Strabo 504, but he regarded the Amazons of myth as 'monstrous and far from credible'. Arrian is more typically Greek in regarding 'myths' as protohistorical.

[40] Such parties (πότοι) were a feature of the King's hospitality to his Companions. There is no reason for supposing that Aristobulus would 'hardly have mentioned them' (Brunt *L* II 248 n. 1), for they were a matter of common knowledge and general acceptance.

[41] Arrian's writing here is difficult to interpret. The contrast is between the fullness of the stadium (τὸ μὲν στάδιον) and the hurried response of A to the report (ἐπεὶ δὲ ἐξηγγέλλετο), presumably because A presided over a full stadium at the boys' events. Arrian used the apodotic δέ to stress the action of A in hastening to Hephaestion. Perhaps because Arrian added the explanatory sentence in the narrative form he failed to continue with the accusative and infinitive in the last sentence, which should have depended on λέγουσι.

4 τίθεμαι; 5 οὐδαμῇ πιστὸν ἔμοιγε; 6 μοι δοκεῖ). The accounts by Ptolemy and Aristobulus were certainly among the many that Arrian considered.

Arrian divided the accounts into two main categories, those inspired by goodwill towards Hephaestion and/or A, and those inspired by malice towards Hephaestion and/or A. In fact Arrian concerned himself mainly with accounts about A. In the first category Arrian reported A lying for a large part of that day on the corpse and then being forcibly removed by the Companions, and A cutting off his hair in mourning – both being commendable in that Hephaestion was 'A's closest friend' (7.14.3). Arrian interjected his own point, that the cutting of the hair was not unlikely in view of A's rivalry with Achilles from boyhood up. In the second category Arrian reported A lying all day and all night on the corpse; A hanging the doctor Glaucias, some said for the wrong prescription, others said for not stopping Hephaestion filling himself up with wine; and A driving the funerary car (Arrian interjected his own disbelief). These excesses were censured as 'unbecoming in a king and in A' (7.14.3). In both categories there was mention of Asclepius: in the first that in sending an offering to Asclepius at Epidaurus A added the words 'Yet Asclepius has treated me unfairly in not saving for me the companion whom I valued as much as my own life' (Arrian thought this 'not utterly unlikely'); and in the second that A ordered the burning down of Asclepius' shrine at Ecbatana (Arrian rejected this as not characteristic of A).

Of these accounts Diodorus chose that which attributed Hephaestion's death to over-drinking, and his phrase was that Hephaestion indulged in 'ill-timed bouts of drunkenness' (17.110.8 ἀκαίροις μέθαις χρησάμενος), his source on my interpretation being Diyllus (*THA* 73). Justin censured A for excessive mourning 'contrary to the dignity of a king' (12.12.12 'contra decus regium'). Plutarch reported that Hephaestion had a fever and that in the absence of his doctor, Glaucus, at the festival he downed a huge beaker of chilled wine and shortly died; A's grief passed all reason; he crucified the unfortunate doctor, had the manes of all horses and mules shorn, ordered the removal of battlements from the nearby cities, and banned all music-making in the camp (72.1–3). I argued above (pp. 137–9) that Plutarch was here following the account of Cleitarchus.[42]

The great majority of writers reported that A ordered the paying of sacrifice suitable to Hephaestion as a hero for ever. Some say (οἱ δὲ λέγουσιν) that he sent men to the oracle of Ammon to ask the god whether he would permit sacrifice to Hephaestion as a god, and that the god did not grant permission. Ptolemy and/or Aristobulus were among that majority; for they were the source of Arrian 7.23.6 which reported the return of the men and the answer of the god.[43]

Arrian then listed a number of matters on which all writers agreed (7.14.8–10), which means that he himself reckoned to have consulted all who wrote on this subject. He noted that A ordered a colossal funerary pyre, costing 10,000 talents (so P*A* 72.3, probably drawing on Cleitarchus; see above, p. 139), and even more 'as some reported' (so Diod. 17.115.5 and Just. 12.12.12, both following Ephippus on my analysis in *THA* 75 and 108). He referred back to the quarrel between Hephaestion and Eumenes (7.13.1), using some source critical of Eumenes as the first to engage in 'the trick' (τοῦ σοφίσματος) of dedicating himself and his arms to Hephaestion (presumably a Macedonian writer, as the practice seems to have been peculiar to Macedonians). At 7.14.10 Arrian resumed his narrative, based on Ptolemy and/or Aristobulus, to report that 'A did not appoint anyone else in place of Hephaestion to be Chiliarch over the Companion Cavalry[44] ... but the Chiliarchy was called (that) of Hephaestion and the standard which preceded it was that made at his order' (7.14.10). It seems that Arrian has here so abbreviated his source that he has fused the

---

[42] Arrian was no doubt familiar with the original accounts on which Diodorus, Trogus and Plutarch had drawn. He left his readers to make their own decision which, he hinted, depended on the attitude of each to A (7.14.2).

[43] Arrian did not mention the view, which was probably that of Ephippus, that A had Hephaestion worshipped 'as a god' (see above, p. 139).

[44] Arrian usually wrote ἐπί with the genitive for an actual command (e.g. at 6.13.1 ἐπὶ τῆς στρατιᾶς). The construction with the dative is less precise; see L–S–J⁹ ἐπί B III 6. It is certain that Hephaestion was not in command of all the Companion Cavalry, because A had abandoned that command post in 330 B.C. (3.27.4).

two offices which we know (ultimately from Hieronymus)[45] that Hephaestion had held: 'the Chiliarchy of Hephaestion' (this being 'the charge of the entire kingdom', i.e. of Asia; Arrian, *Succ.* 1a 3) and the command of the 'most distinguished Hipparchy of the Companions, which Hephaestion first commanded'[46] (Diod. 18.3.4 οὖσαν ἐπιφανεστάτην), i.e. the Royal Hipparchy, analogous presumably to the Royal Brigade of Hypaspists.[47]

The brevity of Arrian has contributed to some misunderstanding of Hephaestion's position.[48] In 330 B.C. he and Cleitus commanded the Companion Cavalry as 'Hipparchs' (3.27.4). In and after 328 B.C. he often commanded an army group, sometimes together with Perdiccas. Then during A's recovery from his wound Hephaestion alone was in command of the army (6.13.1). He acted as A's second-in-command on campaigns thereafter (6.17.4, 6.21.3, 6.28.7). The Hipparchy which he commanded was named first of the three Hipparchies at 5.12.2, and it retained his name after his death (7.14.10). We owe to Hieronymus, the author behind Diodorus 18.48.4f., the knowledge that the Chiliarch was second-in-authority (δευτερεύοντα κατὰ τὴν ἐξουσίαν) and that his office had been taken over from the Persian system by A at the time when he admired Persian customs (*c.* 330 B.C. in Diod. 17.77.4). Hephaestion approved of A's policy towards the Asians (P*A* 47.9, probably following Aristobulus; see above, p. 83), and he married a daughter of Darius. There is no doubt that A intended to leave Hephaestion in Asia as Chiliarch during his own campaigns in Arabia and later in the Mediterranean theatre. It was partly because of Hephaestion's position in the Kingdom of Asia that A ordered mourning throughout Asia (7.14.9; cf, Diod. 17.114.4) and planned an Asian type of funerary monument.

Next A's winter campaign of 324/3 B.C. against the Cossaei

---

[45] See *HM* III 95f.

[46] After A's death Perdiccas took both these offices (see references in the text and add Plu. *Eum.* 1.2). Incidentally R. M. Geer mistranslated οὖσαν ἐπιφανεστάτην at Diod. 18.3.4.

[47] In each case the *agema* survived alongside the larger Royal unit.

[48] Brunt *L* II 511ff. gives a brief account.

was reported as narrative derived from Ptolemy and/or Aristobulus. Here the main source was evidently Ptolemy, who coupled himself as commander of a part of the army with Alexander himself; for neither of them was deterred by difficulties. The final comment that A found nothing impossible in his military operations would come best from Ptolemy as one of A's experienced commanders (7.15.3). Whereas the Cossaei had thwarted all previous attacks by their guerrilla tactics, 'A destroyed the tribe of them'.[49] Other surviving accounts mentioned the founding of cities by A (Diod. 17.111.4, following Diyllus according to *THA* 74; and Arr. *Ind.* 40.8, following Nearchus),[50] and the massacre of all male Cossaeans from youth up, this being an offering to Hephaestion as a hero (P*A* 72.4, following probably Cleitarchus, see above, p. 140). It is interesting that Arrian here concentrated only on the military aspect and the destruction of the tribe. The later statement, that Peucestas brought Cossaeans to fight for A (7.23.1), a statement drawn from Ptolemy and/or Aristobulus, shows that Arrian did not accept the account of a massacre as recorded by Plutarch and probably Cleitarchus.

The embassies which met A on his way to Babylon were reported in two categories: those of the Libyans, Bruttians, Lucanians and Etruscans congratulating A on 'the Kingship of Asia'[51] (in the narrative from Ptolemy and/or Aristobulus), and those of Carthaginians, Ethiopians, European Scythians, Celts and Iberians, hitherto unknown to 'Greeks and Macedonians' (being a *legomenon*, evidently from a Greek writer, since Macedonians had seen Celts at the Danube and Euro-

---

[49] The word ἐξεῖλεν is stronger than Brunt's translation 'A reduced the tribe.' Polyaen. 4.3.31, who may well have drawn on Ptolemy's account, wrote that A 'mastered the country' of the Cossaei by his adroit use of cavalry forces.

[50] The evidence of A's contemporary Nearchus, that in founding cities A intended to convert Cossaeans from nomads to settled people, is very valuable; for it shows that they were to be populated by Cossaeans (for such native cities founded by A see *AG²* 231 in India and 233 in Oreitis). See *AG²* 242 and Hamilton *C* 201. Diod. 17.111.6 called these cities 'important' and situated in difficult country (πόλεις ἀξιολόγους ἐν ταῖς δυσχωρίαις). The Loeb translation by C. B. Welles 'strong cities at strategic points' is misleading; so too is Bosworth's remark 'military settlements to control insurgency' (Diod 17.111.6) in *CE* 165.

[51] For A's position as King of Asia and not King of Persia see H*KA*.

pean Scythians beyond the Jaxartes). In a summary account of these and later embassies Diodorus commented that this was the first time the Greeks knew of 'the Galatae [i.e. Celts] near the Thracians' (17.113.2). It is evident that Diodorus' source – Diyllus according to *THA* 74 – might have been Arrian's source for the *legomenon*. Another *legomenon* said that the embassies appealed to A to arbitrate, and that 'then especially A appeared to himself and his associates to be master of every land and sea', a sarcastic comment worthy of Cleitarchus (see *THA* 83).[52] Arrian then cited Aristus[53] and Asclepiades of the historians of A for the statement that the Romans also sent envoys, and that A on learning about their constitution and on seeing their bearing prophesied something of their future power (7.15.5). Arrian made his own interjection: 'this I have recorded neither as certain nor as utterly incredible' (see *Preface* 3 for the expression). He showed his own disbelief by remarking that neither any Roman historian, nor Ptolemy and Aristobulus 'whom of the historians of A I rather go along with', nor probability supported the sending of envoys by Rome.[54]

A's plan to explore the Caspian Sea was reported from Ptolemy and/or Aristobulus, and from Aristobulus in fact, if A's 'longing' (7.16.2 πόθος) is a sign of Aristobulus. Arrian continued with the state of knowledge in the time of A:[55] 'the beginnings of the Caspian Sea had not yet been discovered, although ... navigable rivers flow into it'. These rivers were

---

[52] The same idea appeared in Just. 12.13.1f., of which on my analysis the source was Cleitarchus (*THA* 108 fin.).

[53] The writer cited in Athen. 438d was active *c.* 250 B.C., when the experience of Pyrrhus and his envoy Cineas was well known (cf. Plu. *Pyrrh.* 19.4 and 20.4). He may be the writer cited by Strabo 730.

[54] Arrian did not mention Cleitarchus' report of an embassy from Rome (*FGrH* 137 F 31), perhaps because Cleitarchus did not go on to forecast Rome's future greatness; for Cleitarchus will have heard of Rome mainly from the negotiations of Alexander the Molossian with the city in 334–1 B.C. Brunt's deduction from this passage that 'Arrian did not read Cleitarchus' is therefore unjustified (*L* II 498). In fact this is an almost unique instance of Arrian citing the sources of a *legomenon*.

[55] Brunt *L* II 258 n. 3 supposed that Arrian should have given the contemporary knowledge of the river's course, and this is assumed by Bosworth *C* 10 n. 18. See Stadter 187, who shares my opinion.

listed. They ended with 'the general *logos*' that the Araxes flowed from Armenia into the Caspian Sea.

On crossing the Tigris A was met by the learned men of the Chaldaeans, who drew him aside from the Companions and asked him to stop the march to Babylon; for (they said)[56] they had had an oracle from the god Belus that the advance to Babylon then was not to be to his good (7.16.5). The source as usual in the narrative was Ptolemy and/or Aristobulus. Then A's reply followed as a *logos*, i.e. not from Ptolemy and/or Aristobulus. The narrative was then resumed in direct speech, making the Chaldaeans' advice more vivid, and it continued with the reflections that the divine power (τὸ δαιμόνιον) was leading A to an inevitable end, that it was better perhaps for him to die at the height of his fame, and that thereby he would avoid a human disaster such as caused Solon to advise Croesus to call no man happy until his end is at hand. These reflections were those of Ptolemy and/or Aristobulus. For Arrian always marked his own interjections clearly – as indeed he proceeded to do in the next sentence (δοκῶ), his idea being that A would have preferred to die before Hephaestion did.[57]

A's suspicions about the motives of the Chaldaeans were summarised in 7.17.1–4.[58] Apart from two *logoi* which concerned the siting of the new temple, this passage came again from Ptolemy and/or Aristobulus.[59] At 7.17.5 a statement by Aristobulus (i.e. mentioned briefly or not at all by Ptolemy) explained that A did try to obey the instructions of the Chaldaeans but found that the approach from the west side, facing eastwards, led his army into marshy ground with open pools, which was impassable. 'So willy-nilly A disobeyed the god.' Arrian then reported another statement by Aristobulus in an abbreviated form (7.18.1 τοιόνδε τινα λόγον). A diviner

---

[56] Brunt *L* II 259 mistranslated this passage as 'it is said that they had an oracle' etc. The phrase λόγιον γὰρ γεγονέναι σφίσιν is the reported speech of the Chaldaeans.

[57] Stadter 86f. differs in attributing 7.16.7 to Arrian; but the Greek text does not support his view.

[58] Arrian used the word ὕποπτος to mark off this section at the beginning and at the end where he employed hiatus for emphasis.

[59] Nearchus gave a different account; see *PA* 73.1 and above, pp. 140f.; see also Diod. 17.112.4 with *THA* 74 and Just. 12.13.3–6 with *THA* 108.

called Peithagoras deduced from the absence of a lobe in a victim's liver that Hephaestion would soon die, as he did the day after the report was delivered. The same diviner found the same absence of a lobe in reference to A, and he passed the word to his brother, Apollodorus, who warned A. Later, having entered Babylon, A asked Peithagoras what the omen had been, and on being informed A respected Peithagoras for his truthfulness.[60] Aristobulus said that he had this story from Peithagoras himself, and that the same omen occurred before the deaths of Perdiccas and Antigonus Monophthalmus. Arrian then introduced the saying of Calanus (which he had not related at 7.3), that he would greet A at Babylon. As we have suggested above, p. 133, in considering P*A* 69.6–8, the *logos* about Calanus was probably drawn from Cleitarchus.

At 7.19.1 A entered Babylon (in spring 323 B.C.). The business of the Greek embassies which awaited him there 'has not been recorded' (i.e. not by any author).[61] 'I myself suppose' that most were congratulatory and brought wreaths. 'It is said' that he received them with due honour and that he gave them statues which Xerxes had removed, including 'it is said' those of Harmodius and Aristogeiton and that of Artemis Celcea.[62] Here Arrian marked precisely the distinctions between his main source, his personal interjection, and the two *legomena*. At Babylon A found that the fleet which he had ordered was ready. For the details of naval preparations, A's plans to colonise the western coast of the Persian Gulf, and his intention to invade Arabia Arrian cited Aristobulus' account, which was presumably fuller than that of Ptolemy. Arrian then added his own interjection as a comment on A's pretext for war, as in Strabo 741, against the majority of the Arabs: 'the truth in my own opinion (τὸ δὲ ἀληθές, ὥς γέ μοι

---

[60] Appian, *B.C.* 2.152 seems to have drawn directly on Aristobulus and not on his contemporary Arrian; see Brunt *L* II 263 n. 1. See above, pp. 142f. for Cleitarchus being the probable source of Plutarch's version in P*A* 73.3–5.

[61] It is probable that the business of the embassies was recorded in the *Royal Journal*. Ptolemy did not trouble to report it.

[62] Arrian reported the *legomena* as 'not utterly incredible'. No doubt he knew that different accounts had been given for the date of the return of the statues to Athens (Pliny, *NH* 34.70 attributed the return of the statues to A, and Paus. 1.8.5 to Antiochus I).

δοκεῖ) is that A was always insatiable in acquiring something more'.

4. The last weeks and Arrian's assessment of Alexander

'Tradition holds (λόγος κατέχει) that A kept hearing that the Arabs honoured two gods only, Ouranus and Dionysus.' Here Arrian indicated that he was not following Ptolemy and/or Aristobulus alone but was quoting a general tradition;[63] and this applied also to A's intention 'to let the Arabs conduct their states in accordance with their own customs, as indeed he had done with the Indians' (7.20.1 fin.). In the next sections, 7.20.2–21.4, Arrian reverted to his main source, Ptolemy and/or Aristobulus, for the other motives of A which arose from the reported prosperity and size of Arabia, and for the reports about two islands in the Persian Gulf. Aristobulus was said by Arrian to be his source for one of the islands being named Icaros on the order of A. The report about the other island and the attempts to circumnavigate the Arabian peninsula (7.20.6–21.9) were evidently from both authors, who were concerned with reports to A. Nearchus was then cited by Arrian for his earlier rejection of Onesicritus' proposal to sail not into the Persian Gulf, as A had ordered, but across the mouth of the Gulf to the Arabian coast.

In 7.21 Arrian adopted a different procedure. He described the system of rivers and waterways in Mesopotamia, and then had this description reported to A, who initiated improvements for flood-control and irrigation as he sailed from Babylon via the Euphrates and Pollacopas canal to the lakes towards Arabia. For this and for A's founding of a city at the end of the voyage Arrian was following Ptolemy and/or Aristobulus.[64] He continued with them for A's return up river and his having Babylon 'on his left' despite the warning by the Chaldaeans not to enter 'facing the setting sun' (7.16.6); for A thought that the warning had been belied by his earlier entry

---

[63] This tradition included among its authors Aristobulus, as we see from Strabo 741.
[64] Strabo 741 cited Aristobulus for part of A's voyage.

into Babylon without any harm. He then reported a *legomenon* (λόγος λέγεται τοιόσδε), that A's cap (καυσία) and diadem were blown off and fell into the water, and that the diadem was retrieved by a sailor who swam with it on his own head. For the sequel of the *legomenon* 'Aristobulus says the sailor received a talent and a beating for fastening the diadem round his head', but the majority of writers on A had A give him a talent but order his decapitation on the advice of the diviners. A further difference was that Aristobulus called the sailor a Phoenician, but some said it was Seleucus; and that, they held, meant death for A and the great kingdom for Seleucus. Arrian left his readers to choose between the different versions. The only comment, which he interjected (οὔ μοι δοκεῖ), was that Seleucus did inherit the largest kingdom.

Back in Babylon A found Peucestas with a large force of Persians, Cossaeans and Tapurians, reinforcements from the West, and envoys from Greece who were wearing crowns and crowned A, 'they having come indeed on a sacred mission to honour a god'. 'Yet the end for him was verily not far off.' Military and naval arrangements followed in 7.27.3–5, and then the arrival of envoys from Ammon. The answer of the god that it was right to sacrifice to Hephaestion as a hero pleased A, who thenceforth honoured him as a hero. A sent a letter to Cleomenes, 'a bad man (ἀνδρὶ κακῷ) who committed many crimes in Egypt' (7.23.6, ἐπιστέλλει using the vivid present tense). Thus far Arrian was drawing on Ptolemy and/or Aristobulus. We may refer back to 7.14.7, where Arrian summarised the position immediately after the death of Hephaestion and reported the different views of writers on the subject (see above, p. 294).[65] The emphasis imparted by the use of the vivid present leads on to Arrian's own interjection.

'I do not myself condemn this letter in view of A's loving remembrance of Hephaestion, but I do condemn it on many other grounds' (ἄλλων δὲ πολλῶν ἕνεκα μέμφομαι). Arrian

---

[65] Plutarch foreshadowed the answer of the god at P*A* 72.3 and reported its arrival and effect at 75.3.

then summarised the contents of the letter: the preparation of shrines for Hephaestion as a hero in Alexandria and on Pharos – shrines of great size, to be called after Hephaestion – and the commemoration of Hephaestion by having his name inscribed on all commercial contracts.

That I cannot censure except for the huge scale in a matter of no great importance. What follows I do condemn very much. 'If I find the shrines in Egypt and the *heroa* of Hephaestion well organised,' the letter said, 'I shall acquit you of any offence you have previously committed, and in future, whatever the scale of the offence you may commit,[66] you will not suffer anything unpleasant at my hands.' I cannot approve this missive from a great king to a man ruling over a large territory and many people, especially since he was a bad man (κακῷ ἀνδρί).

In these last words Arrian resumed those of the sentence based on Ptolemy and/or Aristobulus.

That Arrian found an account of this letter in the work of Ptolemy is beyond serious doubt.[67] There is no evidence that Cleomenes had committed any offences before the sending of this letter, or that A expected him to commit any later. For A was severe in punishing misgovernment at this time, as Aristobulus stated (7.18.1), and he had had no reason hitherto to make any exception for Cleomenes. What was worthy of condemnation was the offer of *carte blanche* for the future. It was an irresponsible offer, perhaps made in an excess of emotion, and in its implications culpable.[68] The subsequent history of Cleomenes was that he was executed by Ptolemy for suspected support of Perdiccas against Ptolemy in 322/1 (Paus. 1.6.3) and no doubt for other offences, whether alleged or true; for Arrian presumably derived from Ptolemy's work his own assertion that Cleomenes was 'a bad man'. Two possi-

---

[66] Cleomenes' position was primarily fiscal (3.5.4, receiving the tribute from the Nomarchs), and this is indicated too by his control over commercial contracts, presumably for exports. See Tarn 303 n. 1 for the evidence about his position. Brunt *L* II 285 translated ἀδικήσαντι as 'had been guilty', for which he would have to read ἠδικηκότι.

[67] Despite the assertion of Tarn 'that he found the letter in Ptolemy's book seems to me out of the question' (306). For the literature on the subject see Tarn loc. cit., Hamilton in *CQ* 3 (1953) 157, and Brunt *L* II 533.

[68] One has to remember that A pardoned Harpalus for some offence which caused him to take flight to Greece, and even reinstated him in charge of large amounts of treasure (3.6.7 αὖθις).

bilities may be stated. The letter which Ptolemy provided in his work was genuine,[69] and Ptolemy cited it to suggest that Cleomenes did take advantage of the *carte blanche*, and that Ptolemy was justified in executing Cleomenes. The other possibility is that Ptolemy inserted the *carte blanche* into the letter, in order to show himself as the punisher of Cleomenes in a better light than A.[70] The first possibility is, I think, more probable.

Resuming the theme from 7.23.2 that A's end was near, Arrian cited Aristobulus for another portent, which occurred when A was presiding over the admission of the new troops into the existing Macedonian units. When A left the dais, a man sat on A's throne, and the eunuchs in attendance[71] tore their robes and beat their heads in lamentation for a great disaster. On hearing of this A had the man put on the rack, in order to learn whether he had acted in accordance with a plot. The man said only that the idea came into his mind. This made the diviners more inclined to presage no good for A.

'Not many days' later, A celebrated 'good events' as he had done at Ecbatana (7.14.1 ἐπὶ ξυμφοραῖς ἀγαθαῖς) by making sacrifices, feasting with his friends and drinking far into the night. The celebrations no doubt covered some days, as at Ecbatana. 'It is said' that he gave victims and wine to his army (mentioned by a source other than Ptolemy and/or Aristobulus, and consistent with past practice). 'There are some who wrote' that A wanted to retire from the drinking-party to bed, but that Medius, then most trusted of his Companions, asked A to join his party; for, he said, it would be pleasurable. As we saw above, p. 145, in considering P*A* 75.3f., one of these writers was Aristobulus. In the early summer heat of southern

[69] If so, Ptolemy found a copy of it in the *Royal Journal* in my opinion. Brunt *L* I xxvi, having denied that Ptolemy had access to the *Royal Journal*, supposed that Ptolemy found the letter 'in the provincial archive of Egypt' (*L* II 533), of which the existence in A's period is hypothetical, as contrasted with the frequently attested *Royal Journal*.

[70] This was my view in *AG*² 264; see *AG*² 4 and 128 for an example of Ptolemy altering the record to win favour in Egypt.

[71] Since the parade included more than 20,000 Asian troops (mainly Persians), A employed Asian ceremonial as well as the Macedonian practice in which A was attended by Companions.

Mesopotamia parties took place after sundown, proceeded fa⟨r⟩ into or throughout the night, and relied not on water of doubt⟨-⟩ful purity but on wine (as did the Greek troops of Cyrus i⟨n⟩ Xen. *Anab*. 1.10.18). The drinking-party was 'a normal socia⟨l⟩ gathering for the king and his associates',[72] at which ther⟨e⟩ were often recitations and other entertainments. The partici⟨-⟩pants, having been up all night, slept during the following da⟨y⟩ (see P*A* 23.8). The parties are not to be equated with drunke⟨n⟩ orgies.

In 7.25.1–26.1 Arrian cited, implicitly as evidence of A's ill⟨-⟩ness, the account in the *Royal Journal* (αἱ βασίλειοι ἐφημερίδε⟨ς⟩ 'the king's dailies'). He introduced the citation with the phras⟨e⟩ 'they are thus' (ὧδε ἔχουσιν) and he ended it with 'thus it ha⟨s⟩ been written' (οὕτως ἀναγέγραπται). He had used the sam⟨e⟩ expression in citing A's reply to Darius at 2.14.4 (ἔχει ὧδε) and he had ended his citation with a similar expression (2.15.⟨1⟩ ταῦτ' ἐπέστειλεν, 'that [is what] he wrote'). As we saw i⟨n⟩ that case (above, p. 221), Arrian did not quote verbatim bu⟨t⟩ used his own words and his own style. Even so he kept his tex⟨t⟩ in the form of direct speech. In citing the *Royal Journal* h⟨e⟩ similarly employed his own words and his own style; but h⟨e⟩ put the text into indirect speech, which indicated that he wa⟨s⟩ summarising the account of the *Journal*.

Arrian was certainly aware that Plutarch – and indee⟨d⟩ others[73] – had cited '*The Royal Journal*' on the subject of A'⟨s⟩ illness. It is interesting to compare Plutarch's form of citation⟨.⟩ He limited himself explicitly to 'the details of the illness' (P*A* 76.1 τὰ περὶ τὴν νόσον). He began with the expression 'the⟨y⟩ have been written thus' (οὕτως γέγραπται), and he ended wit⟨h⟩ a different phrase 'the most of this has been written thus wor⟨d⟩ for word in the Dailies' (77.1 κατὰ λέξιν ... οὕτω γέγραπται)⟨.⟩ Thus he claimed to be repeating phrases of the *Journal* fo⟨r⟩ the illness, and the claim was of course correct, since othe⟨r⟩

---

[72] The quotation is from E. N. Borza, 'The symposium at Alexander's court', *Anc* *Mac*. III 54. The transportation of wine in Mesopotamia was less difficult than h⟨e⟩ supposed: see Xen. *Anab*. 1.10.18.

[73] Ephippus (*FGrH* 126 F 3) and Nicobule (*FGrH* 127 F 1 and F 2) must have done s⟨o⟩ in writing about the end of A.

scholars could have checked his version against the original. On the other hand, he merely summarised the final part of the citation, which concerned the actions of the soldiers, the inquiry in the Sarapeum and the death of A (similarly Arrian paraphrased this latter part, at 7.26.1–3).

The larger scale of Arrian's work was reflected in the size of his citation. For he provided 48 lines of Loeb Greek text as compared with Plutarch's 21 lines of Loeb Greek text for the same part of the illness, i.e. up to A losing the power of speech; and he mentioned a number of things which Plutarch chose to omit. Thus each author dealt freely with the document. Yet the resemblances are such that they were clearly drawing on the same original.[74] Both authors believed the *Royal Journal* to be genuine; so did others who cited the *Journal*, namely Philinus and Strattis of the mid-third century B. C., and Aelian and Athenaeus, who flourished *c*. A.D. 200. There is no indication whatever that they believed that several varying versions of the *Royal Journal* were in circulation, as some scholars have proposed.[75] In particular, Strattis wrote a commentary in five books on *The Journal of Alexander*, a title which assumed that there was one such *Journal* and not several variants. A papyrus fragment, which almost certainly was a copy of Strattis' work, gives us an insight into the nature both of that *Royal Journal* for some events in 335 B.C. and of the commentary itself.[76] Some modern scholars, although they do not possess a word of the original *Journal* (or of several different versions as well), have asserted that these ancient scholars who did have access to the *Journal* failed one and all to realise that it was a forgery.[77] The task of writing a false *Journal* to cover thirteen

---

[74] This was obvious for instance to Jacoby, who insisted on 'die übereinstimmung beider excerpte', and G. Wirth 'nahe liegt, beide Autoren haben, jeder in seiner Weise und nach eigenen Absichten, den Text verkürzt'.

[75] Recently, for instance, by Brunt *L* I xxv 'the so-called journals ... circulated in different versions'; E. Badian 'an official publication, no doubt fully accepted, would later be re-edited in different versions' (in *Zu Alexander d. Gr*. I (Amsterdam, 1987) 621), and A. B. Bosworth in *CQ* 21 (1971) 121 'the texts used by our two authors must have been different', to which should be added his chapter in *AA* (on which see my review in *CR* 39 (1989) 22).

[76] See H*PF*.

[77] The theory was started by L. Pearson in *Historia* 3 (1954/55) 429f.

years of activity day by day and of substituting it for a genuine *Journal* is to me staggering. I have argued elsewhere[78] and also above, pp. 201–4, that these authors were indeed drawing on a genuine *Journal of Alexander*, which, like later *Royal Journals*, was available to them both in the original and in copies in Libraries of the Hellenistic and Roman world.[79]

Having completed his citation, Arrian wrote οὐ πόρρω δὲ τούτων οὔτε ᾿Αριστοβούλῳ οὔτε Πτολεμαίῳ ἀναγέγραπται: 'not far from this is what has been written by Aristobulus and Ptolemy'.[80] He made this point because he went on to mention other versions of A's last days in which A was still able to speak, and yet others which alleged poisoning. His statement shows that he had before him three texts: the *Royal Journal*, the *History* of Aristobulus and the *History* of Ptolemy. The fact that these two authors, who were contemporaries and possibly eyewitnesses, wrote independent accounts which tallied with that of the independently composed *Royal Journal* is certain evidence that the *Royal Journal* cited by Arrian was genuine and correct.

As we saw above, pp. 137f., Plutarch reported that A went to join the party of Medius, drank all next day and began to have a fever. The connection between drinking and fever led Plutarch to deny the account of Cleitarchus, that A downed 'a beaker of Heracles' and collapsed in pain, and to report on the other hand the statement of Aristobulus, that 'when A was madly feverish[81] and thirsty he drank wine excessively (σφόδρα πιεῖν οἶνον),[82] became thereupon delirious and died'. The implication is that Plutarch preferred the version of Aris-

---

[78] See especially H*RJ* 129–50 and H*AAJ*.

[79] For such originals and such copies see my article in *Historia* 40 (1991) 382f.

[80] A different translation has been given for instance by Brunt in *L* II 295 'Aristobulus and Ptolemy have recorded no more than this' with his n. 4 'evidently they stopped with A's death'. See my discussion of the passage in H*RJ* 142f.

[81] This corresponded with the excessive fever of A's very last days (P*A* 76.6f. and Arr. 7.25.6).

[82] I take it that σφόδρα went not with δίψαντα (so Perrin's translation 'very thirsty') but with πιεῖν, because Plutarch was writing about such excessive drinking as he had just mentioned, when A was said to have downed a beaker of Heracles. The word order supports my translation, because σφόδρα being emphatic should precede the word it emphasises.

tobulus, which limited excessive drinking and consequently delirium to A's final days.[83] Plutarch then began his citation of the *Royal Journal*, which did not mention drinking at all. On the other hand, Arrian went straight from the invitation by Medius to the citation, beginning 'that he was drinking with Medius at his party'. It was only later, in 7.26 fin. and 27, that Arrian wrote of other versions of A's illness and death. He chose this course because he was confident that the record in the *Royal Journal* was true.

At 7.26.1, where Arrian was paraphrasing and abbreviating the account of the *Journal*, he made an interjection: the soldiers, 'as I think' (ὡς ἔγωγε δοκῶ) supposed A's death was being concealed by the Bodyguards. Otherwise Arrian added nothing.[84] The last words of the citation 'he died, as this indeed was actually the better thing' referred back to the Companions' question to the god (what is 'better'?) and to the god's answer (to stay where he is will be 'better'). Thus it was in the *Royal Journal*.[85]

At 7.26.3 fin. Arrian mentioned that 'some have written that when the Companions asked him to whom he was leaving his kingdom, he replied 'to the best man', and others (have written that) he added to these words the remark that he saw 'there would be a great funerary contest over him'. Both of these spurious *dicta* had been reported by Diodorus as genuine (17.117.4). As I argued in *THA* 77f., the source of Diodorus here was Cleitarchus; and no doubt others (e.g. Curtius 10.5.5; see *THA* 109) took their line from Cleitarchus.

At 7.27.1 Arrian interjected the remark: 'I know that many other things have been written about the end of A'; and at the end of the chapter he stated his motive in recording them 'so that I may not be thought to be unaware of them rather than that I regard them as credible enough to report' (7.27.3 fin.). He

---

[83] This was not at Medius' banquet, as Bosworth stated in *CQ* 21 (1971) 115. I see no justification for inferring, as Bosworth *AA* 167 does, that 'Aristobulus argued that A drank only after the onset of fever'.

[84] He emphasised the fact that he was using the *Royal Journal* by repeating λέγουσι in 7.26.1 and 2.

[85] Here I have revised the opinion I gave in H*RJ* 146, that Arrian added the comment.

gave three accounts of poison being administered to A. One involved Aristotle, Antipater and Cassander; the second the conveying of the poison in a mule's hoof, and the administering of the poison by Iollas, the king's cupbearer, who had been offended by A; and the third Medius as lover of Iollas and proposer of the party, at which A suffered acute pain on drinking a cup and the pain caused him to leave the drinking-party.[86] As Arrian introduced each account with 'they reported', he drew on more than three sources. The evolution of the poison-versions may have been the following. As we argued above, pp. 145–8, and earlier in *THA* 109f., allegations of poisoning were made publicly by Olympias who accused Antipater and his sons, and Antigonus Monophthalmus asserted that it was Aristotle who organised the plot and provided the poison. It is probable that Hieronymus was the first historian to record the allegations of Olympias, but only after the death of Cassander in 297 B.C. Plutarch provided the name Hagnothemis as the publisher of Antigonus' version (*PA* 77.3; above, p. 146). Rumours that Medius was involved were inevitable and early, since Onesicritus did not dare to name those present at his party (*FGrH* 134 F 37 'fugiens simultatem'), but an elaborated account of poisoning which included the involvement of Medius as lover of Iollas was probably written by Satyrus in his *Life of Alexander* in the middle of the third century B.C.[87] Thus Arrian may have drawn upon Hagnothemis, Hieronymus and Satyrus, and other sources too, for these *legomena*. At 7.27.3 'actually someone was not ashamed to record' that A attempted to commit suicide but was stopped by Roxane. That much was told in the Greek version of *The Alexander Romance*,[88] which was no doubt

---

[86] Other accounts of this drink overcoming A attributed his illness to over-drinking (Nicobule, *FGrH* 127 F 1 and F 2, Ephippus, *FGrH* 126 F 3, Diod. 17.117.1f. and *PA* 75.5). Just. 12.13.7–10 improved on this by having A's friends publish that attribution, but he added that it had been a plot and poison had been added to the drink (12.14.9). Arrian also had Medius involved in 'the act' (τοῦ ἔργου), i.e. in the poisoning (7.27.2).

[87] See *THA* 109–11.

[88] Section 268 in the translation by A. M. Wolohojian. See R. Merkelbach, *Die Quellen des griechischen Alexanderromans* (Munich, 1954) 253ff.

known to Arrian, but there were additional points in Arrian's account which mocked A's aspirations to be thought to be a god.

The text of 7.28.1 is defective in that the month of the Attic year is not included. Arrian then cited Aristobulus for the length of A's life. He stated the length of his reign without citing Aristobulus. He then embarked on his own assessment of A. He may have taken as his model Thucydides' assessment of Themistocles (1.138.3), and we may compare the assessments of Philip and A in Justin 9.8, of A in Curtius 10.5.26–36, of A in Livy 9.18, and of A and Julius Caesar in Appian, *BC* 4.2.149f. Arrian's assessment is not indebted to any source but it is his own, as he repeatedly stressed with such phrases as 'in my opinion', of which eleven occurred in 29f. He cited Aristobulus in support of his view that A did not drink 'a lot of wine' (7.29.4 πολὺν οἶνον), and he mentioned only as *legomena* oracles, apparitions and dreams following on the death of A. He ended with the statement that where he criticised A's acts it was due to his respect for the truth and also for the good of mankind, and that it was with that purpose that he too 'not without God' embarked on the history. Many of Arrian's judgements had been stated already at various points in the work. Thus the final assessment throws some light on Arrian's own approach to his subject, and this we shall consider in the next chapter.

PART FOUR

17

THE PERSONALITY OF ARRIAN AND HIS CHOICE AND USE OF SOURCES

1. The principles of Arrian

Arrian had a strong religious faith. He embarked on the writing of the *Anabasis Alexandrou* 'not without God' (7.30.3 οὐδὲ ἄνευ θεοῦ). He reported with credulity events which Ptolemy and Aristobulus regarded as divine manifestations: for instance, the dream in which Heracles led A into Tyre (2.18.1 καί τι καὶ θεῖον), a bird of prey dropping a stone on the head of A outside Gaza, and two crows guiding A to Siwa. Of the last he wrote in the first person: 'I can state confidently that some divine power helped A' (3.3.6 θεῖόν τι ξυνέλαβεν). He was therefore able himself to understand and to convey to his readers the importance which religious belief had for A and A's Companions and for the Macedonians on the campaign. Thus he chose to report from Ptolemy and/or Aristobulus such statements as the following. When the wind changed near Perge and the army passed along the shore it happened 'not without the divine power, as A himself and his entourage interpreted the event' (1.26.2 οὐκ ἄνευ τοῦ θείου). At Gordium A himself and his entourage believed the oracle to have been fulfilled (i.e. that he would become King of Asia), and thunder and lightning that night were signs from heaven that this was so (2.3.8 ἐξ οὐρανοῦ ἐπεσήμηναν). At Issus 'some divine power chanced to lead Darius' into a cramped position where his numbers were of no avail, and 'it had to be that the Persians would lose the rule of Asia to the Macedonians' (2.6.6).[1] Because Arrian had this faith, he was uniquely able to convey to us the beliefs of A and of his Companions, including Ptolemy and Aristobulus, and also of the Macedonians, to whom the favourable prognostications of Aristander were no doubt relayed (e.g. at 3.7.6 on the eclipse of the moon and the omens of the subsequent sacrifice). In his final assessment Arrian expressed his own belief that A, as a man like no other human being, would have been born 'not without divine agency' (7.30.2 οὐδὲ ἔξω τοῦ θείου).[2]

Arrian shared the belief of A and his contemporary Macedonians in the veracity of traditions which a modern reader may regard as fiction. His own trust was apparent in his digression at 2.16.1–6. The traditional details concerning Heracles, Dionysus, Cadmus, Eurystheus and Geryones were stated as historical events,[3] and Arrian concluded that the Heracles of Tyre was the same as the Heracles of Tartessus. Similarly, as regards the traditions that Dionysus invaded 'India', Arrian expressed his disagreement with Eratosthenes, who was incredulous (5.3.1–4), and he firmly stated his own view, that ancient myths concerning 'the divine' (ὑπὲρ τοῦ θείου) should not be subjected to precise criticism but should be accepted as 'not wholly incredible' (5.1.2).[4] He was more in tune with Hecataeus and Herodotus than with Eratosthenes. Consequently he understood and repeated from Ptolemy and/ or Aristobulus A's wish to believe that Dionysus had reached Nysa, and A's expectation that the Macedonians would willingly join him in going farther east to outdo Dionysus (5.2.1). For Arrian, like A and his Macedonians, thought of Heracles and Dionysus as historical human figures of great stature,

---

[1] Arrian here combined divine intervention and chance in his phrase καί τι καὶ δαιμόνιον τυχὸν ἦγεν αὐτόν, and predestination in his use of ἐχρῆν γὰρ ἤδη. His religious sense was probably not based on philosophical theories.

[2] This phrase has a general significance, rather than a particular one suggesting that A had been conceived by Olympias after copulation with a snake or a god, as in The Alexander Romance.

[3] This was common in antiquity. Even Thucydides regarded Eurystheus as a historical person (1.9.2).

[4] A point of view which has modern analogies.

whom it was possible for outstanding men to emulate and even to surpass.

Arrian attached the utmost importance to truth. He embarked on the writing of the *Anabasis* for the sake of the truth as he saw it (7.30.3 ἀληθείας τε ἕνεκα τῆς ἐμῆς). In order to establish the truth as far as possible, Arrian chose to draw primarily upon the accounts of Ptolemy and Aristobulus because he judged them to be the most trustworthy of the historians of A (*Preface* 2). He added that it would have been more shameful for Ptolemy being a king than for anyone else to tell a lie; perhaps he had in mind the words of Nestor in *Iliad* 2.79–82. In the course of the history he recounted from Ptolemy and/or Aristobulus the saying of A that the king must speak the truth to his subjects and that the subjects must believe that he is speaking the truth (7.4.2). He made it clear that he judged truth to be the foundation both of historical writing and of social cohesion.

Pursuit of the truth led Arrian to praise A, where praise was truly due in his opinion. 'It did not seem right to me to leave unmentioned a noble deed by A ... and I approve it as an indication of endurance and generalship' (6.26.1–3). He realised that many whose feelings towards A were those of envy and malice (7.14.2 φθόνος having both meanings) would object to a favourable estimate of A. But Arrian was not deterred. 'No one man has accomplished among Greeks or barbarians achievements so many in number and so great in magnitude' (1.12.4). 'I am not ashamed of expressing admiration for A himself' (7.30.2). On the other hand, he criticised and sometimes condemned A for actions which Arrian considered to be blameworthy. 'I do not approve this excessive punishment of Bessus ... nor the fact that he, a descendant of Heracles, took on Median dress instead of traditional Macedonian dress' (4.7.4). 'My opinion also is that A did not act sensibly nor was this [burning of the palace at Persepolis] any punishment of the Persians of long ago' (3.18.12). In the final assessment Arrian listed faults as well as merits in A. He asserted that the criticisms which he made were due to his own respect for the truth (7.30.3 ἀληθείας τε ἕνεκα τῆς ἐμῆς).

That a knowledge of A's achievements, and of A's merits and A's faults, would be of value to mankind, was stated at the end of his book (ἕνεκα ... ὠφελείας τῆς ἐς ἀνϑρώπους). At 1.12.4 he had mentioned his own interest in A from the time of his own youth (ἀπο νέου ἔτι), and the need to make A's incomparable achievements known to the world in a worthy manner – something that had not been done in Arrian's opinion despite the large number of varying accounts by earlier writers (*Preface* 2). In claiming that his work would be of value to mankind he may have had the claim of Thucydides in mind (1.22.4), that a precise understanding of the past will enable us to understand present matters of a similar nature. But it seems more probable that Arrian was thinking primarily of A as an exemplar of human conduct and capability; for he directed the attention of his readers to A's fine qualities (7.28.1f. zest, judgement, courage, love of honour and danger, religiosity, perception, leadership etc.) and to A's faults with such attenuating merits as remorse and such attenuating circumstances as his youth, his exposure to flatterers and his continuous 'good fortune'.

Arrian's title was an accurate one: 'the expedition inland of Alexander'. He did not concern himself with the Macedonian people and state, nor with the institutions that produced the army which alone made A's achievements possible. He paid little attention to the Greek participation in the campaign and in the new cities founded in Asia, and none at all to the spread of the Greek language and Greek ideas, though Plutarch had touched on it in *Mor.* 328d. He seems not to have been interested in such wider issues as the symbiosis of Macedonians, Greeks and Asians in the Kingdom of Asia. Thus he reported but did not enlarge upon the significance of A's prayer for 'concord and partnership in rule between Macedonians and Persians' (7.11.9). Indeed, he was somewhat embarrassed by A's acceptance of Persian ways and Persian troops, and he suggested that A's motive was to offset the quick temper and the arrogant pride of the Macedonians by the promotion of Asians in his army. The focus was firmly set on Alexander.

2. The experience of Arrian

Of the five surviving historians of A only Arrian had a lifetime of experience in three capacities: as a military commander, a leading administrator and a recognised man of letters.[5] Born at Nicomedia (Ismit) on the north-eastern shore of the Sea of Marmara in A.D. 89, he served in Roman forces for more than twenty years, and he commanded the army which dealt with the threat of an invasion of Cappadocia by the Alani in 135. As an administrator he became proconsul of Southern Spain (c. 126), consul at Rome (c. 129), and governor of Cappadocia (c. 131–7); and in addition to his career as an outstanding Roman he held offices in his own Greek-speaking city, sat on a council at Delphi, and was eponymous archon at Athens in 145–6.[6] As a writer he was prolific. He wrote specialist works on philosophy, geography, hunting, biography, military training and tactics, comets and local history (Bithynia and India). His most substantial histories were *Anabasis Alexandrou* in seven books, *Events after Alexander* in ten books and *Parthica* in seventeen books. He embarked on the *Anabasis Alexandrou* when 'his name was not unknown to mankind' (1.12.5 τὸ μὲν ὄνομα ... οὐδὲ ἄγνωστον ἐς ἀνθρώπους ἐστίν), an expression which implied that he had already been consul c. 129. Although the matter is far from certain, it appears that the *Anabasis Alexandrou* was a work of Arrian's maturity, being written in his forties or fifties.[7]

Arrian's experience was of immense value to him in writing the *Anabasis*. As a soldier with much service in the countries of the Middle East, familiar with forms of warfare which had changed very little since the days of A, and versed in the specialist literature on military tactics, to which he himself contributed the *Tactica*,[8] he was infinitely better qualified to

---

[5] Little is known about the career of Q. Curtius Rufus. He may have been the orator mentioned by Suetonius (see J. C. Rolfe in the Loeb edition I xix).

[6] I am following the dates suggested by Stadter 173f.

[7] This is the view of Stadter 180f. He discusses in 184f. the arguments of Bosworth for the *Anabasis* being an early work of Arrian's youth.

[8] Arrian wrote this work in 136–7. He was certainly familiar with earlier works on Tactics, whether he wrote his own *Tactica* before or after the *Anabasis*. These military manuals are of great value to the military historian. I had the advantage

weigh one account of a battle of A against another account than any armchair historian of the past such as Diodorus or any of his modern counterparts. Let us take the battle of the River Granicus as an example. Arrian knew the battlefield, which was not far from his birthplace. As a cavalryman he understood the difficulties of charging up a steep river-bank and the reasons for the success of A and his Companion Cavalrymen. As a writer on Infantry Training (*Tact.* 32.3 τὰ πεζικά sc. γυμνάσια) and a commander of infantry forces, he understood the ability of the Macedonian infantrymen with their long pikes to drive the enemy cavalry back from the top of the bank and to overwhelm the more numerous Greek mercenary infantry. With knowledge based on experience he had no difficulty in seeing that the account of the battle in Ptolemy and/or Aristobulus was far superior to the account of Diodorus, which was based probably on that of Cleitarchus, available to Arrian but not to us.[9]

Equally as the governor of a province in Spain and of Cappadocia he was able to appreciate the special arrangements which A made for the administration and for the naval and military protection of Egypt (3.5.2−7, with his own comment at 7). He understood the need to remove incompetent or corrupt governors, to punish violation of the religious shrines of subject peoples, and to demonstrate to those peoples that their rights would not be abused. 'Nothing did more than that to keep order among them, extremely numerous as they were and separated one from another by great distances' (6.27.5) − this being a comment by Ptolemy and/or Aristobulus which Arrian chose to repeat. If he was a curator of public works at Rome,[10] as seems likely, he had a knowledge of public expenditure and of contracts, which stood him in good stead when he read accounts of A building new cities such as Alexandria in Egypt, digging out artificial harbours in Babylonia or con-

---

of discussing them with A. M. Devine, when I supervised him for the Cambridge Ph.D. See now his fine translation of Aelian, *Tactica*, in *The Ancient World* 19 (1989) 31–64.

[9] See H*GR* 87 for the choice which Arrian and modern writers have to make, and H*GR* 74 for modern versions based on Diodorus.

[10] See Stadter 11 for the possibility that Arrian held this position.

tracting for the construction of large warships in Phoenicia, Babylonia and the Caspian Sea.

He had no need to borrow from other writers in his assessment of A's abilities, merits and defects. He had known many men in high places in the Roman military and administrative service. He put A far ahead of them and indeed ahead of any man in ability and in achievement. His assessment is not to be taken lightly. Few have quarrelled with his analysis of A's brilliant intellect in the field of practical affairs (7.28.1-3). Some have doubted Arrian's assertion that A was most dependable in keeping pacts and agreements, because they have supposed that he broke the terms of his pact with the Greeks of the Common Peace;[11] but that was something which Arrian must have considered. The same is true of the assertion that A was most secure against being taken in by those who sought to deceive him;[12] but Arrian may have seen that in a war of liberation from Persia the offer of open neutrality by a Greek state in Asia (1.19.1) was a form of deception which A did not tolerate. Living himself in a time of ruler-cult, Arrian saw that A's willingness to attribute his own origin to a god was understandable perhaps as a means of impressing the subject peoples (7.29.3).

3. Arrian's choice of sources for the *Anabasis*

According to Arrian more accounts had been written about A than about any other person and moreover with wider variations (*Preface* 2). The implication is that Arrian had read them; and this implication is supported for instance by the very numerous *legomena* from different authors which he supplied for the killing of Cleitus and A's remorse (4.9.2-5), the Pages' Conspiracy and the fate of Callisthenes (and 'many

---

[11] On this subject see my comments in *AG*² 253-9. Because Arrian's subject was the *Anabasis* ('The Expedition Inland'), he paid little attention to A's dealings with the Greek mainland. The agreements which Arrian mentioned most frequently were concluded in 'India'.

[12] The attempt of the Indian mercenaries at Massaga to break the agreement to serve in A's army was a case in point, for Arrian was clear about their intention to abscond (4.27.3).

other accounts' not cited, 4.14.4), and A's mourning for Hephaestion (7.14.2–10). When he wrote of friction between Antipater and Olympias he remarked that 'no overt act or word at all on A's part was reported from which anyone would have deduced that Antipater was not as much to A's liking as ever' (7.12.7). Arrian had presumably checked in the numerous accounts to ensure that his remark was correct.[13]

His principles and his experience alike led him to choose as his main sources Ptolemy and Aristobulus. He gave his reasons. They were in his judgement the most truthful of all the writers, and they had campaigned throughout with A. He made the additional point which was familiar to any Roman who had read the work of Tacitus that since they wrote after the death of A there was neither compulsion nor hope of gain to distract them from 'writing of anything in any other way than as it happened' (*Preface* 2 τοῦ ἄλλως τι ἢ ὡς συνηνέχθη ξυγγράψαι). In the same way Arrian chose as men of truth and as participants at a high level Nearchus and Hieronymus to be his chief sources respectively for the *Indica* and for *Events after Alexander*. I see no grounds for doubting the reasons Arrian gave in choosing Ptolemy and Aristobulus. He was concerned primarily to record each event 'as it happened'. Let us then consider first how he used these authors' accounts and how dependable those accounts were for his own narrative of events.

As we have seen in our detailed analysis, Arrian was scrupulous in distinguishing for his reader the three chief components of his history: what he drew from Ptolemy and/or Aristobulus, what he drew as *legomena* from other authors, and what interjections he himself made. If we abide by those distinctions,[14] we see that Arrian derived the great bulk of the narrative of events in his books 1 to 6 from Ptolemy and/or Aristobulus. The question then arises: how dependable were their accounts,

---

[13] Otherwise contemporary scholars and writers could easily have proved him wrong. They had special reason to criticise him if they could, because he had claimed that his work surpassed those of everyone else (*Preface* 3 and 1.12.2 fin.).

[14] Some commentators have failed to do so and made incorrect attributions; see for instance above, pp. 192, 208, 210 and 261f.

written long after the events themselves? The amount of detail is staggering. For instance, in books 1 to 6 one hundred and forty-seven orders by A were recorded, a few in direct speech and some not fulfilled. In the same books precise intervals by days were recorded seventy-eight times. In books 1.11.1 to 4.30.9 two hundred and fifty officers were named, usually with a specification of their posts or duties. There was a great mass of military detail, for which Arrian cited Ptolemy more often than Aristobulus. It is inconceivable that either or both of them could have held such material in their memory.[15] The only hypothesis which provides an explanation is that Ptolemy had access to the *Royal Journal* in which such detail was recorded day by day. On the other hand, Aristobulus lacked that access. Where they differed over such matters as casualties, Arrian always preferred Ptolemy.

The *Royal Journal* was a document of state in the sense that it was a precise record of the king's activities day by day and that it was not made public during his reign.[16] We can see from the two citations of A's last days by Plutarch and by Arrian that it was an unadorned and precise statement of events (see above, p. 204). As a record of events 'as they happened' (ὡς συνηνέχθη), it provided a bedrock of facts for Ptolemy in composing his history. On the other hand, it is unlikely that Ptolemy included excerpts from the *Journal* in his own history, for that was not the practice of ancient historians. They regarded themselves as artists, and they transformed their material into an artistic composition. They were no more concerned to report the origin of the components than a painter is concerned to report an analysis of his paints. Thus it was enough for Arrian to say that he found Ptolemy to be trustworthy. For Arrian was a literary artist. He rated himself among 'the masters in Greek literature' (1.12.5 τῶν πρώτων ἐν τῇ φωνῇ τῇ Ἑλλάδι), and that rating was confirmed by Photius (Bibl. cod. 92. 46, reproduced in Roos, *Arrian* II lxvi, in the Teubner edition). Because Arrian aimed

---

[15] Or indeed in a diary which it must have been very difficult to keep under the conditions of campaigning.

[16] See my articles in *Historia* 37 (1988) 147f. and 40 (1991) 382f.

to draw a true and not an impressionistic or sensational picture of A, he reported accurately the events which he found in the histories of Ptolemy and Aristobulus.

The second interest of the historian is why things happened, and in the *Anabasis Alexandrou* very often why A acted in a particular way. Here too Arrian gave priority to the views of his main sources, no doubt because they best knew the circumstances and the personality of A. We may speculate that he preferred to follow Ptolemy for military matters and Aristobulus for some matters of motivation, but Arrian undertook only to report their shared views and himself to make his own choice where he found that their views differed (*Preface* 1).[17] To take an example, why did A attack at once at the River Granicus? Arrian provided in his own words and style a discussion between Parmenio and A for which he derived the material from his main sources. We cannot tell whether Ptolemy and/or Aristobulus cast an account in the form of a discussion in direct speech or not; but that is no ground for doubting the accuracy of the points which were made in Arrian's account (1.13). Or why did the mutiny occur and why did A handle it as he did at Opis? Arrian provided from the accounts of Ptolemy and/or Aristobulus an announcement by A, his aim therein, the reaction of the men, their accumulated grievances, their demands and mockery, A's quickening temper and his action and order. No one was better qualified to know these matters than Ptolemy as a Bodyguard beside the king and Aristobulus who seems to have had a special insight into A's frame of mind. Arrian has presented the material in his own form of words. There is no reason to doubt the truth of what Ptolemy and/or Aristobulus had recorded. In particular it is to be noted that they were not uncritical of A: he thought he would please the men 'indeed' (7.8.2 δῆθεν) but he displeased them; the men were angered 'not without reason' (οὐκ ἀλόγως); and A was then 'more quick-tempered and, as a result of the barbarian style of his court, no longer as reasonable towards the Macedonians as he had been in the past'.

[17] See above, p. 189.

Arrian made it clear that he had read the works of all writers on the deeds of A. He wrote of them as a group.[18] Sometimes all of them were in agreement (e.g. 7.14.8); often a majority took a particular line (e.g. 6.24.1 οἱ πολλοὶ τῶν ξυγγραψάντων τὰ ἀμφ᾽ Ἀλέξανδρον); occasionally none of them supplied some particular information (7.19.1). It was from the works of this group that Arrian derived his *legomena* 'on the subject of A' (*Preface* 3 ὑπὲρ Ἀλεξάνδρου). Because he attached importance to those who had lived during the years of A's achievements, it seems that he had in mind primarily writers with that qualification. There is no indication that he drew *legomena* from later writers of universal histories such as Diodorus and Trogus, or even from Curtius. In the course of our analysis it has been possible to suggest with varying degrees of probability the names of those writers from whom Arrian drew the individual *legomena*. Much the most frequent was Cleitarchus (fourteen times) and after him Onesicritus thrice, Chares thrice, Callisthenes twice, Ephippus once, Hieronymus once and Hagnothemis once; all of these were alive in the period of A. In addition he drew *legomena* probably from writers of the next generation: Diyllus five times, Eratosthenes once and Satyrus once (here he may have drawn on the (unknown) sources of Diyllus and Satyrus). His general principle in regard to the *legomena* was to leave it to his readers to decide where the truth lay; for by his own definition in *Preface* 3 they were 'not utterly incredible'.[19] Quite apart from the *legomena* Arrian cited authors by name for particular incidents or views: Hecataeus, Herodotus, Ctesias, Nearchus, Megasthenes, Aristus and Asclepiades. He commented on Ctesias 'if indeed anyone finds him competent as a witness' (5.4.2 ἱκανός). He evidently included, without naming him, Cleitarchus among those whom he judged incompetent as witnesses in the matter of A meeting the Amazons (7.13.4). He showed little respect for Aristus and Asclepiades, who alleged that Rome sent envoys to A in 323 B.C. (7.15.6).

---

[18] His usual expression was οἱ τὰ Ἀλεξάνδρου γράψαντες.
[19] When he departed from this practice, he was careful to inform his readers, e.g. at 7.27.3 fin.

Arrian's own interjections, of which I have noted twenty-five, were always clearly marked by the use of the first person. Where he made a judgement, as at 3.10. 2–4, 4.8.5 with 4.9.1f., or 6.26.3, he stated his reasons in a precise manner. In some passages Arrian departed from his standard procedure of drawing on Ptolemy and/or Aristobulus, of inserting *legomena* from other authors, and of adding his own interjections. At 4.8.1 he stated that he would provide his own narration of the Cleitus affair (ἀφηγήσομαι), and he built it upon a variety of accounts, which included that of Aristobulus (see above, pp. 240f.). In 4.10–14, in writing about obeisance, the Pages and Callisthenes, he drew on the general tradition to compose his own account, which was derived from many accounts, including those of Aristobulus and Ptolemy (4.14.1); see above, 245f. He presumably took this course in these two cases because he did not think that his two main authors had covered the topics objectively and entirely. In this he was probably correct. At 5.5.2–6.8 he wrote his own account of 'India', and at 4.7.1–8.1 he speculated about the bridging of the River Indus.

4. The wisdom or otherwise of Arrian's choice

The final question is whether Arrian was wise in his choice of authors. Having read all the accounts which were extant, Arrian was in a unique position to select the most thorough and dependable writers. If one has respect for the judgement which he showed in *Anabasis*, *Events after Alexander* and *Indica*, one will agree that his choice of Ptolemy and Aristobulus was the best possible for recording what A did and why he did it.

Ptolemy was ideally placed to know what happened because he was a personal friend of A, served throughout the campaigns, and in the latter part of the expedition held high commands. As an exact contemporary with shared experience in the School of Pages, he was well placed to understand the mind of A and his developing ideas. Moreover, he had access to the *Journal of Alexander* and derived from it a mass of correctly recorded detail. As a Macedonian he had a thorough understanding of Macedonian ideas and practices; but he was probably less interested in Greek affairs and in Greek courtiers such as Callisthenes.[20] Surprise has sometimes been expressed that Ptolemy's history was very rarely cited by writers other than Arrian. We may conjecture that his work was not of a high literary quality, and that its concentration on military affairs was distasteful to those who were not addicted to military history.[21]

Aristobulus was a Greek, probably of Phocis, and his interest in Greek affairs (e.g. in the fate of Thebes; see above p. 207) compensated for Ptolemy's lack of interest. He was one of those enterprising Greeks who accompanied A as philosophers, scientists and technicians. He was evidently a privileged person, since he had access to the Tomb of Cyrus and was able to observe in detail the contents of the Tomb before it was plundered (6.29.4 to the middle of 6.29.7). When A returned to Pasargadae, he entrusted to Aristobulus the important task of restoring the Tomb to its previous state (6.29.10), a task which required artistic sensitivity and the handling of precious materials. Aristobulus was cited for his descriptions of geographical conditions by Arrian (e.g. 6.22.4–8), and even more so by Strabo. For such matters Arrian's choice was clearly excellent. In commenting on the personality of A it seems that Aristobulus was equally observant. For instance, he reported that the long drinking-parties were not given for the sake of wine by A, who indeed 'did not drink much wine', but to show friendliness towards the Companions (of whom we may assume that Aristobulus was one). It was probably he rather than Ptolemy who observed that A was seized by a compulsive 'longing' to take some action – go beyond the Danube, see the waggon of Gordius, plan the layout of Alexandria and so on.

If I am correct in maintaining that the account of Aristobulus was followed for the Cleitus affair by Plutarch (*PA*

---

[20] For the various accounts of his death see above, p. 100. If Callisthenes died of disease 'when A was wounded in India', it is probable that Ptolemy was engaged in military operations and was not present with the baggage-train, where prisoners were kept (3.14.5).

[21] It is of interest that a Hellenistic history of contemporary events treated battles in a perfunctory manner; see *FGrH* 148 Col. 3 (cf. 151 F 1, 3).

50–52.7), Aristobulus noted that both A and Cleitus were the worse for drink, that Cleitus was removed by the Friends, and that Cleitus returned by himself and was killed by A. Aristobulus concluded that the error was that 'of Cleitus alone' (Arr. 4.8.9), i.e. in returning, since otherwise the calamity would not have occurred. That is not to say that Aristobulus exonerated A;[22] for he described A as 'enraged and leaping towards Cleitus to kill him' just before Cleitus was forcibly removed (Arr. 4.8.9) and as killing him when he did return. The overall explanation which Aristobulus gave was that the death of Cleitus was predestined and foreshadowed by a dream and an omen (see above, pp. 91–4); and that was a form of double determination[23] (at the divine level and at the human level), which did not relieve the participants of responsibility for their individual actions.

Was Arrian justified in regarding as less 'trustworthy' the authors from whom he took his *legomena*? He had the advantage that he knew their entire works on A, whereas we have only a few fragments. Even so, we can see that he was wise not to use Callisthenes. For Callisthenes, whose aim was to magnify the achievements of A, especially for a Greek readership, was not hampered by considerations of the truth. In his description of the Battle of Issus he said that A positioned himself to engage in personal combat with Darius, that Darius did the same, but that Darius panicked and moved to another position (Plb. 12.22.2). This is clearly a lie; for A positioned himself at the point where he intended to break through the weak place in the enemy line; and that was not the point where Darius was defended, as at Gaugamela, by the best cavalry and the best infantry in depth.[24] In the battle of Gaugamela the failure of A to catch Darius was attributed by Callisthenes to a plea for help from Parmenio, whose slackness was said to

---

[22] *Contra* Bosworth *CE* 115 'Aristobulus' account is slanted to exculpate the king as far as it could be done.'

[23] For this concept in Greek tragedy see Hammond in *JHS* 85 (1965) 44f.

[24] According to Plb. 12.17.9 Darius was in the centre of his line 'when the enemy were drawing near'. Polybius complained at 12.22.3 that Callisthenes did not say what new position Darius adopted. For the course of the battle see *AG*² 95–110, which is based on my inspection of the site and analysis of the sources.

be due 'to envy and abhorrence of the authority and of the massiveness of A's power' (*PA* 33.10; see above, p. 40); his purpose was presumably to blacken the name of Parmenio after Parmenio's death, without reference to the truth that Parmenio prevailed in the battle and was not helped by A.[25] Equally propagandist was Callisthenes' attempt to represent the sea off the coast of Pamphylia doing obeisance to A as a deity (*FGrH* 124 F 31). Callisthenes was rightly scorned as a 'flatterer' of A by Timaeus (Plb. 12.12b.2).

Chares, a Greek from Mitylene and probably a non-combatant since he was a court official, was no better. He reported that A engaged in single combat with Darius and was wounded in the thigh by Darius at the Battle of Issus (Plu. *Mor.* 341c.). That Darius inflicted the wound is certainly untrue. Then A's horse, Bucephalus, was said to have carried him into personal combat with Porus, to have been wounded and to have carried A out of danger, and then to have succumbed; here again Chares was romancing (see above, p. 111).[26] He was one of those who falsely described Calanus as 'having thrown himself into the fire' (*FGrH* 125 F 19a). Ephippus attributed the fatal illness of A to an act of over-drinking, wherein Dionysus took revenge for the sack of Thebes (*FGrH* 126 F 3). This attribution, we have argued, was false (see above, pp. 308f.). Arrian certainly thought so, and he must have distrusted Ephippus on that account and for the portrayal of A as 'unendurable and murderous' and a terror to those at court (F 5). As a citizen of Olynthus Ephippus had a hatred of Macedonia and of A.[27] Onesicritus, a Greek islander, surpassed everyone in the tallness of his stories about India (*FGrH* 134 T 10, F 7 and F 16); and like Chares he had Calanus leap into the

---

[25] Diod. 17.60.7; Curt. 4.16.4–6; *PA* 33.11; Arr. 3.15.3. See *AG*² 147.

[26] This passage reveals the nature of the mistake made by Lucian in *Hist. Conscr.* 12. He wrote that when A was sailing down the Hydaspes Aristobulus read aloud his description of a single combat between A and Porus, whereupon A threw 'the book' into the river in disgust. 'Aristobulus' was clearly a mistake for 'Chares', a mistake not untypical of Lucian since he substituted Olynthus for Methone in reporting the blinding of Philip's eye in *Hist. Conscr.* 38. I take it that 'the book' was Chares' notebook.

[27] So too Bosworth *CE* 283 'he was certainly hostile to Alexander'.

fire (F 18), incorrectly. He lied about his own position, claiming that he was admiral, whereas he was chief helmsman (Arr. 6.2.3).[28] This lie might have been accepted in the Greek islands at the expense of Nearchus; for he came from Crete, the home of proverbial liars. Onesicritus may be one of the authors who hinted that the death of A was due to poisoning at the party of Medius; for he refused to name the guests there, 'fearing their animosity' (F 37), i.e. in the period of civil war between the generals.

Since we know nothing more of Hagnothemis, we are left with Cleitarchus. 'No critic of antiquity has a good word for him as a historian', wrote Tarn.[29] Cicero rated him among those rhetorical writers to whom it is permitted in writing history to lie outright ('ementiri'), in order to be able to say something more brilliantly ('argutius'); and at the same time Cicero reckoned that there was a puerile quality ('puerile quiddam') in his work. Quintilian's judgement on Cleitarchus was that he was praiseworthy in his talent (for writing) and notoriously untrustworthy ('probatur ingenium, fides infamatur'), while Longinus found him to be a 'superficial windbag' (φλοιώδης κτλ.).[30] Cleitarchus told the lie that Ptolemy had been one of those who saved the life of A at the city of the Malli (Curt. 9.5.21), his motive being no doubt to curry favour as a resident at Alexandria with the king of Egypt. But Ptolemy published the truth in his own book. Cleitarchus propounded the false stories that A was visited by the Amazon queen (PA 46.1 and Strabo 505; see above, p. 81), and that the Athenian courtesan Thaïs at a drunken party initiated the unpremeditated burning down of the palace of Xerxes at Persepolis (FGrH 137 F 11).[31] Both stories are 'fables' as Wilcken called them. Then Cleitarchus asserted

---

[28] So Brown Ones. 8f.

[29] Tarn in OCD² 249 and Wilcken 129 'it was Cleitarchus who introduced into literature the falsification of history' (re Siwa).

[30] These passages are in FGrH 137 T 7 and T 13 (Cicero), T 6 (Quintilian) and T 9 (Longinus).

[31] The excavators found that valuables had been removed from the Palace before it was burnt. The burning was therefore premeditated. See E. F. Schmidt, Persepolis (Chicago, 1953–70) I 157, 220 and II 3.

that Rome sent an embassy to A (F 31), something which is generally rejected as untrue (see above, p. 299).[32] As an example of a writer dressing up an incident in 'a rhetorical and dramatic manner' Cicero cited the invention of Stratocles and Cleitarchus, that Themistocles did not die a natural death as Thucydides had reported, but that he committed suicide by drinking poisoned bull's blood (F 34, the invention being 'rhetorically and dramatically presented', 'rhetorice et tragice').[33] It seems that Cleitarchus dramatised the end of A by introducing 'the beaker of Heracles' and the immediate collapse of A – 'making a tragic and moving finale as it were of a great play' (PA 75.5; see above, p. 137 and p. 308).

No one who has read the fragments of these authors and is interested in discovering the true course of events will deny that Arrian was wise to prefer the accounts of Ptolemy and Aristobulus. For the evidence is incontrovertible that these authors sometimes wrote fiction rather than history. As Greeks they were profoundly affected by the animosities of the Lamian War and then, if they stayed in Asia, by the wars between the generals. We can see why they chose to represent A and his Macedonians as drunkards, and to assert that A was poisoned by a group of Macedonian generals, led by the hated Antipater, who deprived Athens of her liberty. The most unscrupulous of these authors was Cleitarchus. This was clear to Cicero, Quintilian, and Longinus; for independently of one another they condemned him as a historian for his outright lying, puerility, superficiality and disregard of the truth. The surviving fragments support those denunciations. Indeed there is not a single statement by an ancient author, nor a single fragment in Jacoby's collection of thirty-six genuine fragments, which speaks to the contrary.

The opposition to this evaluation of Ptolemy and Aristobulus as compared with the authors behind the *legomena* has taken several forms. The first is to reject Arrian's estimate of Ptolemy's truthfulness and to suggest that Ptolemy misrepre-

---

[32] Bosworth *AA* 89–93 argued that it was authentic.
[33] Diodorus probably used Cleitarchus when he gave this version at 11.58.3.

sented situations in order to praise himself and denigrate his rivals.[34] The difficulty about the situations is that Ptolemy was writing primarily for Macedonians. He would therefore have been a fool to lie about events which they were likely to remember, such as his part in the capture of and handing over of Bessus, when Ptolemy commanded some 7,000 men and delivered Bessus 'naked, bound and wearing a wooden collar' in the presence of the rest of the army (Arr. 3.29.7–30.3).[35] That Ptolemy was able to describe his own actions was due to his own memory, because they were not described in the *Royal Journal*. The actions of other generals holding an independent command (such as Perdiccas and Hephaestion) were neither known to Ptolemy nor recorded in the *Royal Journal*. It is erroneous to suppose that Ptolemy 'suppressed' accounts of the latter in order to praise himself.

The theory of denigration has been applied to the episode in which, according to Ptolemy, Perdiccas initiated the attack at Thebes without having received an order from A (Arr. 1.8.1). The argument seems to be that Ptolemy, who fought against Perdiccas after A's death, lied in saying that Perdiccas acted without any order from A, and that the aim of the lie was to taint Perdiccas with an act of 'ill discipline' or 'an unparalleled piece of insubordination'.[36] The initiative of Perdiccas, whether ordered or not, is then taken by one critic to result in 'the stigma of failure' for Perdiccas and by another critic to result in the capture of Thebes. Let us choose the latter. If it is correct, it did Perdiccas credit, and we can see why Perdiccas commanded a brigade again at the River Granicus and was promoted to the rank of a Bodyguard of A. However, the argument of the critic is that in having Perdiccas attack without an order Ptolemy was 'partially absolving Alexander of the blame for Thebes' destruction'.[37] This is very far-fetched:

[34] I take as an example the article of R. M. Errington, 'Bias in Ptolemy's History of Alexander', *CQ* 19 (1969) 233–42.

[35] Bosworth *CE* 108, for instance, maintained that what he calls 'the romanticism and self-glorification of Ptolemy's account' is to be rejected in favour of Aristobulus' account at Arr. 3.30.5.

[36] The quotations are from R. M. Errington, op. cit. 237 and Bosworth *CE* 32 n. 22.

[37] Errington, loc. cit.; see my criticisms in *THA* 166 with n. 14 on p. 195.

for the razing of the city was decided by the order of the Council of the Greeks of the Common Peace and was carried out by A as Hegemon.[38] Perdiccas had nothing to do with that; for he was seriously wounded at the time, and no ancient author associated him with the destruction.

To take another example, it has been argued that Ptolemy disliked Aristonoüs and therefore omitted his actions – a view which assumed that what Arrian included from Ptolemy's history was all that Ptolemy wrote –[39] and that this resulted in a depreciation of Aristonoüs.[40] Yet if this was so successful, why did Ptolemy not omit the actions of Perdiccas? In fact in passages which were derived by Arrian from Ptolemy and/or Aristobulus Perdiccas was named unusually often, and sometimes it seems unnecessarily in association with Ptolemy at 4.16.2, 4.21.4 and 5.13.1 and with Hephaestion at 4.22.7, 4.28.5 and 4.30.9.[41]

Another way of downgrading Ptolemy as a source of information was to maintain that the *Royal Journal* which Ptolemy used was a forged document, and that it therefore conveyed false information. I hope that my earlier arguments in *Historia* 37 (1988) 129f. and 40 (1991) 382f. and those in this book have demolished that theory.[42] Where it was conceded that Ptolemy did use a genuine *Royal Journal*, it was argued that the *Journal* was 'an official court journal', and that Ptolemy therefore

---

[38] See Diod. 17.14.1 τῷ κοινῷ συνεδρίῳ and 4 ἀκολούθως τῇ τοῦ συνεδρίου γνώμῃ; Just. 11.3.8 'in concilio de excidio urbis deliberaretur'; Arr. 1.9.9 τοῖς δὲ μετασχοῦσι τοῦ ἔργου ξυμμάχοις and 1.9.10 οἱ ξύμμαχοι ἔγνωσαν.

[39] As Brunt *L* II 562 observed with reference to Ptolemy 'nor can we properly hold that what is not in Arrian was not in Ptolemy'. Contra Errington, op. cit. 234 'it is not in Arrian, and the reasonable conclusion is that it was not in Ptolemy'. There is abundant evidence that Arrian abbreviated the accounts of his main sources, Ptolemy and Aristobulus.

[40] Errington, op. cit 235, and Bosworth *CE* 136 'Ptolemy was silent about the achievements of his enemy Aristonous.' By a strange coincidence the name of Aristonous was omitted from the Index of Brunt *L* II.

[41] In particular when A split his army into two groups, he commanded one half and he gave the command of the other half to Perdiccas (6.9.1); and in 325 B.C. a separate operation was conducted by Perdiccas, when A was convalescing from his serious wound. On these occasions he was the senior general with A.

[42] On the other hand Bosworth *CE* 299 accepted the existence of the *Ephemerides* but held that neither Ptolemy nor any primary source used the *Ephemerides* systematically.

wrote an official version of events; but, as I argued above, p. 203, that is to misunderstand the nature of the *Journal* (it was the task of Callisthenes and his successor to publish the official version), and therefore to misjudge the purpose of Ptolemy's history.

Aristobulus too has been downgraded by the attachment to him of such labels as 'adulatory and apologetic',[43] labels which reflect the prejudices of the labellers. What we have to realise objectively is that Aristobulus and Ptolemy had a genuine admiration for A, some of their reasons for that admiration having survived in Arrian's text, and at the same time that they were not uncritical of him. Arrian also has been labelled as 'encomiastic'; yet he too gave his reasons for admiring A and was not uncritical of him. The proper course for the modern historian is to give Arrian a fair hearing, analyse his sources of information, and investigate the nature of those sources.[44]

The corollary to the downgrading is the upgrading of what has often been called 'the Vulgate Tradition'. As I pointed out in *THA* 1f., the term 'Vulgate' was originally used of some elements common to Diodorus, Trogus and Curtius, but it was expanded to cover not only the works of these three authors but also Plutarch's *Life of Alexander*, the *Metz Epitome* and almost anything not found in Arrian.[45] Another attachment to this so-called Vulgate Tradition was the name of Cleitarchus as its original and chief source, so that E. Schwartz, F. Jacoby and many others wrote of 'the Cleitarchan Vulgate'. This theory is now seen to be simplistic. P. Goukowsky observed in his commentary that Diodorus used many sources beside Cleitarchus, J. E. Atkinson in his commentary noted that 'Curtius used several sources', of whom one 'may have been Cleitarchus', and in *THA* I analysed the sources of

---

[43] Bosworth C 29 and in CQ 21 (1971) 115 'the notoriously apologetic'. Brunt too in L II 561 found Aristobulus 'an apologist' and 'biased' in favour of A.

[44] A good example of such an approach is Brunt's summary of Aristobulus' contribution, in L. II 556f.

[45] Thus Brunt L I 43 n. 4 'vulgate' unless 'they' are Ptolemy and Aristobulus; I 47. n. 1 'others say' = vulgate; I 49. n. 5 'vulgate' for 1.11.6–8; and so on.

Diodorus, Justin and Curtius and found that they all used writers over and above Cleitarchus. It is thus clear that the term 'the Vulgate Tradition' in the sense of a single tradition to be set against the work of Arrian is obsolete and should be abandoned. What is needed is an assessment of the various writers who have been so often grouped under the umbrella of the Vulgate Tradition.

Fortunately we have already made that assessment both in *THA* and in this book. It remains only to point out that much recent writing has been based on a form of circular argument, that the Vulgate Tradition contained both good and bad material, that its ultimate source was Cleitarchus, and that the good, defined as 'factual and relatively sober reporting', as well as the bad, was to be attributed to Cleitarchus.[46] When we see that the Vulgate Tradition was a euphemism for many writers of diverse qualities, this circular argument collapses. Cleitarchus must be judged by the opinions of Cicero, Quintilian and Longinus, who knew his works, and by the surviving fragments. The sum of these leaves no room whatever for 'factual and sober reporting'. Arrian, in fact, was correct in not forcing all the *legomena* into the frame of a Vulgate Tradition but in citing each *legomenon* separately. Moreover, in most cases he left his readers to choose between what was derived from Ptolemy and/or Aristobulus and what came from other writers, and sometimes between variant versions provided by those other authors. In my opinion his methodology was superior to that of some of his critics.

---

[46] The quotation is from Bosworth *CE* 298. He has gone farther than most in accepting the material based on Cleitarchus in the vulgate and rejecting the version of Arrian based on Ptolemy and/or Aristobulus. I cite a few examples and my comments: the capture of Thebes (*C* 8of.; my *THA* 13f.), the Battle of the River Granicus (*C* 115f.; H*GR* 73f. and 87f.), siege of Halicarnassus (*C* 144f.; my *AG*² 42), and the revel in Carmania (*CE* 147; my *AG*² 236).

INDEX

(Ancient authors are not generally included.)